Hostile Takeovers of Large Jewish Companies, 1933–1935

Lexington Studies in Modern Jewish History, Historiography, and Memory

***Series Editor*:** Carsten Schapkow, University of Oklahoma

Modern Jewish history is an essentially interdisciplinary field. This series aspires to transcend disciplinary and methodological boundaries, welcoming original scholarship that advances our understanding of the modern Jewish experience. The series will cover all geographical areas and all periods in modern Jewish history by welcoming scholarly contributions including cultural history, intellectual history, transnational Jewish history, global Jewish history, and memory studies. We welcome original monographs and edited volumes as well as English-language translations of manuscripts originally written in other languages.

Titles in the Series

Britain, the Bible, and Balfour: Mandate for a Jewish State, 1530–1917, by Jonathan Immanuel

Judaism for Christians: Menasseh ben Israel (1604–1657), by Sina Rauschenbach

Jewish Studies and Israel Studies in the Twenty-First Century: Intersections and Prospects, edited by Klaus Hödl and Carsten Schapkow

Modern Spain and the Sephardim: Legitimizing Identities, by Maite Ojeda-Mata

Eastern European Jewish American Narratives, 1890–1930: Struggles for Recognition, by Dana Mihailescu

Hostile Takeovers of Large Jewish Companies, 1933–1935: Reassessing Aryanization of Jewish-Owned Firms, by William M. Katin

Hostile Takeovers of Large Jewish Companies, 1933–1935

Reassessing Aryanization of Jewish-Owned Firms

William M. Katin

LEXINGTON BOOKS
Lanham • Boulder • New York • London

Published by Lexington Books
An imprint of The Rowman & Littlefield Publishing Group, Inc.
4501 Forbes Boulevard, Suite 200, Lanham, Maryland 20706
www.rowman.com

6 Tinworth Street, London SE11 5AL, United Kingdom

British Library Cataloguing in Publication Information Available

Library of Congress Control Number: 2020943935

ISBN 9781793606822 (cloth) | ISBN 9781793606839 (epub)

Contents

Tables

Acknowledgments

It is a great privilege to acknowledge my indebtedness to UCLA Professor Albion Urdank. As chair of my dissertation committee and mentor, he gently urged me to refine my ideas. His favorite analogy was to compare my many drafts to the process whereby Karl Marx clarified his *Grundrisse der Kritik der politischen Ökonomie* to *Das Kapital*. Although Dr. Urdank never intended to imply any comparison of my revision of "Aryanization" with the widespread influence of *Das Kapital*, my book has nevertheless left the notebook stage, thanks to his repeated exhortations.

I am also grateful that I had the opportunity to study with Saul Friedländer before his retirement from UCLA. His emphasis on comprehending the Shoah from the perspective of the victims is reflected in my focus on Jewish companies. Many thanks should also be expressed to two other scholars for my business history methodology. In my early stages of research, Northwestern Professor Emeritus Peter Hayes helped me to grasp the problem of understanding large, Jewish-owned conglomerates. In addition, former University of Redlands Professor Jeff Fear encouraged the habit of reading microfilm copies of business documents.

I want to express appreciation for my funding sources. The Paul Turovsky Research Fellowship enabled me to examine both Hermann Tietz and Leonhard Tietz documents in the Federal Archive in Berlin; the Benjamin Nickoll Research Fellowship allowed me to examine private Jewish manuscripts in the Leo Baeck Institute in New York; and the Albert Hoxie Research Fellowship permitted me to utilize Centralverein deutscher Staatsbürger jüdischen Glaubens's legal defense records of terminated Hermann Tietz employees. Appreciation must also be extended to archivists who located original manuscripts for me.

I also want to pay tribute to family members of German department store owners, who provided me with helpful background material. One of these generous individuals was Otto Schiff who informed me about Kaufhaus Schiff in Höchst. Others associated with department stores were introduced to me by UCLA dissertation committee member, Professor Todd S. Presner. I am grateful to Dr. Presner for arranging for me to interview Walter Arlen, who was the grandson of the Warenhaus Dichter owner in Vienna as well as Julius Rothschild who worked for the Leonhard Tietz branch in Aachen.

A third member of my dissertation committee was Professor Mary A. Yeager, for whom I served as a reader in American economic history. I am thankful for the context from which to evaluate German financial history in this book. A fourth committee member was Professor Russell Jacoby. Along with Dr. David N. Myers and Dr. John McCumber, his expertise in intellectual history prepared me to become a lecturer in modern European intellectual history at California State University.

I am especially indebted to my wife, Janet, who has continually encouraged me. I am also extremely grateful to my children Paul, Rebekah, and Deborah, who endured a father overly engrossed in German history and the Shoah.

In conclusion, I would like to dedicate this volume to my grandfather Moritz Katin, who was murdered; to my grandmother Johanna (née Rülf) and her youngest child Leone, who perished in the Kovno Ghetto; as well as to my uncle Benjamin Stein and aunt Jeannette (née Katin), who perished in Sobibor. May their names be a blessing.

Chapter 1

How Cheap Purchases of German-Jewish Firms Occurred

"Aryanization" is the Nazi term for the cheap purchase of Jewish firms during the Third Reich with the ultimate goal of eliminating Jews from the German economy. Eleven of the largest such companies in Germany are examined in this study and a pattern becomes evident. In an atmosphere of anti-Semitism, conservative non-Nazi businessmen approached Germany's three largest banks to request that they withdraw existing loans from a Jewish-owned company. Although this study focuses on the large Hermann Tietz and Leonhard Tietz retailers, it presents a new paradigm of Aryanization through analyses of the patterns of acquisition of massive publishing houses, as well as an enormous private bank, brewery, and a gun manufacturer.[1]

The financial institutions participated because they earned fees, appointed bank executives to the formerly Jewish firms' supervisory boards, and became the house banks conducting all future transactions. Courts were unwilling to intervene in the coerced acquisitions, because they shared the same conservative mindset as the businessmen and financial institutions. By focusing on the Jewish enterprises, it appears that the largest enterprises were frequently purchased in 1933–1935, whereas the tiny "mom-and-pop-shops" usually went out-of-business in 1938. This insight has not been noticed by the traditional model, since it does not differentiate between large and small companies.[2]

The cheap purchase of Jewish-owned companies occurred during the 1933 through 1938 timeframe. Saul Friedländer keenly observed a radical break in its implementation during these six prewar years, with the pre-1936 period being a time of "relative moderation." He discerned a "new phase on the internal German scene" in 1936 in its manner of actualization, which had profound consequences. The 1936 break in the style of execution occurred due to Germany's economic growth and return to full employment as well as Göring's appointment to the Four Year Plan to prepare the nation for war. With regard to the Jewish citizens, the resulting "internal radicalization" in 1936 necessitated that in the opinion of the Reich, "their assets [be] impounded for the benefit of German rearmament." Furthermore, Schacht's dismissal in 1938 also contributed to the government replacing private opportunists as the key player in Aryanization.[3] There were two periods of Aryanization. The 1933–1935 period, discussed in this study, was characterized by an ad hoc private initiative perpetrated by non-Nazi businessmen. In contrast, the 1936–1938 period was an organized state activity leading to the exclusion of Jewish businessmen from the German economy.

Many historians have successfully elucidated the later 1936 through 1938 period of Aryanization directed from Berlin for the benefit of the state or private parties. By observing that the largest of Jewish-owned companies were taken during the earlier 1933 through 1935 period, this volume seeks to make a contribution to scholarship. The responsibility for the 1933–1935 Aryanizations is placed firmly on the private sector, rather than on either the Nazi political party or on the central government in Berlin as has been characterized for the 1936–1938 timeframe. Another comprehensive break in the Aryanization process came later with the focus on tens of thousands of mid-sized and small businesses as contrasted with the earlier conglomerates. The later timeframe additionally also concentrated on houses, apartments, acreage, and even synagogues.[4] This interval coincides with Friedländer's far-reaching break between the two periods of Aryanization. Although the following quotation concerns the difference between the prices paid for large versus small firms, perhaps Friedländer could accept my interpretative inclusions. He affirmed: "As noted in chapter 1, recent research indicates that the considerable scope of [later] Aryanization at the medium- and small-business level was not indicative of the [earlier] situation at the higher level of the economy."[5]

My interpretive adaptation of Friedländer illustrates that although this investigation is indebted to him for an Aryanization paradigm, with a thoroughgoing differentiation before and after 1936, there are some significant contributions in this research. Another such example concerns the role of conservatives in the process of expropriating Jewish companies. Friedländer viewed conservatives, such as Schacht, as a protection for the continuation of Jewish ownership or at least that fair market value would be offered.[6] However, research uncovered in this analysis indicated that in the earlier 1933–1935 period, conservative businessmen without any capital were extended loans by conservative bankers to coerce a sale in which conservative judges were unwilling to ensure that justice was achieved.

For the most part, one does not find documentation in the archives concerning intervention by Adolf Hitler, Hermann Goering, or Rudolf Hess in the seizure of large Jewish-owned department stores, publishing houses, banks, and breweries during the 1933–1935 timeframe. The key participants in the acquisition of such Jewish firms are non-Nationalsozialistische Deutsche Arbeiterpartei (NSDAP) members, such as Joachim Tiburtius, Georg Karg, Max Winkler, Walther Frisch, and Herbert Hoffmann.

Two significant differences immediately emerged between my 1933–1935 bottom-up approach in the investigation of seizing Jewish firms and a later top-down procedure. First, I discovered that in building his financial colossus, Göring had no interest in acquiring firms from the consumer sector as the private Aryanizers did. Göring's NSDAP-inspired technique involved acquiring control over firms in the Autobahn construction, car manufacturing and synthetic fuel and fiber replacement industries. Second, following Friedländer's observation, Göring's Four Year Plan commenced in 1936, which took place after the period from 1933 to 1935 in which the major Jewish companies had been "purchased."

Private "purchases" of Jewish-owned businesses for personal benefit occurred years before Göring's acquisition of war-related industries for the state's benefit. This exploration does not seek to answer the question of whether comparatively smaller private sector Aryanizations influenced the later NSDAP's public infrastructure acquisitions. In addition, neither Friedländer nor I attempt to address the quantitative issues of what percentage of rearmament funding originated with Hjalmar Schacht's Metallurgische Forschungsgesellschaft promissory notes (also known as Mefo bills) as opposed to the requisition of Jewish assets. The hesitancy to be more quantitatively precise in both Aryanization and the funding of German rearmament is indirectly acknowledged by Friedländer's admission: "It is difficult to assess what was paid . . . to the tens of thousands of Jewish owners."[7]

This assessment merely seeks to contribute to the understanding of early Aryanization. Neither the Aryanization by the state nor by private individuals in the later 1936–1938 period are addressed. Numerous other economic issues remain for future research, including other private to public transitions such as the private pre-1933 building of the Autobahn to the later Organisation Todt construction of the roads.[8]

The banks played a key role in the early enrichment of conservative businessmen. One of the three largest financial organizations was the Dresdner Bank. Its executive Karl Rasche was made a scapegoat by his firm in the subsequent war crimes trials at Nuremberg.[9] In contrast, less is known about other Dresdner Bank executives, not to mention the numerous local bank managers who organized lists of local businessmen seeking a quick profit. Similarly, little is known about German businessmen, who were not Nazi Party members, but who nevertheless took advantage of the political circumstances to enrich themselves. Germans viewed postwar denazification proceedings as "victor justice," and thus these postwar processes are replete with whitewashed assessments of how German businessmen acquired Jewish firms. Since the original Jewish proprietors were usually unaware of the confidential negotiations between the three largest banks and the new Gentile owners, the restitution trials are often unhelpful to the historian. Nevertheless, the common perspective of a "perpetrator" as one carrying a weapon is expanded in this book to include "ordinary" non-Nazi businessmen who enriched themselves at Jewish expense.

A. THE ROLE OF ANTI-SEMITISM IN PREPARING THE WAY FOR ARYANIZATIONS

Long before Adolf Hitler's assumption of the reins of government on January 30, 1933, anti-Semitic businessmen had sought support for German boycotts against Jewish stores and youths had desecrated synagogues and Jewish cemeteries. Saul Friedländer has distinguished between an earlier, less violent religious-based anti-Semitism and a later murderous racial anti-Semitism in the Third Reich. The topic of German boycotts against Jewish-owned firms will be addressed in chapter 4 section B through an examination of three of Kurt Zielenziger's economic analyses during January–February 1930. Here the emphasis will focus on newspaper reportage of boycott events from the 1920s in the *C.V. Zeitung*. As early as August 3, 1922, the Jewish media reported on the ironic situation of a German newspaper attempting to profit from both Jewish and anti-Semitic customers. On the one hand, advertisement revenue was sought from Jewish companies, but on the other hand, the same presses printed cards reading: "Buy no sewing supplies from the enemy; Don't buy from Jews!"[10] Lest one imagine that boycotts were restricted to small towns, such as this example from Zeitz in Saxony-Anhalt; the Centralverein deutscher Staatsbürger jüdischen Glaubens specifically mentioned confronting boycotts three months later as part of its strategy. The largest German-Jewish organization announced on the front page of its official organ:

> The content and goal of the Centralverein is appealing to courts and administrative authorities in anti-Semitic infringements of the law; seeking relationships with youth and elderly; with producers and the military class; with knowledge workers and craftsmen to oppose boycotts and pogroms.[11]

After a few years, the attorney Bruno Weil was able to identify a number of features of the anti-Jewish boycotts, most strikingly that they were instigated by nationalistic völkisch groups in the northeastern states of Pomerania and Prussia and not by the fledgling Nazi Party in the southern state of Bavaria:

> The modern boycott movement does not stop with economic issues as in the prewar period, but rather seeks from political motives to bring about the economic harm of jobs. . . . The politically motivated boycott against the Jews reached its zenith at the end of the inflation and the beginning of the stabilization period. It took various forms. Publicly disparaging declarations from local nationalistic groups were relatively seldomly issued. On the other hand, secret mergers could frequently be detected in which every business contact with Jews was to be avoided, for example in the Pomeranian Landbund and in the local group in Rummelsburg. Especially noticeable were the boycotts in Pommerania and East Prussia and especially severe in all the rural areas and small towns as well as in the Voigtland.[12]

By the end of 1928, the location of the most severe boycotts remained in East Prussia. However, two new factors included the greater participation of National Socialists as well as the attempt to obtain relief from Nazi economic oppression through the courts:

> In the December 21, 1928 edition of the *C.V. Zeitung*, we reported on the harsh fashion in which the NSDAP exercised the Christmas boycott in Königsberg and that the department stores and consumer associations which were affected by the boycott acquired interim relief from the District Court, which prohibited the National Socialists from asking for a boycott and treating the affected firms contemptuously. In spite of the legal decree, the National Socialists disobeyed the prohibition in public assemblies and leaflets by calling for a boycott and renewed treating the firms contemptuously. So, Dr. Lepehne filed for fines in two cases.[13]

German-Jewish businessmen were threatened not only by boycotts but also by physical violence, which might accompany the desecration of synagogues and cemeteries during the 1920s. Iron Cross First-Class recipient Leo Löwenstein founded the Reichsbund jüdischer Frontsoldaten on February 8, 1919, after having been mistaken that all prejudice against the Jewish people would be eradicated because of combat for the sake of the German Fatherland in World War I. Instead "unscrupulous defamers greeted us upon returning as cowardly shirkers." In response the Jewish frontline veterans established self-defense units to protect synagogues and passersby. Before coming to the public's attention through the fatal wounding of one plunderer during the November 25, 1923 looting of Berlin's Jewish ghetto, known as the Scheunenviertel, the protection offered by the former soldiers had been reported in the Jewish press:

> Several members of the Federation of Jewish Frontline Soldiers took on guard duty for synagogue attendees [in Görlitz] . . . . But a few minutes after the last

worshipper had left the synagogue, a procession of German nationalists passed by the synagogue.[14]

Interior Minister Karl Jarres admonished in April 1924 that Jewish defense measures must cease. By May 15, 1924, all members of the Berlin squad stood before a large jury trial, although only Löwenstein and two other veterans were fined 50 RM for the possession of illegal firearms.[15]

The discontinuance of armed Jewish self-defense patrols played a role in the dramatic increase of synagogue and cemetery desecrations. A Masonic Lodge publication noted that by the beginning of December 1928, there had been sixty-five desecrations in Germany of Jewish cemeteries and had observed "The true responsibility for such deeds . . . is not only borne by people such as Erich Ludendorff, but also by those who remain silent."[16] The statistic may have attracted the attention of the Jewish media because thereafter they tracked the number of profanations scrupulously. As the incidents increased, the locations moved south from East Prussia to Franconia and also included National Socialists:

> The series of desecrations of Jewish cemeteries will not end. We already counted to the shocking numbers 77 and 78 . . . . In the small village of Preußisch-Holland in East Prussia, a shroud was taken from the Jewish mortuary and burned. Eight days later five tombstones were toppled and smashed with a hammer. The police charged 17–year-old Walter Werner . . . . On January 21st tombstones were overturned and damaged in the Jewish cemetery in Georgensgmünd near Nuremberg . . . Georgensgmünd is one of the areas, where the National Socialist movement has strongly agitated and *Der Stürmer* is widely read.[17]

The Jewish publication continued to lament as the number of defilements increased to 109 at the end of 1931. Although perpetrators were seldom caught, the participation of Nazis had been documented in eight of those incidents, including Göttingen on August 10, 1924, Gerolzhofen near Schweinfurt on August 28, 1927, Gladbeck on January 19, 1929, Berlin on February 16, 1930, Trebnitz in November 1930, Freistett in Baden on April 21, 1931, Schriesheim on June 5, 1931, and Buchen in Baden on August 11, 1931.[18]

B. WERE ARYANIZATIONS ATTEMPTS TO "CAMOUFLAGE" JEWISH OWNERSHIP?

Ludolf Herbst's and Thomas Weihe's research in the Commerzbank's archive questioned whether the bank's true motives were anti-Semitism or to help Jewish proprietors. Weihe's perspective would challenge the methodology introduced in this book. As non-Jewish firms refused to issue contracts to their Jewish counterparts, these two German scholars claim that Jewish entrepreneurs attempted to "camouflage" ownership by means of alleged sales to Aryan employees or friends. The evidence for this provocative interpretation rests on a November 7, 1935, issue of the Chamber of Industry and Commerce's internal publication. Commerzbank supervisory board member Friedrich Reinhard looked favorably on the exposé of sham sales undertaken by business registration courts as reported in the Chamber's internal organ. Herbst and Weihe had access to the files of mid-sized Jewish firms with fewer than 1,000 employees. These historians' goal was to demonstrate that the owners devised negotiation strategies in long-term processes between 1933 and 1938 and were thus actors and not mere victims.[19]

The proposal of sham sales by virtuous German colleagues to protect the actual Jewish owners introduces a tantalizing theory. However, it neither reveals names nor the number of Jewish companies, which attempted to camouflage their true ownership. There is an internal methodological inconsistency between positing that Jews attempted to conceal the true ownership of their businesses with the expectation of discovering written records of the secret transactions, especially in the files of a non-Jewish bank. Nevertheless, the question regarding Jewish actions remains valid.

C. FIVE JEWISH STRATEGIES DEPICTING CUSTOMARY RESPONSES, RATHER THAN CAMOUFLAGE

Rather than seeking Jewish entrepreneurs' responses in the customer files of the Commerzbank, or in the NSDAP's 1935 *Green Address Book*, or in Chamber of Industry and Commerce's lists from the end of 1937 or in the Gau Economic Advisors files or in Aryanization companies, such as LEGA GmbH from 1938 as Ludolf Herbst did,[20] it seemed more appropriate to seek a Jewish response in the weekly editions of Germany's largest Jewish newspaper, the *C.V. Zeitung* from January through December 1933.

Instead of finding any evidence for concealing the Jewish ownership of a business as the camouflage theory claims, I discovered advertisements for "property management" from the Fall of 1933 as well as five different Jewish strategies to attempt an offsetting of the economic persecution. These tactics reoccurred in feature articles and large display ads throughout the year.

The October 4, 1933, issue of the *C.V. Zeitung* provided one of two unambiguous small personal advertisements. It concerned Dr. G., who was a retired senior civil servant seeking employment. His qualifications included fluency in French and English, which he had undoubtedly gained via business experiences abroad. He sought to assume a trusteeship of any kind of company, including managing an organization or buildings or assets. What is most startling about this ad was that Dr. G explicitly stated that he was an Aryan. Rather than an attempt to provide camouflage for the true Jewish ownership, this example extended the Aryan nature of Dr. G as a benefit to the Jewish firm. Having an Aryan executive as the company trustee was considered as a means of continuing the firm's existence as early as the Fall of 1933.

The other unambiguous ad was published in the November 2, 1933, edition by a thirty-seven-year-old Jewish man, who had been expelled from the civil service. He was seeking a property management position. In comparing the two advertisements, it is clear that the former Jewish civil servant was seeking a job, whereas the retired official was seeking either control of the operations or control over the ownership. Whereas the first two illustrations make it explicit whether the applicant was a Gentile or a Jew, it is not as clear in a third case. Because the candidate described himself as a "retired attorney and notary," it would appear as though he was not Jewish. The position for which he applied was the management of many rental properties. Combining the two facts leads to the conclusion that he was an Aryan, who thought he could come out of retirement and quickly earn large sums of money. The final instance is even more ambiguous. Since it appeared on both October 4 and 11, 1933, perhaps the persistence indicates a true need for an income, rather than an enhancement to a retirement paycheck. It may be concluded that this final job search was by a Jewish aspirant. In contrast with a paradigm, suggesting the desire to conceal Jewish ownership, these examples indicate a willingness to reveal identity in the public media. In addition, Dr. G and the retired attorney were clearly concerned about exploiting the opportunity for their own benefit, not about assisting Jewish businesses in distress.

In contrast with the recently proposed paradigm of concealment, I discovered five strategies by Jewish people to offset prejudice in the economy in 1933. The most frequently offered and availed strategy in the *C.V. Zeitung* was the provision and use of advice for Jews forced to adopt a new career. The reference to the Centralverein's Legal-Economic Counseling Center occurred for four weeks before the passage of the Law for the Restoration of the Professional Civil Service. The cause for this new service, commencing on March 16, 1933, was the "radical change" (Umwälzung) in the economy occurring in the first two weeks of March. At its inception, consultations were only available to members of the Centralverein.[21] But weeks before the Law for the Restoration of the Professional Civil Service, Jewish businessmen were flocking to these six-days-a-week counseling appointments. A front-page article in the following week depicted the "radical change" as a "National Revolution," in which private beneficiaries (Nutznießer) had used "the historical events as the basis for personal revenge." Forming an analogy between the 1933 Revolution and World War I, the newspaper correspondent adopted an expression from the war: "hyenas of the battlefield." The beneficiaries of the March 1933 Revolution, he now termed as "Hyenas of the Revolution."[22] I interpret the newspaper expression as the "Economic Opportunists of the March 1933 Revolution against the Jews." Centralverein counseling was not provided to enable Jewish businessmen to cooperate with Gentile "helpers," but to protect Jews from those trying to fleece them.

In the first week of career counseling, the clientele was enlarged from merely Centralverein members to all Jewish men and women, who represented diverse groups. A first group seeking advice included physicians, medical interns, attorneys, artists, teachers, businessmen, and other white-collar employees. The persecuting Aryan beneficiaries must have either been employers or competing Germans in white-collar careers, since the newspaper specified that those seeking advice had been terminated without notice. The article indicated that a second group seeking practical recommendations consisted of students prior to their graduation, who were confronted by an unpromising future. A third group consisted of those who were afraid of losing their economic existence in the coming weeks and months. Ironically, the modern camouflage theory portrayed Jewish businessmen as active participants, some of whom concealed the ownership of their firms. In contrast, the newspaper account from March 1933 depicted male and female employees of all ages in the direst of financial circumstances. The description from 1933 portrayed unemployed Jews in a more passive mode: "with the deepest worries concerning their economic existence, regarding how they should construct a new life."[23]

Because the caseload grew nearly every day in March 1933, another German-Jewish organization began offering advice concerning jobs, namely the Wirtschaftsausschutz des Preußischen Landesverbandes jüdische Gemeinden (Economic Committee of the Prussian Regional Association of Jewish Congregations).[24] Non-Jewish employers took advantage of the circumstances, becoming beneficiaries as evidenced in the April 6, 1933, reportage. German employers not only preceded the April 1 Civil Service Law but also misapplied it to the detriment of their Jewish workers. Aryan employers reduced their payroll expenses by firing their Jewish private sector employees without notice or cause. In the front page, featured article historian Ismar Elbogen depicted how a law regarding government officials was greatly extended by Aryan opportunists: "Ten thousand from us have been forced out of our bread and profession. Numerous independent existences have been uprooted . . . . One can condemn us to hunger, but not starvation!"[25] A second article also noted that the Jewish organization had done more than merely provide counseling. The agency had also implemented countermeasures with the private sector of the economy: "In the last hour, the Centralverein reached an interpretation of employee terminations with the responsible committee of retailers."[26] Unfortunately dismissals of Jewish employees extended far beyond merchants and salesmen to the realm of the artisans. Thus, a twenty-year veteran in the typesetting industry appealed for justice after his firing.[27] Hundreds of sacked workers of all disciplines were advised each week as the newspaper reported: "In our waiting rooms and counseling rooms, high officials sit next to the worried apprentice, the human resources manager of a large business next to terminated shorthand typist."[28] The evidence of large numbers of Jews from diverse professions awaiting career counseling cannot be harmonized with a modern theory of Gentiles with high-minded motives, seeking to aid Jewish businessmen.

In the prior quotation from Professor Elbogen, one might wonder whether his reference to "starvation" was an unfortunate example of hyperbole by a historian, since most scholars depict the economic destruction of German Jews as occurring in 1938 and not as early as 1933. Yet, in the emergence of career advisement by a third organization, the Zentralausschuß der deutschen Juden für Hilfe und Aufbau, the same degree of indigence is affirmed: "Certainly, it is our primary task that none of ours should need to starve and to be deprived of the roof over his head."[29]

A development in the structure of the job counseling facility indicates an improvement in the quality of advice as well as in the efficiency in advising an ever-increasing number of unemployed workers. This trend is observable in the period May–June 1933. On May 11, there was only one Centralverein law office providing services for civil servants, physicians, university students, artists, independent businessmen, and members of the other free professions. One week later the fields of dentists and journalists were added. However, by June 22, 1933, not only had the *C.V. Zeitung* started a new column entitled "For Help and Building-Up," but also the sole office had been expanded into the six departments of white-collar workers, attorneys, physicians, civil servants, college instructors, and artists, as well as journalists. In addition to the intensification of Jewish countermeasures, a fourth organization was established to assist the previously existing three agencies of the Centralverein, the Wirtschaftsausschutz des Preußischen Landesverbandes, and the Zentralausschuß der deutschen Juden für Hilfe und Aufbau. The new association was the Reichsverband des jüdischen Mittelstandes, which saw its chief task as "contributing to the preservation of the Jewish people and advocacy in economic and vital issues."[30]

Instead of enlisting fair-minded non-Jewish colleagues to camouflage Jewish ownership of businesses, the 1933 issues of the *C.V. Zeitung* record a second measure, which Jewish people implemented to counteract the economic oppression in the German economy. In addition to job counseling, unemployed Jews developed new companies. The most well-known example was the Kulturbund Deutscher Juden (Cultural Federation of German Jews). Berlin Rabbis joined in the assistance to thousands of terminated producers, directors, actors, singers, and other artists, who lost their creative positions.

After four publicity evenings in July and August, the next marketing step was to sell memberships in the August 17, 1933, *C.V. Zeitung*. The monthly fee of 2.50 RM allowed the subscriber to attend one theater performance, one concert and one lecture per month during the 1933–1934 artistic year.[31]

Kurt Singer obtained permission from Hans Hinkel, who had been the editor of the *Völkischer Beobachter*, before becoming the president of the Prussian Theater Committee in the Ministry of Culture. Councilor Otto Laubinger of the Propaganda Ministry joined Hinkel in providing government authorization in July, on the condition that only Jews could be members and only members would be admitted to the events, which would otherwise be closed to the public. From the 10,000 attending the marketing evenings, advertisements were sent to a few thousand and Singer's staff grew from five to twelve members. Publicity was not only given by the *C.V. Zeitung*, but also by four other Jewish newspapers, including the *Jüdische Rundschau*, *Hamburger Familienblatt*, *Jüdisch-Liberale Zeitung*, and *Schild*. Branches of the Federation were also formed in large cities.[32]

In analyzing this second strategy, whereby German Jews responded to economic discrimination in 1933, the camouflage hypothesis once again appears improbable. When government authorization was received from both Hans Hinkel and Otto Laubinger, four Rabbis gave public support to the self-help endeavor, including Rabbis Baeck, Prinz, Warschauer, and Wiener. In order to sell memberships, five newspapers provided publicity, including the *C.V. Zeitung*, *Jüdische Rundschau*, *Hamburger Familienblatt*, *Jüdisch-Liberale Zeitung*, and *Schild*. Instead of being a camouflaged response, the Berlin Bund's activities were so well-known that it inspired similar cultural responses in many large cities.[33]

A third reaction, which opposes the camouflage hypothesis, concerns advertisements for moving companies both warehousing and transporting furniture to Palestine. The timeframe for this third strategy is limited to the period from July 6 through October 4, 1933. This would appear to indicate that counseling for new careers in Germany as well as the creation of new jobs in the Fatherland were the first choices for Jews. Emigration became a possibility only after the first two coping mechanisms had proved to be less than ideal.

Advertisements were placed by Neumann and Schneider, who claimed that they were specialists in moving furniture to Palestine and Paris.[34] By August 10, 1933, two other moving companies were seeking Jewish customers, namely the Block and the S. Simonowitz firms.[35]

Three new moving companies began advertising in the same newspaper issue, including the large display ad by Brasch and Rothenstein, which specified in large type: "Transport to and from Palestine." A second firm was the public corporation Transhand in Munich, which had previously been Falk & Foy. A third business was the Treuhand-Gesellschaft, which specifically marketed itself as a "Christian" company. Two new moving companies began advertising in the September 20, 1933, edition of the newspaper. One was named "Möbeltransport Merkur" and specified that its owner L. Abraham would bring furniture to Paris or Berlin. Another new feature in the September 28, 1933, edition was Italian steamers taking Jewish passengers on information trips to Palestine as in the case of Amtliches Italienisches Reisebüro. A variation was provided by the Consulich Line, which transported immigrants to what became Israel.[36]

In contrast to the camouflage theory, a fourth public strategy, which Jews utilized to counter the effects of job dislocation was training on farms. Two objectives were simultaneously employed. First the number of Jews engaged in law and medicine was reduced along with attempting to diminish the criticism that Jewish men performed the "disreputable" work of trading, rather than the "honest labor" of farming. Second, Palestine's economy required agricultural workers, rather than professors, physicians, and attorneys. Photographs by Herbert Sonnenfeld depicted voluntary labor service on the Neuendorf training farm outside Berlin in the January 19, 1933, edition of the newspaper. The 927-acre farm was leased in 1932 by the jüdische Arbeitshilfe with financial support from the Prussian Welfare Ministry to train sixty unemployed youth, who would stay for twenty weeks. Not only was financial support from the Prussian government obtained but also public acclaim from the mayor of Lobetal in this openly acknowledged Jewish self-help program.[37]

Sonnenfeld photographed not only the Neuendorf training farm outside Berlin but also the Israelite Horticulture School in Ahlem, the labor camp in the Berlin suburb of Waidsmannslust, the labor redevelopment camp in Niederschönhausen, the facility in Ahrensdorf, which prepared young people to operate a Kibbutz together in Palestine, the religious facility in Steckelsdorf uniting Orthodoxy with work, and the two schools in Rüdnitz and Schniebinchen preparing fifteen- to seventeen-year-old teenagers for emigration to Palestine.[38]

A fifth and final strategy utilized by Jews was the establishment of settlements other than in Palestine for German-Jews. The previously mentioned organization the Zentralausschuß der deutschen Juden für Hilfe und Aufbau advocated this approach. This tactic was not advocated by the Centralverein, which warned about the financial risks. Nevertheless, it was included in their organ's newspaper.[39]

The claim that Commerzbank executives or loyal colleagues helped conceal the ownership of Jewish companies is improbable. If this had occurred, one would have expected that thousands of Jewish owners would have flocked back to Germany after the war to resume their businesses. But after the war, the "non-Jewish caretakers" did not reveal that they had merely been concealing the true ownership of the company and restore ownership to the true proprietors. In contrast, chapter 6 of this book will discuss the Dresdner Bank's Aryanization of Bankhaus Gebrüder Arnhold. After the war, Walther Bernhard revealed that after the sales price had been accepted, the Dresdner Bank "used every opportunity to accuse the Arnholds of contract violations . . . thereby the Bank destroyed the hopes of having found a friendly and fair contract partner."[40]

Instead of an unproven and unlikely camouflaging of Jewish possession of firms by honest bankers and businessmen, I have uncovered cooperation among non-Nazi businessmen, the three largest German banks, and the courts. This occurred due to their shared conservative ideology and the opportunism of the Dresdner Bank and ambitious entrepreneurs, aided by the judiciary's laissez-faire mindset. Transitioning from a refutation of the camouflage theory to the role of the banks, a sixth strategy can be noted, which was not discerned by examining the *C.V. Zeitung* from 1933. Some talented Jewish individuals were able to move from a large Aryan firm to a Jewish-owned company. Such was the case with regard to Walther Bernhard, who foresaw that he no longer had a future with the Dresdner Bank and therefore transitioned to the Berlin branch of the privately owned Bankhaus Gebrüder Arnhold.[41] In contrast with the camouflage proposal, which focused on the Commerzbank, Aryanization from 1933 to 1935 was made possible due to the Dresdner Bank.

D. ROLE OF THE BANKS IN ARYANIZATION

The three major German banks were essential to all businesses due to their short-term loans, which made the purchase of new inventory possible. Before becoming economics editor of the *Vossische Zeitung* in 1926, Kurt Zielenziger published major business essays in Jewish periodicals. He stressed the necessity of cash in a front-page feature: "A business class without operating capital is an economic impossibility." Joseph Goebbels distorted the need for liquid assets in support of his propaganda: "Department stores and large banks work closely together. The banks provide credit whereby new purchasing palaces can always be formed on the earth." Anti-Semites perversely recognized long before Hitler's ascension that loans from Germany's three major banks were crucial for the financial success of large Jewish commercial enterprises. Later chapters of this text will illustrate the centrality of loans for the Hermann Tietz department store chain and the Mosse publishing house when both firms possessed collateral in the form of fixed assets. In his disinformation campaign, Joseph Goebbels distorted the legitimate relationship between Jewish firms and large banks. Goebbels had merely incorrectly assumed that the banks would have to be "stormed" in order to break the bonds binding the financial institutions with large Jewish entrepreneurs.[42] Goebbels had failed to take into consideration that the banks would obtain fees and commissions by extending loans to the new proprietors. The banks viewed the assessment of new costs as a higher priority than maintaining traditional relationships with Jewish clients. Nazi propaganda claimed that Jews sought to dominate the world through global capitalism, whereas in actuality, German banks were eager to pocket additional fees for extending credit.

Another important factor in the banks' involvement in the inexpensive acquisition of Jewish firms was the interlocking nature of German financial institutions. For example, as a member of the Dresdner Bank's Loan and Personnel Committee, Bernhard Dernburg played the decisive role in convincing the Dresdner Board of Directors to accept a fusion with the Danat Bank. Because Dernburg was simultaneously a member of the Akzeptbank's supervisory board, he convinced the hesitant minister of the economy that Germany's bank of acceptance was able to repay the Dresdner Bank's loan for acquiring the Danat Bank, in case the former defaulted. Because of the cartel-like nature of German public and private lending institutions, one individual was able to endorse the Dresdner's takeover of the Danat by ensuring guarantees from the Akzeptbank. This cooperative spirit is evident in the fact that the acceptance bank's liability for the merger was reduced from 440 million RM at the beginning of 1932 to 280 million by the conclusion of 1932.[43]

The successful collaboration of German financial repositories is supported by the Dresdner Bank's 1932 annual report, which surprisingly stated that the merger was successfully implemented "in a few weeks." Despite fifty-two Dresdner offices being "folded into Danat Bank branches" as well as a 20.9 percent reduction in employees from 13,898 to 10,994, Dresdner management recommended a 31.8 percent devaluation in the value of shareholder equity from 220 million RM to 150 million RM. The Dresdner Bank attempted to increase revenue, because the profit margin from lending declined, since the gap between the interest rate they were charged and the amount they could charge borrowers had decreased. One method of increasing bank income was to implement the Reich President's October 6, 1931 Ordinance, which allowed the Bank to reduce unproductive reserves from 30 million RM to 15 million RM.[44] The elucidation of the Dresdner Bank's coordination with the Akzeptbank and the loan amount guaranteed provides the background for understanding the Dresdner Bank's quest to leverage more of its reserves and arrange new loans at higher interest. Bank commissions and higher interest rates provided much of the motivation for Germany's largest financial institutions to participate in the takeover of Jewish-owned businesses. A prominent example was the inexpensive acquisition of the Hermann Tietz department store chain by means of Georg Karg's 14 million RM Akzeptbank-guaranteed loan through the Dresdner Bank consortium.

By extending capital to a new non-Jewish owner, the financial institution became the primary lending institution of the acquired company. Thereby, they were able to obtain supervisory board seats in the firms, which provided the banks with voting rights and insider information. An example of the value of insider information for Aryanization is revealed in the takeover of the Vereinigten Papierwerks Heroldsberg-Nuremberg. As will be discussed in chapter 7, as early as 1934, the Dresdner Bank branch manager recommended that Gustav Schickedanz purchase the paper company's stock housed in the bank's vault as security, in order to pay off the Jewish firm's loan with the bank.[45] Because the branch managers had detailed information about local Jewish-owned firms, the mid-level managers were frequently involved in Aryanizations. Despite more widespread involvement, the Dresdner Bank was willing to sacrifice one top executive, such as Karl Rasche, as the scapegoat during the Nuremberg Trials. A fuller discussion of Rasche will appear in chapter 2.

In addition, individual Deutsche Bank and Dresdner Bank executives were able to garner more personal power, not only within their own lending firms, but also in the Aryanized business. One illustration of personal enrichment occurred when Schickedanz acquired a second Jewish firm in order to serve as a supplier for the Vereinigten Papierwerk. He bribed a second Dresdner Bank Branch Manager in order to force the payment of the entire pension fund obligation of the Jewish company. The requirement to pay the entire amount to the retirement fund would provide the opportunity for Schickedanz to make another quick purchase. Examples of these benefits obtained by the Dresdner Bank will be seen in the examination of Aryanizations contained in Chapters Six and Seven.

E. ROLE OF OPPORTUNISTIC GERMAN BUSINESSMEN

My perspective is that the banks enabled inexperienced German businessmen to become instantly wealthy. But Gregor Schöllgen's biography of Schickedanz characterized him quite differently. It narrated that after the July 13, 1929 death of his wife in a car accident and the temporary closure of the Dresdner Bank on July 14, 1931, Schickedanz "went on the offensive as he had in the crisis of the early 1920s" and "he again acted counter-cyclically."

He acted in a completely opposite manner to the prevailing business trend by buying a former 8,000 m^2 shoe factory from the state of Bavaria, when the market had bottomed-out. Since his mail-order business needed to expand its circle of customers during the crisis, Schickedanz hired the free-lance artist Otto Steinlein in 1930 to increase catalog sales. Sales grew because of Schickedanz's "no-questions-asked return policy" as well as by selling a five-piece men's suit for only 9.95 RM as unemployment rapidly increased. He made a lowball cash purchase of high-quality wool from a Westphalian mill, when an English firm failed to accept delivery of the cloth.[46] No American could fail to be impressed by a Horatio Alger rags-to-riches novel, but does merely hard work and determination actually bring success in the modern capitalistic business world? The German biographer claimed that Schickedanz had "an excellent reputation throughout Germany" among suppliers. However, the historian failed to notice Schickedanz's twice-depicted character of offering ridiculously low bids, when the seller was undergoing a crisis. It would be the same strategy, which he used a few years later in buying several Jewish-owned businesses facing the economic downturn.[47]

There is a methodological problem in analyzing the actions of Aryanizers, beyond viewing the buyers as helpfully intending to camouflage the Jewish identity of the company owners. A second difficulty is the sources used to depict the motives behind the participants in the transfer of assets. After World War II, most Germans began a frantic search for Socialists, Jews, or religious leaders, who could write a letter of recommendation attesting to their upright character. These ubiquitous letters were called Persilscheine after the name of the German laundry detergent, "Persil." Postwar German character needed to be washed "as white as snow" in Denazification Trials in order for society to continue.

When reviews of Schöllgen's book appeared, both Dieter Ziegler and Ralf Ahrens observed that Schöllgen had eschewed footnotes, which would have required him to document whether his sources were the exculpatory letters from Denazification Trials, since Schickedanz had joined the Nazi Party on November 1, 1932. In addition, the large number of files containing these whitewashed attestations did not address the issue of whether any of them were credible. The Restitution Cases in the Bavarian State Office pose the different problem of providing the two opposing perspectives from the German opportunist, who acquired the firm during the Third Reich, and the original Jewish owner. By failing to document the source, it could become unclear whether a statement represented an opinion of one of the opposing parties or a judicial conclusion. Postwar evidence came from the Schickedanz family and company archives, to which no historian other than Schöllgen has been given access. Ziegler was suspicious that these sources were also designed to exonerate Schickedanz.[48]

Ziegler also raised an issue with regard to his acquisition of the Rosenfelder brothers' Vereinigte Papierwerke company. Similar to the universal recognition of the brand names "Kleenex" and "Tampax" in the United States, so the Rosenfelder's corresponding "Tempo" and "Camelia" were household terms and as such had an economic value. The name was an asset, which was not recognized as possessing its own economic worth, which needed to be paid for by all the Aryanizers in the 1930s. To concretize: the purchase price for a factory, which manufactures 100,000 Kleenex, should be far more than for a factory that produces 100,000 facial tissues.

Although Schöllgen's book on Schickedanz is one of the most recent productions on an Aryanizer, Ziegler sadly concluded that it "represents a relapse in the writing of German business history." Ziegler ruefully forecast: "Historians, who are not contracted by the family, will probably not be given access to the family archive."

F. ROLE OF JUDGES IN ARYANIZATION

One might have imagined that the German judiciary would have interceded on behalf of Jewish entrepreneurs, who had been coerced into signing sales contracts at give-away prices, either on the legal grounds of physical or economic duress. But such an interpretation would been founded on a lack of understanding of the Weimar era judiciary. One main school of interpretation views judges in light of their conservative monarchic upbringing and training. A second major perspective explicated judges in terms of rejecting natural law in favor of legal positivism. Emil Julius Gumbel is perhaps the most prominent proponent of the former view and those contrasting Gustav Radbruch's pre- versus postwar understanding of jurisprudence may be viewed as advocates of the latter view.

Gumbel taught statistics at the University of Heidelberg, but he is most well-known for examining 376 murders committed from January 1919 through the killing of Walther Rathenau on June 24, 1922. Of these killings occurring out of political motivations, 354 had been committed by right-wing perpetrators of whom 326 went unpunished and the remaining few punished received an average sentence of four months. In contrast, left-wing murderers numbered only twenty-two, of whom merely four went unpunished and the remaining were sentenced to an average imprisonment of five years. By publishing a book disclosing these details, Gumbel demanded a public investigation of the one-sided judiciary from Minister of Justice Gustav Radbruch.[49]

Gumbel decried the one-sided convictions in which two right-wing adherents had been convicted for theft of the deceased's possessions and two had been sentenced for manslaughter. In addition, officials had been unable to trace a single assassin despite being given specifications of the perpetrator and the surrounding circumstances. Furthermore, the offender was frequently acquitted because he assumed that he had been ordered to shoot the victim. Moreover, Gumbel depicted that "the legal situation of the surviving dependents is as unfavorable as possible." The law had recognized that when the sole wage earner had been shot, the fate of the family was dire and therefore the state would assume the burden of court costs. But through the "devices" of the judiciary, the Arbitration Court imposed this burden on all cases on the surviving family members. Gumbel specifically precluded the possibility that the financial imposition could have been the "artifice" merely of Bavaria. He provided the illustration that when Max Maurer was shot while "attempting to escape," near Bottrop, his widow was informed that she would have to prove that he had not been fleeing when killed, in order to avoid the imposition of court costs.[50]

In his sociological analysis of the lack of punishment for right-wing homicides, Gumbel observed that World War I had "blunted the value of human life." Nevertheless, the onus fell squarely on the lack of impartiality in the German judiciary, and without its collusion, "these circumstances would naturally be inconceivable."[51]

The prior edition of this pamphlet, entitled *Two Years of Murder*, had already sold 18,000 copies and thus Gumbel had noted that it had "by no means remained unnoticed." He had assumed that either the judiciary would have believed that he had told the truth and would prosecute the 300 murderers or that it would be convinced that he had perjured himself and sentence him for libel. Perhaps since neither occurred, Gumbel's expanded *Four Years of Political Murder* attempted to provoke a prejudiced judiciary to reform its ways:

> If a supporter of the left-wing Parties is killed by someone in the right-wing, the judge will simply be unable to detach himself from the thought that the murdered individual was his enemy and by his attitude was already deserving of a severe punishment. The murderer is actually preempted from punitive justice and therefore is to be treated mildly. Thus, it frequently occurs that ethically the murdered, rather than the murderer, stands before the judge. The murderer belongs to the same social class and life as the judge. Innumerable social bonds tie the officer-assassin to the judge, who will acquit him, and to the public prosecutor who will suspend the proceedings and to the witness who described in detail the "attempted escape." They are of the same flesh and blood. The judge understands their language, feelings and thoughts. Under the pretense of formality, his soul tenderly resonates with the murderers. The murderer is acquitted.
>
> But woe, when the murderer is left-wing.[52]

Gumbel's contemporary assessment of Weimar's judiciary is confirmed by current scholars, who contrast how Bavarian Minister of Justice Franz Gürtner and Bavarian Supreme Court counselor Theodor von der Pfordten adjudicated two trials: the trial against Felix Fechenbach in 1922 and the proceedings against Adolf Hitler in 1924. Several weeks before becoming the Justice Minister, Gürtner publicly joined Hans Hilpert's Middle Party, which welcomed nationalistic associations, but rejected the parliamentary democracy of the Weimar Republic. The party never established boundaries to distinguish itself from radical right-wing activities out of fear of losing votes. Gürtner's cunning ability to remain ambivalent was key to his decade-long career in the Bavarian Cabinet, which was rewarded by his promotion to Minister of Justice for the entire Reich under Franz von Papen and Hitler.[53]

In October 1922, Kurt Eisner's private secretary Felix Fechenbach was sentenced to eleven years in jail for treason. He had given a diplomatic document from before 1918 to the foreign press as well as news about the activities of illegal arming of militant right-wing organizations and its toleration by the government. In November 1922, the Bavarian Parliament upheld the court's decision. Fechenbach's Defense Attorney Max Hirschberg filed an appeal for clemency, observing among other items that Theodor von der Pfordten had previously opined that disclosing documents to a foreign newspaper did not constitute treason. Although the Bavarian State Court's October 30, 1923, opinion recognized several violations of the law by the District Court, von der Pfordten ruled that all Hirschberg's objections against the Lower court's verdict were unfounded. Ten days later, von der Pfordten was killed while participating in the November 9, 1923, Hitler Putsch.[54]

In contrast with Fechenbach's sentence of eleven years of imprisonment for treason, Hitler was sentenced on January 12, 1922, to merely three months for "disturbing the peace," when his followers bombed the Bavarian Federation meeting. By the end of July 1922, Hitler was released on probation after serving one month. However, the probation faced revocation since various paramilitary organizations threatened an armed deployment against a peaceful May 1, 1923, rally in Oberwiesenfeld by labor unions and Social Democrats. Although the public prosecutor objected to Hitler's probation, the Bavarian Supreme Court rejected the complaint. Admittedly the court reduced Fechenbach's sentence to the three-and-a-half years already served. However, Minister of Justice Franz Gürtner postponed Fechenbach's pardon as long as Bavarian state policy required it. With regard to equal treatment under the law, current scholarship concluded: "In this sense, Gürtner subordinated the law to politics, a mindset more pronounced as his behavior with regard to the illegal activities of the radical nationalistic associations and Hitler in 1923 proves."[55]

Although judges' unconditional loyalty to a conservative state and strong monarchic convictions did not correspond with the political ideals of the Republic, less than 0.15 percent of all judges retired, despite guarantees of financial claims. They were characterized by a love for authority and nationalism, which "was not far from the path of racism" and with regard to politics there was no question of independence. In the April 1924 Hitler-Ludendorff trial, the same Bavarian court suspended Hitler's five-year sentence after he had served six months in prison. Ludendorff left the courtroom as a free man. Although Fechenbach was pardoned in 1924, he was arrested by the Nazis in March 1933 and was shot on August 7, 1933, while being transported to Dachau. At the conclusion of the German Lawyers Conference in Leipzig on October 3, 1933, more than 10,000 attorneys gave the Hitler salute and swore an oath to follow Hitler until the end of their days. Thus, contemporaries are able to conclude that "it was unnecessary for the new rulers to exert a direct influence on the judicial system."[56]

Even before Gumbel observed the lack of fairness in the German judiciary, *Vorwärts* Editor Erich Kuttner published a book entitled *Class Justice* in which he had provided reasons why German judges were biased in favor of right-wing defendants. The first reason was due to the small unrepresentative stratum of the society from which judges were selected. Due to the requirements of a lengthy university education followed by unpaid internships, prospective judges needed to come from wealthy homes in order to afford the costs incurred. Three to four years of education were followed by a similar length of time as a trainee in the civil service, which in turn was followed after the Second State Exam by a five to ten-year probationary period. During the time in training and probation, the individual worked gratuitously and only at the age of about thirty-five to thirty-eight would the person be paid a salary. Kuttner estimated the required investment as between 30,000 and 50,000 Marks, thus requiring extremely large family financial backing. Prussia reinforced this selective process by further requiring a cash deposit in a bank of 7,500 Marks. A left-leaning worker or liberal middle-class family hardly possessed such wealth to support an aspiring judge.

Kuttner provided additional reasons why the German judiciary was exclusively conservative in political orientation by observing that "an unpopular trainee could be dismissed from judicial service without further ado and with no legal procedure." This was not a theoretical hurdle. Wilhelm Liebknecht's sons, Karl and Theodor, were rejected as trainees even though they had not yet been personally active in politics.

Furthermore, Kuttner observed that judges were the most monarchic in orientation of all German civil servants. Nevertheless, he graciously concluded that judges were unaware of their own bias and thus their injustice was due to naïve innocence.[57]

To demonstrate that this right-wing interpretation of the German judiciary is not merely the view of left-wing individuals such as Emil Gumbel and Erich Kuttner, the Jewish weekly *C.V. Zeitung* will be briefly surveyed. Admittedly, the organ for the Centralverein deutscher Staatsbürger jüdischen Glaubens is an unlikely source to find substantiation for a broader public acknowledgment of inherent prejudice in the judges of the Weimar Republic for two reasons. First, in their attempt to prove their loyalty to Germany, this newspaper could be quite nationalistic. For example, the June 27, 1930, headline read: "Frei ist der Rhein!" and the front-page article commenced with the patriotic sentiment: "When the sun rises on July 1st, its rays will greet a freed land. On June 30th the last foreign soldier will leave the Rhineland. The German people on the Rhine are redeemed from decades-long hardship."[58]

German Zionists were infuriated that the Centralverein was overly zealous for the Fatherland. Unfortunately, this determination to prove their loyalty to Germany was evident in their unwarranted expectation that their civil rights would be protected by the courts. This unfortunate Jewish assumption remained even after the July 1932 Preußenschlag in which Chancellor Franz von Papen dismissed the SPD government of Prussia. This unsettling attack against the Republic occasioned the Centralverein to seek reassurances from Reich Minister of the Interior Wilhelm von Gayl, since the Jewish population viewed the circumstances as a "civil-war-situation." Jewish leaders reaffirmed their faith in Germany as a nation of laws, when the minister promised to uphold the laws with all means.[59]

Despite this over-confidence in Germany's adherence to the law, a brief survey of the major German-Jewish newspaper exposes some doubts about the right-wing judiciary. In January 1926, Max Warburg sued Theodor Fritsch for his slanderous articles in his newspaper *Hammer*. One article was entitled "The Secret Kaiser" and another was captioned "Who Is Guilty of the Defeat?" Fritsch claimed that during World War I, Warburg had behaved as an advocate of "Jewish world capital" instead of as a German. The first trial resulted in a verdict of three-month imprisonment for Fritsch. On appeal, the sentence was reduced to a 1,000 RM fine. The *C.V. Zeitung* commented that "Contrary to expectations, Fritsch received an exceedingly mild punishment."[60] In the following days, additional insight was provided regarding the Jewish perspective on the trial. Although the newspaper was clearly perplexed by the unexpected outcome of the appeal, nevertheless the reporter went to the extreme length of making German judges seem to be passive victims, in order to avoid assigning them a share of the responsibility for the political bias evident in both the trial proceedings as well as in the outcomes.

> In the course of many years, the political trial has come into fashion with us. One can certainly not say that it is a gratifying achievement. The judge is given

> tasks for which he has not been trained and misuses a judge's authority for purposes of political propaganda. . . . . One may well say that this judgment was not understood by either the Hamburg nor the German public.[61]

More frustration with German courts appeared in an article dealing with vigilante murders as well as ascribing this negative feeling to a population much greater than merely the newspaper staff.

> The German courts, both in the Schwerin and in the Berlin murder trials, have unfortunately continued to veil the vigilante murder organizations. . . . But by no means have the courts satisfied the feelings of the people. The German people of all political Parties demand a full investigation, including who are the instigators and financial sponsors of the vigilante movement.[62]

Legal and educational works were the prime activities by which the Centralverein guarded Jewish civil rights. Thus, the organization was able to assemble nearly 400 attorneys from throughout Germany for a conference. Julius Brodnitz, the President of the Centralverein, wrote the feature article, which in part addressed the problems in the German legal system:

> We see an interaction between the courts, politics and the intellectual and cultural worlds. Serious political work must pay attention to the signs of the time. What until now could have been described in prevailing public opinion as a miscarriage of justice or a legal error of individual agencies, currently seems to the vigilant and more aroused public as the conscious and intentional enforcement of political worldviews assisted by the law and the administration of justice. . . . It is no longer the old Fatherland.

Brodnitz also focused attention on what lay within and what was outside the scope of the delegates' purpose in responding to the organization's appeal to attend the legal conference:

> Our conference of attorneys should not increase the number of declarations, which gave rise to the slogan: "crisis of confidence in the courts." . . . We are constantly confronted by an alarming lack of knowledge of Jewish life and the Jewish worldview. Here the obligation arises for German Jews to . . . enlighten German judges about phenomenon which to the detriment of their reputations are unknown and without us would perhaps remain unknown.[63]

Beyond Brodnitz's concern that Jewish civil rights were being disregarded by the courts, lay the fear that rights for all left-wing and liberal citizens were imperiled by judicial favoritism of right-wring Defendants. The issue of minimal penalties for right-wing thugs reoccurred in the resort town of Bad Salzbrunn. Whereas in past cases in which the emphasis had been on who were the leaders behind such assaults and who were the financiers, who paid the criminals' fines, by the end of 1929 the focus had changed to the broader issue of the damage occasioned to the sense of justice in the German courts.

> The fine of 100 RM was less than what had been proposed. . . . The imposed fine will naturally be paid for by the Party and will more likely be encouragement, rather than a detriment. When will the courts finally summon the energy to impose prison sentences in such cases.[64]

A final illustration of Jewish awareness of the injustice of the German Judges was occasioned by the September 27, 1929, assault by National Socialists against a Socialist conference in Schweidnitz. Damages included ninety-five smashed chairs and thirty-eight tables as well as thirty-four broken windows. Fifty attendees went to the hospital. Their injuries were so serious that at the time of the trial on January 3, 1930, many were still undergoing medical treatment. Most scholars will be interested in this case because Adolf Hitler became befuddled in his courtroom testimony. Thus, the significance for many will be in an earlier rendition of Hans Litten's May 1931 entrapment of Hitler in the Tanzpalast Eden Trial. But in the present book, the emphasis is on the Centralverein's growing disillusionment with German courts due to its lack of justice:

> As we reported in the December 20, 1929 *C.V. Zeitung*, nine of the sixteen National Socialist Defendants in the blowing up of the Socialist assembly and disturbing the peace in Schweidnitz have been acquitted. A few have been punished. This punishment seemed very mild for the brutal, well-organized raid by the "Brown-shirts" against the Socialist assembly in Schweidnitz. Of the originally 50 injured, some are still in the hospital. The chief perpetrator Mr. Thielmann received a sentence of three months in prison. The other six National Socialists received either lesser prison sentences or even fines. In contrast the ringleader, the Gau's business leader Mr. Herda and his brother Trzeciak, were completely exonerated. Of 200 invited witnesses, only 39 were heard. If only the Defendants had been handled more sharply and if only the hours of agitated speech by the National Socialists, which blurred the picture, had not been allowed with angelic patience and if only the theme of evidence had been more strictly maintained, the result would probably have turned out differently. One can hardly understand it.[65]

The Jewish newspaper confirms the Socialist affirmation that German judges sympathized with conservative Defendants. The judiciary consistently ruled in favor of those with similar backgrounds and ideologies. There was little hope that Jewish business owners could expect that either a German courtroom or Reich Minister of Justice Gürtner would recognize that they had been coerced into selling their firms at ridiculously low prices. Conservative German businessmen were able to collude with the nation's largest banks in a society willing to tolerate anti-Semitism, without any concern that the judiciary would intervene. A few newspaper examples will be provided to illustrate judges' lack of impartiality also extended into the business world.

For example, one year before Joseph Goebbels obtained immunity from prosecution due to his election to the Reichstag,[66] he assailed the Hermann Tietz department store. His first edition of *Der Angriff* on July 4, 1927, was a slanderous assault against Mr. Levy, who had managed the former Jandorf store on the Große Frankfurter street, since Hermann Tietz acquired the retail facility in 1926. A sales lady apparently approached Mr. Levy, requesting a pay increase. Allegedly he gruffly responded that if she wanted to earn more money, she knew where the Friedrichstraße was located. The street was known in Berlin for prostitution.[67] Goebbels could print such libel without fear of a judicial proceeding, due to the judiciary holding a similar conservative mindset.[68] A victory by the Jewish-owned large retailers provoked a front-page reaction by Goebbels. Small businessmen in Leipzig had formed an association printing leaflets decrying department stores "luring" the masses through "cheap junk" and publishing "deceptive" advertisements. Goebbels claimed that when the wealthy owners were unable to factually respond, they sought injunctive relief. Goebbels editorialized that a more annoying mockery of the middle class could not be imagined. Any further distribution of the fliers would be met merely with a court fine.[69]

A third example of Jewish businessmen unable to find justice in the German judiciary was reported in three weekly issues of the *C.V. Zeitung*. Theodor Fritsch had libeled Max Warburg and Carl Melchior in the May 1923 edition of his newspaper *Hammer*. He claimed that the Hamburg bankers had aided in the defeat of Germany in World War I by representing Jewish world capital, rather than the interests of the Reich.[70] During the January 15–18, 1926, trial, Warburg and Melchior sought a prison sentence of three weeks for Fritsch. Instead, the newspaper publisher "received an exceedingly mild punishment" of merely a 1,000 RM fine. In addition, the judge assessed Melchior with the majority of the court costs and charged Fritsch with two-thirds and Warburg with one-third of the remainder.[71] In a front-page editorial, a member of the Lower House of Parliament affirmed that "the judge misused his authority for purposes of political propaganda." He concluded that the trial was a "fiasco," understood neither by the populace of Hamburg nor the German public and thus would require an appeal.[72] As the German-Jewish historian Arnold Paucker concluded decades ago: "A democratic state, which could no longer defend itself, was hardly able to protect a helpless minority."[73]

Postwar historians have often exculpated judges during the Weimar Republic by maintaining that they were bound by statutes. Judges were excused for their verdicts, because there was no other alternative. Scholars have claimed that only after the war was there a pendulum swing in Minister of Justice Radbruch's philosophical approach from prewar legal positivism to postwar natural law. Radbruch's legal philosophy during the Weimar Republic may be summarized as maintaining that even an unjust law produced certainty and security in human interactions. To maintain the highest goal of certainty and security, courts might frequently pronounce sentence on an individual, who had acted on the basis of his sacred convictions. Radbruch held the courts would be correct in meting out punishment to such a sincere offender, because the judiciary's primary responsibility was to maintain the inviolability of the positive legal order.[74]

Immediately following the war, Radbruch appeared to acknowledge a tension between a moral conception of justice and his positivistic view of law. In part, his quandary was occasioned by a trial in which Mr. Puttfarken was accused of denouncing Mr. Göttig to the Gestapo. In 1946, Mr. Puttfarken was sentenced to life imprisonment in the Russian zone of occupation for having informed on Mr. Göttig in 1942. Thuringian chief public prosecutor Friedrich Kuschnitzki raised the question of whether Puttfarken was the perpetrator or whether the judges were the murderers. The Thuringian Court ruled that Puttfarken was merely an accomplice, but the Nazi judges were guilty of murder.

In Radbruch's assessment, "Positivism, with its principle that 'a law is a law,' had in fact rendered the German legal profession defenceless against statutes that are arbitrary and criminal." Astonishingly Radbruch turned to the New Testament as a source for the conflict between legal certainty and justice, since the Book of Hebrews admonished Christians to submit to rulers, whereas the Book of Acts commanded obedience to God as a higher obligation than to man. Radbruch's solution was to maintain that positive law was more important

> unless the conflict between statute and justice reaches such an intolerable degree that the statute, as "flawed law," must yield to justice . . . . Where there is not even an attempt at justice, where equality, the core of justice, is deliberately betrayed in the issuance of positive law, then the statute is not merely "flawed law," it lacks completely the very nature of law . . . . Measured by this standard, whole portions of National Socialist law never attained the dignity of valid law.[75]

In H. L. A. Hart's April 1957 lecture at Harvard, he startlingly depicted Radbruch's resolution in religious terminology as a conversion:

> Radbruch had himself shared the "positivist" doctrine until the Nazi tyranny, but he was converted by this experience and so his appeal to other men to discard the doctrine of the separation of law and morals has the special poignancy of a recantation.[76]

On the other hand, Stanley L. Paulson not only rejected Hart's understanding of religion as the cause of Radbruch's radical change in perception but also denied a major distinction between his Weimar era and later democratic writings. In Paulson's comprehension, Radbruch's "earlier and post-War writings reflect different aspects of a single position."[77] Paulson's explication is unconvincing, since Radbruch's transformed thought became the basis not only for adjudicating the actions of Nazi criminals but also more recently of East German border guards.[78]

Radbruch lost his only daughter Renate on March 22, 1939, in a mountain avalanche and his only son Anselm on December 5, 1942, due to an embolism following a battle injury in Stalingrad.[79] Nevertheless, I reject both Hart's religious experience as well as Paulson's view of continuity in Radbruch's positivism. Instead, I interpret Radbruch's dramatic transformation as regret for his limited activity during the Third Reich. At one end of the spectrum stood his former student, Georg Dahm, who joined the NSDAP in May 1933 and became a member of the Law Enforcement Committee in Hans Frank's Academy of German Law. He attained a position as a full Professor of Law in Kiel and served as the vice chancellor from 1935 to 1937. In 1955, he resumed his professorship in Kiel.[80] Since Dahm had "turned to the new gods" in the 1930s, Radbruch "remained on the battlefield until the last hour" in order to debate criminal law with him. In the spring of 1933, Radbruch was dismissed from the University of Heidelberg and worked on a biography on the criminologist Anselm Feuerbach, which was published in 1934. Although he was allowed to travel for professional reasons to Zurich, Geneva, and Lyon, the Foreign Office required him to cancel his acceptance of a teaching position at the University of Kovno, but he was allowed to spend a year as a guest of University College in Oxford.[81]

Fritz Bauer exemplifies the more active role, which Radbruch could have adopted. In contrast to Dahm, who studied under Radbruch in Kiel, Bauer studied law at Heidelberg, before Radbruch arrived. As a law student he never had classes with Emil Julius Gumbel. Nevertheless, Bauer was attracted to Radbruch's *Introduction to Jurisprudence* as well as his *Philosophy of Law*. At age twenty-seven, Bauer became the youngest magistrate in Germany on May 15, 1930, a circumstance which only lasted until March 1933, when he was interned in the Heuberg Concentration Camp for eight months. In contrast, as Radbruch was dismissed from Heidelberg in the spring of 1933, he began a twelve-year "internal exile."[82]

Fritz Bauer's sister Margot moved to Copenhagen with her husband Walter Tiefenthal in 1934, to establish a new existence in the textile industry. After the enactment of the Nuremberg Laws in 1935, Bauer joined her in Denmark. On February 11, 1936, Bauer received police certificates, recognizing him as an employee of the Zurich Social Democrat newspaper *Volksrecht* and the Berlin Jewish newspaper *C.V. Zeitung*. On November 24, 1938, Walter and Margot Tiefenthal were able to telegram Ludwig Bauer the good news that their son Fritz had obtained an entry permit for them to come to Copenhagen. Bauer endured a second imprisonment at the Horserød Concentration Camp but was released on December 4, 1940. He was imprisoned for the third time during June 23–30, 1941, and after he was released, he spent the next twenty-eight months moving from one hiding place to another. Having been informed of the German plans to round up all the Jews of Denmark, fishing boots took the Jewish people to Sweden during the night, including Fritz, his seventy-two-year-old father and his sixty-two-year-old mother, his sister Margot with her husband Walter Tiefenthal, as well as their two sons Peter and Rolf.[83]

Already in his November 11, 1943, letter to SoPaDe (Socialist Party of Germany) leader Kurt Heinig, Bauer was planning his postwar academic career in Denmark, since it seemed humanly dismal to return to Germany, In the November 15, 1944, issue of the Communist newspaper *Politische Information*, Bauer wrote:

> The problem of war crimes can be legally resolved . . . . According to the applicable international law, a criminal of war is one who begins a war illegally and therefore is guilty of war . . . . Christianity and humanism have established the terms just and unjust war and the one who begins a war for the sake of expansion or religion or prestige is branded as a war criminal and the attacked state is granted the right to punish him . . . With the beginning of the war against Poland, Nazi Germany broke the Kellogg Pact and therefore on the basis of international law is guilty of war. The terrible murder of hostages, mass murders in Poland and the Soviet Union; the deportations, the devastations and the plundering of occupied countries are clear violations of the Hague Convention, which Germany signed. According to the prevailing view of lawyers in the entire world, murder, manslaughter, false imprisonment, property damage, theft, etcetera can all be punished according to the applicable criminal law.[84]

After three imprisonments in concentration camps and immigration in two foreign countries, Bauer was focused on punishing perpetrators. In contrast,

Radbruch viewed justice for the victims in light of existing statutes as an exception to the general rule of law. I interpret Radbruch's change in legal philosophy as in part due to the influence of former judges, such as Fritz Bauer. Radbruch's safe and peaceful existence in Heidelberg paled in comparison with the persecution meted out to judges, such as Bauer, who were persecuted for merely being Socialists or Jews.

The paradigm presented in this investigation perceives that the judiciary did not intervene when Germany's three largest banks enabled non-Nazi businessmen to acquire Jewish-owned companies at bargain prices in the first three years of the Third Reich. The large financial institutions earned fees by extending new loans as well as inside information from recently acquired supervisory board seats. The new Aryan proprietors did not object to fees since they became owners with little to no investments of their own equity. Prevailing scholarship has traditionally understood inexpensive acquisitions of Jewish firms within a top-down, Berlin-inspired, intensification of anti-Semitic political measures. My contribution to the academic interpretation is to explicate a period from 1933 to 1935 in which the private sector was responsible for large companies in Germany from their Jewish owners. Opportunism was a major motivation, not NSDAP ideology.

The remaining chapters will examine the largest German-Jewish companies from the perspective of the proposed paradigm.

NOTES

1. By the expression "Jewish firm" or "Jewish company," I am referring to a commercial enterprise that is owned by Jewish partners. Quite often these partnerships were based on family or extended clan relationships. Most of the firms discussed in this book were not corporations, so whether stockholders were Jewish or not is usually not relevant. Although the Leonhard Tietz chain of department stores was incorporated, most major stockholders came from the extended family. None of the surveyed large enterprises sold Jewish religious items, so the merchandise plays no role in determining whether the organization can be defined as Jewish. The examined entrepreneurs defined themselves first and foremost as Germans as did the Centralverein deutscher Staatsbürger jüdischen Glaubens, the largest German-Jewish organization throughout the Empire and the Weimar Republic. Thus, it is fitting that this volume frequently quotes from this institution's organ, the *C.V. Zeitung*, which was intentionally neither Orthodox nor Zionist in orientation. To explore the basis on which German-Jewish entrepreneurs self-identified as Jews is beyond the scope of this study. Please note that I bear the responsibility for translating *C.V. Zeitung* articles as well as all other German publications and unpublished documents cited in this book.

2. Interest in the Jewish-owned department stores in Germany remains high, even to this day, as evidenced by Racheli Edelman's response to David Motadel's

"What Do the Hohenzollerns Deserve?" in the March 26, 2020, issue of the *New York Review of Books*. As the granddaughter of Salman Schocken, she mentioned how four German banks had replaced Jewish directors by Aryans as a first step in eventually selling stock in the Schocken Department Stores to the Hohenzollerns (See Christopher Clark and Racheli Edelman, "Helping Hitler: An Exchange," *New York Review of Books*, April 9, 2020). I have not included the Schocken retail establishment in my book, because of its small size in comparison with either the Hermann Tietz or Leonhard Tietz chains. Schocken's February 28, 1933, balance sheet itemized that the firm had earned a 1.86 million RM net profit, based on 10 million RM in registered capital. By December of 1933, the structure of the company had changed from a limited partnership, with Salman Schocken being the solely liable individual, to a joint stock company with share capital of 4.2 million RM. In comparison with the largest businesses evaluated in this book, Schocken was mid-sized and therefore not included. For additional information, see "Warenhaus Schocken als AG," *Vossische Zeitung*, December 15, 1933, 14.

3. Saul Friedländer, *Nazi Germany and the Jews, Volume I; The Years of Persecution, 1933–1945* (New York: HarperCollins Publishers, Inc, 1997), pp. 178–179.

4. Admittedly, Avraham Barkai observed that the Viennese *Reichspost* newspaper reported such sales as early as December 1935. See, Avraham Barkai, *From Boycott to Annihilation; The Economic Struggle of German Jews 1933–1945* (Hanover: University Press of New England, 1989), p. 108.

5. Friedländer, *Nazi Germany*, p. 233.

6. Friedländer, *Nazi Germany*, p. 236.

7. Friedländer, *Nazi Germany*, p. 233.

8. The May or June 1942 ninety-eight-page evaluation of Göring's first Four-Year Plan contained in BA R26 I/18 may be a profitable starting point for such future research. I am indebted to Gerhard Weinberg for this citation in "Hitler's Memorandum on the Four-Year Plan: A Note," *German Studies Review*, Vol. 11, No. 1 (1988), pp. 133–135.

9. On Karl Rasche, see Chapter 1 page 21 as well as Chapter 2 pages 67–69.

10. "Die Neuesten Nachrichten in Zietz," *C.V. Zeitung*, Vol. 1, No. 13 (August 3, 1922), p. 164.

11. "Gegen Rassenhaß, Klassenhaß und Massenhaß," *C.V. Zeitung*, Vol. 1, No. 27 (November 9, 1922), p. 164. All translations of German sources throughout this book are my own.

12. "Völkischer und jüdischer Boykott," *C.V. Zeitung*, Vol. 5, No. 14 (April 1, 1926), p. 193.

13. "Ausschreitungen der Nationalsozialisten in Ostpreußen," *C.V. Zeitung*, Vol. 8, No. 2 (January 11, 1929), p. 14.

14. "Deutschnationale Sammlungspolitik," *C.V. Zeitung*, Vol. 1, No. 26 (November 2, 1922), p. 1.

15. Jacob Rosenthal, *Die Ehre des jüdischen Soldaten. Die Judenzählung im Ersten Weltkrieg und ihre Folgen* (Frankfurt am Main: Campus Verlag GmbH, 2007), pp. 145–147.

16. "Die wahren Verantwortlichen. Gegen Friedhofsschändung und politische Hetze," *C.V. Zeitung*, Vol. 8, No. 11 (March 15, 1929), p. 132.

17. "Wieder Friedhofsschändungen in Ostpreußen und Franken," *C.V. Zeitung*, Vol. 9, No. 5 (January 31, 1930), p. 1.

18. "Und die Folgen," *C.V. Zeitung*, Vol. 10, No. 50 (December 11, 1931), p. 573.

19. Thomas Weihe, "'Wahre' Motive: Antisemitismus oder Hilfe," in Ludolf Herbst and Thomas Weihe (Eds.), *Die Commerzbank und die Juden 1933–1945* (München: C.H. Beck, 2004), p. 70.

20. Ludolf Herbst, "Banker in einem prekären Geschäft: Die Beteiligung der Commerzbank an der Vernichtung der jüdischen Gewerbetätigkeit im Altreich (1933–1940) in *Die Commerzbank und die Juden*, pp. 74–78.

21. "Juristisch-wirtschaftliche Beratungsstelle," *C.V. Zeitung*, March 16, 1933, p. 91.

22. "Staat ist Ordnung," *C.V. Zeitung* (March 23, 1933), p. 1.

23. "Eine Woche juristisch-wirtschaftliche Beratungsstelle des C.V.," *C.V. Zeitung* (March 23, 1933), p. 99.

24. "Täglich wirtschaftlich-juristische Beratung," *C.V. Zeitung* (March 30, 1933), p. 107.

25. "Haltung!," *C.V. Zeitung* (April 6, 1933), p. 1.

26. "Massenandrang in der Beratungsstelle des C.V.," *C.V. Zeitung* (April 6, 1933), p. 121.

27. "Fristlos entlassen," *C.V. Zeitung* (April 20, 1933), p. 141.

28. "Helfen, helfen, helfen," *C.V. Zeitung* (April 20, 1933), p. 141.

29. "Unsere Pflicht!; Der Zentralausschuß der deutschen Juden stellt uns den nachfolgenden Aufruf zur Verfügung," *C.V. Zeitung* (April 27, 1933), p. 147. For details about this organization, see "Der Zentralausschuß der deutschen Juden für Hilfe und Aufbau," *C.V. Zeitung* (May 11, 1933), p. 166.

30. Compare "Alltag der Hilfe," *C.V. Zeitung* (May 11, 1933), p. 171 with "Aus der Arbeit des Centralvereins," *C.V. Zeitung* (May 18, 1933), p. 178 and "Für Hilfe und Aufbau," *C.V. Zeitung* (June 22, 1933), p. 240 and "Der Reichsverband des jüdischen Mittelstandes gegründet," *C.V. Zeitung* (June 22, 1933), p. 240.

31. "Wir rufen Euch! Tretet ein in den Kulturbund Deutscher Juden," *C.V. Zeitung* (August 17, 1933).

32. Kurt Singer, "Vor der Premiere des Kulturbundes," *C.V. Zeitung* (September 28, 1933).

33. Trude Rosenthal, "Der jüdische Kulturbund Rhein/Ruhr," *C.V. Zeitung* (October 19, 1933).

34. Compare "Möbeltransporte," *C.V. Zeitung* (July 6, 1933), p. 265 and "Möbeltransporte," *C.V. Zeitung* (July 20, 1933), p. 290 with Ignaz Maybaum and Friedrich Brodnitz, "Deutsches Judentum und Palästinawanderung," *C.V. Zeitung* (July 27, 1933), pp. 297–298; and "Theorie oder Leben?" *C.V. Zeitung* (July 27, 1933), pp. 298–299.

35. Compare "Block" and other advertisements, *C.V. Zeitung* (August 10, 1933), with "Die neuen Devisenvorschriften für Auswanderer," *C.V. Zeitung* (September 7, 1933).

36. Wirtschaftstatsachen über Palastina," *C.V. Zeitung* (September 14, 1933). Compare "Vorsicht–Achtung," *C.V. Zeitung* (September 20, 1933), with "Amtl. Italien. Reisebüro," *C.V. Zeitung* (September 28, 1933); and "Consulich Line," *C.V. Zeitung* (September 28, 1933).

37. E. G. L., "Freiwilliger Arbeitsdienst im Landwerk Neuendorf," *C.V. Zeitung* (January 19, 1933), p. 21.

38. Maren Krüger, *Herbert Sonnenfeld; Ein jüdischer Fotograf in Berlin 1933–1938* (Berlin: Nicolaische Verlagsbuchhandlung, 1990), pp. 104–137.

39. "Siedlungspläne im Ausland," *C.V. Zeitung* (October 11, 1933).

40. Ingo Köhler, "Unternehmenserwerb auf eigene Rechnung: Die Übernahme des Bankhauses Gebr. Arnhold, Dresden–Berlin," in Dieter Ziegler, *Die Dresdner Bank und die deutschen Juden* (München: R. Oldenbourg Verlag, 2006), p. 145.

41. Dieter Ziegler, "Entjudung und Nazifizierung 1933–1937," in Klaus-Dietmar Henke et al., *Die Dresdner Bank im Dritten Reichs. Band 1* (München: R. Oldenbourg Verlag, 2006), p. 89. See further details in Chapter 6 of the present work.

42. Contrast Kurt Zielenziger, "Der Untergang des jüdischen Mittelstandes," *C.V. Zeitung*, Vol. 4, No. 46 (November 13, 1925), p. 1 with "Ochse, siehste Wertheim nicht?" *Der Angriff*, Nummer 24, December 12, 1927, and "Warenhaus und Baupalast," *Der Angriff*, Nummer 24, June 11, 1928.

43. Dieter Ziegler, "Der Ordnungsrahmen," in Klaus-Dietmar Henke, *Die Dresdner Bank im Dritten Reich*, Band 1, 54.

44. This is the data supplied for the 1932 fiscal year in "Dresdner Bank–Geschäftsbericht für 1932," *Vossische Zeitung* (June 18, 1933), p. 15. Although the information was published in June 1933, it is safe to assume that the delay was caused by the time required to close the annual books and summarize the statistics. More uncertain is the trend reported in a table on July 26, 1933, that the Dresdner Bank's shareholder capital still remained constant from May 31, 1933, to June 30, 1933, at 220 million RM. Similarly, their reserves continued to remain at the 30 million level during the same time period. This may either mean that the recommendations submitted by the Board at the 1932 annual meeting were rejected or that the bank made an astonishing financial recovery during the period January through March 1933. This uncertainty in the accounting arises because the theme of the July article is that there had been a 6 percent decline in the dollar rate in June, which caused a 72.87 million RM loss in assets among Germany's five largest banks. The Dresdner Bank's share in the loss of assets during June was 25.49 million RM. The newspaper attempted to inspire financial confidence by reporting that the five banks had lost considerably more in assets during May 1933 (139 million RM) and April 1933 (184 million RM). It is difficult to perceive how total assets could decline on the left side of the Balance Statement for three consecutive months and yet both the shareholder capital and the reserves remained constant on the right side of Statement. See "Neue Bilanzkürzung der Großbanken; Eine Folge des weiteren Dollarrückgangs," *Vossische Zeitung* (July 26, 1933), Evening Edition, 10.

45. Maren Janetzko, "Die Arisierungs–Vermittlung," in Klaus-Dietmar Henke et al., *Die Dresdner Bank im Dritten Reich, Band 2* (München: R. Oldenbourg Verlag, 2006), pp. 199–201.

46. Gregor Schöllgen, *Gustav Schickedanz; Biographie eines Revolutionärs* (Berlin: Berlin Verlag, 2010), pp. 61–66.

47. As a result of the coronavirus, the Hertz rental car company entered bankruptcy. Their stock plummeted from 16 dollars per share to 1.25 dollars per share. In a business gamble mirroring Gustav Schickedanz's actions, day traders began purchasing Hertz shares in June 2020.Whether current investors will replicate Schickedanz's windfall profit is unclear, but it does indicate that counter-cyclical practices are still being utilized to this very day.

48. Dieter Ziegler. Review of Schöllgen, Gregor, *Gustav Schickedanz: Biographie eines Revolutionärs*. H-Soz-u-Kult, H-Net Reviews. March, 2011.

49. Emil Julius Gumbel, *Vier Jahre politischer Mord* (Berlin: Verlag der neuen Gesellschaft, 1922), p. 81.

50. The most common figurative translation of the German noun "Kniff" is "trick," but not wanting to over-emphasize Gumbel's theme, I have employed the less pejorative terms "device" and "artifice." See Gumbel, *Vier Jahre*, pp. 114–116.

51. Gumbel, *Vier Jahre*, pp. 146–147.

52. Gumbel, *Vier Jahre*, p. 149.

53. Lothar Gruchmann, *Justiz im Dritten Reich 1933–1940; Anpassung und Unterwerfung in der Ära Gürtner* (München: R. Oldenbourg Verlag, 1988), pp. 24–25.

54. Gruchmann, *Justiz*, p. 28.

55. Gruchmann, *Justiz*, pp. 28–29.

56. Jürgen Vortmann, "Juristischer Widerstand gegen den Nationalsozialismus," *Zeitschrift für Rechtspolitik*, Jahrgang 23 Heft 5 (May 1990), 193–194.

57. Heinrich Hannover and Elisabeth Hannover-Druck, Politische Justiz 1918–1933 (Berlin: Metropol Verlag, 2019), pp. 27–30.

58. Bernhard Falk, "Frei ist der Rhein!" *C.V. Zeitung* (June 27, 1930), p. 1.

59. Zusammenhänge und Hintergründe–Der C.V. beim Reichsinnenminister–Weitere Maßnahmen," *C.V. Zeitung* (August 12, 1932), p. 342.

60. Compare "Der Warburg-Fritsch Prozeß vor der Urteilsverkündung in Hamburg," *C.V. Zeitung* (January 22, 1926), p. 41 with "Der Ausgang des Warburgs-Fritsch-Prozesses; Fritsch zu 1000 Mark Geldstrafe verurteilt," *C.V. Zeitung* (January 29, 1926), p. 52.

61. Rudolf Michael, "Der Hamburger Prozeß," *C.V. Zeitung* (February 5, 1926), p. 1.

62. Ernst Lemmer, "Reinigung!," *C.V. Zeitung* (February 26, 1926), p. 98.

63. Julius Brodnitz, "Unserer Juristentagung zum Gruß!," *C.V. Zeitung* (June 17, 1927), p. 1.

64. Nationalsozialisten vor Gericht; Mildes Urteil gegen Störenfriede in Bad Salzbrunn, *C.V. Zeitung* (May 3, 1929), p. 234.

65. Felix Heimann, "Der Schweidnitzer Nationalsozialistenprozeßen; Hitler und Herr von Pfeffer als Zeugen," *C.V. Zeitung* (December 20, 1929), p. 679 and Felix Heimann, "Wo steht Hitler; Die Lehren des Schweidnitzer Nationalsozialisten-Prozesses," *C.V. Zeitung* (January 3, 1930), p. 5.

66. Further details will be provided in Chapter Four Section B.

67. "It was the city's pleasure palace, not only because it was called the 'street of 107 cinemas,' but also because of the many prostitutes who plied their trade here." Kyle James, "Berlin's Friedrichstrasse: where city's history played out," www.dw .com, December 8, 2006.

68. "Jüdische Warenhausethik," *Der Angriff*, July 4, 1927. Goebbels's expectation that the courts would not intervene was repeated one week later, when he attacked the Jewish-owned Wertheim department store chain for purchasing a real estate parcel in Steglitz for the preposterous sum of 1 million RM in order to erect a "department store palace." This occurred at a time when hundreds of thousands of "productive Germans" were unsuccessfully searching for a home and hundreds of small shopkeepers were on the brink of ruin. See "Die Warenhauspomp," *Der Angriff*, July 11, 1927.

69. "Warenhausbluff und Justiz," *Der Angriff*, October 31, 1927.

70. "Der Warburg-Fritsch-Prozeß. Vor der Urteilsverkündung in Hamburg," *C.V. Zeitung*, Vol. 5, No. 4 (January 22, 1926), p. 41.

71. "Der Ausgang des Warburg-Fritsch Prozesses. Fritsch zu 1000 Mark Geldstrafe verurteilt," *C.V. Zeitung*, Vol. 5, No. 5 (January 29, 1926), p. 52.

72. Rudolf Michael, "Der Hamburger Prozeß," *C.V. Zeitung*, Vol. 5, No. 6 (February 5, 1926), p. 61.

73. Arnold Paucker, *Der jüdische Abwehrkampf gegen Antisemitismus in den letzten Jahren der Weimarer Republik* (Hamburg: Leibniz-Verlag, 1969), p. 84.

74. Anton-Hermann Chroust, "The Philosophy of Law of Gustav Radbruch," *The Philosophical Review*, Vol. 53, No. 1 (January 1944), p. 45.

75. Gustav Radbruch, "Statutory Lawlessness and Supra-Statutory Law (1946)," *Oxford Journal of Legal Studies*, Vol. 26, No. 1 (Spring 2006), pp. 1–6, 10.

76. Stanley L. Paulson, "On the Background and Significance of Gustav Radbruch's Post-War Papers," *Oxford Journal of Legal Studies*, Vol. 26, No. 1 (Spring 2006), p. 18.

77. Stanley L. Paulson, "Radbruch on Unjust Laws: Competing Earlier and Later Views?" *Oxford Journal of Legal Studies*, Vol. 15, No. 3 (Autumn 1995), p. 493.

78. Peter E. Quint, "Judging the Past: The Prosecution of East German Border Guards and the GDR Chain of Command," *The Review of Politics*, Vol. 66, No. 2 (Spring 1999), pp. 303–329; Peter E. Quint, "The Border Guard Trials and the East German Past–Seven Arguments," *The American Journal of Comparative Law*, Vol. 49, No. 4 (Autumn 2000), pp. 541–572; and Adrian Künzler, "Judicial Legitimacy and the Role of Courts: Explaining the Transitional Context of the German Border Guard Cases," *Oxford Journal of Legal Studies*, Vol. 32, No. 2 (Summer 2012), pp. 349–381.

79. Gustav Radbruch, *Der Innere Weg; Aufriß meines Lebens* (Göttingen: Vandenhoeck & Ruprecht, 1961), p. 139.

80. Ernst Klee, *Das personen Lexikon zum Dritten Reich* (Hamburg: Nikol Verlagsgesellschaft, 2016), p. 100.

81. Radbruch, *Op. Cit.*, pp. 134–137.

82. Irmtrud Wojak, *Fritz Bauer 1903–1968; Eine Biographie* (München: Verlag C.H. Beck, 2009), pp. 96–115.

83. Wojak, *Fritz Bauer*, pp. 122–155.

84. Wojak, *Fritz Bauer*, pp. 164–180.

Chapter 2

History of Research on Cheap Purchases of Jewish Firms

A. METHODOLOGICAL CONSIDERATIONS

Hostile takeovers of Jewish-owned companies during the 1930s have been frequently researched by German scholars under the technical term "Aryanization."[1] This chapter will survey six researchers in four stages of academic development during the past six decades in order to propose a new interpretation based on the experiences of large Jewish companies. Most of the prior research has been done by German scholars. Unfortunately, the topic has been investigated by very few English-speaking academicians.[2] The topic was investigated later and by fewer historians than the study of the Holocaust. Although the topic of Aryanization is not as significant as the murder of six million European Jews or something less than half a million German Jews during the Holocaust, it is one indication of the demise of German-Jewish civilization.

Existing scholarship has never told the story of the demise of Jewish businesses from the perspective of the companies. Thus, a monograph on a Jewish-owned department store chain as the foundation for understanding how and when hostile acquisitions occurred during the Third Reich is useful. Consumers sought material pleasure in large retail establishments. Proprietors of large Jewish firms had business relationships with an extensive network of German businessmen and government officials. Not only did such mass merchandisers provide thousands of jobs per company and pay millions in taxes and social welfare benefits, but they also had commercial arrangements with banks for loans, manufacturers for products, railroads for shipping, and primarily with millions of customers. If merely 5 percent of all employees, customers, and merchandise providers were Jewish, then this business sector not only carried significant weight in Weimar's nascent economic recovery but also greatly influenced daily Jewish existence.

Academic interest in Jewish-owned companies during the Nazi era lagged behind research into German corporations by two decades. Investigation of the collaboration of large German firms with the Nazi regime began immediately after World War II with the examination of the Flick companies, I.G. Farben, and Krupp as the fifth, sixth, and tenth of the twelve criminal proceedings in the Subsequent Nuremberg Trials conducted in 1947. The German population either convinced themselves that all twenty-four "bad Nazis" had been previously tried by the International Military Tribune in 1945–1946 or they became weary of "victor justice" and desired to restore their own personal, social, and economic lives instead of admitting any role in National Socialist policies against Jews or their assets. Chancellor Konrad Adenauer was unconcerned with whether the postwar German economy was rebuilt in part by German businessmen using the remnants of Aryanized Jewish firms.[3]

After two decades of disinterest in the German role in the expropriation of Jewish-owned assets, Helmut Genschel pioneered the academic study of the hostile takeovers in 1966. In a wide-sweeping survey on "The Dispelling of the Jews from the Economy of the Third Reich," Genschel devoted more attention to Nazi-supporting, Gentile industrial giants than to Jewish entrepreneurs. This irony probably occurred due to the lack of Jewish sources. Thus, twenty-three pages were dedicated to the Flick Conglomerate, four pages to I.G. Farben, and one page to Krupp. In comparison, only three pages were dedicated to the Hermann Tietz and one page to the Leonhard Tietz department store chains. In the same fashion, the world famous Mosse advertising agency and publishing house was never mentioned and merely one page devoted to the Ullstein Publishing Company. Similarly, merely two pages related to Bankhaus Gebrüder Arnold, the largest Jewish private financial institution.[4] This treatise seeks to promote a shift in this academic perspective.

One simple methodological principle shapes this review. If the low-cost acquisition of Jewish-owned companies became the focus of six decades of German academic studies on Aryanization, then the Jewish firms should have provided the framework for the timing and method by which low-ball "purchases" had been made. Instead the following survey of six scholars will demonstrate that a chronology of Berlin-inspired, Nazi political events had more often provided the framework for understanding the Aryanization of Jewish firms. This approach may have been adopted either because the political acts were better understood or due to the lack of Jewish company records. This inspection will begin to rewrite this history utilizing Jewish records preserved by German banks, Jewish diaries and memoirs, as well as contemporary newspaper articles.

The traditional academic interpretation ascribed Aryanization as a process in which progressive Nazi legislation from 1933 to 1938 finally allowed "old fighters" from the NSDAP to reap the financial benefits of years of unpaid service. In contrast, the new operation recognized in this book shifts the onus from the party to "ordinary" Germans. The new procedure suggested here is a bottom-up, rather than a customary top-down approach. The general mechanism whereby Jewish firms were purchased at extremely low prices early in the 1930s entailed four participants: (1) conservative, exclusively profit-focused German businessmen, (2) large German banks, (3) Jewish company owners intimidated either through boycotts or a general climate of anti-Semitism, and (4) Right-wing judges, who lost sight of impartiality in the immediate aftermath of World War I.

B. OVERVIEW OF THE HISTORY OF RESEARCH

An examination of the academic study of Aryanization will commence with Helmut Genschel, in which the historians' approach may be usefully divided into four stages. The review of prior scholarship will indicate the usefulness of this work. The distinction between this analysis and Genschel's strategy is evident from his table of contents. Genschel's chapter titles display a top-down perspective in an evolutionary development in which the central government's role in Berlin dictated the speed and course of the action. After two chapters on the situation of the Jews in the German economy of the Nineteenth Century and its role in anti-Semitism, his progression commenced with Interior Minister Wilhelm Frick's pronouncements against non-sanctioned, individual actions. It continued with the Hitler-Goebbels initiation of the Boycott against Jewish stores on April 1, 1933, to offset the foreign embargo of German manufactured goods.[5] The political orientation is additionally demonstrated in the following two chapter headings with slow rate of Jewish persecution in 1933–1935 and the Nuremberg Race Laws of 1935. Two subsequent chapters entail further slow Jewish persecution in 1936–1937 and the transition to complete Jewish elimination from the economy in 1938. The book reaches its highpoint with the Kristallnacht of November 1938. Genschel's political orientation is interrupted by a two-and-one-half page excursus on a cigar chain in Hannover and five pages on the admittedly very important Simson Weapons Factory in Suhl.[6]

The documentation for his brief excursus was political in nature, not business. One of Genschel's repeatedly used sources was the series of brochures entitled the *Thuringian Investigation of the Jewish Question* and the other reference was from the fifth Subsequent Nuremberg Trial on the Friedrich Flick Company. Records for investigating Jewish firms were scarce when

Genschel wrote in 1966 as the most recent German study of Aryanization admits.[7] Company owners often emigrated with almost no personal property and thus their accounting ledgers were probably the last thing on their minds as they attempted to preserve their lives. In addition, bookkeeping records would frequently have been destroyed by the new proprietors either to avoid paying wind-fall profits taxes to the Reich or to conceal that the new owners had made their fortune by means of cheap acquisitions. Furthermore, if such Jewish documentation survived the 1930s, it would have often been destroyed during the Allied bombing of German cities.

Twenty-one years lapsed before the second academic book was published in 1987 on the theme of hostile takeovers. As a Zionist, Avraham Barkai escaped the Jewish section of Berlin, known as the Scheunenviertel, by fleeing to Palestine.[8] Although the preface acknowledged "the excellent, still indispensable 1966 study by Helmuth Genschel," Barkai established a second phase in the academic research. A reader, hoping that an Israeli scholar would structure his methodology on the basis of the seized Jewish firms, will be disappointed. Barkai accepted Genschel's 1933 Boycott through 1938 Kristallnacht chronological perspective, rather than focusing on the dispossessed Jewish proprietors. He merely refined Genschel's structure by objecting to Genschel's periods of "creeping displacement."[9] Additionally, he dissented from Genschel's positive assessment of Reichsbank President Hjalmar Schacht's "protection" of Jewish businesses in the German financial recovery after the worldwide economic crisis. Barkai furthermore rejected the view of examining Jewish owners as passive victims and highlighted the role of Jewish self-help organizations. Such assistance was necessary, as Barkai highlighted, because in 1933 more than 33 percent of the non-Aryan German population was older than age forty years, resulting in the percentage of Jews receiving welfare benefits being twice as high as that of Gentiles. In such declining economic circumstances, 34 percent of Jewish employees were women.[10]

Barkai intended to address the hostile takeovers from a Jewish perspective. However, he uncovered few sources detailing that viewpoint. He was only on occasion dependent on the Duisburg City Archive, the Federal Archive in Munster, and the Leo Baeck Institute. He frequently utilized Kurt Jakob Ball-Kaduri's secondary source *Das Leben der Juden in Deutschland im Jahre 1933*. His desired goal was shared by other Israeli scholars, including UCLA's Saul Friedländer. But unlike Barkai, Friedländer employed dozens of Jewish diaries from Germany, Poland, and the Czech Republic, which have been published subsequent to the Holocaust.[11] The wide acceptance of Friedländer in contrast with the more limited appeal of Barkai is in part due to the latter's limited documentation. The primary sources often must be found in the files of German companies or ferreted out-of-business sections of contemporary German newspapers.

This book has searched for additional sources. For example, it has employed Hans Schaeffer's diary entries regarding the Jewish-owned Ullstein Publishing House in chapter 6, section C. A further source was unknown even in 1989 as Barkai's volume was translated from German into English. In 1990, it was discovered that the Centralverein deutscher Staatsbürger jüdischen Glaubens records seized by the Gestapo were later taken by the Red Army to Moscow. Part of these Jewish records were subsequently microfilmed and made available in Jerusalem. Barkai read large numbers of these documents and later composed a volume on this Jewish umbrella organization. Unfortunately, he had insufficient time to revise his book on the Jewish place in the German economy, before composing his memoir and passing away.[12] In contrast, chapter 5, section E of this study not only utilizes the Centralverein records from Moscow, which attempted to assist fired Jewish department store employees but also department store financial records preserved in the Federal Archive in Berlin. Company data has also been gleaned from the *Vossische Zeitung* and the *Berliner Börsen-Zeitung* in chapter 6 in addition to the diametrically opposed articles in Joseph Goebbels's *Der Angriff* and the Centralverein's *CV Zeitung* in chapter 4.

It required an additional five years until Barbara Händler-Lachmann launched the third stage in the study of hostile takeovers in 1992. This third period in the academic investigation should once again be viewed as a refinement of Genschel. Händler-Lachmann accepted the chronological development in hostile takeovers from the 1933 Boycott through the 1935 Nuremberg Race Laws.

The unique feature of this stage was its focus on city history. This had the advantage of having records in the local archive, but with the resulting disadvantage that Lachmann's monograph on Marburg examined modest shops in a small university town and automatically excluded research on large, regional businesses with branches across Germany. She even admitted that as of January 1, 1933, the tiny locale had a population of 29,259 inhabitants of whom only 340 were Jewish. Barkai had previously generalized that Jewish businessmen were overly represented in the retailing niches of shoes, clothing, department stores, and private banking. By restricting the scope of inquiry and utilizing the city's business registry as her source, Lachmann was able to specify that of the forty-three ready-made clothing, fabric, and accessory shops in Marburg, nine were Jewish-owned. In addition, out of the six fashion and department stores, four had Jewish proprietors. Since the small city was surrounded by farms, she was able to add to Barkai's understanding by observing that out of the five grain, flour, fodder, and fertilizer shops, three were owned by Jewish entrepreneurs. She also noted that Jewish participation in the trades was under-represented. There had been only one Jewish tailor, one cobbler, and one carpenter, but by 1933, these shops were no longer in operation. Similarly, the kosher butcher Metzgerei Jonas had gone out-of-business at the end of the 1920s as did three private banks, namely the Baruch Strauß, Menke Eichelberg, and Karl Haas.[13]

Accessing personal and local history of the Holocaust received its institutional impetus with the formation of the Fortunoff Video Archive for Holocaust Testimonies at Yale University in 1981. This investigative approach received international recognition with the establishment in 1994 of the USC Shoah Foundation. From the Fortunoff inception with 183 testimonies, the oral history method has grown to a collection of 55,000 recordings at USC. Although recordings of survivors are extremely popular in the United States, Händler-Lachmann preferred to access three contemporary local newspapers: the *Hessische Volkswacht*, the *Oberhessische Zeitung*, and the *Kurhessische Landeszeitung*. Local historians enjoy the advantage of employing journalistic material not deemed sufficiently important to be microfilmed or digitized in larger national archives. Part of Lachmann's significance is the utilization of these rare, contemporary sources.

Such contemporary accounts dispel the notion that the Boycott of Jewish-owned businesses was merely a one-day affair on April 1, 1933. Newspaper articles recording that Alfred Rosenberg spoke on the theme of "The Destructive Influence of Talmud Teaching" in Marburg on March 2nd and the March 13th report of a boycott in the neighboring Hessian city of Kassel are both significant for denying a one-day event inspired by Adolf Hitler or Julius Streicher.

The motivation for purchasing Jewish firms, below the value of their fixed assets, has usually been viewed as the result of the Nazi ideology of anti-Semitism. In contrast, this exploration perceives that although anti-Semitism provided the pressure for Jewish proprietors to sell, the primary motive of non-NSDAP Party Members was the self-centered greed for profit. Händler-Lachmann clearly depicts the dark side of capitalism: profit took precedence over ideology, even when Nazi racial theory would lead to the destruction of Jewish businesses and ultimately to the murder of coreligionists. Lachmann's subtitles in chapter 3 use the traditional German words for "displacement," "Aryanization," and "liquidation." But a surprising novelty is her subtitle "Fraud against Jews" in which she refers to the lack of a morality to pay, as well as the haggling of prices, and deceit by German customers.[14]

Clearly not all anti-Semites were opportunists. There were individuals who became anti-Semites due to ideological reasons. From a similar perspective of desiring to clarify the social situation in the early years of the Third Reich, this research has focused on the careers of such businessmen as Georg Karg. Karg's chief goal was to make a profit by expanding a usurped empire. Business ethics played no role in his transactions. However, this disregard for any influence of morality within the economy was not derived from National Socialism. Although his assumed conglomerate would have benefited by his membership in the NSDAP, he never joined this right-wing political party. Similarly, in a time when refusing to give the Hitler greeting may have served as the basis of a denunciation, he did not employ such ideological language.

There is a historiographical problem in attempting to utilize anti-Semitism as the exclusive explanation for Jewish-Gentile interaction in Germany or the Third Reich, since it "has prompted frequent speculative generalization but little systematic exploration."[15] For example, much could be made about the fact that in 1850 approximately 13 percent of Bavaria's population "opposed" Jewish emancipation. However, when the state investigated it determined that many of the petitioners were actually indifferent and had no contact with Jewish people, but had merely been influenced by a priest. During the Weimar Republic and the beginning of the Third Reich, the völkisch movement added a racial anti-Semitism to this type of traditional religious anti-Semitism. In a rebuttal to Lucy Dawidowicz, it was noted that scholarship had countered her opinion that generations of German pathological hatred of the Jewish people had prepared the Volk to accept Hitler as their "redeemer." For a later generation of Holocaust students, Dawidowicz' 1975 theory could sound similar to Goldhagen's 1996 view.[16]

There is an ongoing need for historians to identify the different types of anti-Semitism in the Third Reich and identify the diverse motivations behind political, social, and economic acts. A blanket attribution of anti-Semitism is of little value:

> Though Hitler himself apparently regarded anti-Semitism as the most important weapon in his propaganda arsenal, it seems in fact, far from being the main motive force in bringing Nazism to power, to have been secondary to the main appeal of the Nazi message. A contemporary Jewish assessment [Arnold Paucker] of the spectacular gains in the 1930 Reichstag elections emphasized that millions of Nazi voters were in no sense anti-Semites, adding pointedly however that their rejection of anti-Semitism, on the other hand, was evidently not great enough to prevent them giving their support to an anti-Semitic party.[17]

Since a theory of anti-Semitism is unable to explicate the motivation for all acts by Germans during the later years of the Weimar Republic and the first years of the Third Reich, then new driving forces must be uncovered from the events themselves. Although all businessmen in a capitalistic economy must earn a profit, the welfare of the workforce and returning something of value to the local population had long been part of the German characterization of the company owner as a father figure. As early as 1871, the employer had borne the legal and financial responsibility for an injured worker.[18] A group of business opportunists in the Third Reich thus becomes a distinct group with a specific motivation, not a universal characteristic necessitated by capitalism.

The third phase in the academic study of Aryanization continued with Frank Bajohr's 1997 publication on inexpensive purchases in Hamburg. Although Bajohr referred to the 1933 Boycott and the 1938 Kristallnacht, Genschel's political framework no longer supplied the structure for understanding business history. From the outset of his book, Frank Bajohr changed the direction of scholarship through three key insights. First, he assessed that a focus on nationwide activities such as the April 1, 1933 Boycott was in need of refinement because anti-Jewish practices were adopted on the local level long before the national basis. Second, he noted that the local appropriation of Jewish assets differed from one city to another. Third, he maintained that hostile seizures did not occur by means of obeying policies established in Berlin.[19]

Another crucial contribution was Bajohr's focus on larger companies such as Max Warburg's Bank, which he accomplished by examining the files of M.M. Warburg. But the significance was not merely restricted to the size of the firm. It also entailed elucidating the role of the large businesses in the overall German-Jewish economy. Admittedly, the window of opportunity that such an economic contributor possessed in possibly altering the course of both Jewish survival and also National Socialism's power was limited. Adding to the problem of the brief time, which National Socialists required to consolidate power, was that diverse Jewish constituencies had opposed each other. But cooperation was necessary because as early as 1933 Jewish employees, terminated by Gentile firms, sought new positions in Jewish-owned companies that had large enough payrolls to afford a sudden influx of new personnel. Another reason, requiring such accord, was the lending constraints of large German banks. Small Jewish retailers sought new loans from private banks as well as community self-help agencies, when credit from the large financial institutions ceased. A further reason for harmony stemmed from Jewish teenagers seeking apprenticeships in either larger Jewish-owned firms or from community institutions. But in addition to the problem of lack of solidarity, there was also the hesitation on the part of Jewish merchants to isolate themselves from Gentile businessmen. Furthermore, there was the moral issue of whether an Aryan boycott should be repaid by Jewish retribution.[20]

Bajohr's highlighting of large Jewish firms also led to the recognition that Jewish-owned firms provided more donations and employment to the Jewish community than what they received in return. Because 15,000 Jewish inhabitants of Hamburg were unable to be the sole customer base of 1,000 Jewish businesses, two slight-of-hand procedures were devised by non-Gentile firms for survival. One employed by Von der Porten & Frank continued to obtain government contracts by establishing a company under Hartmann von der Porten's Aryan attorney. The second scheme, utilized by the Familie Delmonte & Koopmann wholesale fish business, entailed accepting a non-Jewish partner.[21]

In contrast with these means of surviving, Max Warburg strove to create an economic and political window of opportunity in the first months of 1933. Warburg drafted a memo in the spring of 1933 with former Undersecretary of State Hans Schäffer regarding the need to preserve Jewish firms as a component of rebuilding Germany's economy. This idea became incorporated in a memo emanating from a June 28, 1933, meeting among Gustav Krupp von Bohlen, Carl Friedrich von Siemens, and Economics Minister Kurt Schmitt. A second aspect in this window of opportunity involved assisting Jewish emigration. M.M. Warburg's capital funds of 18 million RM and balance sheet of 120 million GM gave it the strength as one of Germany's ten largest private financial institutions to assist Jewish families to move to Palestine. Although those fleeing preferred to live in either the United States or Great Britain, the Haavara Agreement, signed in August 1933, enabled 52,000 German Jews to leave the Reich with 140 million RM. The Warburg Bank was responsible for 75 percent of this arrangement to sell German products abroad, ensuring that newcomers to Palestine would not be penniless.[22]

This review's strategy of focusing on large Jewish-owned companies is rewarded by observing the reoccurring roles played by key figures in various political and economic sectors. Thus, the Warburg Bank will be reexamined in chapter 5, section A's discussion of the attempted defense by the Hermann Tietz department stores against a hostile takeover by Georg Karg and a banking consortium. Similarly, Hans Schäffer will be readdressed in chapter 6, section C's discussion of the fate of the Ullstein Publishing Company.

Chronologically and methodologically there is an overlap between stages three and four in the academic approach to comprehending the demise of Jewish companies. This last stage in scholarly research is characterized by a desire to be all-inclusive through such means as investing a decade of research in the project, employing a team of investigators, and utilizing computers to establish a database. The last phase in this historiographical survey commenced with Wolfram Selig's 2004 massive 960-page publication on inexpensive purchases in Munich. Selig's study was so lengthy due to his goal of achieving comprehensiveness. Despite conducting research for a decade, his stated objective of examining all Jewish-owned businesses required Selig to limit the period of his investigation only to the years between 1937 and 1939.

Instead of following Genschel's series of political events, Selig examined Jewish involvement in the retail, department store, wholesale, agricultural, art, publishing, services, and manufacturing business sectors. This structure promotes some confusion as merchandise such as textiles, leather goods, tobacco, and groceries are examined in four separate chapters of the book regarding commercial agents, retailers, wholesalers, and firms incorporating both retail and wholesale clients. The Jewish connections between manufacturers, wholesalers, middlemen, and retailers of any one product are obscured. Furthermore, Selig's goal was to examine all of the 1,800 businesses in Munich. However, the index provided a list of "only" 517 Jewish companies.[23]

Despite being considered in this fourth stage of research, Selig was also influenced by Genschel's top-down approach from the first phase. Selig thus emphasized that Gauleiter Adolf Wagner established the private collection company Vermögensverwertung München GmbH on November 25, 1938, whereby Jewish proprietors surrendered their right to dispose of their businesses. Wagner's private enterprise temporarily stopped cheap purchases and enhanced the pressure on Jewish firms, initially carried on by the Nazi labor union, known as the Deutsche Arbeitsfront (DAF). Selig repeated the methodological problem of focusing on non-Jewish companies to explicate the demise of Jewish businesses. For example, Wagner's liquidation firm received more attention than any Jewish company. Ninety pages were devoted to it. A similar structural approach was displayed by Selig's examination of the non-Jewish trustee agency, known as the Deutsche Allgemeine Treuhand AG. It received the second-greatest emphasis with seventeen different pages referring to it. In contrast, the superficial survey of Jewish companies is evident from their customary treatment on part of one page. This structural orientation is also evident in Selig's discussion of five Nazi agencies involved in the inexpensive acquisitions, including the collection company, the trustee agency, the commercial office, the lending office, and the apartment office.[24] Selig's emphasis on Nazi bureaucracies conflicts with his goal of thoroughly examining Jewish firms in Munich. Although Selig follows Barkai's methodology from stage two by utilizing Yad Vashem records, he rejects Bajohr's emphasis on a bottom-up approach, which formed part of stage three in the survey of academic research.

In Selig's brief overview of the years from 1933 through 1935, the Papierfabrik August Neustätter was mentioned as having lost its government contract to supply paper to the City of Munich. In this first reference to a Jewish business, it was noted that all twenty-five employees were Aryans. However, their appeal to preserve non-Jewish jobs was dismissed. The second Jewish business to be mentioned by Selig was the Firma Merk & Mainzer, which Wilhelm Schütte desired to purchase. However, Selig's purpose in referring to this enterprise was to provide an example of how the Bavarian Chamber of Commerce intervened because Schütte's daily visits to the Jewish establishment implied far too much personal contact. Both of the first two allusions to Jewish firms are made in order to support a top-down approach, rather than presenting a company approach to understanding purchases below asset value.[25]

In addition, the methodological emphasis on tiny details regarding 517 small firms may cause the reader to lose sight of the overarching problem of when and how the cheap purchases occurred. Selig may have shown awareness of this problem as he addressed Jewish textile wholesalers halfway through his tome:

> Even in wholesale, the majority of Jewish firms were small operations without great economic significance in which the owner, often without staff was able to earn his livelihood. But there was also a series of significant businesses, leading in their sectors, which snatched the interest of Aryans.[26]

Instead of arranging the Jewish textile wholesalers in order of importance, Selig chose an alphabetical approach. Of the twenty-seven textile wholesalers, the reader must make his or her own analysis to discover that the five principal operations were Firma Goldschmidt & Fränkel, Firma J. Heilbronner & Guggenheimer, Gebrüder Heine, Firma D.M. Neuburger, and Firma Max & Leo Weil.

The largest of these twenty-seven wholesalers was Goldschmidt & Fränkel. Goldschmidt wholesaled the same types of merchandise in the 1930s from which department stores had their original sales in the 1880s, namely lace, buttons, embroidery, and trimmings. With a staff of nineteen, the wholesaler had sales of 566,509 RM in 1936 and 655,492 RM in the following year, an increase, which Selig described as "astonishing," due to the boycott measures. The Jewish partners were able to sell their business to Paul Jakob at the end of August 1938 before Emil Goldschmidt and Eduard Fränkel emigrated to Switzerland. In early 1942, the National Socialist Asset Recovery Agency transferred 11,235.60 RM for the benefit of the Reich, since the former Jewish owners had "moved away" to enemy foreign countries. With Selig's focus on governmental activity, no data is provided on how much the firm was worth in 1938, nor how little Paul Jakob paid for it, nor the circumstances in which the company was acquired. Although both prewar city records and postwar restitution applications were utilized, it was merely noted that Goldschmidt was paid 228.60 RM for articles of silver, which he delivered to the lending office before fleeing to Palestine via Switzerland.[27] It may be that Selig meant that Jakob only paid 11,235.60 RM, which was a fraction of the company's worth.

In contrast with the two-and-one-third page explication of Goldschmidt's wholesale business, Selig devoted fourteen pages to Firma Heinrich Uhlfelder. This concentration is most welcome, since this investigation perceives the large department store chains as central to explicating the overall picture of when and how Jewish-owned firms were purchased below the costs of their fixed assets. Because Selig restricted his investigation to the period of 1937 through 1939, he merely mentioned that after the multi-facility Tietz complex was Aryanized in 1934, the stand-alone Uhlfelder store became the focus of Nazi anger. However, he also acknowledged that as early as March 10, 1933, a student had kidnapped the owner Max Uhlfelder, driven him through the streets of Munich and repeatedly stopped to see if various trees were strong enough to hang Max on them.

Selig supported the customary understanding of Aryanization reaching its pinnacle in 1938. However, another support for the early Aryanizations of Jewish firms is Selig's acknowledgment that Max considered in 1935 withdrawing from his operation and appointing a non-Jewish managing director. With 450 employees in Munich, this retailer was a small operation in contrast with the 15,000 employees of the Leonhard Tietz chain, discussed in chapter 6, section A, or the 14,000 in Hermann Tietz, analyzed in chapter 5. In elaborating how Max was unwilling to accept a low purchase price, from the businessmen who had already "purchased" the Hermann Tietz chain, Selig employed the local Bavarian Economic Archives. Thus, authors evaluated in stage four, follow the prior phase in utilizing local sources.[28] Archives in small cities and towns may contain important data on local businesses but appear ineffective in disclosing the activities of national or regional companies.

Academic interest in the Aryanization of Jewish-owned companies has not waned. The last volume in this survey was published by Christoph Kreutzmüller in German in 2012 and translated into English in 2015. It forms the concluding part of stage four's team and computer-generated database approach. Similar to Selig, Christoph presents an all-encompassing view albeit of the most significant economic hub of Germany, namely Berlin. Similar to the structural problem observed in Selig's repetition of themes, Kreutzmüller's organization by subject resulted in a nonchronological arrangement. Thus, Chapter 4 concerned "Violent Persecution" and Chapter 7 involved "The Destruction of Jewish Commercial Activity," whereas Chapters 8 and 9 covered the "Institutional" and the "Individual Counter-Strategies" respectively. Since Jewish self-help activities could not logically occur after the destruction, Kreutzmüller retraced the events of 1933 from a different perspective, whereas viewing Jewish activities as responses to Nazi measures would have been illuminating.

To his credit, Kreuztmüller surveyed an unusually diverse spectrum of sources from the Berlin City Archives including newspapers and diaries. The expanse ranged from the liberal *Berliner Tageblatt* and *Die Weltbühne* to the National Socialist and right-wing *Der Angriff*, *Völkische Beobachter*, and *Der Stürmer* as well as including the Jewish publications *Jüdische Rundschau* and the *C.V. Zeitung*. However, the amassing of details interferes with the train of thought. Various scintillating statements are neither reconciled with existing scholarship nor harmonized with each other. Kreutzmüller fourth chapter commenced with an assertion that provides a powerful impetus for this assessment:

> It is a well-known fact that anti-Semitic stereotypes were widely spread long before 1933. Envy and resentment rose dramatically during the financial crisis of the late nineteenth century, which was one fundamental source of modern anti-Semitism.[29]

The motivation caused by financial envy is key to this volume's comprehension of how German businessmen were able to "purchase" a business from a former employer or "friend" at far below the value of the fixed assets. In contrast, Kreuztmüller emphasized violence. However, it appears that he erred in both the original nature of the violence as well as the original target of that violence. First, Kreutzmüller disregarded the distinction between Germany's pre-1933 "traditional religious anti-Semitism" and the Third Reich's "racial anti-Semitism."[30] As a UCLA dissertation, written for the academic institution where Saul Friedländer taught the Holocaust for several decades, the reader will understand the dozen references emphasizing this text's indebtedness to his distinction between a pre-1933 "religious" and a post–Nuremberg Laws "racial" anti-Semitism. In discussing the judiciary's favoritism of right-wing politics, the "Introduction" to this book mentioned that German-Jewish journalist Felix Fechenbach was shot while being transported to Dachau on August 7, 1933. Jewish men, including Wilhelm Aron and Louis Schloß, were murdered by Dachau guards in May 1933.[31] It is clear that a development in anti-Semitism occurred from smashing synagogue windows and breaking cemetery gravestones before 1933 to killing of individual concentration camp inmates during 1933 to the murder of millions by soldiers' bullets or Zyklon B after the outbreak of war.

Kreutzmüller's valuable publication was accomplished through a team of researchers, limiting their efforts to the city of Berlin. Since their investigation encompassed the pre–Third Reich period through the Late Third Reich,[32] it seems justified that the investigative team should have noted Friedländer's differentiation in types of anti-Semitism. In contrast, this monograph attempts to make a small contribution only to Aryanization in the 1933 through 1935 period.

Christoph's inattention to this differentiation is evident in a following assertion: "Hitler's appointment as Reich chancellor [*sic*] on 30 January 1933 may not unambiguously represent a dividing line where anti-Jewish violence is concerned."[33]

Second, Kreuztmüller failed to observe that the original target of the Berlin violence had been Communists and Socialists. In narrating the "Violent Persecution" in Chapter 4 and the "Bureaucratic Persecution" in Chapter 5, Kreutzmüller indicated that in the more than 150 concentration camps in and surrounding the capital, at least sixteen Jewish men were murdered between February and September 1933. He acknowledged that Hans-Norbert Burkert's research was the source for this fact. Although I would not want to trivialize anyone's death, the number of Jewish deaths appears small for so many camps. What was not disclosed was a comparison with the number of Socialists, Communists, and "work shy" individuals executed during the same eight-month period. Since Berlin had been a stronghold for Socialists and Communists in which the SA had to fight more violently to gain power over the streets, it would seem highly plausible that far more supporters of left-wing politics than Jews were killed. The interpretation that camps primarily focused on Communists and Socialists in 1933 is supported by Kreutzmüller's prior assertion that "Jews were not the party's primary enemies in the years of its rise" as well as his subsequent statement that Jewish people were first arrested in large numbers in June 1938.[34]

This need to refine Kreuztmüller's understanding of the violence in the capital is supported by other researchers who noted that the concentration camps in the Berlin sections of the Tiergarten, Prenzlauer Berg, Kreuzberg, Charlottenburg, Köpenick, and Spandau were often located in Communist neighborhoods. Permission from higher authorities was neither necessary nor desired, since each SA was a political soldier who was conscious of his task under the motto of "extermination of the Marxist plague."[35]

Already in March 1933 Rudolf Diels and Kurt Daluege had to calm Berlin's SA after the Foreign Office was called into action due to complications with the Soviet Union. Further support of the prominence of left-wing casualties over Jewish victims was the June 1933 Köpenick Blood Week. Anton Schmaus was a Socialist, who occasioned the escalation in violence by shooting three SA men when they forcibly entered his father's house. In retribution for the killing, SA Storm Troop number 15 murdered the father Johann that evening and the son was wounded. The SA was provided with names and addresses of KPD and SPD members. Under the guise of searching for weapons and pamphlets, approximately 500 were abducted and at least 23 were murdered, including the Socialists Richard Aßmann and Paul von Essen as well as the Communists Josef and Paul Spitzer, Erich Janitzky, and Karl Pokern. Although there were Jewish targets, those primarily suffering were Socialists and Communists.[36]

Kreutzmüller's subtitle is *The Destruction of Jewish Commercial Activity*. In his narrative, the multimillion-dollar enterprises such as the Hermann Tietz department store, the Ullstein Publishing Company, the real estate developer and apartment complex builder Adolf Sommerfeld, and the Engelhardt Brauerei AG are mentioned alongside Philipp Moschkowitz's egg business, Judka Jankel Kopelmann's café, Michalski & Striemer's linen shop, and Erich Felix's fruit stall. Rarely is the reader informed of specific business facts such as the Christian Wilhelm Kayser & Company smelting works employed 160 people or the Albert Labus paper factory's capital was 100,000 RM. Thus, there exists an unfortunate amalgamation of businesses without regard to founding capital, number of stockholders, net sales, value of fixed assets, or number of employees. Yet it appears self-evident that an egg business, café, linen shop, and fruit stand might have all been one-person operations. Thus, all four might have easily gone out of existence without affecting the larger issue of the "destruction of Jewish commercial activity." In contrast, the department store, publisher, builder, and brewery together undoubtedly employed tens of thousands and had millions in annual sales. The loss of such magnitudes did mean destruction.[37] It is questionable whether the large amount of space Keutzmüller allotted to compounding examples of tiny businesses is capable of attaining his objective of depicting "the destruction of Jewish commercial activity."

Perhaps there was a brief window of opportunity in 1933 during which high unemployment made the preservation of large German-Jewish companies important to National Socialism.[38] Such a favorable economic moment could only be exploited if the decades-long divisions between assimilationists versus Zionists as well as the cultic Orthodox as opposed to the *religious Reform Jews* could be quickly overcome. Bajohr's discussion of this favorable moment was mentioned earlier in the treatise's reference to the Warburg Bank, but will now be reexamined under the unified organization known as the Reichsvereinigung der deutschen Juden. Kreutzmüller saw the origin of this institution under the impetus of the previously mentioned Carl Melchior[39] of the M.M. Warburg Bank and Hans Schäffer of the Ullstein Publishing Company as well as through Wilfrid Israel of the Berlin department store bearing his surname. Among other self-help activities, this umbrella agency used funds from the American Joint Distribution Committee to establish twenty-two micro banks in 1933. In addition, the Economics Department of another association, the Wirtschaftshilfe, assisted 3,500 distressed businessmen with information in the second half of 1933. The Department's financial aid was modest with merely one-fifth of the despairing obtaining loans, of whom one-third received less than 50 RM and a second-third obtaining less than 150 RM and the majority of the remainder receiving less than 600 RM. In addition, "loans" were not customarily cash, but rather bicycles, sewing machines, clothing, and other products from Jewish wholesalers.[40] Alongside the examples provided by the Reichsvereinigung and the Wirtschaftshilfe, the number of people rescued and the amount of funds involved were enhanced due to the capability of one large Jewish-owned firm, the M.M. Warburg Bank.

This investigation's focus on large commercial enterprises is justified. If cooperation had existed among the diverse Jewish orientations, Max Warburg's financial connections with the Reichsbank and Palestine may have been able to preserve some of the financial stability of the Jewish community for a number of months. Warburg's association in 1933 with three Jewish organizations—the Haavara, Reichsvereinigung, and Wirtschaftshilfe—has already been mentioned. The January 27, 1936, Liquidationsbank proposal was quickly retracted. Thus, the outcome for any counterfactual thesis must be restricted to three years or less.

C. A PROPOSED NEW METHODOLOGY

This research intends to inaugurate a fifth phase in the academic study of Aryanizations of Jewish-owned companies. The three prior stages have made valuable revisions to Genschel's pioneering efforts. This assessment will benefit from central concepts gleaned from the preceding six authors. One of the most strategic ideas was discovered by Alex Bruns-Wüstefeld, who identified how Genschel had erred in his developmental schema by not distinguishing between the Aryanization and the liquidation of Jewish firms. It is important to determine whether Jewish companies were "purchased," or whether they went out-of-business. Bruns-Wüstefeld observed a pattern in Göttingen, Marburg, and Heidelberg that although there was a heightened activity in 1938, it was due to Jewish businesses being liquidated. In Göttingen, during 1938, thirty-five non-Aryan operations had been allowed to expire and only seven had been purchased. In Marburg, during 1938, twenty Jewish companies had gone out-of-business, whereas merely three had been bought. The paradigm was repeated in Heidelberg for 1938 in which forty-one firms had ceased operation, but only twenty-one had been acquired. Thus, Genschel's flurry of activity in 1938 was occasioned by Jewish mom-and-pop shops that were allowed to dissolve, because no Gentile entrepreneur wanted to buy such a struggling enterprise. The demise of the tiny operations merely reduced the competition for the non-Jewish survivors.[41]

For private German businessmen to be able to acquire large Jewish-owned enterprises with little to no capital, banks needed to be involved either to force the sale through recalled loans to Jewish entrepreneurs or by supplying the capital to German businessmen. The two banks most involved in Aryanizations were the Deutsche Bank and the Dresdner Bank. Both of the two largest had between two and three billion RM, which was sufficient to enable the acquisition of the largest Jewish firms. The assets of these two

Table 2.1 Financial Institutions Enabling "Purchases" of Jewish Firms

	Deutsche Bank		*Dresdner Bank*	
	Assets in billion RM	*Staff*	*Assets in billion RM*	*Staff*
1933	3.04	16,789	2.68	11,157
1934	2.96	17,588	2.57	11,760
1935	3.02	17,619	2.44	12,374
1938	3.75	17,947	2.79	11,902
1942	7.50	21,000	5.74	13,622
1944	11.37	NA	8.61	13,573

Source: Material obtained from *Dresdner and Deutsche Banks; Special Report of the Military Governor, U.S. Zone*. 1947, 25.

largest financial institutions more than doubled during the period from 1933 through 1943, which may be due to their cheap acquisition of existing Czech, Austrian, Polish, French, Belgian, and Dutch banks. However, the procurement of such non-Jewish and non-German companies is outside the scope of this book (Table 2.1).

Perhaps the brief thirty-four-page Office of Military Government, United States (OMGUS) report was researched in preparation for Karl Rasche's eleventh Subsequent Nuremberg Trial in which the Dresdner Bank's spokesman was sentenced to seven years. The American military accumulated abundant facts, leading the June 1947 OMGUS report to arrive at a swift indictment:

> Another phase of National-Socialism from which the banks benefited was the "Aryanization" of the German economy. Both the Deutsche and the Dresdner Banks were active in acquiring for themselves Jewish banking houses and industrial enterprises, although their major efforts in this field were focused on the selection of "targets" for Aryanization and on the financing of purchases of Jewish property. The Dresdner Bank distinguished itself especially by utilizing its close ties with the SS and by exercising political duress in effecting Aryanizations.[42]

However, decades later, when Harold James was granted access to the Deutsche Bank Archive, he urged extreme caution in utilizing OMGUS files:

> Those who uncritically based their work on the material provided in the post-war US military government (OMGUS) reports, relied on a narration of the banks' and bankers' business and social contacts. Following the unsubstantiated assumption that such connections inevitably meant political pressure, these analyses went on to imply that political leverage was constantly being exercised by business. They took for granted the conclusion that they claimed to be proving, they forgot about the way in which power functioned in a totalitarian state.[43]

The circumspect Professor James maintained that OMGUS had erred in claiming that a German bank had room to maneuver during the Third Reich. He contended that there was no possibility for moral considerations in opposing the anti-Semitic ideology of the Third Reich. Apparently, the dictatorship required the banks to cooperate in seeking new owners of Jewish companies. James's perspective could lead to the troublesome conclusion that the fact that the Deutsche and Dresdner Banks had benefited financially must be sheer coincidence.

Opposing James's interpretation is the previously mentioned Warburg Bank utilization of a small window of opportunity in the Haavara Agreement. The Jewish financial institution perceived the opposition to Jewish companies, whereby loans were recalled and new owners were sought within the ranks of existing Deutsche Bank and Dresdner Bank customers. In contrast, Warburg enabled 55,000 Jews to immigrate to Palestine with 140 million RM. In addition, Max Warburg proposed to Hjalmar Schacht the creation of a Liquidationsbank with initial funding of 250 million RM for the purpose of transferring all Jewish property. Officials of the Economic Ministry were surprised by a large amount of cash and interested in how many German Jews would emigrate. Unfortunately, this January 27, 1936, scheme was later withdrawn.[44] Nonetheless, it certainly raises the issue of whether OMGUS's 1947 assessment of the Deutsche and Dresdner Banks is not more impartial than what James allowed.

A correct interpretation of the banks' role in hostile takeovers of Jewish firms is clouded by pre- and post-Nuremberg testimony given by Carl Goetz of the Dresdner Bank. Scholars after James have argued two main points: False testimony had been given against Karl Rasche and he had been tried as a proxy for the Dresdner Bank's exploitation of the Czech and Dutch economies. What is the correct interpretation of the conflicting evidence? Before Rasche joined the Dresdner headquarters in Berlin in January 1935, his redevelopment activities on behalf of the Westfalenbank in Bochum may have entailed the Aryanization of Jewish firms in cooperation with Gau Economic Advisor Paul Pleiger. In March 1947, fellow Dresdner Board member Carl Goetz provided testimony against Rasche, allegedly ignoring the fact that the Bank needed mid-sized business clients in the provinces. Instead, he emphasized that Rasche had been hired due to the repeated interventions by Wilhelm Keppler, founder of the Circle of Friends of Heinrich Himmler. By joining the Board, massive political influence from the NSDAP had been avoided. Goetz considered that both Rasche and another Board colleague, Emil Meyer, were trusted by the Nazi Party elite. After Goetz was released from prison and no longer included as a possible defendant in Nuremberg, he altered his testimony and maintained that Rasche was appointed solely on the basis of his expertise in reorganizing businesses.[45] The best interpretation may be that Rasche had been guilty in the Aryanization of Jewish-owned companies, but Goetz and other Dresdner Bank executives allowed him to be the "scapegoat" for their collective offenses. Goetz changed his testimony after the danger of punishment for war-time activities had passed and the new era of German whitewashing of the past had begun.

James appeared more willing to disclose the Deutsche Bank's actions against its own Board Members than its participation in Aryanizations of Jewish companies. Thus, he provided an extensive translation of Spokesman Georg Solmssen's (originally the Jewish surname was Salomonsohn) April 9, 1933 correspondence to Supervisory Board Chairman Franz Urbig in which the actions of German businessmen against Jewish colleagues were emphasized:

> Dear Herr Urbig . . . I fear that we are only at the beginning of a conscious and planned development which is aimed at the indiscriminate economic and moral destruction of all members of the Jewish race living in Germany. The complete passivity of the classes which do not belong to the National Socialist Party, the lack of any feeling of solidarity on the part of those who have up to now worked in business shoulder to shoulder with Jewish colleagues, the ever more evident pressure to draw personal advantages from the free positions created by the purges . . .[46]

In addition to underscoring the motivation of greed of one colleague against another, James highlighted the termination of Jewish employees in the private sector during 1933. He specifically noted that of the 1,500 Jewish employees in the Hermann Tietz chain, 500 had already been fired by August 1933.[47] This significant detail will be reexamined in chapter 6. If James has been overly cautious in accepting the OMGUS Report, it nevertheless provided the important fact that by 1935, the Dresdner Bank had a revolving fund of five million RM for the hostile takeover of Jewish firms. In addition, the Report mentioned that Hermann Göring's brother-in-law Franz Hueber requested his half a million Swiss Franc fee for negotiating the cheap sale of the Gebrüder Arnhold Bank to the Dresdner Bank be deposited in Switzerland. This element will be readdressed in chapter 6, section D. Furthermore, the Dresdner Bank induced the Gestapo to imprison the proprietor of the Engelhardt Brauerei AG until he agreed to a low sales price.[48] This too underscored the lack of business ethics by the Bank in the Aryanization of one of Germany's largest breweries. This brewery will be investigated in chapter 6, section E.

A sketch of the following chapters will now conclude the history of research. Since department stores were not only large economic entities, but a business sector dominated by Jewish entrepreneurs, chapter 4, Section A will focus on the history of economic opposition to the Hermann Tietz chain by disgruntled Plauen lace manufacturers, smaller retailers, and the banks. Chapter 5 will concentrate on the 1933–1934 activity by Georg Karg and a banking consortium in acquiring the Hermann Tietz department stores with almost no financial collateral.

Chapter 6 will support the claim that Aryanizations occurred as early as 1933 and occurred as conservative, non-Nazi businessmen were supported by large German banks. This will be maintained by examining the Leonhard Tietz department store chain. To withstand any possible allegation that department stores provide an isolated example of hostile takeovers, two of Germany's largest publishing houses will be investigated, namely Mosse and the Ullstein Verlag. Additional evidence that firms from other business sectors were purchased below the value of their assets is provided by one of Germany's largest private banks, Gebrüder Arnhold as well as the Engelhardt Brewery. The Simson rifle, bicycle, and motorcycle factory will be the sixth Aryanized firm examined in chapter 6.

Chapter 7 will briefly mention four large companies, which support the model of early Aryanization. The exploration will conclude with a suggestion for further research.

NOTES

1. On this first occasion of the Nazi neologism, the term has been placed within quotation marks. To avoid being overly pedantic and as an aid to easier reading, the quotation marks will be deleted in all future occurrences.

2. The role of non-Jewish businesses has been of greater interest to American and British scholars. See, for example, Peter Hayes, *Industry and Ideology; IG Farben in the Nazi Era* (Cambridge: Cambridge University Press, 1987); Bernard P. Bellon, *Mercedes in Peace and War; German Automobile Workers, 1903–1945* (New York: Columbia University Press, 1990); Gerald D. Feldman, "The Deutsche Bank from World War to World Economic Crisis 1914–1933," in Lothar Gall et al., (Ed.), *The Deutsche Bank 1870–1995* (London: Weidenfeld & Nicolson, 1994); Neil Gregor, *Daimler-Benz in the Third Reich* (New Haven: Yale University Press, 1998); Gerald D. Feldman, *Allianz and the German Insurance Business, 1933–1945* (Cambridge: Cambridge University Press, 2001); Harold James, *The Deutsche Bank and the Nazi Economic War Against the Jews; The Expropriation of Jewish-Owned Property* (Cambridge: Cambridge University Press, 2001); Peter Hayes, *From Cooperation to Complicity; Degussa in the Third Reich* (Cambridge: Cambridge University Press, 2004); Francis R. Nicosia (Ed.), *Business and Industry in Nazi Germany* (New York: Berghahn Books, 2004); and Harold James, *Krupp: A History of the Legendary German Firm* (Princeton: Princeton University Press, 2012). However, a few English-speaking scholars have addressed Jewish companies in English: Ron Chernow, *The Warburgs; The Twentieth-Century Odyssey of a Remarkable Jewish Family* (New York: Random House, 1993); Martin Dean (Ed.), *Robbery and Restitution;*

The Conflict over Jewish property in Europe (New York: Berghahn Books, 2007); and Martin Dean, *Robbing the Jews; The Confiscation of Jewish Property in the Holocaust, 1933–1945* (Cambridge: Cambridge University Press, 2008).

3. If Chancellor Adenauer had no qualms of including high-ranking Nazis into his postwar democracy, he certainly did not object to seeing those who had profited from low-cost acquisition of Jewish firms from continuing to financially benefit after the war. See the exposes of Nazi elite in the Federal republic: Klaus Gotto (Ed.), *Der Staatssekretär Adenauers. Persönlichkeit und politisches Wirken Hans Globkes* (Stuttgart: Verlagsgemeinschaft Ernst Klett, 1980). Philipp-Christian Wachs, *Der Fall Theodor Oberländer (1905–1998). Ein Lehrstück deutscher Geschichte* (Frankfurt am Main: Campus Verlag GmbH, 2000); and Jürgen Bevers, *Der Mann hinter Adenauer. Hans Globkes Anstieg vom NS-Juristen zur Grauen Eminenz der Bonner Republik* (Berlin: Christoph Links Verlag, 2009).

4. Helmut Genschel, *Die Verdrängung der Juden aus der Wirtschaft im Dritten Reich*. Göttinger Bausteine zur Geschichtswissenschaft (Göttingen: Musterschmidt Verlag, 1966).

5. Genschel, *Verdrängung der Juden*, pp. 45–47.

6. Genschel, *Verdrängung der Juden*, pp. 97–104.

7. Christoph Kreutzmüller, *Final Sale in Berlin. The Destruction of Jewish Commercial Activity 1930–1945* (New York: Berghahn Books, 2015), p. 190.

8. Avraham Barkai, *Erlebtes und Gedachtes; Erinnerungen eines unabhängigen Historikers* (Göttingen: Wallstein Verlag, 2011), p. 7.

9. Genschel repeatedly used the German adjective "schleichend." Since Genschel was never translated into English, his volume is known to the English-speaking world only through the citations by Barkai, which were translated into English by William Templer. Although it can mean "creeping," this rendition is a bit ambiguous. The simple word "slow" is another acceptable translation and it removes all vagueness. This exploration is arguing that half a dozen of Germany's largest, Jewish-owned companies were all "purchased" in the period 1933 through 1935. Numerous one-person Jewish operations may have gone bankrupt in 1938, but surely this does not justify the depiction of a slow demise of Jewish businesses. Utilizing the word "slow" highlights the departure from Genschel's perspective in this analysis.

10. Avraham Barkai, *From Boycott to Annihilation; The Economic Struggle of German Jews 1933–1943* (Hanover: Brandeis University Press, 1989), pp. 2–5.

11. Saul Friedländer, *Nazi Germany and the Jews, Volume I: The Years of Persecution, 1933–1939* (New York: HarperCollins Publishers, Inc., 1997).

12. Barkai's previously mentioned *Erlebtes und Gedachtes.*

13. Barbara Händler-Lachmann und Thomas Werther, *"Vergessene Geschäfte verlorene Geschichte"; Jüdisches Wirtschaftsleben in Marburg und seine Vernichtung im Nationalsozialismus* (Marburg: Hitzeroth, 1992), pp. 47–48.

14. Händler-Lachmann, *Vergessene Geschäfte*, pp. 49–61.

15. Ian Kershaw, *Popular Opinion & Political Dissent in the Third Reich*; *Bavaria 1933–1945* (New York: Oxford University Press, 1983), p. 224.

16. Kershaw, *Popular Opinion*, p. 229. Compare Lucy S. Dawidowicz, *The War against the Jews 1933–45* (New York: Holt, Rinehart & Winston, 1975) with

Daniel Jonah Goldhagen, *Hitler's Willing Executioners; Ordinary Germans and the Holocaust* (New York: Alfred A. Knopf, 1996).

17. Arnold Paucker, *Der jüdische Abwehrkampf gegen Antisemitismus und Nationalsozialismus in den letzten Jahren der Weimarer Republik.* 2. Verbesserte Auflage (Hamburg: Leibniz-Verlag, 1969), pp. 194–195.

18. Gerhard A. Ritter and Klaus Tenfelde, *Arbeiter im Deutschen Kaiserreich 1871 bis 1914* (Bonn: Verlag J. H. W. Dietz Nachf. GmbH, 1992), p. 697.

19. Frank Bajohr, *'Aryanisation' in Hamburg; The Economic Exclusion of Jews and the Confiscation of their Property in Nazi Germany* (New York: Berghahn Books, 2002), p. 5.

20. Bajohr, *Aryanisation*, pp. 114–117.

21. Bajohr, *Aryanisation*, pp. 118–119.

22. Bajohr, *Aryanisation*, pp. 122–127.

23. Compare Chapters 1 through 4 in Section B of Wolfram Selig, *"Arisierung" in München. Die Vernichtung jüdischer Existenz 1937–1939* (Berlin: Metropol Verlag, 2004), pp. 6–7, 946–955.

24. Selig, *"Arisierung" in München*, pp. 43–49, 52–57.

25. Selig, *"Arisierung" in München*, pp. 17–21, 23–24.

26. Selig, *"Arisierung" in München*, p. 455.

27. Selig, *"Arisierung" in München*, pp. 455–491.

28. Selig, *"Arisierung" in München*, pp. 370–371.

29. Kreutzmüller, *Final Sale,* p. 99.

30. Recall Friedländer, *Nazi Germany*, pp. 82–83.

31. Timothy Ryback, *Hitler's First Victims; The Quest for Justice* (New York: Alfred A. Knopf, 2014), pp. 125–139.

32. The reader will recall that Kreutzmüller's subtitle is *The Destruction of Jewish Commercial Activity 1930–1945.*

33. Kreutzmüller, *Final Sale*, p. 102.

34. Compare Kreutzmüller, *Final Sale*, p. 101, 113 and 127.

35. Irene Mayer-von Götz, *Terror im Zentrum der Macht. Die frühen Konzentrationslager in Berlin 1933/34–1936* (Berlin: Metropol Verlag, 2008), pp. 241–244.

36. Stefan Hördler, "Ideologie, Machinszenierung und Exzess: Taten und Täter der 'Köpenicker Blutwoche,'" in Stefan Hördler (Ed.), *SA-Terror als Herrschaftssicherung. "Köpenicker Blutwoche" und öffentliche Gewalt im Nationalsozialismus* (Berlin: Metropol Verlag, 2013), pp. 83–87. Also note Stefan Hördler, "Kooperation der Gewalt. Anmerkungen zur 'Köpenicker Blutwoche' und zum SA-Sturm 33," p. 105 as well as Hördler, "Entgrenzung und Eingrenzung der Gewalt. Berliner SA, SS und Polizei (1933–1939) in Michael Wildt and Christoph Kreuzmüller (Eds.), *Berlin 1933 – 1945* (München: Siedler Verlag, 2013), p. 299.

37. Kreutzmüller, *Final Sale*, pp. 101–111, 127.

38. Avraham Barkai's views were previously examined in stage two of the academic research on Aryanization. In contrast with Bajohr's "small window of opportunity" for the Jewish-owned Warburg Bank, Barkai claimed that Hitler had personally approved a loan for the Hermann Tietz department stores in the period from 1934 to

1937, which he depicted as a time with "the illusion of a 'grace period.'" This treatise observed a lack of archival documentation by Barkai, which will be ameliorated in part in chapter 5, section A of this assessment. The Wolfgang Reichart versus Hjalmar Schacht disagreement regarding a proposed loan to Hermann Tietz will be discussed based on the Bundesarchiv document R43 II/369, originally from the Reich Chancellery files and now in Lichterfelde. Unlike Warburg's average loan of 2,700 RM to 52,000 Jews fleeing to Palestine (discussed earlier in Chapter One), the July 1933 loan or 14.5 million RM to Hermann Tietz "preserved jobs" by enabling Georg Karg to take control of the department store chain. Although the two sets of bank loans both occurred early in the Third Reich, their purposes and outcomes were quite disparate.

39. Carl Melchoir's gloomy political and financial impact on John Maynard Keynes during the Versailles peace discussions is noted in Niall Ferguson, *The Pity of War. Explaining World War I* (New York: Basic Books, 1999), pp. 400–412.

40. Kreutzmüller, *Final Sale*, p. 227, pp. 233–235.

41. Alex Bruns-Wüstefeld, *Lohnende Geschäfte; Die Entjudung der Wirtschaft am Beispiel Göttingens* (Hannover: Fackelträger Verlag, 1997), p. 115, pp. 124–125.

42. OMGUS, *Dresdner*, Office of Military Government, United States, pp. 2–3.

43. Harold James, "The Deutsche Bank and the Dictatorship 1933–1945," in Lothar Gall et al., (Ed.), *The Deutsche Bank 1870–1995* (London: Weidenfeld & Nicolson, 1995), p. 283.

44. Avraham Barkai, "German Interests in the Haavara-Transfer Agreement 1933–1939," *Leo Baeck Institute Year Book*, Vol. 35 (1990), p. 257.

45. Although Ralf Ahrens does not employ the German term "Sündenbock" from Leviticus Chapter 16, he implies this concept depicting Karl Rasche as the "example candidate" in the title of his journal article. As the sole bank executive placed before the tribunal during the Subsequent Nuremberg Trials, the American military viewed him as a "symbolic figure," representing the three largest financial institutions. Other members of the Dresdner Bank's Board distanced themselves from their former spokesman and held that there was no further need to examine the activities of the organization's management. After Rasche's early release from his seven-year prison sentence, he perceived that his prior colleagues would "by no means" accept his return to employment. Thus, the more explicit use of the Biblical term "scapegoat" both here and in chapter 7 appears appropriate. See Ralf Ahrens, "Der Exempelkandidat. Die Dresdner Bank und der Nürnberger Prozess gegen Karl Rasche," *Vierteljahrshefte für Zeitgeschichte*, Vol. 52, No. 4 (October 2004), pp. 637–643.

46. James, *Deutsche Bank*, p. 296.

47. James, *Deutsche Bank*, p. 303.

48. OMGUS, *Dresdner*, pp. 15–16.

Chapter 3

New Approach to Comprehend Aryanizers

A. SURVEY OF PRIOR RESEARCH

The four stages of academic development employed in the introduction to survey the topic of Aryanization are similarly useful in examining the corollary issue of determining the precise identity of Aryanizers and the chief motivation of their actions. Helmut Genschel's first stage of scholarly investigation in 1966 emphasized the role of the NSDAP and state legislation. Within his top-down paradigm Adolf Hitler, Hermann Göring, Joseph Goebbels, Heinrich Himmler, Reinhard Heydrich, and Hjalmar Schacht understandably received most of the attention. Admittedly, Friedrich Flick, the coal magnate convicted in the fifth Subsequent Nuremberg Trial, is examined. However, the business activities of steel magnate Gustav Krupp, the I.G. Farben executive Carl Krauch and the Dresdner Bank spokesman Karl Rasche are not mentioned, so the middle-class Aryanizers of Jewish businesses emphasized in this volume were naturally excluded.

Avraham Barkai's 1987 publication in the second stage of research produced a few detached remarks, which still bore the imprint of Genschel's influence. Although Barkai moved the focus in the early years of the Third Reich from Party elites, he still contended that "Old Guard party stalwarts and middle-class party functionaries were the principal gainers." By 1936, these NSDAP members had been superseded by "respected industrialists and heads of firms." Although the socioeconomic standing of the Aryanizers had changed, their conduct had not: "well-educated 'Aryan' large entrepreneurs behaved no differently from the small middle-class Nazis." Barkai addressed the motivation of these "shrewd and profit-conscious businessmen, who attempted to hew out of the given situation as much profit as possible." Although he acknowledged that some of them were not anti-Semitic, "economically motivated opportunism" was insufficient to explicate the cheap acquisitions. He maintained that "occupational envy and greed" were added to anti-Semitism.[1] In contrast, this study observes that most early Aryanizations occurred at the hands of non-Nazi Party members.

Frank Bajohr's 1998 volume in the third phase of the academic investigation produced a schema. Despite perpetrators attempting to conceal the details of their lives and their business acquisitions in the postwar restitution files of the Hamburg District Court, Bajohr observed that the individuals involved included three types: former employees of the Jewish firm, newcomers to the business sector, and Party members who used their political connections for their personal benefit. From 300 files, he noted that 40 percent of the Aryanizers were "unscrupulous profiteers," whose personal involvement led to a decrease in the already-low sales price. He used Barkai's term "sleeping partners" to depict a second group of 40 percent, who wanted their cheap purchases to appear as proper transactions although they sought their own profit. Ironically, these individuals claimed to be "victims" in postwar reparation trials initiated by the original Jewish proprietors. Only a remaining 20 percent of the individuals purchasing Jewish firms attempted to make secret payments for goodwill.[2]

Not only did Bajohr deviate from Barkai with respect to replacing disconnected ideas with a typology, Bajohr also diverged from Barkai's fallback to anti-Semitism as the primary motivation for German businessmen's cheap purchases of Jewish firms. One example originated with the State Police in Aachen, who remarked that in many anti-Jewish actions National Socialist attitudes played less of a role than did the business competitors' jealousy. Another illustration arose in Baden and Württemberg's leather and shoe industries:

> Even though the majority of boycott initiatives originated from middle class industrial companies, especially retailers and craft businesses, it would nevertheless be inappropriate to classify the middle-class economy across the board as anti-Semitic. This is shown by a comparative examination of the middle-class shoe and leather industry in southwest Germany. . . . it was the consensus of the leather industry to exclude the racial question from business life.[3]

A third indeed altogether counter-example stemmed from the early years of the Third Reich in which "the enticement of profitable business with Jewish companies was greater than the influence of anti-Semitic propaganda or the danger of being publicly denounced as a friend of Jews." A fourth source of support arose with farmers, who clung to their business connections with Jewish cattle dealers and preferred to buy from the Jewish-owned department stores in the cities.[4]

A further line of investigation inspired by Bajohr was the insight that a businessman's acceptance or rejection of anti-Jewish measures in the commercial sphere could be traced back to the generation in which the individual was born. The older generation was composed of Liberals, who had become financially successful during the empire. This generation rejected racial anti-Semitism because it opposed the image of personal competence. In contrast, stood the generation born at the turn of the twentieth century, which was unable to replicate their fathers' financial success. The younger generation adopted a National Socialist and anti-Semitic orientation. The pattern from the business world was paralleled by middle-class academic youth, who were socialized in the völkisch movement.[5]

One aspect of Barkai's methodology adopted by Bajohr was the use of Jewish sources. Bajohr employed memoirs from the Hamburg banker Max Warburg as well as the Berlin stylish clothing proprietor Franz V. Grünfeld. Warburg had hoped to defend his establishment as a fortress, which Bajohr observed was already in the spring of 1933 an "illusion." Part of the reason for the swift demise was the lack of loyalty by Gentile employees on the payrolls of Jewish firms. Instead of being grateful for a regular paycheck during the worldwide economic depression, non-Jewish staff would engage in eavesdropping on Grünfeld's telephone conversations, surveillance of his mail, and sifting through his wastepaper basket. He lamented that "the number of loyal employees could be counted on the fingers."[6] Without doubt, Bajohr advanced the academic understanding of those cheaply acquiring Jewish-owned companies. However, a dichotomy has been exposed in his oeuvre. Was the generation born about 1900 fated to anti-Semitic acts against Jewish entrepreneurs, because economic conditions were unfavorable in replicating the financial success of their fathers, or does the lack of gratitude for a salary and failure to demonstrate fidelity indicate a weakness in their responsibility to take ownership for their actions? Is society or each individual accountable?

Scholars, business representatives, and the media, who met on June 20–21, 1997, in I.G. Farben's former headquarters extended the number of possible explanations beyond the two mentioned above. The doyen of German historiography Hans Mommsen rejected the two proposed approaches in favor of examining Germany's political culture:

> The analysis of individual businessmen's behavior will not lead very far and requires a statistical analysis of common characteristics of collective biography. . . . Under the conditions of the Third Reich, the state of mind of industrial companies to resist the impositions of the regime in boundary situations was low. Even in the case of Robert Bosch, who was personally connected with the July 20, 1944 event, the activity of his firm did not deviate. The entanglement in the tyranny and the crimes of the regime are therefore least of all to be sought

> in individual psychology of each businessman than in determining German political tradition, which was molded by authoritarian attitudes and an overestimation of the value of abiding by the law.[7]

Both Barkai and Joachim Scholtyseck took exception to Mommsen's remarks. With the influence that German businessmen were accorded, due to their place in the economy, Barkai affirmed that they bore a greater responsibility than the average citizen.[8]

The fourth phase of the academic investigation of German businessmen, making cheap purchases of Jewish firms, parallels the desire for completeness already discussed in this text's introduction. A series of massive biographies on National Socialist elite and German businessmen began to be composed as the third phase concluded. Hannah Arendt's model of a nameless bureaucrat as the perpetrator was being replaced. Ian Kershaw depicted the new paradigm in which "responsibility and culpability [were being restored] to the center of the story."[9] Ulrich Herbert's study of Werner Best launched the methodology of prosopography and individual biographies as the dominant mode by which perpetrators of mass executions as well as German businessmen would be viewed by contemporary German historians. Academia's epistemological return to biographies of individuals requires a brief explanation, since social history of the 1960s and 1970s had replaced the focus on an individual with an emphasis on group developments. Well into the 1980s, composing a biography would terminate a career in the German university system. However, the cultural turn inspired a renewed scholarly acceptance of biographies.[10]

With academia's reacceptance of biography, this treatise will produce a spectrum of perpetrator behavior in order to better understand the identities of Aryanizers of Jewish-owned firms. Six German personalities from the Weimar Republic through the Third Reich will be situated on a five-node spectrum in order better to comprehend the range of behavior. After recounting Ulrich Herbert's biography on Werner Best and Michael Wildt's on Erwin Schulz, three recent, massive studies on the banker Hermann Josef Abs, the engine parts manufacturer Robert Bosch, and the coal and steel magnate Friedrich Flick will be surveyed. Due to the Hauptgemeinschaft des Deutschen Einzelhandel's opposition to the Hermann Tietz and Leonhard Tietz department store chains, its President Joachim Tiburtius will also be placed on the continuum. The survey of Gestapo administrator Best and killing squad leader Schulz is presented only in order to introduce a generation of German men, who accepted no limits to their actions. This lack of behavioral boundaries will then be utilized to better understand businessmen's interactions with Jewish people and the Aryanization of their companies.

Werner Best began his career as an attorney by writing the August 1931 Boxheim Document calling for a National Socialist putsch and before his death in June 1989 sought to amnesty all Nazis. The historian Ulrich Herbert explained that viewing the common threads of the post–World War I generation would clarify the apparent inconsistency of highly educated German youth espousing mass murder:

> The combination of a gifted, well-read and "level-headed" young lawyer with a fanatical SS ideologue and organizer of mass murder as appearing in other biographies of Best represents a political and moral challenge, since it doesn't fulfill the classical pattern and expectations of a leader of a National Socialist terror apparatus. On the other hand is the assumption made in my biography that it is this combination of radicalism (ideological drive and a specific form of reason) . . . with the ideological basic assumptions of "objectivity" on the other hand which must be historically and individually explained. One wants to understand why an apparently not small part of intelligent young Germans in the 1930s and 1940s was prepared to endorse, design and put into practice (to a previously unknown degree) policies of oppression and extermination?[11]

Best concluded his service for the Third Reich as the Plenipotentiary for Denmark and after the war was put on trial there. Herbert reconstructed Best's adolescence on the basis of ten personal accounts during a 1945 interrogation. These records are significant for tracing the noteworthy experiences of Best's life, especially the incorporation of his personal development within a political framework. Best's father was wounded in France and succumbed to his injuries. At age eleven, Werner felt responsible for his mother and younger brother. In 1918, at the age of fifteen, he considered that his responsibilities included the restoration of Germany. He felt that he was accountable for the resurgence of the nation. Politics gave meaning to the events of his life and were constitutive for the self-image of postwar middle-class males.

Herbert interpreted Best's generation, born between 1900 and 1910, as being molded through direct postwar contact with the enemy by living in either East Prussia or the Rhineland. These individuals were too young to have had any personal experiences of warfare, but instead were shaped by hunger, deprivation and the complete collapse of their fathers' world. All values of the prior generation were reassessed. Civilization, progress, and humanity were despised and Best's generation did not shudder before the barbarization of life.[12] They became the fiercest opponents of Liberalism. Best viewed the separation of the Rhineland as a conspiracy, which was realized and protected by the ideals of the French Revolution.[13] At the University of Frankfurt, he joined a college association defining the German "Volk" in a biological fashion. His university friend Ernst von Salomon recruited activists for Captain Hermann Erhardt's violent Organization Consul.[14]

The characteristics of Best's generation included having been non-combatants in World War I, who did not have the financial opportunities of their fathers, while also rejecting Republican values.[15] Working for Herbert, it was natural for Wildt to utilize the same typology as his mentor in analyzing 221 managers of the Reichssicherheitshauptamt (RSHA). Ideological police executives, such as Reinhard Heydrich, Werner Best and Otto Ohlendorf, viewed World War I as a "missed opportunity," robbing them of the opportunity to have become a heroic frontline soldier. The psychological turmoil was worsened by the 1923 inflation, which "turned" the bourgeois world "upside down." Middle-class values were rejected in favor of a type of self-help characterized by "egoism, ruthlessness and violence."[16]

Two-thirds of the RSHA leaders attended college and approximately one-third earned a doctorate in law. For these undergraduates, involvement meant participation in violent conflicts. Those later to become RSHA executives were ambitious, utilizing their university educations to ascend from their parents' lower-middle-class lifestyles. In contrast, society-imposed limitations on other law students with the result that of 12,800 wanting to start legal careers in 1932, only 7.7 percent found jobs in the profession. This led many university students to the depressing conclusion that their generation was superfluous.[17]

One can applaud Wildt's avoidance of a "deterministic biographical model" in part because the state actively exerted pressure on these ambitious individuals while removing the previously existing system of checks and balances. These men were not passive bureaucrats, since they not only adapted to changing war-time circumstances but also developed and implemented plans. However, in the description of this generation, it was mentioned that more than 10 percent of all RSHA officials had joined the Freikorps. These mercenaries had continued fighting after World War I. However, to engage in combat with the Freikorps wasn't an individual usually too old to belong to the generation born in 1900–1910? A second aspect in which Wildt's model lacks consistency is the generation's rejection of social-class distinctions and money in favor of the camaraderie of frontline soldiers, which they expected would arise in the new Volksgemeinschaft.[18] But how would the postwar generation have known about camaraderie, when it was too young to have fought in World War I? It appears that discrepancies have entered Wildt's attempt to specify the qualifications of one generation.[19]

Otto Ohlendorf was a member of the generation born between 1900 and 1910. In addition, he earned a doctorate in law and became a member of the NSDAP years before Hitler came to power in 1933. But has the dominant Herbert-Wildt academic model provided a foundation for the public to move beyond Judge Michael Musmanno's April 10, 1948, depiction of Otto Ohlendorf as Dr. Jekyll and Mr. Hyde? The Nuremberg Court had been confounded by attempting to harmonize how an attorney as the leader of Einsatzgruppe D could murder 90,000 Jewish civilians. In lieu of reviewing Ohlendorf, Wildt's analysis of Erwin Schulz will be surveyed.[20]

Wildt's examination of Schulz, instead of Ohlendorf, is significant because all twenty-four defendants in the Nuremberg Einsatzgruppen Trial, with the exception of Schulz, sought exoneration by following Ohlendorf's recreation of the mass shootings of civilians. Schulz broke off his law studies in the spring semester of 1921 in order to fight with the Freikorps Oberland against Poles in Upper Silesia. By November 1923, he was accepted as an officer candidate with Bremen's Municipal Police. He began informing the NSDAP of the planned actions by Bremen's political and counterespionage police starting in 1931 and was appointed the acting director of the Gestapo in the city on November 13, 1933. He joined the Nazi Party, due primarily to his anti-Communistic attitudes, although career opportunities also played a role. On July 5, 1941, Schulz's force killed 2,500–3,000 Jews in a forest near Lviv, although during an October 8, 1947, interrogation in Nuremberg, Schulz maintained that he was reluctant to do so. Although he denied in postwar questioning that his group killed Jewish people in Dubnow on July 6, a subsequent West German trial proved his claim to be false. On August 24, 1941, Schulz traveled to Berlin to personally complain to Bruno Streckenbach how difficult it was psychologically for his men to comply with Otto Rasch's order to murder Jewish women and children from Zhtomyr. SS Situation Report Number 111 listed the murder of 207 political functionaries, 112 saboteurs, and 8,800 Jewish civilians. Schulz was replaced because he was not "hard enough." In opposing the academic perspective that there was allegedly no room to maneuver under a dictatorship,[21] Schulz was not killed, punished, or demoted by Heinrich Himmler for balking at an order to shoot Jewish women and children. Schulz returned to his former position as the director of the Leadership School of the Security Police in Berlin-Charlottenburg.[22]

There was also room for maneuver, without reprisals, in the commercial sector of the Third Reich according to Tim Mason.[23] In the building, glass and wood industries' demands for wage increases were combined with collective threats of quitting. Full employment emboldened the average employee to move every twelve months in order to obtain better pay. In late 1937 through early 1938, shop assistants were successful in closing stores early on Saturdays and coal miners and paper makers were so strong that they compelled the German Labor Front (DAF) to make wage demands for them. From February 1936 to July 1937, the Nazi labor union listed 192 strikes or protests, although admittedly they averaged only thirty employees in a single company.[24] The threat of a strike enabled industrial workers on average to increase their pay by 17 percent between 1936 and 1939. Despite increases in pay, inexpensive food in the canteen and company sports teams, productivity declined by 10 percent in coal mines between 1935 and 1938 and between 15 percent and 30 percent throughout Saxony.[25] The situation of German workers illustrates that Schulz was not the sole example of an individual having a measure of freedom in the Third Reich.

Schulz was typical of this cohort by replacing the "glory" of World War I with deployment in Austria or the Sudetenland in 1938 or Czechoslovakia and Poland in 1939. He shared the feature of being part of Germany's intellectual elite by earning a degree in law. His ambition was displayed through his rapid advancement in Bremen's police department. But depicting similarities with Schulz's RHSA peers does not explicate how his conscience allowed him to conspire against his Bremen employer or why he had no objection to later killing unarmed Jewish men, but baulked at shooting women and children. Wildt also leaves unexamined why Schulz was concerned about the psychological state of his men, but was unconcerned that men without weapons were being shot by his order. Wildt also avoids addressing why Schulz differed from his colleagues in objecting to shooting women and children. Wildt also leaves the question unresolved regarding why Schulz would deviate from the defense proposed by Otto Ohlendorf and followed by all other defendants during the Nuremberg Trial. Although the Herbert-Wildt generational model is widely accepted in academic circles, perhaps modifications can offer fresh insights, especially for Aryanizers.

The careers of German businessmen Hermann Josef Abs, Robert Bosch, and Friedrich Flick will be analyzed. Unlike the concentration on committed Nazi ideologues, born within one decade, it is hoped that businessmen's biographies will enable a differentiation between conservative actions and anti-Semitism as well as indicating that a range of ethical actions was available for Aryanizers, living under a dictatorship.[26]

The first five-stage schema attempting to differentiate Nazi perpetrator behavior was initiated by the German states in December 1945. When it was later approved by OMGUS, it became part of the March 5, 1946, "Law for the Liberation from National Socialism and Militarism." The number of exonerated or "non-offenders" in Group V comprised the vast majority of the adult German population, although 13.8 million adults had voted for the NSDAP in 1932.[27] By July 1947, 12,025,659 Germans had completed questionnaires regarding their activity during the Third Reich. Of these adults, 8,735,000 were categorized as "non-offenders" and were placed in Group V. Of the remaining 3,290,659 only 2,308,458 had been charged by July. Responsibility for assessing the status of those of legal age, residing in the American zone of occupation, shifted from the American Army to German "Spruchkammer" Courts. The original model in graphic form appeared thus:

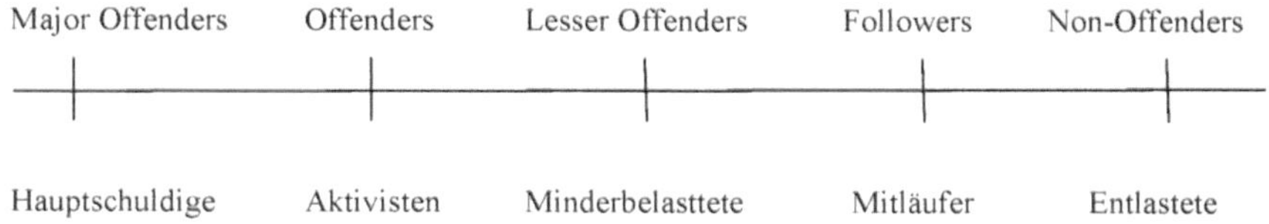

Of the more than two million charged, 1,998,958 were amnestied by the American governor at Christmas 1946. This left 201,019 as "followers" in Group IV. To clarify academic usage, it should be noted that when German scholars wrote in English, they coined the phrase "fellow travelers" for the fourth group. In addition to the amnesty, there were 59,787 trials, which were discontinued before reaching sentencing. Of the final 48,694 individuals, approximately 26,200 had been SS members, 12,150 had been Nazi Party leaders and 1,150 had been Gestapo. As punishment, the Americans intended that persons in Group I might face trial as a war criminal and were to be sent to a labor camp for between two and ten years and should not be employed in a profession for ten years. For Group II, the offenders were restricted from serving in a profession for up to five years and lesser offenders in Group III were limited to working as laborers two years. Followers in Group IV were to be fined.[28]

Since merely 1 percent of denazification trials had been settled in Bavaria by the end of October 1947, the *Indianapolis Star* bewailed that at that rate, the Germans would drag out the procedures until 2018. The lament was not confined to disgruntled American newspaper reporters, but shared by Denazification Officers within the American government in Bavaria, who observed that 40–80 percent of government bureaucrats in southern Germany during the late 1940s were "reinstated former Nazis." One former military officer teaching at Harvard confessed that "denazification had failed—failed to come near achieving *any* objective ever set for it. . . . The German people never really favored the implications of denazification."[29]

This review would like to propose a modification to the five-stage graph characterizing perpetrator behavior, based on an analysis of Abs's, Bosch's, and Flick's biographies:

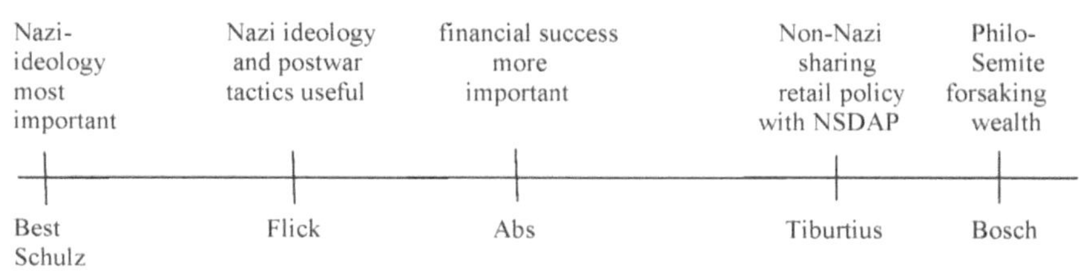

A five-stage schema for classifying degrees of involvement has been part of the understanding of perpetrator behavior since its introduction by the German states as a legal device in December 1945. This tool provided a framework for the German courts in determining the level of guilt or innocence of millions of Germans after the war. Fifty years later, the depiction of a perpetrator was refined by the historian Ulrich Herbert. Herbert revised Aronson's, Buchheim's and Höhne's prior view of the average member of the Gestapo and Einsatzgruppen as "an opportunist and careerist without political convictions."[30] Because of a revival in biography, Herbert was able to identify a völkisch identity in this younger generation of elites, which was not present in the older generation of businessmen, characterized as being emotional and personal.[31]

More precise knowledge of perpetrators made the five-step graph more useful to historians. In a similar fashion, it is anticipated that more exact knowledge of Aryanizers will alter the chart and simultaneously allow comparison of their actions and degree of responsibility.

As additional Aryanizers are discussed in this analysis, the chart is repeated as an aide for the reader's overall understanding. But it must be admitted that there are limits to all graphical illustration. To avoid over-complicating the oft-used five-stage diagram, it has been presented in this monograph, as well as in legal and historical publications for over seventy years, as static.

Some much-studied Holocaust protagonists outside the scope of this inspection, such as Oskar Schindler or Kurt Gerstein, are deserving of being placed in a gray area between two nodes or indicating the restrictions, which an image can graphically represent. Schindler is the most well-known German Aryanizer of Jewish-owned firms. Oskar's prewar spying activities for Admiral Wilhelm Canaris' Abwehr was the occasion for his interrogation by Dr. Sobotka, the director of the Czech Police in Brno in November 1945. Supplying intelligence was important for the inclusion of the Sudetenland in the Reich, thus appearing to indicate that Schindler earned a position on the left end of the spectrum along with members of the RSHA, studied by Herbert and Wildt. However, the most extensive biography on Schindler concluded that he "was not motivated by Sudeten German patriotism." This surprising judgment was based on Sobotka's report that his "only aspiration [was] to obtain easily and without work a lot of money."[32]

Schindler has been evaluated as an opportunist by both Nazis with whom he worked and Jewish concentration camp inmates. In his 1983 British documentary, *Schindler: The Real Story*, Jon Blair was able to interview Ruth Kalder, Commandant Amon Goeth's mistress. The footage recorded her interpretation: "He was a lovable opportunist."[33] Commemorating his July 1967 designation as one of the Righteous among the Nations, Yad Vashem recently affirmed that Oskar's "revulsion" of Nazi inhumanity against the

Jewish prisoners occasioned "a curious transformation in the unprincipled opportunist."[34]

But businessmen such as Georg Karg or Joachim Tiburtius have been so little researched that a depiction of over-lapping areas would appear to cause unnecessary complication, unless the publication of this book spurs future study of the secretive lives of Aryanizers. On the other hand, the image of a quick comparison is a useful generalization and additionally quickly indicates that businessmen had a wide range of possible actions within a "totalitarian society."

B. HERMANN JOSEF ABS BANKER AS AN ARYANIZER

Hermann Josef Abs was born in Bonn in 1901, thus resembling the depiction of the Herbert-Wildt model since both the date of birth was within the targeted decade and the location lay in territory occupied by French troops in 1919. But the strong Catholicism of his mother Katharina (née Lückerath) also molded his life, as had the acceptance of foreign culture based on his father's two-year sojourn in England. His two older brothers died in World War I. But instead of relieving his disappointment of having been too young for "glory" in World War I, by fighting Poles with the Freikorps, Abs performed auxiliary military service on an aristocrat's East Elbian estate. In 1923, Franz Koenigs asked Abs whether he would work in the foreign currency exchange for Rhodius Koenigs Handel-Maatschappij in Amsterdam. Rather than be disloyal as Erwin Schulz had been to the Bremen Police, Abs informed his Dutch employer that the manager in charge of the stock and bond division had embezzled 800,000 RM worth of securities. Because of his Catholic upbringing, he agreed with Schulz in distrusting the Protestant middle class. However, from Abs's perspective, Germany's defeat in war had been self-inflicted, and the Weimar Republic drew his sympathy as an economist.[35]

Also, unlike the RSHA leadership in the Herbert-Wildt model, the banking sector in the Weimar Republic offered Abs a highly promising career. When the leading executive of the private bank Delbrück Schickler & Company passed away on October 9, 1928, the board selected Abs as a future partner. His three concerns in 1929 were the increased need for credit by the Nordwolle wool company, the Jewish-owned Hermann Tietz department stores and the Karstadt chain. From Abs's short-term profit-oriented perspective, this meant withdrawing the financial institution's backing from companies, which did not appear to have a future, as quickly as possible and forcing other businesses to reorganize.[36]

Abs converted ninety million RM in reserves into liquid cash and thereby earned Delbrück Schickler & Company a one million RM fee. Abs's employer acknowledged his deal-making ability on January 1, 1935 by promoting him to the status of a partner with an annual salary of 670,000 RM. To illustrate the enormity of Abs's salary, a skilled worker earned on average 1,900 RM; a mid-level white-collar worker earned between 2,600 and 3,900 RM; and a civil servant earned between 3,200 and 11,400 RM per year.[37]

His fourteen seats on other firms' supervisory boards, including the Karstadt Department Stores, further demonstrated Abs's rise to wealth and power. The Berlin Stock Exchange, which appointed him to its board at the end of 1936, also acknowledged his influence. In addition, in the summer of 1937, the Deutsche Bank offered Abs a position on its board.[38]

On March 17, 1938 five days after the annexation of Austria, Abs arrived in Vienna to negotiate the Deutsche Bank's takeover of Austria's largest bank, the Österreichische Creditanstalt-Wiener Bankverein. He was accompanied by innumerable directors of German industrial companies, who were seeking profitable acquisitions. By March 26, Abs had signed a "friendship agreement," whereby the Deutsche Bank would take almost all of the Creditanstalt's nominal shares of stock from the Austrian government and assume the bank's financial business in southeastern Europe.[39] Interpreting the motivations behind Abs's financial activities has been fraught with difficulties, since as Gerald Feldman explained Abs "covered his tracks very effectively." After World War II, OMGUS gathered evidence for a proposed trial. This planned Subsequent Nuremberg Trial intended to dissolve the Deutsche and Dresdner Bank and try their executives as war criminals.[40]

Abs's contract with the Creditanstalt met with the sharpest rejection from Hitler's economic advisor, Wilhelm Keppler. The 1947 Annex to the OMGUS Report quoted Keppler as affirming: "The Deutsche Bank wants to rob; it came to Vienna with twenty men to take over the Creditanstalt." Hjalmar Schacht personally informed Abs that his intentions could not be realized.[41] Abs did not back down from the combined power of Keppler and Schacht, but threatened to build a network of Deutsche Bank branches throughout Austria. Austrian Minister of Finance Hans Fischböck was able to frustrate Abs's takeover bid only until December 30, 1938. Abs's goals were fulfilled in nine months, whereupon he announced the cost-cutting streamlining of the Austrian bank on January 11, 1939.[42]

Simultaneous with the March 1938 takeover of the Viennese bank, Abs arranged the Aryanization of the Jewish-owned Mendelssohn & Company Bank. The opening of the Moscow and East German archives in Potsdam after 1990 shed important light on his activities. By 1935, Rudolf Löb led the Jewish bank. It had not been previously Aryanized due to concerns by the Third Reich of losing foreign loans, although the government-owned

Reichs-Kredit-Gesellschaft informed the Reichsbank of its interest in taking over the Jewish firm. Reichsbank Vice President Friedrich Dreyse informed Löb in March 1938 that he could expect increasing problems. Löb responded with the white lie that he was already in discussions with the Deutsche Bank regarding a transfer of ownership. Immediately thereafter he went to Abs, although the basis for this trust remains unclear. Negotiations began in April 1938. On December 20, 1947, Löb recalled that the significant demand made by the Jewish proprietors was that no NSDAP-friendly partners should be adopted. On the basis of the June 30, 1938 balance sheet, the Deutsche Bank would assume 65 million RM and the non-Jewish employees. Rudolf Löb fled the country with 210,000 RM and another partner Paul Kempner emigrated with 50,000 RM. From the sale of 150,000 RM in company stock, fifty-three Jewish white-collar workers and retirees hoped to be compensated.[43]

A simple condemnation of Abs's behavior has been clouded by two separate streams of evidence. The first is aspersions cast on OMGUS's legal investigation. Christopher Kopper decried:

> These [Reports] distinguish themselves through an unambiguous political interest in the liquidation of the large banks and the abolition of universal banking, which the Anglo-Saxon's separation of lending from stocks did not recognize. Out of ignorance of the monopolistic-appearing universal banking system, the Reports . . . assessed the role of the banks in the Third Reich too highly. One must reproach them for having consciously not considered exonerating statements in the seized documents and testimonies. The investigators of the Financial Investigation Section assumed the premise to expose the active participation in the National Socialist seizure of power; the organization of the German war economy; and the management of the war.[44]

It is universally acknowledged that the OMGUS Report was written to determine if sufficient evidence existed to place bankers on trial. It is also possible that the investigators overestimated the role of private bankers in accepting Mefo bills so that the Reich could camouflage rearmament spending. It is additionally possible that economists such as Colonel Bernard Bernstein did not fully understand the different functions between American and German banks. However, the accusation that at times the American investigators deliberately disregarded exculpatory evidence is a charge demanding reference to specific Deutsche Bank records in which officers deliberately utilized negative data while consciously obscuring exonerating information.

If OMGUS had seized Deutsche Bank documents, which could have acquitted the firm but had failed to cite them, Abs's defamation lawsuit against East German historian Eberhard Czichon would have provided a perfect opportunity to bring this alleged vindication to public attention. In September, Abs filed an interim injunction to prevent a second edition of *Der Bankier und die Macht. Hermann Josef Abs in der deutschen Politik* from being published by Czichon and his West German publisher, Manfred Pahl-Rugenstein. Abs maintained that there were twenty falsifications in the book. Czichon brought to the courtroom suitcases filled with documents from 218 file folders and volumes of Deutsche Bank correspondence dating from the 1930s and 1940s, but housed in the East German archive in Potsdam. In contrast, Abs merely brought letters in his behalf and sworn affirmations of his character, written for the trial. Czichon claimed that Abs had personally benefited through his Aryanization of the Petschek's brown coal conglomerate and that he was one of the initiators of the immediate dismissal of Jewish employees in the Karstadt Department Store. During the 1971 trial in Stuttgart's District Court, Abs prevailed based on his defense that the sales of the Mendelssohn's and Petschek's companies were "friendly Aryanizations." Abs was able to impose a 20,000 DM fine on both the author and publisher based on the July 31, 1970 letter from Robert von Mendelssohn and other expropriated German-Jews.[45]

The reason why Robert von Mendelssohn would defend Abs, who had negotiated for the cheap acquisition of his private bank, is still debated by scholars. But the Potsdam historian Julius H. Schoeps surmised: "Robert was compensated after 1945 with the stipulation that he would not demand the Mendelssohn Bank back from the Deutsche Bank." Unfortunately, confirmation of this theory seems impossible since Robert died in 1996 and his attorney referred the newspaper correspondent to the professional code of silence. Subsequent to advising Mendelssohn heirs, Schoeps critiqued Kopper for reintroducing Wilhelm Treue's old conception of a "friendly Aryanization" as well as Harold James for "not clarify[ing] what role Hermann J. Abs had in the Arianization of Mendelssohn and Co."[46]

One of the many documents, read by Harold James in the Frankfurt archive of the Deutsche Bank, was scanned and emailed for my use, when the 2020 corona virus prevented travel from the United States to Germany. It is a December 20, 1947 letter written by Rudolf Löb in exile in Buenos Aires for the benefit of Abs. Several factors warn against any historian's exculpation, based on this and presumably any other postwar letter by a surviving Jewish businessman. First and foremost is the fact that this letter was written at Abs's request to defend himself in a denazification trial. This record was not written on Löb's initiative. Second is the non-effusive nature of the letter. A standard format, if the author had been American, would have been something similar to:

> It is my privilege to write a letter recommending the character and actions of Hermann Josef Abs during the sale of the Mendelssohn Bank to the Deutsche

> Bank. During the tumultuous events in Germany during 1938, Mr. Abs gave Jewish owners the best possible cash sales price, which he deposited in an account exclusively in their names in the neutral country of Argentina.

Instead of this imaginary effusion, the short eleven paragraphs in the actual three-page letter commenced:

> According to the wishes of Mr. Hermann J. Abs, I submit the following explanation regarding the Fall and Winter 1938 negotiations, which occurred between the Mendelssohn & Company Bank in Berlin and the Deutsche Bank.

The sixth of the eleventh paragraphs at the top of page two should have urged either American prosecutors in Subsequent Nuremberg Trials or Germans engaged in denazification trials to express caution. Löb depicted the Jewish owners' assessment of their takeover partners in the Deutsche Bank of 1938: "according to our impression almost the entire Board of the Bank were far-removed from the Nazi Party." Such cautious language was being expressed even though Löb's third paragraph contained the two non-negotiable stipulations that the name of the Jewish firm would continue and that no Nazi would be accepted as a new partner. The Jewish owners must have conceded that they were in such a weak position that they were unable to negotiate for any of their basic requirements.

Beginning in the seventh, continuing in the ninth and concluding in the eleventh paragraphs, Löb finally was complimentary toward Abs:

> With full conviction I can affirm that the negotiations, which resulted from our initiative, were led by Mr. Abs in an exemplary manner. . . . The differences were based in our personnel, who were probably much better off than anyone from another German bank. We demanded the maintenance of the previous income and the other benefits of our personnel. It is reasonable that the Personnel Department of the [Deutsche] Bank had great concerns about the fulfillment of this demand and I know that it strongly asserted its opposition.

This seventh paragraph reveals at least as much about Löb's self-sacrificing character as it does about Abs's personality. Löb was quick to agree with his non-Jewish wife that their three children should not grow up and study in a Germany altered by Nazi ideology. So, he settled his family in the Netherlands by June 1933, although he remained in the Fatherland to care for the welfare of his employees.

Similarly, Löb's compliment to Abs spoke volumes about the character of bankers in the economic life during the first few years of the Third Reich. After thirty years of employment with the Mendelssohn Bank, Alfred

Manovill left the oppressive atmosphere of Germany for his native Hungary. By March 19, 1934, Löb met with the Minister of the Economy Robert Schmidt out of concern that Jewish financial institutions, such as Warburg and Mendelssohn, would have to be sold. Löb's meeting was occasioned because bankers were running ahead of Hitler's anti-Semitic ideology. They were claiming that it was "too risky" to conduct business with a non-Aryan bank, before the Berlin government imposed any restriction.[47]

> Without doubt, he [exhibited] a great deal of tact, wisdom and strength to assert himself against the pressure, which the situation in Germany at that time must have exerted on him. Despite this pressure, which was more than once visible, he adhered to the line of the basic communication which had prompted us from the beginning.

Mr. Abs was the most desirable personality for such negotiations from the bank's point of view because of his attitudes and characteristics.

Löb's compliment to Abs needs to be interpreted within the context of how Jewish refugees felt about returning to their former Fatherland. In addressing the historian Hans-Joachim Schoeps, who returned to the University of Erlangen after the war, Gershom Scholem famously exclaimed: "I am astonished that you can breathe this air." The original expression in German is so well known that it became the title for a collection of thirteen Jewish intellectuals by Monika Boll.[48] But it did not require an intellectual for a Jewish person to categorically refuse any association with the land of persecution. After Paul Kempner was forced to resign from the Mendelssohn Bank on December 5, 1938, he was allowed to take 50,000 RM with him into exile. Nevertheless, his wife Margarethe von Mendelssohn vigorously opposed any thought of ever returning to postwar Germany.[49]

The value of Löb's unenthusiastic compliment of Abs differs significantly from Abs's self-portrayal of what transpired after Löb was informed by Reichsbank Vice President Friedrich Dreyse on March 14, 1938, that the state-owned Reichskreditgesellschaft was prepared to absorb the Mendelssohn Bank. Allegedly Abs informed Löb that Löb could choose the date to hear the Deutsche Bank's good news for the Jewish bank. This generous offer by Abs only became known with the 1968 publication of Wilhem Treue's book on the Mendelssohn Bank. A second rosy aspect of the negotiations was the claim that the negotiation regarding the takeover only required five sessions, before all details were successfully resolved in the beginning of September 1938. However, this depiction of a cheerful negotiation does include the caveat that the Deutsche Bank required an additional five meetings to determine the wages of ninety-four Aryan employees with high wages, who were being accepted by the Deutsche Bank.

Löb died on January 30, 1966, two years before Abs's self-serving version was published in Treue's book. Löb never had the opportunity to respond to Abs's positive assessment of the negotiations between the Mendelssohn and Deutsche Bank. Nevertheless, there are two points of agreement between Löb's 1947 letter and Abs's recollection in the 1968 volume. Both are consistent in acknowledging that the Mendelssohn Bank initiated the negotiation and that the higher wages of the non-Jewish employees were a difficult aspect to negotiate. Much more disturbing is the end result of the "sale." Did Löb, Kempner, and other Jewish partners receive any cash or did the Deutsche Bank merely adopt the active accounts, leaving the Jewish partners with the non-solvent parts of the company to liquidate? How many Jewish employees were immediately fired and what amount of profit did the Deutsche Bank achieve by the instant cost-cutting? How long after the takeover did the Deutsche Bank maintain retirement payments? In addition to my uneasiness with regard to the lack of financial transparency in Abs's 1968 portrayal, other historians have viewed it as a "defense from East German accusations regarding his activities during the era of National Socialism."[50]

Despite the strong Catholic façade, it appears that the thirty-six-year-old Abs was so absorbed with wielding influence and power that he attempted to absolve himself as he came ever-closer to the Nazi regime. Gall suggested that Abs became "integrated in the economic and political reality of the Third Reich and its further development." This supports the Herbert-Wildt model regarding the role of ambition in this generation, which accepted no restrictions on its behavior.[51] In the preceding review of Deutsche Bank's acquisition of the Creditanstalt and the Mendelssohn Bank, Abs's determination to overcome the resistance of competing financial institutions, government officials and potential new partners became clearly manifested. In building his legacy, Abs displayed no fear of Reich officials. Already in the spring of 1945, he began constructing the memory that history would preserve when he moved from Berlin to Hamburg and began assembling a personal archive. By the time of his death on February 5, 1994, he had assembled more than 5,000 file folders, which shed light only from the perspective of his honorable financial accomplishments.[52]

Where Abs should be placed in the series of perpetrator behavior is difficult to determine, since he has covered his tracks, skewed the evidence in his archives, and bribed the Jewish heirs of the Mendelssohn Bank to secrecy. From the review of the Creditanstalt and the Jewish private bank, Abs appears as a vulture intent on his prey. He did not flinch in the face of high-level officials in the Third Reich. But the extent of his exploitation for personal gain as well as the postwar amount paid to former Jewish proprietors to assure their silence and his status as the premiere banker in democratic Germany remain uncertain. In the scope of behavior, Abs is placed in the center, clearly to the right of Robert Bosch but to the left of Werner Best or Erwin Schulz.

Before leaving the discussion of Abs and the Mendelssohn Bank, I would like to briefly resume my objection toward Ludwig Herbst and Thomas Weihe's claim that Jewish proprietors attempted to camouflage the true ownership of their firms through fictitious sales. Both Alfred and Johann Kurzmeyer became employed with the Mendelssohn Bank and had authority to commit the institution's finances before World War I. Having no Jewish ancestors and wielding more power than any other Aryan employee, Alfred would have been a perfect candidate if Jewish owners had considered fabricated sales as a method of retaining ownership. However, Kurzmeyer overdrew his account by 200,000 RM during the 1930s. Clearly, this would have been a sufficient reason why he would never have been proposed as the "actual owner." Nevertheless, he aggressively pursued a promotion during the months of October through December 1938. Deutsche Bank Directors Ferdinand Kremer and Robi pressed Löb to delay his emigration from Germany until he had calmed Kurzmeyer. The Deutsche Bank feared that Kurzmeyer would "make employees defiant," unless Löb calmed him down.[53]

Since Kurzmeyer had become a director in the Deutsche Bank and held a Swiss passport, Abs sent him to Zurich at the end of 1943. He served as a trustee for the Deutsche Bank's gold, which formed a reserve, in case the Third Reich collapsed as well as a trustee for the SS's most important company, owned by Oswald Pohl, namely the Deutsche Wirtschaftsbetriebe GmbH. On February 16, 1945, Kurzmeyer served as an administrator of 10,843,012 Swiss Francs in assets. Kurzmeyer did not seem to possess the character, which Löb would have selected, if Jewish firms ever sought a faux proprietor. Nevertheless, the narrative has a successful conclusion. Abs "felt uncomfortable" about the bad publicity, which the Deutsche Bank might receive from placing gold from Jewish victims, which Degussa had melted into bars, in a Swiss investment house.[54] Only in March 1998, after forty-one years of remaining deposited in a Swiss bank, were the 323 kilograms of gold sold. The Deutsche Bank gave 2.8 million DM of the proceeds to impoverished Holocaust survivors via the World Jewish Restitution Organization and the other half was donated to the March of the Living Foundation.[55]

C. ROBERT BOSCH, INDUSTRIALIST'S FUNDS FOR JEWISH EMIGRATION

The panorama of perpetrator behavior continues with Joachim Scholtyseck's biography on industrialist Robert Bosch. The translated subtitle *The Liberal Resistance against Hitler* already peaks curiosity, since the Communists are widely acknowledged to have been the main source of German opposition with the Conservatives and generals adding a late contribution through the July 20, 1944, assassination attempt. But a Liberal opposition is previously unknown. Scholtyseck traced a Liberal component back to 1921 when Georg Gothein became the Chair for the Stuttgart chapter of the Society for the Defense against Anti-Semitism. Bosch joined the two hundred strong group, which combated hatred against Jewish people. Scholtyseck admitted that Bosch was not active in public life and "primarily felt a moral responsibility to join." The author also acknowledged that National Socialism prohibited the Society in 1933 and the former members were not in general persecuted. Although the biography extolled the industrialist's role, it frequently seemed to be limited to merely bankrolling Bosch's General Manager Hans Walz's activities.

In May 1933, Walz protested to Wilhelm Keppler about Nazi anti-Jewish policies and was reproached as an "excellent attorney for the Jews." As a member of the Confessing Church, Walz's June 16, 1967 correspondence subsequently documented anti-Semitism "as a precursor of a later anti-Christianity." Because political and economic interventions appeared hopeless, Bosch acted through Walz to assist individual German-Jews. Walz teamed up with former Society member Theodor Bäuerle to aid Karl Adler when the Jewish director of the Stuttgart Conservatory of Music was forced to resign in 1933. A June 9, 1956 letter from Rabbi Leo Baeck's close associate, Otto Hirsch, recorded the recommendation for Adler to continue aiding Stuttgart's Jewish community. Martin Buber began the Resource Place for Jewish Adult Education in 1934, a part of which included Walz and Adler's assistance to Jews willing to emigrate.[56]

In November 1982, Bosch's personal secretary Felix Olpp noted his employer's oft repeated maxim to avoid personal gain through the "misfortune of Jews." One example occurred in 1938 when Kurt Hamann of the Victoria Fire and Life Insurance negotiated with Hans Walz about the sale of the firm. Bosch acquired considerable packets of Victoria stock, the restitution of which Olpp apparently negotiated with Hamaan in Dusseldorf after the war. A second illustration was the "friendly Aryanization" of the Robert Koch Jewelry Store in Frankfurt am Main. Dr. Herbert Goetz of the Goldschmidt-Rothschild Bank was able to negotiate a "generous purchase price" and Willy Schloβstein was able to transfer precious metals and jewels via Switzerland to the United States. Bosch also enabled Goetz to immigrate to Chile with a gift of 3,000 Dutch Gulden. As evidence that these company takeovers were "friendly," Scholtyseck specified that financial assistance was given, allowing Jewish families to flee. In Grete Adler's August 4, 1976, correspondence, she related how her husband Karl was released from a concentration camp after the November 1938 Kristallnacht on the basis that he would accelerate the emigration of the Jewish inhabitants of Stuttgart. Despite the monitoring of Karl Adler's progress by the SD and the Gestapo from within his Resource Place office, money was clandestinely transferred by Hans Walz, Theodor Bäuerle, Albrecht Fischer, and Willy Schloßstein. Since Bosch's funds were provided "under the nose of the Gestapo," no receipts are available for historians to examine. However, Fischer's April 11, 1947 letter suggested that the sealed envelopes customarily contained between 500 and 1,000 RM and on occasion between 2,000 and 3,000 RM. Walz maintained in correspondence from May 13, 1947 that Bosch orally instructed him on all large transactions. Jewish people were illegally smuggled across the borders into Holland, Luxemburg, Belgium, Yugoslavia, and Czechoslovakia. According to James May's November 3, 1966 statement for Yad Vashem, the most spectacular case occurred on August 30, 1939, when his father, mother, and sister, as well as fourteen other Jewish people escaped over the Kehl-Strasbourg bridge.[57]

Scholtyseck's biography of Bosch and his relationship with the July 20, 1944 assassination attempt via his financial advisor Carl Goerdeler has been considered unconvincing.[58] Since Bosch's personal correspondence was destroyed during the war, the biographer has in large measure used postwar documentation as noted in the preceding pages of this book.[59] Attention must return to the Mendelssohn Bank. Fritz Mannheimer had established a subsidiary of the Mendelssohn Bank in Amsterdam in which Bosch had deposited 100,000 Dutch Gulden. After the November 1938 pogrom, Mannheimer withdrew 20,000–30,000 Gulden every three months for the Jewish Relief Committee in Holland. Another rescue clearly substantiated by contemporary documentation concerns the March through June 1936 rescue of Stuttgart author Bernhard Blume and his Jewish wife Carola.[60]

More detrimental to Scholtyseck's biography than the use of postwar sources was the reproof that he accepted the sources uncritically. Cornelia Rauh-Kühne admonished the biographer for having glossed over all references to the fact that Bosch championed the interests of his armament factory, which she affirmed could not be explicated as an attempt to camouflage his resistance activities. Admittedly Bosch's use of slave laborers due to the decrease in available manpower because of the war is another concern to scholarship. Scholtyseck's attempt to glorify Bosch also suffered not only from his obligatory 1.75 million RM donation to the Adolf Hitler Fund, but also from the 553,000 RM contribution to various Party organizations.[61] However, Manfred Overesch provided a comparative survey of financial contributions by which Bosch's intentions could better be assessed. Bosch's true motivations could better be evaluated through the much larger donations of 29,173,000 RM for Bosch Aid or the 6,000,000 RM for the Bosch Foundation Hospital or the 26,829,000 RM for employees and their families. Overesch concluded that in contrast, the sum for the Hitler fund was similar to paying a mandatory "tax."[62]

On October 28, 1940, the first fifty-nine French POWs and on January 27, 1941, the first twelve Belgian POWs came to the Bosch plant in Hildesheim, for which the firm paid Stalag Fallingbostell 11,538.26 RM. In 1948, Bosch Manager Oskar Kies claimed that foreign workers received just treatment and pay, since a humane approach led to the best factory output. Overesch accepted this assessment, even though there were "occasional aberrations." In part, the Hildesheim historian was able to arrive at this conclusion by distinguishing between the actions of the Stalag and the private firm. Thus, it was the internment camp, which determined which POWs would improve forests, work in quarries, or manufacture engine parts for Bosch. In turn, Bosch was authorized to give each Allied prisoner two towels and two coarse yarn blankets. In principle, POW remuneration was 60 percent of the going rate although the Allied soldier only received vouchers valid in the canteen. The business paid the Stalag 60 percent of the wage, while retaining 0.20 RM per day for lodging; from 0.80 to 1.20 RM per day for food; and an allotment for possible work clothes. From the 30 RM earned by a POW in a sixty-hour work week, the company kept 20 RM for room and board, whereas the Stalag received 10 RM for every prisoner per week. At 21 RM, every two weeks, a civilian employee from Eastern Europe did not earn much less than a comparably skilled German staff member. As Overesch concluded, the enterprise's principles became unavoidably less-well adhered to but did not disappear as groups of between 10 and 220 would appear on a single day.[63]

Bosch gave limited assent to a totalitarian regime but also opposed the regime's anti-Semitism. Perhaps he allowed his subordinates to shield him from Nazi punishment. There appears to be an altruistic motive in Bosch's payments for Jewish emigration, which warrants placing him on the far right of the perpetrator scale. Nevertheless, his "friendly Aryanization," the employment of POWs and the payment in canteen vouchers, rather than cash, appear to substantiate his identification in some slight manner as a perpetrator. However, it must be admitted that Bosch was a rare example of an industrialist, who practiced a business ethic far above the norm.

D. FRIEDRICH FLICK, MAKING THE STATE AND JEWS PAY FOR HIS ASSETS

Friedrich Flick's most well-known Aryanization of the Petschek coal mines will form the basis of determining what stage in the five-step model best depicts his behavior, whereas his October 1934 involvement in the Aryanization of Simson Gun Manufacturing will be examined in chapter 6, section F. The descendants of Ignaz and Julius Petschek owned 65 percent of the central German deposits of brown coal, which Kim Priemel depicted as being annexed by Friedrich Flick at "no cost." Lisa Stallbaumer also noted that Flick and Otto Steinbrinck were conscious that the opportunities, which the National Socialist state offered for Aryanization, were "fundamentally unethical." Prior scholarly interpretations stood in agreement by placing the accent on the unscrupulousness of the beneficiaries. Such interpretations explained the takeovers by means of businessmen, who had no inhibitions of preying on other entrepreneurs as long as there was no risk of being punished. This is in agreement with Ulrich Herbert's understanding that perpetrators were not motivated by an ideologically "fanatical behavior" but rather an apathetical, deficit of "moral norms," making Nazi crimes possible. Flick and his managers adopted this deficiency during the period from 1933 through 1937. Jewish owners were excluded from the ethnic community and thus did not enjoy property rights.[64]

In the beginning of November 1937, Flick heard rumors that the Petscheks were willing to sell everything, which Wilhelm Keppler confirmed to Steinbrinck. For some time, the Jewish proprietors had been in sales negotiations with both Wintershall and I. G. Farben. For Flick and Steinbrinck, it seemed an intolerable condition that after five years of Nazi rule, Jews should still own raw materials "essential" for the people and the Four-Year Plan. On November 15, 1937, Herbert Göring disclosed to Steinbrinck that his half-brother was interested in the Jewish firm, thus revealing that Hermann Göring would decide who the new owner would be. Flick began lobbying Petschek, Keppler, and Wintershall and with the assistance of Herbert Göring overcame the advantage, which the Wintershall-I.G. Farben partnership had in potentially purchasing Petschek's holdings. Flick's tactical maneuvering included pitting the half of the Petschek owners, who wanted to ward off any new owner, against the other descendants, who wanted to sell.[65]

A Berlin meeting was arranged on January 22, 1938, in which Julius Petschek's heirs expected to be paid eighteen million U.S. dollars, a sum which Flick could not raise and the Ministry of the Economy would never have approved. In contrast, Flick had composed a written authorization to negotiate, which Göring signed the previous day, empowering Flick as the sole negotiator with both Petschek conglomerates. Under the threat that the state would inflict something far worse, Flick used the document signed by Göring in a take-it-or-leave-it posture. He did not negotiate, but insisted that he would offer no cash, but only preferred shares. In addition, he constricted the window for accepting the offer. But although George Murnane, the Chair of the United Continental Corporation, acknowledged the German difficulty in rearmament and the Jewish problem, he remained firm with regard to the sales price of fifteen to sixteen million U.S. dollars and would not accept either Reichsmarks or any other German commercial paper. In contrast with Flick, Murnane maintained that the American and British holding company was not in a panic mode and rejected any hasty decision. There was a thirteen-million-dollar gap between Murnane's lowest acceptance amount and Flick's highest sales offer. Flick responded by merely limiting the negotiating period to January 31, 1938. The American perceived that Flick threatened an expropriation by the state, should he not capitulate to the German businessman's demands. Instead he retorted that German companies in the United States could face the same problem as Jewish businesses were experiencing in the Reich. In addition, Murnane quantified the amount offered by Wintershall to be eleven million U.S. dollars. The U.S. position could be interpreted in two ways: that Murnane had an alternative to Flick's poor offer, but also that there was room to maneuver a mediating proposal.[66]

Steinbrinck searched for a compromise involving the payment of 7.5 million dollars. Herbert Göring informed the German negotiators that his half-brother was temporarily preoccupied with what would become the March 12, 1938 annexation of Austria. Since Helmuth Wohlthat from the Ministry of the Economy enjoyed good relations with the Americans as well as the Petschek clan, he became Göring's liaison at the end of March. After the incorporation of Austria into the Reich, the danger for the Petscheks skyrocketed since a large percentage of both the Julius and the Ignaz properties lay in the Sudetenland. In addition, a month before the April 22, 1938 Ordinance against Camouflaging Jewish Companies, Steinbrinck had already written a description of its general orientation in his files. The Flick Conglomerate had advance notification of the Reich's intentions. Furthermore, a law instituted four days later required foreign Jews to report their German assets, from which the state derived authorization to access private resources. Meanwhile, Steinbrinck considered countering Murnane's expectation of eighteen million dollars with a counter of six to seven million. But on the basis of recently enacted legislation, Wohlthat insisted on an upper limit of four-and-a-half million. Nevertheless, in the May 17–19, 1938 discussions in Berlin, a sum of $6.325 million was agreed upon which was 48 percent of the Petschek stock's par value. Does the improved offer warrant historians Bernhard Grotto's and Harald Wixforth's conclusion of a "normal sales negotiation"? Scholars of contemporary German history have shifted responsibility from Flick to the astounding ability of Berlin to subvert moral behavior:

> This was a resounding success of National Socialist's social policy, which aimed at the reeducation of the ethnic community, because "completely normal" business people accepted the inferable criteria in their economic calculations: They included the economic predatory pressure on Jews as any other market factor.[67]

German scholarship perceives that the change in the political climate between January and May 1938 left both sides of the negotiating table prepared to make compromises. In addition, Flick had to include the rival team of Wintershall, I.G. Farben, and Salzdetfurth, because he needed their reserves of U.S. dollars to pay both the United Continental Corporation as well as to fulfill his inducement to the Four-Year Plan and the Reichsbank that he would procure hard currency. Flick deviated from his prior Aryanizations in which his purchase price came from the Jewish firm only to the degree that he had to pay the competing team 200 million tons of coal from the former Jewish coal mines. In all documentation, Flick justified his behavior. He underscored his claim that he was supporting the state and had not acquired the Julius Petschek property for personal enrichment. However, it does appear that he intended on justifying the tax-free nature of his acquisition. In addition, Flick had become the vicarious agent of the Reich, whereby he surmised that his reputation as an honorable businessman was not violated. Moreover, his ownership of Julius Petschek's conglomerate made him the logical contender to acquire Ignaz Petschek's properties. As early as May 25, 1938, the Chairman of the Salzdetfurth Board informed Flick that he was ready to participate in the acquisition of the larger Ignaz Petschek business. The takeover of Julius Petschek had merely been an intermediate stage in the building of Flick's expanding empire.[68]

Current scholarship concludes that Flick was always convinced that he acted as a virtuous businessman.[69] However, this must be interpreted from the background of ever-expanding boundaries of irreproachable behavior. On occasion, German scholars view Flick's options as limited and therefore his process of adaption as "inescapable."[70] But a nagging doubt lingers with regard to contemporary German historians. By arresting only Communists and Jews, had not the regime been able within five years to alter the behavior of individuals such as Flick, who had been raised in his first fifty years under a completely different business ethic? Why do the files of the Flick Conglomerate not record that the norms of his first fifty years affected his next five? If the belief system of the Third Reich was so pervasive, did Flick suffer from an inability to recognize the rights of foreigners during the final twenty-seven years of his life?

Since Flick was older, he was not a part of the Herbert-Wildt model. Flick's behavior should have conformed to a prior business ethic and not the unlimited boundaries acceptable to Werner Best and Erwin Schulz. Nevertheless, the bribing of government officials was part of his business practice during both the Third Reich and later in democratic Germany. His third son not only followed him in the management of the steel and coal conglomerate but also in kickbacks to postwar authorities.[71] The unbounded quest for power and financial riches leads to his placement on the left of the spectrum of perpetrator behavior. Although not to be equated with the murder of Jewish civilians as witnessed in Werner Best's and Erwin Schulz's activities, Flick's pre-National Socialist career should have established a foundation for a more principled behavior. However, Flick never incorporated such a potential business ethic. Before examining the takeover of the Jewish-owned Hermann Tietz department stores in chapter 5, the reader should refer back to the preceding figure for the coming trajectory of non-Nazi, conservative Aryanizers, such as Joachim Tiburtius (chapter 4, section B), Georg Karg (chapter 5), Max Winkler (chapter 6, section C), Walther Frisch (chapter 6, section D), and Herbert Hoffmann (chapter 6, section F) later in the analysis.[72]

NOTES

1. Barkai, *From Boycott to Annihilation*, pp. 69–75. Also Avraham Barkai, "Die deutschen Unternehmer und die Judenpolitik im 'Dritten Reich,'" *Geschichte und Gesellschaft*, Vol. 15, No. 2 (1989), p. 246.
2. Bajohr, *deutschen Unternehmer*, pp. 256–259.
3. Frank Bajohr, "Verfolgung aus gesellschaftsgeschichtlicher Perspektive. Die wirtschaftliche Existenzvernichtung der Juden und die deutsche Gesellschaft," *Geschichte und Gesellschaft*, Vol. 26, No. 4 (2000), p. 634.
4. Bajohr, *Verfolgung*, pp. 631–634, 640.
5. Bajohr, *Verfolgung*, pp. 635–636.
6. Bajohr, *Verfolgung*, pp. 636–638.
7. Hans Mommsen, "Konnten Unternehmer im Nationalsozialismus apolitisch blei-ben?" in Lothar Gall and Manfred Pohl (Eds.), *Unternehmen im Nationalsozialismus* (München: Verlag C.H. Beck, 1998), p. 71.
8. Barkai, "Die 'stillen Teilhaber' des NS-Regime," in Lothar Gall and Manfred Pohl (Eds.), *Unternehmen im Nationalsozialismus* (München: Verlag C.H. Beck, 1998), p. 117.
9. Ian Kershaw, "Biography and the Historian; Opportunities and Constraints," in Volker R. Berghahn and Simone Lässig (Eds.), *Biography between Structure and Agency; Central European Lives in International Historiography* (New York: Berghahn Books, 2008), p. 36. Hans Mommsen, "Konnten Unternehmer im Nationalsozialismus apolitisch bleiben?" in Lothar Gall and Manfred Pohl (Eds.), *Unternehmen im Nationalsozialismus* (München: Verlag C.H. Beck, 1998), p. 71.
10. Volker Depkat, "The Challenges of Biography: European-American Reflections," *Bulletin of the German Historical Institute*, Vol. 55, No. 1 (Fall 2014), pp. 39–45.
11. Ulrich Herbert, *Best. Biographische Studien über Radikalismus, Weltanschauung und Vernunft 1903–1989* (Bonn: Verlag J.H.W. Dietz Nachfolger, 1996), p. 12.
12. Herbert, *Best*, pp. 42–50.

13. The Allied occupation of the Rhine illustrated the opposing French need for securing her borders as opposed to the German need to exercise sovereignty within her boundaries. See the negotiations of Aristide Briand and Gustav Stresemann in the signing of the Treaty of Locarno on October 16, 1925, in Ian Kershaw, *To Hell and Back; Europe 1914–1949* (New York: Penguin Random House, 2015), pp. 178–183.

14. Herbert, *Op. Cit.*, pp. 50–58.

15. In formulating the distinctive features of a German generation born between 1900 and 1910, Herbert acknowledged the usefulness of the "best surveys" written by Barbara Stambolis, *Der Mythos der jungen Generation. Ein Beitrag zur politischen Kultur der Weimarer Republik* (Bochum: Ruhr-Universität Bochum, 1982); and Irmtraud Götz von Olenhusen, *Jugendreich, Gottesreich, Deutsches Reich; junge Generation, Religion und Politik, 1928–1933* (Köln: Verlag Wissenschaft und Politik, 1987). However, he held that Robert Wohl, *The Generation of 1914*, Cambridge: (Harvard University Press, 1979) reduced the myth of youth to an intellectual extravagance lacking in political instinct, which distorted the functional connection of the middle class's impending loss of status (*Best*, footnote 3 on p. 546). Wohl focused on German men born between 1880 and 1900, who served as front-line soldiers and after the war became the literary elite, whereas Herbert's attention was directed to men who were too young to have experienced combat, but after the war became men of action. Herbert viewed the generation born between 1900 and 1910 as being excluded from the success, which their law degrees should have imparted. In contrast, Wohl understood that the soldiers viewed the younger generation of 1900–1910 as resembling their non-combatant grandfathers, who could settle comfortably into their jobs. In addition, Wohl affirmed that the younger generation shared no common experiences and no concrete social bond (*The Generation of 1914*, pp. 63–76), whereas Herbert sought the characteristics which caused intelligent Germans to design and implement extermination policies (*Best*, p. 12).

16. Michael Wildt, *An Uncompromising Generation; The Nazi Leadership of the Reich Security Main Office* (Madison: University of Wisconsin Press, 2009), pp. 10–35, 45–47.

17. Wildt, *Uncompromising*, pp. 38–41.

18. Wildt, *Uncompromising*, pp. 27–30.

19. In depicting his departure from Germany to the front, Ernst Jünger described his ninth company as an "enthusiastic group [who] . . . shared a yearning for danger, for the experience of the extraordinary. We were enraptured by war." Returning to his Regiment from Hanover as a junior officer after his wounded thigh healed, his portrayal of the trenches had a nostalgic air: "a feeling of cosy seclusion at the table in my little dugout . . . something of the Wild West . . . and the aroma of toasting bread gradually filled the air. What trench warrior has not experienced the sensation?" If sufficient copies of such memoirs were available in the 1920s, they may possibly have inspired a yearning for war-time comradery of which Wildt's theory is dependent. See Ernst Jünger, *Storm of Steel* (New York: Penguin Random House, 2003), pp. 3, 29–33, 51.

20. Wildt, *Uncompromising*, pp. 272–273.

21. Recall Harold James' hesitancy to accept the OMGUS Reports on the Deutsche and Dresdner Banks in chapter 2, based on the Reich's limitation on moral action. The fallaciousness of the claim that there was no room to maneuver is demonstrated by the fact that "no defense attorney or defendant in any of the hundreds of postwar trials has been able to document a single case in which refusal to obey an order to kill unarmed civilians resulted in the allegedly inevitable dire punishment." See Christopher R. Browning, *Ordinary Men; Reserve Police Battalion 101 and the Final Solution in Poland* (New York: HarperPerennial, 1998), p. 170.

22. Wildt, *Uncompromising*, pp. 274–287.

23. Tim Mason theorized that Hitler was conscious of German workers having allegedly undermined a German victory in World War I. Mason maintained that when Germany reached full employment in 1936, laborers obtained great power by threatening strikes for higher wages and better working conditions. Mason continued his hypothesis by claiming that Hitler was a "weak dictator" in the period 1936 to 1941, who was unwilling to increase consumer prices. He was "forced" to deviate from his time schedule of launching a war in order to obtain manpower and raw materials. This thesis is not generally accepted. However, Kershaw acknowledged that Hitler was concerned about price increases, even though Carl Goerdeler wanted to dispense with his own Commission for Price Surveillance. Other evidence that Mason had a bedrock of economic facts from which he speculated was the acceptance that the Führer did without imports for armaments in 1935 to 1936, in order to avoid food rationing. In addition, Hitler did not mobilize women in order to avoid morale problems, although Kershaw doubted both Hitler's consciousness of the political problem and the severity of the economic crisis. The advent of the war also depended more on Germany's advantage in the arms race, rather than worker unrest. Nevertheless Kershaw concluded that "Hitler was not 'master of the Third Reich' in the implied meaning of omnipotence" and workers did have room to manipulate working conditions for their own benefit Ian Kershaw, *The Nazi Dictatorship; Problems and Perspectives of Interpretation*, 4th Edition (New York: Oxford University Press, 2000), pp. 88–92.

24. Much of Tim Mason's theory on Germany's distressed labor force causing the weak Hitler dictatorship to commence World War II ahead of the Führer's timetable has been rejected by scholarship. Therefore, it seemed prudent to confirm that the details regarding the workforce were accurate. This verification was provided by the German-Jewish historian Francis Ludwig Carsten: "Altogether a total of 179 labour conflicts were recorded for 1936, with a peak in July and fewer during the winter months. But only ten involved between 51 and 100 men, and only nine more than 100; few lasted longer than one day" *The German Workers and the Nazis* (Aldershot: Scholar Press, 1995), p. 54.

25. Tim Mason, "The Workers' Opposition in Nazi Germany," *History Workshop*, 11 (Spring 1981), pp. 122–126.

26. Scholars have debated the nature of the Nazi state and whether the Third Reich is best understood under the rubric of Totalitarianism or Fascism, The origin of the academic disagreement may be traced to Franz Neumann's years of exile, when he penned his perspective on the terror behind the authoritarian facade

Behemoth. The Structure and Practice of National Socialism 1933–1944 (New York: Octagon Books, 1963). After World War II, academicians were split into two opposing perspectives. The intentionalists, as represented by Klaus Hildebrand "Monokratie oder Polykraties? Hitlers Herrschaft und das Dritte Reich," in Gerhard Hirschfeld and Lothar Kettenacker, *Der Führerstaat: Mythos un Realität* (Stuttgart: Klett-Cotta, 1992), viewed all policy as originating in Hitler's master plan. Hitler divided and ruled his subordinates by distributing his power to them. In contrast, the opposing structuralists such as Martin Broszat *The Hitler State: The Foundation and the Development of the Internal Structure of the Third Reich* (London: Longman, 1981) maintained that the Third Reich was a polycracy, in which subordinates fought with each other for power under a weak dictator. Further details regarding the academic discourse are available in Jane Caplan, "National Socialism and the Theory of the State," in Thomas Childers and Jane Caplan, *Reevaluating the Third Reich (*New York: Holmes & Meier, 1993), pp. 98–113. Ian Kershaw wanted to preserve the model of Totalitarianism to elucidate the Third Reich in a "very limited" fashion, despite its inability to cope with change and its inability to address "socio-economic conditions." See both "The essence of Nazism: form of fascism, brand of totalitarianism, or unique phenomenon?" and "Hitler: 'Master in the Third Reich' or 'weak dictator'?" in *The Nazi Dictatorship; Problems & Perspectives of Interpretation*, 4th Edition (New York: Oxford University Press, 2000), pp. 20–46, 69–92.

27. Jürgen W. Fälter, *Hitlers Wähler* (München: Verlag C.H. Beck, 1991), p. 17.

28. Elmer Plischke, "Denazification Law and Procedure," *The American Journal of International Law*, Vol. 41, No. 4 (October 1947), pp. 824–825. Statistics from other sources differ from the number of individuals mentioned here. Thus, the sum of persons in Group I has been given as 1,654 and in Group II as 22,122. However, it is unclear if these figures represent the same time period and whether they combine or separate the U.S., British, and French zones. See Norbert Frei, *Adenauer's Germany and the Nazi Past; The Politics of Amnesty and Integration* (New York: Columbia University Press, 2002), pp. 38–39, 329.

29. William E. Griffith, "Denazification in the United States Zone of Germany," *The Annals of the American Academy of Political and Social Science*, Vol. 267 (January 1950), pp. 74–75.

30. Ulrich Herbert, "Ideological Legitimization and Political Practice of the Leadership of the National Socialist Secret Police," in Hans Mommsen (Ed.), *The Third Reich between Vision and Reality; New Perspectives on German History 1918–1945* (Oxford: Berg, 2001), p. 97.

31. Herbert, *Best*, p. 98.

32. David M. Crowe, *Oskar Schindler; The Untold Account of His Life, Wartime Activities, and the True Story Behind the List* (Cambridge: Westview Press, 2004), pp. 18–19.

33. David Gritten, "The 'Schindler' Everyone Forgot About—Until Now," *Los Angeles Times*, February 27, 1994.

34. Daniel Fraenkel, "Schindler, Oskar; Schindler, Emilie," in Israel Gutman, Editor-in-Chief, *The Encyclopedia of the Righteous Among the Nations; Rescuers*

of Jews during the Holocaust. Vol. 5 Part 1 (Jerusalem: Yad Vashem, 2007), pp. 144–145.

35. Lothar Gall, *Der Bankier Hermann Josef Abs; Eine Biographie* (München: Verlag C.H. Beck, 2005), pp. 14–27.

36. Gall, *Bankier*, pp. 27–30.

37. Gall, *Bankier*, pp. 35, 41–45.

38. Gall, *Bankier*, pp. 45–51.

39. In October 1929, Austrian Chancellor Johannes Schober placed Louis Nathaniel von Rothschild under enormous pressure to merge Vienna's bankrupt Bodencreditanstalt with the Creditanstalt. Combined with the American stock market crash of the same month, these events led to the May 11, 1931, public admission by the Creditanstalt that it had suffered losses of 140 million schillings. However, the actual sum was more than one billion schillings for which the public was responsible, although it represented approximately 10 percent of Austria's national income for 1930. For further details on the crisis suffered by the Credit-Anstalt für Handel und Gewerbe, see the published Habilitationsschrift: Fritz Weber, *Vor dem großen Krach; Österreichs Banken in der Zwischenkriegszeit am Beispiel der Credit-Anstalt für Handel und Gerwerbe* (Wien: Böhlau, 2016).

40. Gerald D. Feldman, "Wer Spinnt? *German Politics and Society*, Vol. 20, No 3 (Fall 2002), p. 44. Through his book review, Feldmann drew attention to the ironic situation that the text of the OMGUS Report is easily accessible in a published edition, but a listing of the exhibits is available only in an older German translation. Compare Christopher Simpson, *War Crimes of the Deutsche Bank and the Dresdner Bank; Office of Military Government (U.S.) Reports* (New York: Holmes & Meier, 2002), pp. 158–159 with Hans Magnus Enzenberger (Ed.), *O.M.G.U.S. Ermittlungen gegen die Deutsche Bank 1946/1947* (Nördlingen: Franz Greno, 1985), footnote 38 and 39 on p. 503.

41. As early as March 19, 1938, Wilhelm Keppler made known to Deutsche Bank executives Eduard Mosler, Hermann Josef Abs and Hellmuth Pollems the competing ambitions of the government's own Vereinigte Industrie-Unternehmungen AG (VIAG) in the takeover of the Creditanstalt. Based on the Keppler's instructions at the end of March, Austria's newly appointed Minister of the Economy Hans Fischböck refused to approve the sale of Creditanstalt shares to the Deutsche Bank. Keppler was defending the Reich's interests in the defense industry, since the Austrian financial institution exerted some financial control over both Czech and Yugoslavian industrial enterprises. See Christopher Kopper, *Zwischen Marktwirtschaft und Dirigismus; Bankenpolitik im "Dritten Reich" 1933–1939* (Bonn: Bouvier Verlag, 1995), pp. 292–294.

42. Enzenberger, *O.M.G.U.S.*, pp. 53–58.

43. Enzenberger, *O.M.G.U.S.*, pp. 58–63.

44. Kopper, *Zwischen*, p. 10.

45. Kopper, *Zwischen*, pp. 271–273. "Prozesse Abs; Noch'n Ruch," *Der Spiegel*, No. 43 (October 19, 1970), pp. 128–131. Also see Enzensberger, *O.M.G.U.S.*, footnote 8, p. 497.

46. Andreas Förster, "Freundschaftliche Übernahme oder 'Arisierung?' Eine Erbengemeinschaft stellt Antrag auf Rückgabe des Eigentums: Das ungeklärte Ende

des Bankhauses Mendelssohn," *Berliner Zeitung* (October 17, 1997). Julius H. Schoeps, "Review of Die Deutsche Bank und die 'Arisierung,'" *Shofar*, Vol. 21, No. 1 (Fall 2002), pp. 171–174.

47. Sebastian Panwitz, *Das Haus des Kranichs; Die privatbankiers von Mendelssohn & Co (1795–1938)* (Berlin: Hentrich & Hentrich Verlag, 2018), pp. 266–267.

48. Monika Boll and Raphael Gross, *Ich staune, dass Sie in dieser Luft atmen können; Jüdische Intellektuelle in Deutschland nach 1945* (Frankfurt: S. Fischer Verlag, 2013).

49. Panwitz, *Haus des Kranichs*, p. 269.

50. Panwitz, *Haus des Kranichs*, pp. 275–276.

51. Recall Ulrich Herbert and Michael Wildt's generational model previously discussed in chapter 2.

52. Enzensberger, *O.M.G.U.S.*, p. 440.

53. Panwitz, *Haus des Kranichs*, pp. 276–278.

54. Harold James, *The Nazi Dictatorship and the Deutsche Bank* (Cambridge: Cambridge University Press, 2004), pp. 179–183.

55. Jonathan Steinberg, *The Deutsche Bank and its Gold Transactions during the Second World War* (München: C. H. Beck), pp. 59–66.

56. Joachim Scholtyseck, *Robert Bosch und der liberale Widerstand gegen Hitler 1933–1945* (München: Verlag C. H. Beck, 1999), pp. 267–268.

57. Scholtyseck, *Robert Bosch*, pp. 269–273.

58. See Cornelia Rauh-Kühne, "Review of "Robert Bosch und der liberale Widerstand gegen Hitler 1933 – 1945," *Historische Zeitschrift*, Vol. 274, No. 2 (April 2002), pp. 520–521.

59. Seven postwar documents have been cited in Scholtyseck *Robert Bosch* chapter III, including: Walz's correspondence of 1967, Leo Baeck's of 1956, Olpp's of 1982, Adler's of 1976, Fischer's of 1947, a second letter of Walz's of 1947, and May's statement in 1966.

60. Rauh-Kühne, *Review*, compare with Scholtyseck, *Robert Bosch*, p. 273.

61. Rauh-Kühne, *Review*, pp. 521–522. Scholtyseck, *Robert Bosch*, p. 147.

62. Manfred Overesch, *Bosch in Hildesheim 1937–1945* (Göttingen: Vandenhoeck & Ruprecht, 2008), p. 22.

63. Overesch, *Bosch*, pp. 220–223.

64. Johannes Bähr, Axel Drecoll, Bernhard Gotto, Kim C. Priemel and Harald Wixforth, *Der Flick-Konzern im Dritten Reich* (München: R. Oldenbourg Verlag, 2008), pp. 322–323.

65. Bähr, *Der Flick-Konzern*, pp. 323–332.

66. Bähr, *Der Flick-Konzern*, pp. 333–335.

67. Bähr, *Der Flick-Konzern*, p. 340.

68. Bähr, *Der Flick-Konzern*, pp. 335–343.

69. The image of Flick as a martyr won importance on the political stage. Nevertheless, his first appeal for a pardon from General Lucius D. Clay in January 1948 failed. Undeterred, Flick petitioned John McCloy with reference to his "moral character throughout his life" as well as opinions from the Red Cross in a second

unsuccessful November 1948 appeal. But Christian Democratic Union (CDU) politician Otto Lenz's claim that Flick was one of the large industrialists, who had never supported Hitler, went to far even for German Justice Minister Thomas Dehler's. Nevertheless, Flick depicted himself before the American Clemency Board as a victim of the war, since his "life work had been nearly destroyed." Flick was released from Landsberg Prison and became a free man on August 25, 1950. See Norbert Frei, Ralf Ahrens, Jörg Osterloh and Tim Schanetzky, *Flick. Der Konzern, die Familie, die Macht* (München: Karl Blessing Verlag, 2009), pp. 430–435.

70. Bähr, *Der Flick-Konzern*, p. 378.

71. For the 26 million Mark bribes, which Flick paid to the CDU, FDP, and SPD Parties in order that the proceeds on the sale of 2 billion Marks in Daimler stock would be considered tax-free, see Frei, Ahrens, Osterloh and Schanetzky, *Flick*, pp. 744–745.

72. The interest in perpetrator behavior has not waned as evidenced by the survey in Peter Hayes's 2017 volume. Hayes held the most recent publication by Felix Römer in highest esteem. Although he provided a sketch of the prior perpetrator debate between Christopher Browning and Daniel Goldhagen, he failed to mention the possibility of a new dispute between Felix Römer and Sönke Neitzel. Similar to the Browning versus Goldhagen controversy in which both authors based their views on Reserve Police Battalion 101 court proceedings, both Römer and Neitzel employ secret recordings by Allies of German POWs. However, Neitzel utilized British transcripts of unnamed prisoners, whereas Römer employed American transcripts of identified Wehrmacht inmates. Neitzel had earlier pleaded for scholars to avoid an over-emphasis on ideology as a motivation for behavior, whereas Römer specifically identified "individual moulding" of captured soldiers as being capable of making a difference in behavior. Compare Peter Hayes, *Why? Explaining the Holocaust* (New York: W.W. Norton & Company, 2017), pp. 137–141 with Felix Römer, *Kameraden. Die Wehrmacht von innen* (München: Piper Verlag GmbH, 2012), pp. 21–25.

Chapter 4

Background to Aryanization of the Hermann Tietz Chain

A. LONG HISTORY OF ECONOMIC OPPOSITION TO DEPARTMENT STORES

1. Anti-Semitism as an Insufficient Cause for Jewish Economic Decline

In discussing perpetrator behavior, chapter 3, section A had noted an undeniable anti-Semitism demonstrated by Werner Best and Erwin Schulz on the left end of the spectrum. But as attention moved toward the right of the panorama in the previous chapter, the degree of anti-Semitism declined and was ultimately replaced by altruism on the part of Robert Bosch and his general manager Hans Walz. During the Weimar Republic, Jewish historians and sociologists had customarily interpreted their community's economic decline at least in part as a result of anti-Semitism, although the mode by which it occurred differed according to each author's perspective.

In 1931, Alfred Marcus observed "a radical process of transformation" in four key sectors, namely metal trading, banking, textiles and the grain trade. He claimed that bankruptcies in these spheres in which Jewish participation exceeded their percentage of the population could not be understood merely from the perspective of the worldwide depression. As the center for metal trading shifted from Europe to New York after World War I, Marcus theorized that Jewish trading companies suffered "extraordinary financial losses" during the inflation, whereas non-Jewish companies in Germany owned the mines and foundries. Manufacturing associations began to form cartels, which excluded Jewish middlemen.[1] Marcus's view continued by maintaining that Gentiles exercised a collective economic mentality in practice, whereas Jewish businessmen demonstrated individualism. The German culture of evolving highly developed forms of cartelization left "no place for Jewish individualism." For German-Jews to offset this trend, Marcus envisioned that they would need to assimilate. The process "would result in the stripping off of all cultural characteristics." As a corollary, Marcus opined that young Jews worked "less intensively" than their German counterparts, because their energy was not directed toward a goal. Thus, Jewish youth would have to accept a lower standard of living, since it would become ever-more difficult to obtain a secure position. However, the responsibility for the deterioration did not lie completely with the younger generation nor with economic developments. Instead, Marcus lamented that Jews were unwanted in the German economy. One hundred years ago, Jewish pioneering activity in new branches of the economy was valued, whereas in 1930, Gentile Germans rejected new business creations by Jews.[2]

These novelties included the establishment of the Hermann Tietz department store chain by Oscar Tietz, which brought new lines of merchandise to proletarians and the middle class, but undermined the profit structure of small shop owners.

2. Antagonism by Displaced Middlemen and Retailers

Oscar Tietz established one of Germany's largest Jewish-owned companies, although the department store chain was named after his Uncle Hermann, who supplied the 1,000 RM in founding capital. Initial success was achieved when Oscar made a revolutionary discovery. He embroidered cotton to the back side of wool and then carefully applied hydrochloric acid to the interspersed sections of wool. The wool was eaten away, leaving a quick and inexpensive method of producing lace. Oscar rented a small, one display-window shop in the city of Gera, which was renowned for weaving wool. The move was initiated to be close to the source of large quantities of wool scraps, which Oscar intended to purchase inexpensively. Oscar located a craftsman in the lace-making capital of Plauen, who could cheaply produce lace by applying acid. Thus the first shop in what later became the Hermann Tietz chain was founded on March 1, 1882. Profits were so great that Oscar traveled to Plauen nearly every other day to order twice the amount of chemically produced lace as previously. In addition to supplying the initial capital, Hermann may have brought four innovations from his prior years of residence in the United States. The business novelties, just beginning to emerge in Germany, included: the profit margin for each piece was small; prices were clearly marked for the customers; bargaining was not practiced; and payment was only in cash.[3] Berlin wholesalers were so furious, that out of fear of retribution, Hermann left the partnership. Oscar repaid him not only the 1,000 RM equity, but also 5,000 RM from recent profits. Non-woven Plauen lace became the backbone and largest bearer of earnings in Oscar's shop.[4] By displaying lace in other formats, Oscar expanded the line of merchandise to include curtains and tablecloths, while unfortunately incurring the wrath of Plauen lace weavers, including the small, middle-class Mutschmann and Eisentraut Company, later founded in October 1907.[5]

Oscar, along with his new wife and son, moved to Munich in 1889, due to the inexpensive property and the fact that the city did not yet have a department store. At first Tietz's customers in the Bavarian capital were laborers and lower level civil servants, with the upper classes seeking to avoid embarrassment by having purchases wrapped in neutral paper rather than the Hermann Tietz emblazoned gift wrap. Up until then, the manufacturers selling to Tietz stores in Gera and Weimar had been small and mid-sized. Although large industrialists were ashamed to meet Oscar in his downtown Munich store, they contracted for unmarked deliveries in his apartment. The line of merchandise further expanded to include school supplies, novels, porcelain and ladies clothing.[6]

Perhaps Oscar's proclivity to diversify his assets by purchasing buildings began as early as 1895. Leonhard and Oscar's widowed mother Johanna convinced Oscar not to reinvest all profits back into the retail stores but to buy an apartment building and make his wife Betty a part owner. No sooner had he purchased the Imperial office building on the corner of Bayer and Schützen Streets, when several tenants terminated their leases claiming they had no desire to have their offices in the Jewish Tietz Palace. Since new occupants were not found, Oscar decided to remodel the edifice by including an atrium, two elevators, and the first electric lights inside a Munich structure. The redesigned office building became the Munich retail outlet.[7]

In addition to this incident of anti-Semitism, there were numerous occasions of opposition, purely out of business concerns. For example, opposition arose to Oscar's challenge to the traditional business model of middlemen marking up wholesalers' prices with small retailers adding their profit as well. To the hostility from Plauen lace manufacturers, retailers attempted to bring an alleged claim of a fire hazard to the attention of the state parliament. They endeavored to curtail sales to the ground and first floor by asserting that prospective customers would not be subject to the risk of being trapped in upper stories during a potential fire. Additionally, retailers requested that police limit the number of people allowed to enter at any one time. Antagonism also arose with regard to the employment of women.

3. Resistance to Women in the Workforce

Although it was becoming common for women to work in retail, during inventory of the Tietz store in Munich on Sunday December 31, 1899,[8] competing retailers induced "hooligans"[9] at the "Augustiner Keller" beer garden at Arnulfstraße 52 (formerly known as Salzstraße)[10] to protest. It is unknown how many of those imbibing beer were persuaded to throw cobblestones through the Tietz display windows and prohibit either customers or staff from entering or departing from the store. However, the 5,000-seat layout of the beer garden in Munich had been minimally altered since 1896 and the police were unable to quell the disturbance. Soldiers were necessary to restore peace.[11]

A smaller, previous incident in Munich occurred when small shop owners incited students in a fraternity to leave a pub and flirt with the Tietz sales girls. Paul Hessling notified the frat boys, that they were trespassing and asked them to leave. But they beat Paul, flung the merchandise around, and smashed the windows. Oscar sought protection from the police, who declined to intervene, because the students represented Munich's finest families. A neighboring baker and his journeymen assisted in restoring order. Paul filed a complaint with both the police and the vice-chancellor of the university. When both declined to take action, Hermann went to the U.S. Consulate, since he had retained his U.S. Citizenship from the years of being in the bakery business in Memphis, Tennessee. The vice-chancellor requested that the matter be resolved out-of-court, which resulted in apologies from both the fraternity house and the university in a joint communique published by the newspapers.[12]

Both of the incidents from the 1890s involving intoxicated mischief-makers and the university students were sponsored by competing retailers according to Tietz accounts. However, the student tumult also included male opposition to women participating in the economy, despite women having predominated the staffs of the related German textile, garment and cigar industries for in a number of years. Female preeminence in the textile industry continued until the outbreak of World War I, with labor increasing by 115 percent between 1873 and 1913. Growth was interspersed with adversity, with Plauen lace producers viewing innovators as the cause of their personal business failures.[13] The various hostile acts against the Tietz store in Munich make it clear that resistance to business innovations must be distinguished from anti-Semitism.

4. Hostility by Plauen Lace Manufacturers and Its Chief Advocate, Martin Mutschmann

The Saxon lace, white and colored embroidery as well as the production of ready-made clothing, was essentially concentrated in the Vogtland area of Plauen.[14] A ready source of skilled artisans was available due to Plauen's trade and art institutions. The Theodor Bickel firm placed the name "Plauen

Lace" in the public domain, preventing it from becoming any one company's trademark, but instead becoming a symbol of quality. Plauen's international recognition broke St. Gallen's monopoly in the lace industry. The high point was achieved on August 18, 1900, when the Plauen pattern received the grand prize at the Paris World's Fair.

Lace wholesalers in Plauen, who had lost much of their importance, tried to regain their influence by separating Hermann Tietz from the manufacturers. Based on his experiences in Paris, Georg Tietz convinced Oscar to open a building in Plauen to purchase and warehouse lace, embroidery, drapes, rugs and other woven items from the Vogtland and thus save on the wholesalers' fees. Georg's centralized purchasing office replaced the prior system in which each store manager in conjunction with his department director would make purchasing decisions.[15] Later in 1923, the Leonhard Tietz chain followed the Hermann Tietz strategy of vertical integration by purchasing a lace factory in Plauen, a weaving mill in Augsburg and establishing a laundry workshop, which was managed by the Wolff brothers, their nephews.[16] Some opposition to Herman Tietz arose due to anti-Semitism. However, many other instances had nothing to do with ideology. Instead much antagonism arose due to department stores elimination of the need for middlemen, refusal to accept women in the labor market, and opposition by Plauen lace-makers to the replacement of handmade lace by chemical means. Small retailers sought government assistance both in Imperial Germany and in the Weimar Republic by instituting a tax on the bigger enterprises.

5. Prussian Department Store Tax and Its Unintended Consequences

The Prussian tax on department stores may appear to have been motivated by anti-Semitism. However, the tax predated the February 1919 formation of the Deutschvölkischer Schutz- und Trutzbund (German National Protection and Defense Federation) by nearly two decades. A second reason for assessing the German tax law as motivated by economics, rather than anti-Semitism, is the simultaneous opposition of small shop owners against stores such as Macy's in New York City, Wanamaker's in Philadelphia, and Marshall Field's in Chicago. Both Indiana and Wisconsin legislatures had passed laws licensing and regulating department stores in 1897. Missouri imposed a 300–500-dollar tax for each class of merchandise in a department store.

Germany followed suit with a Bavarian tax on department stores introduced on June 9, 1899, and Prussia was requested "to come to the rescue of the small tradesman" by leveling the playing field through an assessment on their larger competitors. Frank H. Mason, Consul-General in Berlin from 1898 to 1905, provided American businessmen with a report on Prussia's

June 18, 1900 law, which imposed a progressive tax when department stores' annual sales exceeded 400,000 RM. Whereas the implementation of the Bavarian tax appeared to be based on the specific interpretation of the civil servant involved in each incident, the Prussian law specified a progression from 1 percent of 400,000 RM in annual sales to 1.8 percent of 650,000 RM to 2 percent of 1,100,000 RM. But before his death on September 8, 1901, Johannes von Miquel, Prussian Minister of Finance, expressed doubt regarding the wisdom of taxing department stores and concerns about the consequences. A third reason for rejecting anti-Semitism as the motivation for the tax was provided by the economic interpretation given at that time. Scholarship at the turn of the century did not interpret taxes on American, German, and French department stores in an anti-Semitic vein:

> Hardly any attempt has been made to disguise the motive of such taxation as this. The aim is not fiscal, but political and social . . . they have been openly advocated and justified as a means of protecting one industrial class against the competition of another.[17]

The department store taxes did not prevent either the Hermann Tietz or the Leonhard Tietz department store chains from expanding. In fact, the tax produced the opposite unintended consequences. The Prussian tax law had been based on a classification of merchandise into four categories: groceries, yarn and twine, household goods, and jewelry. Competitors who had considered or recently expanded their line of merchandise into more than one classification, unlike the Tietzes, returned to sales of more restricted range of wares, in order to avoid incurring the tax. A fourth reason for interpreting this tax as an economic reaction, rather than an anti-Semitic act, is the fact that it also adversely affected Gentile companies, including the four chains owned by Rudolf Karstadt, Ernst Karstadt, Theodor Althoff,[18] and the partnership between Johann Theodor Peek and Adolph Cloppenburg. The tax further ensured that multistory, stand-alone department stores such as the non-Jewish Warenhaus Jacobsen in Kiel as well as the Warenhaus St. Florian in Oberzipfelhausen did not expand into a regional string of commercial establishments. Uwe Spiekermann's conclusion with regard to the middle-class opposition to department stores appears prudent: "In the two decades before the worldwide economic crisis, large segments of the retail business rarely argued in an explicitly anti-Semitic fashion." Instead anti-Semitism was espoused by some small political parties and the associations of shop assistants.[19] Middlemen, hand lace makers and small shop owners were not the only adversaries of department stores. Since bankers also played a role in deciding whether to extend loans, they could conceivably be viewed as foes. But during Imperial Germany's and the Weimar Republic's turbulent times was the imposition of high interest rates on commercial loans an indication of an adversarial relationship or merely an appropriate method to compensate for financial risk?

6. Sub Rosa Activity of Banks

A severe financial setback occurred as a 1901 economic crisis struck Germany. Not only did the Kassel kiln drying company Trebertrocknungsanstalt go bankrupt, but it also forced its lending bank the Leipziger Bank into insolvency on June 26, 1901. The Pommernbank, from which Oscar had accepted a three million RM mortgage,[20] had collapsed as did the Berliner Bank. This occurred at the time when Tietz had placed large orders for its Berlin store. In order to pay creditors, Oscar obtained a loan of 1 million RM from Bankhaus Hardy & Company at 10 percent interest and 20 percent of the profit. Eugen Landau's extension of a half million RM unsecured loan with the Nationalbank für Deutschland cost Landau his Supervisory Board seat with the Nationalbank, whereupon he founded the Berliner Disconto-Gesellschaft.

Business began to expand. In the following year, Oscar repaid the one million RM loan to the Hardy Bank as well as the 20 percent demanded in profit sharing. The world decried Hardy as a usurer, but Oscar described the terms of the loan as an appropriate risk premium and remained in intimate personal friendship with the Hardy Bank owners, James and Ludwig Hardy as well as Fritz Andreä and Richard Pohl almost until 1933, when they lost ownership control of the bank.[21] As Jewish executives of the financial institution, neither Hardy nor Andreä can be accused of perpetrating an anti-Semitic act against the Tietz department store. Perhaps the best explanation regarding why a Jewish bank charged such an excessive rate to a Jewish company lies in the fact that it too was in a precarious financial state. Many people had no sense of compassion for the department stores' opposition from middlemen, lace-makers and small retailers, believing that the large merchandisers squandered huge profits on costly edifices and large personal salaries.

7. General Economic Status of Department Stores

The palatial structures and the rapid pace of expansion led the general urban public to imagine that the stores were achieving enormous profits for their owners. A contemporaneous source recorded that only in the last three or four years had A. Wertheim achieved astonishing total sales of 33 million RM with a profit of 800,000 RM. Hermann Tietz had sales of merely five to six million RM, whereas the general public speculated that both firms would have had twice that amount of turnover. The same journalist also responded to the fear that small shop owners were being put out of business by the department stores, by calling this depiction a "cock-and-bull story" (Ammenmärchen). The newspaper reporter attempted to present a balanced story by acknowledging that the turnover in employees was rapid.[22] In a self-disclosure, twenty years later (1929), the Leonhard Tietz chain of seventeen stores acknowledged 5,243 of its 7,431 employees (70.6 percent) had not yet been with the company for five years. Nevertheless, the firm attempted to put a positive interpretation on this fact by also indicating that a further 1,359 staff members (18.3 percent) had been employed between five and ten years and the remaining 829 white-collar workers (11.2 percent) had been on the payroll for more than ten years.[23]

The popular newspaper reportage by Leo Colze was substantiated by Johannes Wernicke's academic research. Using data from the 1908 *Statistisches Jahrbuch für den Preußischen Staat*, Wernicke noted that the ninety-three department stores that paid the Prussian tax in 1905 had total sales of 176.12 billion RM from which they earned a 5.3 percent profit of 9.42 billion. Although the number of stores decreased to 90 in 1906, the profit margin of 5.1 percent remained similar as did the profit of 5.7 percent in 1907 when the number of stores increased to 107.

Not only did Wernicke examine department store profits in Prussia, but he also examined total sales in Germany. To the 101 Prussian department stores, he added 41 in Bavaria, 150 in Prussia, which were too small to pay the special tax, as well as 100 throughout the remainder of the country. He estimated the total 1907 sales by German department stores according to the 1911 value of the Reichsmark as being approximately 525–550 million RM, which indicates that caution must be exercised in the use of conflicting financial data. He concluded that department stores accounted for a mere 2.2 percent of the total German retail sales of 25 billion RM.[24]

Public outcry against the department stores appears far in excess of the redistribution of sales. Perhaps the best explanation for this disproportionate response may be ascribed to blaming one retail innovation for the general upheaval in the German economy. Without retracing the economy of the Second Empire, one could simply indicate that a recent German social history listed five depressions between 1873 and 1908 before reaching the crisis of 1913. The five downturns encompassed eighteen of the forty-year span. The department store became the convenient target for the numerous upheavals caused by Germany's late industrial revolution and the migration of the rural population to the urban areas.[25] Not only did the economic disruptions, for which Tietz was faulted, affect the department store, but also overly ambitious executives desirous of stake in the firm's ownership.

B. WEAKNESSES AND ATTACKS LEADING TO ECONOMIC DECLINE AND ARYANIZATION OF HERMANN TIETZ

1. Attempted Takeover Prior to Georg Karg and the Deutsche Bank

Self-centered company executives desirous of being promoted co-proprietors in the Hermann Tietz Company became an issue when Oscar and Betty Tietz went on a three-month, pre–World War I cruise to India. The purchasing manager for the Berlin stores together with the manager of the Alexanderplatz branch and the finance director seized the opportunity to try overwhelming the owners' lesser experienced son Georg. The three executives demanded that the firm become incorporated, giving them the opportunity to acquire partial ownership. The executive in charge of purchasing threatened to resign unless Georg made the decision in an hour. After accepting the resignation, Georg mistakenly assumed the issue was settled, but the three department store executives had conspired with Carl Klönne, who was on the Board of Directors at the Deutsche Bank from 1900 to 1914. Klönne suggested transforming Hermann Tietz into a corporation and allowing the Deutsche Bank to sell the shares under the threat of having to repay a recently negotiated three-year loan from the bank within eight days.[26] Georg turned to the firm's General Counsel, Isidor Dzialoszinski, who suggested obtaining a loan from Richard Pohl at the Hardy Bank. When Pohl could only extend a temporary loan of 1 million RM, Georg responded that would be of no assistance. Thus, Georg, Isidor, and Richard inquired of Hermann Waller at the Disconto-Gesellschaft, who extended the same terms for a 3 million RM loan as the Deutsche Bank had offered. As Tietz and Löwenberger returned the unused 3 million RM to Carl Klönne, the Deutsche Bank Board Member was furious. Upon Oscar's return from India, Georg was rewarded by receiving the office adjacent to his father's.[27] The first attempted takeover of Hermann Tietz by one of Germany's largest financial institutions had failed. Unfortunately, it became the pattern whereby the Deutsche or Dresdner Bank would assist conservative businessmen in Aryanizing large Jewish-owned companies in the first years of the Third Reich.

German corporations utilized a two-board system, entailing internal executives on the Board of Directors and bank managers, large shareholders, government officials and other experts on the Supervisory Board. Carl Klönne's actions against the privately owned Tietz chain illustrated German banks' desires to wield power in the economy. In a study of seventy-eight companies in the five business sectors of textiles, breweries, iron and steel, electrotechnical, and automobiles, the impact of Germany's largest banks was demonstrated. Among textile firms sampled, 47 percent of Supervisory seats were held by banks and only 14 percent by large shareholders. In breweries, the ratio was 37 percent to 13 percent; in iron and steel, 25 percent to 17 percent; in automobiles, 31 percent to 9 percent; and in electro-technical, 38 percent to 3 percent. On average, banks constituted one-third of all Supervisory Board members during the 1920s, thereby possessing insider knowledge of the companies as well as being able to influence the firms' futures by means of voting.[28] Supervisory boards are unknown to American businesses, but U.S. department stores' introduction of catalog sales was emulated by the Hermann Tietz chain.

2. Expansion into Mail Order Business

Georg unsuccessfully attempted to follow the American pattern of establishing purchases via mail order. The turnover in the Hermann Tietz warehouse was so rapid, that by the time an order had been received, the inventory in the warehouse had already been sold. In response Georg stationed a fleet of forty ton-and-a-half trucks every fifty kilometers, which were supplied with customer orders from vehicles constantly shuttling between Berlin and Hamburg. The fleet of 40 lorries was increased to 100 trucks as new customers from villages and rural areas were added. In addition, an in-house print shop was established to produce an eight-page advertisement of three-day specials. Ever more aspects of the business fell upon Georg's shoulders, enabling Oscar to focus on public and charitable activities. Georg's younger brother Martin did an internship with the British department store chain Selfridge and demonstrated an aptitude for detecting where expenses could be limited. Martin had adopted one of Harry Gordon Selfridge's dicta: "No part of an intricate machine such as the retail trade can ever be so 'well' that it cannot be better."[29] Unfortunately, improvements in department stores led to the resentment that the chains had amassed exorbitant profits at the expense of the common people.

3. Unsubstantiated Claims of Tietz's War Profiteering

Although Harry Gordon Selfridge catered to the upscale market, he hired Martin Tietz, whose family-owned chain focused on the working-class population. Immediately prior to the outbreak of World War I, department stores still displayed a transnational cooperation. However, that international retail assistance soon dissolved in the wake of the political upheaval.[30]

On Sunday, August 2, 1914, Georg and Martin Tietz drove to their office and opened their sealed military orders regarding the delivery of blankets, cots, shoes, dried peas, lentils, dried fruit, tea, coffee, cans of meat and other articles to army field depots. The Hermann Tietz firm was further assigned to process gauze into belts and ammunition pouches. On Monday August 3, 1914, there were practically no sales, allowing Georg to assign employees to the mobilization orders. Business became very busy as people stocked up on supplies and purchased gifts for departing soldiers. Everyday Georg received contracts for new supplies for the military. All trucks capable of carrying more than one ton of supplies were appropriated by the army and even Georg's motorboat was commandeered and sent to the Vistula River. Tietz's Self-Service Division was transformed and worked day and night on military contracts for hospital gowns, military shirts, sandbags and tarpaulins. The space where the print shop had been was converted into a leather shop, where pouches for bullets, belts, bridles, saddles and machine gun harnesses were produced. Special machinery was purchased with the funds obtained from the delivered supplies and the requisitioned cars and trucks. Retail employees were retrained to handle government procurement. By year's end, the effects of the British blockade had become noticeable through scarcer merchandise and increased prices. Bread was rationed in 1915 and the Hermann Tietz warehouse on the Lehrter Straße was rented by the army. Coffee beans only accounted for a third of ground coffee, inducing Georg to travel to Switzerland and Holland to buy merchandise. The government established prices for both distributors and consumers. Before the war, the department stores had made their profit by fast turnover of large amounts of merchandise. In seeking to exclude profiteering, Hermann Tietz purchased 1,500 tons of dried peas at 17.50 RM per hundred pounds and was required by the government to store them for eighteen months before rationing them out at 24 RM for 100 pounds. In addition, a new staff was required to complete numerous forms in an eight-copy format. Competition between department stores, wholesalers and smaller specialty shops in the retail sector disappeared.[31]

Foreign currency with which to pay for merchandise from abroad became scarcer. Switzerland instituted an embargo of silver five Franc pieces from Belgium and France into Germany. In an attempt to counter the lack of silver coinage, Georg agreed to conduct fashion shows in Bern and Geneva and on his return trip to Germany, he was able to smuggle several million Francs worth of silver coins into the Fatherland in order to be able to convert them into Swiss currency.[32]

Germans first experienced famine during the winter of 1916–1917. The ill-effects could be circumvented through acquisitions on the black market. Occasionally Georg made illicit private purchases not allowed by his ration card, rather than dipping into the stores' warehouses, despite the disapproval of his future father-in-law, Ludwig Grünfeld of F.V. Grünfeld Landeshuter Leinen und Gebildweberei. On one occasion, Hermann von Stein, the Prussian Minister of War, asked Oscar how to alleviate the popular cry for cooking oil. Oscar sent Georg to Stockholm to purchase 3,000 tons of American lard and smuggle it back into Germany aboard a Norwegian freighter. Half went to the military administration and the remainder was sold in one-pound packages to lines of customers forming in the atriums of all three Berlin flagship stores of Hermann Tietz. Oscar's reputation with the War Department grew immeasurably, resulting in his promotion as the Ministry's special delegate for economic affairs. During the second winter of famine, women were seen everywhere standing in lines for items on the ration cards. Oscar loaned all three 200 horsepower diesel motors from Munich stores and six motors from Berlin so that the Post Office would have sufficient energy for radio and transatlantic cables. Thereby, Oscar incidentally benefited by knowing the international rates in the commodity markets.[33]

However, the Tietz's relationship with the Foreign Office cooled when Georg was given a diplomatic passport for travel to Constantinople where he was to secure food supplies during the spring of 1917. By attending Sabbath services in the synagogue, he met one of the Sultan's physicians, who had an insight regarding Turkey's intentions regarding English Major General Charles Townsend, who had been taken prisoner in April 1916. The British General was negotiating with the Macedonians and it was clear to an insider, that Turkey wanted something from Britain.[34] Thus, the physician advised Georg to sell the Hermann Tietz purchasing office in Stambul and take the proceeds back to Germany, since the following year he would obtain nothing for the property. In less than three weeks, Georg took the proceeds and traveled back to Germany via Sophia. In the capital, he met the representatives of the *Frankfurter Zeitung* and Krupp, both of whose expressions confirmed Georg's insights. However, when Georg attempted to report the adverse situation to the Foreign Office, he was informed that the Kaiser[35] did not appreciate pessimistic news.[36]

There were three socio-economic reasons why the urban population would have mistakenly accused the Tietz department stores of war profiteering. Even prior to World War I, consumers in cities opposed protective tariffs, benefiting large-scale agriculture. Resentment would have spiked in the knowledge that despite these indirect subsidies, the nation needed to import 33 percent of its basic commodities including 42 percent of its fat. In spite of the fact that large retail chains offered metropolitan customers a wide variety of food products at prices cheaper than in small neighborhood shops, patrons would have lost the relationship of trust established with local grocers, butchers and bakers. In lieu of personal relationships, city dwellers ruminated over affluent landowners seeking exorbitant profits and government officials willingly accepting bribes. It was easy to imagine that lords over the chain stores were charging the helpless city populace a hefty markup. The British blockade against German civilians was part of England's wartime strategy.

Berliners suffered from shortages of bread in the fall of 1914 and potatoes in early 1915. Already by February 1915, Berlin Police Commissioner Traugott von Jagow warned the government that the city's inhabitants were more absorbed by the British blockade than German battlefield successes.[37] The department stores were a defenseless target. Therefore, the angry hunger of urbanites was focused on them long before outrage brought the downfall of the Kaiser and his generals. The existence of the black market confirmed the public's suspicions about collusion between the farmers and the government.

During the winter of famine in 1917–1918, women publicly sold their services for food and soldiers deserted. Hermann Tietz sold fabric for clothing made of paper; soles for shoes fabricated from cardboard; and broth from turnips, whereas on the black market everything was still available. On the evening of November 8, 1918, members of the groups seeking an end to World War I met at Oscar and Betty Tietz's house. Before Paul Hirsch and Otto Wels left the Tietz residence, Hirsch said that on the following morning, he would either be hanging from the gallows or appointed as Prussia's Prime Minister with Philipp Scheidemann serving as Chancellor and Otto Wels as Commandant of the City of Berlin. The following day the Hermann Tietz stores displayed signs proclaiming that they were under the authority of the workers' and soldiers' Council. This step was taken to protect against looting, although the stores lacked both customers and merchandise. Oscar and Georg were both elected to leadership positions in the Councils formed within their stores. Since the items sold in the stores during the last years of the war were inferior, on December 23, 1918, Georg met with Mr. Eugster, the owner of an embroidery factory in Altstätten Switzerland in the attempt to purchase merchandise on credit. But Eugster confronted Georg with an already incurred bill of half a million Francs. Georg responded that if Eugster would supply him with a one-year loan of 600,000 RM, he would cover the prior debt and would acquire 100,000 RM worth of finished English goods. On the basis of Eugster's personal guarantee, the Rheinische Kreditbank in Altstätten granted Georg a one-year loan of 600,000–700,000 RM and the Kreditanstalt in St. Gallen similarly extended a loan. Although company executives accused Georg of accepting a 20 percent loss in the value of the Mark against the Swiss Franc, Georg defended his actions maintaining that other firms had remained solvent only by becoming limited liability companies or by becoming corporations.[38]

Stuttgart's revolutionary labor minister claimed the Hermann Tietz branch as government property. In order to resolve this issue, Georg took the train to Stuttgart and checked into the Hotel Marquardt. However, he had to barricade himself in the basement in order to avoid arrest from the armed sailors, who had mutinied. The next morning Georg negotiated a collective agreement, which resulted in the cancellation of the nationalization of the store.

In Berlin, the employees assembled in the stores' courtyards, where Oscar urged them to return to work, since only the sales' proceeds could pay their wages. Although it appeared that calm had been restored in the Berlin stores, on January 8, 1919, the Spartacists entered the Alexanderplatz flagship as part of the workers seizure of downtown Berlin. Revolutionaries attempted controlling the neighboring newspaper publishing district on Kochstraße, pride of place, which was assigned to Hans, Franz, Louis, Rudolf, and Hermann Ullstein's *Berliner Morgenpost*.[39] Nearby Kochstraße newspapers also included Rudolf Mosse's *Berliner Tageblatt* and August Scherl's *Berliner Lokal-Anzeiger*.[40]

By offering the hundred sailors cigars and alcoholic beverages, Georg and his nine night-watchmen were able to disarm the mutineers from their rifles, pistols and hand grenades. The left-wing sailors left the store only to be replaced by an adolescent naval cadet leading thirty-four members of the right-wing Freikorps, who were armed with four machine guns. But Georg was able to frighten them into leaving by reporting that the Communists had returned. Wilhelm Pieck and other Reds had occupied the police headquarters and promised Georg protection from the Freikorps as well as safe passage as he traversed the downtown area. Similarly, Georg received promises of protection from Hermann Ehrhardt, leader of 5,000–6,000 man Marine Brigade Ehrhardt, who later played a prominent role in the March 1920 Kapp Putsch. With weapons from fleeing Spartacists and Freikorps, Georg defended the store for six days with five night-watchmen in two-hour guard duty shifts, until the regular army joined the Freikorps and began shooting mortars in buildings housing Spartacists. Georg thought he escaped with little damage, since only the display windows along the Alexanderstraße were destroyed. Taking sheet metal from Degner's unoccupied iron warehouse, Georg protected the store from looting. After eight days, the struggle between left-wing and right-wing forces ended at the Alexanderplatz, but continued for a few more days in Kochstraße's publishing district. As the Mark suffered further losses in value, Hermann Tietz purchased merchandise or when no goods were available, the conglomerate acquired foreign currency or shares of stock. Laws establishing price ceilings promoted further losses. Goods not rationed during the war were now included in a strictly allocated system.[41]

Contemporary newspapers sold large numbers of issues blaming a few companies of "earning" outrageous profits at the public's expense. In contrast, contemporary scholars Joerg Baten and Rainer Schulz examined the profits in the tax records of 140 businesses in the cities of Essen, Düsseldorf, Elberfeld and Duisburg. Joint stock companies represented 47 percent of the sample, mining firms were 14 percent of those surveyed, limited liability operations constituted 8 percent and large family enterprises amounted to the remaining 31 percent. The sample included internationally renowned conglomerates, such as Krupp, Stinnes, Thyssen, and Beckerath. Although Hermann Tietz had no stores in these industrial areas, these were the locations where Oscar's older brother Leonhard operated his chain of retail establishments. When Baten and Schulz adjusted profits for inflation, they discovered that for the seven chemical businesses, profits in 1917 were 144 percent of the 1913 baseline. Similarly, for the twenty-six firms in the war-necessary metal and machinery sector, profits had increased in 1917 to 121 percent of the 1913 level. However, Paul von Hindenburg's strategy of introducing a massive armament program reduced products for civilian consumption. Thus, for the thirteen businesses in merchandising, 1917 profits were reduced to 55 percent of the 1913 niveau. Similarly, for the food and tobacco sector, profits declined to 53 percent of the prewar quantity and similarly for textiles and clothing, it also dwindled to 53 percent.[42] Accusations of war profiteering against either Hermann Tietz or Leonhard Tietz were spurious. Angered by a lack of food and clothing, consumers merely reacted against a convenient target. Although shoppers immediately after World War I probably did not express a political ideology in venting their anguish, Joseph Goebbels did.

4. Goebbels's Attack on Jewish-Owned Department Stores

Although Goebbels was the Leader of the Gau of Berlin, he neither had the physical power to domesticate the city's SA nor was he ideologically willing to do so. In fact, in August 1928, the Party needed to pay the SA 3,500 RM to restore some degree of tranquility between the NSDAP and its brawlers. But prior to Hitler's termination of Walther Stennes, the SA did not view itself as an aside to the Party, but rather as its center. Tensions between the paramilitary and the NSDAP skyrocketed when Hitler fired Stennes and the terminated SA leader occupied the Party's Berlin headquarters. Out of loyalty to Hitler, Goebbels sided with Munich's assent to a legal approach to power over the SA's path of violence to political power. Since even the so-called Jewish press of Berlin craved the excitement that street bloodshed occasioned, Goebbels exploited news-hungry publications for the NSDAP's propaganda purposes. In addition to the SA's physical disturbances, verbal assaults in *Der Angriff* also played a role in Goebbels's strategy.[43]

Only two themes had encroached on the masthead in as many as five issues of *Der Angriff*. One topic was the glorification of the Rathenau assassins and the second theme of the department stores will now be examined, commencing with the December 12, 1927 edition. Unfortunately, Goebbels's diaries contain a seventeen-month gap between his last entry on October 30, 1926 and the following record on April 14, 1928, thus depriving historians of any commentary by Goebbels on his first two department store issues.

Under the front-page headline "Berlin Department Stores' Tax Evasion," six different companies were attacked, commencing with the accusation that although the proprietors were wealthy, they had avoided their obligation to pay taxes. It was claimed that Karstadt was a Jewish joint stock company with 250 million RM in earnings. Nevertheless, the supposed Jewish firm was fined 20,000 RM in 1903 for reporting income of 120,000 RM as being merely 22,000 RM. Although the article began with a critique of Karstadt, it quickly expanded to entail four other chains in which annual sales amounted to 1 billion RM annually, including Hermann Tietz, Wertheim, Wronker and Leonhard Tietz. These Jewish enterprises were initially addressed as conglomerates, accounting for most of the 1.5 billion RM in department stores' yearly sales. Later in the argumentation, their origin was addressed in terms of stemming from an "Oriental bazaar" or from the American model of the five-and-ten cents stores. Goebbels linked the term "bazaar" with junk and purported to provide specific examples as his "reportage" continued on the inside pages. Allegedly quoting a long-standing employee of the Potsdamer Platz store, it was claimed that cow meat was sold as beef and pork originated "from unsuitable animals." Referring to the Jewish banker Carl Fürstenberg of the Berliner Handels-Gesellschaft led to the final recrimination against advertisements and funding from powerful capital.[44]

In addition to the lead article, another titled "Tietz Doesn't Have to Pay Taxes," referred to the Prussian Diet's plan to reintroduce the pre–World War I tax on department stores. However, the intervention of large banks overturned this proposed legislation, due to the poor economic climate. This provoked the editorial comment that in all other situations, the Ministry of Finance was "frantic for every new source of taxes" and thus the "very rich Jewish money pigs" were somehow not "slaves" to the Dawes Plan as all other Germans were.[45]

A third article in the December 12, 1927 issue appeared under the heading "The Christ-Child by Tietz" claimed that Jesus had unloaded gifts for children, which "department store Jews obligingly accepted." As though offending Jewish people was insufficient, one would have imagined that all Protestants and Catholics in Germany would have been incensed by the statement that "the Christ-Child must have His own taste" in leaving Christmas presents with the Jewish Wertheim and Karstadt chains.[46]

But who was to blame for this woeful state of consumer affairs? The easy answer was the Weimar Republic for not re-imposing the department store tax and the Social Democrat newspapers for running the stores' deceptive advertisement. But such a response would still have left the conundrum that large numbers of Germans must have believed that they were purchasing quality merchandise at inexpensive prices or else the chains would have never opened or would have quickly become bankrupt. Thus, Goebbels was forced to disparage the German people by asserting that Karstadt's ninety stores "thrived through the stupidity of the masses." Probably as a mollification to potential voters, he later added that the Wilmersdorfer Straße branch had recently failed "because the German instinct fights back against these cut prices and trash places."

The appeal to additional voters can best be seen in the front-paged cartoon by Hans Schweitzer entitled: "Workers and middle-class members! Whom are you fattening with your coins?" The caricature depicted a German couple throwing coins into the mouth of an obese figure, labeled as "department store capital," who was crushing a half-concealed individual, labeled as the small businessman. This thesis was frequently found in *Der Angriff* but scarcely if ever in Goebbels's diary.[47] The newspaper was reserved for external enemies, whereas the diary addressed internal competitors.[48] Schweitzer was a close friend of Goebbels, who assumed the nom de plume "Mjölnir," from the mythology of Thor's hammer. As Goebbels confided, "He has the great gift to tell the essential in a few strokes of the pen." But the pen and ink drawings crossed the line in what the Jewish people were willing to tolerate. The left side of a second December 12, 1927 illustration depicted Jesus being spit upon while hanging on the cross, while the right side rendered a crooked-nose department store owner beckoning customers to his Christmas sale. The inflammatory caption read: "He who allows Christ to be beaten on the cross, today makes his deceitful profit with the Christmas festival." In case a reader should somehow not recognize the assault on Jewish character, the term "deceitful profit" was of Yiddish origin.[49]

After Willi Schäfer was sentenced to 2.5 years imprisonment on April 16, 1928 for beating up Communists in the Lichterfeld train station, Goebbels confided in his diary that it was high time that he obtained immunity. The editor of Goebbels's diary interpreted Goebbels's evaluation of the 1928 German elections as a success because it resulted in Goebbels becoming a Member of the Reichstag, which to a large extent brought him immunity from criminal prosecution as well as free travel courtesy of the Republic's train service. The immunity was immediately useful, because his June 6, 1928 diary entry disclosed that he and his editor Dagobert Dürr had been fined 200 RM for slandering six members of the Political Police as associates of the Soviet secret police. The following day's entry noted Goebbels's concern that a department store trial would commence.[50]

By combining data from several editions of *Der Angriff* along with Goebbels's diary, the following picture emerges: About one week after the publication of the December 12, 1927 issue, "Jewish" Assistant Police Chief Bernhard Weiß was accompanied by two policemen in his visit to *Der Angriff's* business office. They attempted to impound the mass edition of the publication. The articles did not specify how many copies were printed. But at this time, there were only 200 paid subscriptions, although other special editions prompted runs of 50,000–60,000 copies.[51] Goebbels appears to have won the propaganda war, since he was only able "to humbly hand over the publisher's copy," since all others had already been sold. Goebbels viewed the edition as "a punch to the counting house of the fortress of Jewish money," whereas the police viewed it as blasphemy. "From reliable sources" the newspaper learned that the Centralverein deutscher Staatsbürger jüdischen Glaubens had endeavored to oppose the *Angriff*'s "work of enlightenment." The largest Jewish umbrella organization in Germany urgently turned to the Association of Department Stores[52] with the inquiry regarding what could be done. Department store executive Isidor Bach's hope for an indictment of blasphemy was reduced to the charge of "gross mischief." Months before the second special edition of the *Angriff* against department stores or the trial against the newspaper, Goebbels threw down the challenge: "Jewish department stores should remember: We are only at the beginning of the battle."[53]

Additional details were provided after the June 8, 1928 department store trial by the third anti-department store special edition of *Der Angriff* on June 11. Perhaps because Isidor Bach had been one of the seventeen hostages taken by Freikorps Oberland on November 9, 1923 during the Hitler Putsch, he immediately took action. As the managing director of the Association of German Department Stores, he wrote Dr. Schmitz on December 15, 1927 regarding *Der Angriff*'s accusation that Karstadt had evaded paying taxes in 1903. After company management in Hamburg displayed no interest in undertaking a lawsuit, Bach was apparently contacted by the Centralverein, but he doubted there was any legal basis on which the Association could sue. Nevertheless, the two agencies joined forces in contacting the Public Prosecutor regarding the provocation against a religious community. In Goebbels's perspective, "the Public Prosecutor hurried to launch appropriate steps from such prominent agencies."[54]

In his June 9, 1928 diary entry, Goebbels recorded the right-wing's pleasure that the magistrate allowed him during the previous day's trial to harangue for an hour. Goebbels affirmed that the judge stated: "Business is business" and appeared to substantiate this claim by mentioning in a prior newspaper that if a defendant had stated that "a Jew is a Jew," how could that be any different from stating that a Protestant was a Protestant? Even more mystifying to a modern historian was the diary claim that the prosecuting attorney had not recognized the incriminating nature of the cartoon. Goebbels mentioned that he had been fined 20 RM and Dagobert Dürr 10 RM. Immediately thereafter, he indicated the mildness of the punishment by noting that a spectator, who had cheered the verdict, was fined 30 RM for being out-of-order. In a demonstration against the trial, Goebbels assembled business people, merchants and blue-collar workers to protest the department stores' "murders of German industriousness," since the stores and banks enjoyed their palaces, whereas the people were hungry. Goebbels made full use of his Reichstag immunity and the July 14, 1928 Amnesty Law. For his incitement of bodily injury against Pastor Fritz Stücke, his original six weeks of imprisonment was reduced to a fine of 600 RM and had it not been for the Jewish Judge Löwenstein, Goebbels held that he would have gone entirely free. Indeed, after passage of the Law, he divulged in his diary: "Now I am once again as pure as an angel," although four months later he feared that the Reichstag would revoke his immunity.[55]

Goebbels printed the fourth issue in the series against department stores on December 10, 1928. But one week before its appearance, he announced a sale of bulk quantities through the use of an enclosed payment card. The discounted prices were ten copies for 1 RM, fifty copies for 3.50 RM, but 1,000 copies for only 35 RM in order to ensure as wide a circulation as possible. He reprinted the pen and ink drawing, which caused the first issue in the series to be impounded and reflected that the judge had been "unable to decide for a conviction or an acquittal because of his conflict between his assignment and his conscience." Goebbels had filed an appeal, which made no progress, because his "crime" was amnestied. In order "to demonstrate the connections between justice and Jewish capital," the inflammatory cartoon was being reprinted in order that the issue might appear at a higher court and thus "open the eyes of tens of thousands." Goebbels was looking forward to the propaganda battle.[56]

The fifth and final issue in the anti-department store series carried the headline: "Ritual Murder: Department Stores and Large Banks Butcher German Economic Life." In each of the five editions, a correlation between the stores and banks had been drawn. However, the frequency and intensity of the consequences became shriller. For example, fifteen months earlier, the relatively factual statement had been made:

> Department stores and large banks work closely together. The banks provide credit whereby new purchasing palaces can always be formed on the earth. But where does the money originate? From the broad masses of the employed from whose pockets the large banks route the laboriously created savings into their vaults. In this way, the department stores and their allied banks achieve dominion over the workers.[57]

The sole statement in the second issue associating department stores with banks was even more straightforward in mentioning that the small chain H. Wronker A.G. in Frankfurt sought funding from Lazard, Speyer-Ellissen, and Teixeira de Mattos. Although the prior sentence noted that the department store was a lustrous business for the Jewish entrepreneur and the headline read "Department Store Owners Enslave German Workers," no slur was made that both the American and Dutch bankers, assisting the store, were Jewish financiers.[58]

By the third issue, two front-page articles addressed the linkage between banks and department stores. The first sentence in the lead article decried:

> Although for years the catastrophic dangers of bank capital bound racially with the Jewish department stores (which threaten our economic life) have been made known by responsible people, nothing in the slightest has been done through taxes or administrative measures to prevent the unrestrained spreading of the destruction of innumerable lives.[59]

It then provided the example that although Karstadt had sales of 231.5 million in 1927, the conglomerate offered a "correspondingly small dividend of 6 million RM." A second, front-paged article posed the rhetorical question: "Do department stores and bank palaces serve the welfare of the people or much more the money bag of international Jews?"[60] However the fourth edition in the sequence attacked Hjalmar Schacht's salary of 310,000 RM as president of the Reichsbank and also his provision of loans for recently constructed department stores and the Epa Single-Priced stores.[61]

With the fifth and final installment in the succession, the accusations reached their pinnacle in the headline: "Ritual Murder: Department Stores and Large Banks Butcher German Economic Life." The Deutsche Bank, the Karstadt and Tietz department store chains, and the Republican government, all came under assault for destroying the German economy:

> Besides the large banks only the department stores operate with vast profits . . . department stores and large banks have not undergone displacement in the ownership of their share capital. Department stores' and large banks' capital are, remain and will be combined in the hands of fewer Jews (such as Wassermann, Salomonsohn, Karstadt, Tietz, etc). But the remaining actual German economy will deteriorate, become desolate and will vanish through the systematic fleecing until the state of financial anemia. . . . Can a genuine Government accept responsibility to nurse department stores and banks back to health?[62]

5. Continuity of Anti-Department Store Legislation

The final special department store issue of *Der Angriff* had appeared on March 5, 1929, but Nazi agitation against the large chains had not ceased. A shrill headline at the end of 1930, drew a parallel between young people working in the department stores and the medieval peasants' drudgery in providing compulsory agricultural labor for a feudal lord. In using the old German term "fronen," Goebbels claimed that governmental authorities had allowed a large Jewish department store in Berlin to hire children "in order to arrange Christmas sales as cheaply as possible." Three days later the newspaper announced that the Parliament in Braunschweig had decided to increase the tax on department stores by 300 percent since the large retailers were practically the sole businesses, which had good sales. The article threatened that where National Socialists enjoyed power, they would strongly engage against the forces of capital.[63] But there were also non-Nazi conservative forces engaged in protecting German shop owners from the loss of sales by department stores.

In a March 13, 1933 letter to Hans Lammers, Joachim Tiburtius pleaded for a period of undisturbed activity for German retailers, since retail sales were a "characterizing barometer of the entire economy." On the grounds that the Hauptgemeinschaft des Deutschen Einzelhandels (Main Association of German Retailers) comprised 670,000 independent German businessmen and almost that many white-collar employees, Tiburtius requested a meeting for a delegation from the Hauptgemeinschaft with Adolf Hitler as soon as possible. Archival records indicate that the Hauptgemeinschaft wanted to demonstrate its support for the draft version of what later became the May 12, 1933 Law for the Protection of Retail Trade. Through the Law, the Hauptgemeinschaft wanted to ensure their protection against the increasing competition from large retailers and from further transition in retail trade, since their figures evidenced that total retail sales from 1929 through 1932 had fallen 36 percent, whereas the total costs had merely declined by 20 percent. The continuity of anti-department store policies between the Weimar Republic and the Third Reich was expressed via several corroborating factors. First and foremost was the extension of the December 23, 1932 Emergency Ordinance's ban against constructing any large retail building. The legislation from 1932 had originally prohibited any further construction until April 1, 1934, but before the Hauptgemeinschaft's March 13 correspondence, amendments were filed with the Reichsrat, Parliament's "upper house," which sought a continuation of the ban.

Joachim Tiburtius's compilation of complaints to be brought to the attention of Hitler included new marketing approaches utilized by department stores:

> Advertisement must be free of misleading statements and exaggerations. Enticing low price come-ons and bonuses must be abolished. Special events and close-out sales must be limited in order to be able to maintain a steady, low price range in the regular course of business.[64]

Nazi courtship of conservative businessmen was evident in Goebbels's front-paged cartoon in which a German stared into the sky at balloons labeled as "end of season sale," "linens week," as well as "Christmas, Easter and Pentecost sales." The caption to the pen-and-ink drawing was "Blinding work—Germans, how long will you still fall for it?" The message was repeated four months later in another front-paged caricature in which a multistory building had the word "advertisement" printed between the display windows of every story, while an obese man had the store names "Wertheim, Tietz, Karstadt" emblazoned with a Star of David on his chest. The March 18, 1929 edition of *Der Angriff* printed a lampoon, making the anti-advertisement intent even clearer. One individual was reading the liberal Ullstein newspaper *Berliner Morgenpost*, which advertised the end-of-season sale; while a second was perusing the Socialist's *Vorwärts*, which was emblazoned with Tietz's special sale; and a third was absorbed with the Communists' *Die Rote Fahne*, which mentioned linen week prices. The caption claimed, "Middle class coins build the palaces of department store capital."[65]

The Hauptgemeinschaft paralleled themes found in *Der Angriff* through its desire for a unification with the Chamber of Commerce in order that "its powers against outsiders" would be strengthened. Both the conservative Hauptgemeinschaft and the Nazis desired that retail competition be "cleansed," although the non-Nazi perspective often feared that a large marketing budget would sway the public to the giant stores.[66] In contrast, the term "cleansing" meant for Goebbels the replacement of German-Jewish businessmen by "native" Germans with supposedly pure heritage and culture:

> The next issue of the *Angriff* will fight against the department stores. . . . Think again and again that Jews have abused their rights as guests and not only oppress and cheat Germans, but also destroy our brothers, the German businessmen. Indeed, the Jewish department stores put Christmas trees in their display windows, but love for the festival of Christmas remains banished. Ensure that our department store issue penetrates everywhere and comes to the right hands and enlightens. Not a penny for the department stores, but every support for the German businessman.[67]

Another sphere in which the Hauptgemeinschaft's tenets were similar to National Socialism was in the significance, which smaller German retailers placed on a sales apprenticeship. Tiburtius continued:

> Persons, who are technically or morally unfit for an apprenticeship, must be withdrawn from this privilege. The retail trade along with the white-collar associations will bring about an Agreement concerning the Law Regarding Vocational Training, which is now being drafted. A legal action to exclude from commercial activity will be carried out against those businessmen, who stubbornly contravene the rules of good professional practices.[68]

Goebbels had protested that Tietz attempted to interest girls, before graduation from school, to become saleswomen. The attraction lay in the fact that a wage of 40 RM could be earned, without completing an unpaid apprenticeship.[69]

A final continuity between the Hauptgemeinschaft and *Der Angriff* was the Association's claim that small, family-operated retailers sold quality merchandise in contrast with department stores and other large retailers. Tiburtius's Angst induced him to falsely conclude that low prices offered by the chains could only be the result of selling second-rate merchandise:

> If the retail trade is to fulfill its task of delivering inexpensive and useful merchandise in the long run, it must be protected by the public sector from unreasonable competition through consumer associations, factory stores as well as peddlers.[70]

Goebbels had often made the accusation that department stores were no different than Oriental bazaars in which the buyer had to be cautious of being deceived:

> The department store Jews enticed dumb Gentiles by means of screaming advertisements to Christmas junk in the palaces of money. . . . Each Tietz palace ruins hundreds of small merchants and artisans. One does not buy more inexpensively at Jewish department stores, but worse than at specialty shops. The department stores are an imitation of the Oriental bazaars with much junk, stimuli and items of poor taste.[71]

Although *Der Angriff* frequently employed the same language as Joachim Tiburtius did, their motivations were different. As president of the Hauptgemeinschaft, Tiburtius's intent was to eliminate "immoral" marketing techniques. In contrast, Goebbels's goal was to eliminate any role for Jewish businessmen in the German economy. Tiburtius's reaction to the introduction of advertising, close-out sales and bonus items opposed the marketing campaigns of both Jewish and Gentile large retailers. His aversion impacted both the Jewish Hermann Tietz and the non-Jewish Karstadt chains. His objection was not motivated by anti-Semitism. This elucidates his placement on the right side of the five-stage perpetrator graph presented at the conclusion of chapter 3, section A (table 4.1).

A progressive radicalization of the Hauptgemeinschaft des Deutschen Einzelhandels can be traced, beginning with the preparations for the November 15, 1932 retail association's general assembly. This development in Tiburtius's organization will be traced in chapter 5, section A. But before the discussion of the exclusion of department stores from retailers' umbrella organization, the study will examine businesses' greater dependence on

Table 4.1 Twelve Wealthiest Prussians, 1912

Name	*Jew or Gentile?*	*Assets in millions of RM*	*Income in millions of RM*
Bertha Krupp von Bohlen	Gentile	187	17
Prince Hendel von Donnersmark	Gentile	177	12
Christian Kraft Prince of Hohenlohe–Oehringen	Gentile	151	7
Baron Max von Goldschmidt–Rothschild	Jew	107	3–4
Hans Heinrich XV Prince of Pleß	Gentile	84	1.9
Hans Ulrich Earl of Schaffgotsch	Gentile	79	4–5
Baroness Mathilde von Rothschild	Jew	76	2–3
Eduard Beit von Speyer	Jew	76	2–3
Franz-Hubert Earl Tiele-Winckler	Gentile	74	3–4
Engelbert Duke of Arenberg	Gentile	59	2.6
Earl Franz von Ballestrem	Gentile	56	2-3
August Thyssen	Gentile	53	2.6

Source: Kurt Zielenziger obtained this data from Page 1 of Rudolf Martin's, *Jahrbuch des Vermögens und Einkommens der Millionäre in Preußen,* which was published in Berlin in 1912.

financial institutions during this period of economic uncertainty as depicted by Kurt Zielenziger.

6. Weakened Status of German-Jewish Business Forced Greater Reliance on Banks

Financial information on German-Jewish businessmen from the late 1920s through the early 1930s often stems from Kurt Zielenziger's accounts. After earning a doctorate in economics in 1912, he became the economic editor for the *Vossischen Zeitung* in 1926. During the 1920s, he also contributed feature-length articles to the Centralverein deutscher Staatsbürger jüdischen Glaubens's newspaper. Thereafter, he composed a volume of twenty-one Jewish entrepreneurs at the pinnacle of German business, including Oscar Tietz. In response to the völkisch movement's campaign against department stores, Zielenziger maintained that the Jewish middle class had been "doomed to destruction" because of World War I and its consequences. Although Jewish entrepreneurs had held a dominating position in metal, grain and textile trades, the wartime economy had benefited industry and large-scale agriculture. Inflation meant the demise of those who were unable to flee into tangible property, namely the Jewish middle class involved in the free professions. Although all businessmen were confronted by limited cash due to their "patriotic" losses in investments in government bonds, this most seriously affected those circles in marketing, which required a rapid circulation of cash.[72]

These successful Berlin Jewish businessmen lived along Berlin's elegant Kurfürstendamm, whereas their proletarian brothers lived near the

Alexanderplatz. Contrasting developments in these disparate neighborhoods allowed Zielenziger to forecast the results of the occupational data contained in the not-yet released June 1925 Census. On the basis of the number of previous Jewish employers, residing in the Kurfürstendamm, who were forced to become white-collar workers as well as the numerous Jewish women, who were currently "forced to work in offices and accounting bureaus in order to contribute to the subsistence of their families," Zielenziger claimed the "downfall of the Jewish middle class."

Beyond Zielenziger's decline of Berlin's middle class was the dissipation of Jewish multimillionaires. Utilizing Rudolf Martin's published data from 1912 regarding the twelve Prussians with assets of more than 50 million RM, the editorial staff supported Zielenziger's prior articles by printing the names of the non-Jewish industrialists Bertha Krupp and August Thyssen and seven estate owners. Only three Jewish names appeared on the list of the dozen wealthiest Germans, including two Rothschild family members and the banker Eduard Beit von Speyer of Lazard Speyer-Ellisen.[73]

After Goebbels had published his fourth anti-department store edition of *Der Angriff*, during Christmas 1928, Zielenziger responded to the anti-Jewish economic agitation provoked by this recent retail innovation:

> But with the development of the department stores, a lively trend immediately was deployed against it. The middle class, retailers and artisans felt their existence threatened and called for the State's help. The anti-Semitic movement fomented this battle. . . . It is not a new thought, when the Völkisch today believe they perceive in the department stores the mortal enemy of the middle class.[74]

Zielenziger continued that with the printing of a völkisch pamphlet entitled *Shun the Department Store*, he recognized that "once again the ghost of a Boycott arose . . . [and] here it is the task of the Centralverein to resort to counter-measures."[75]

Three weeks later the Jewish newspaper assumed the challenge issued by Zielenziger through both the print media and the courtroom. Rabbi Felix

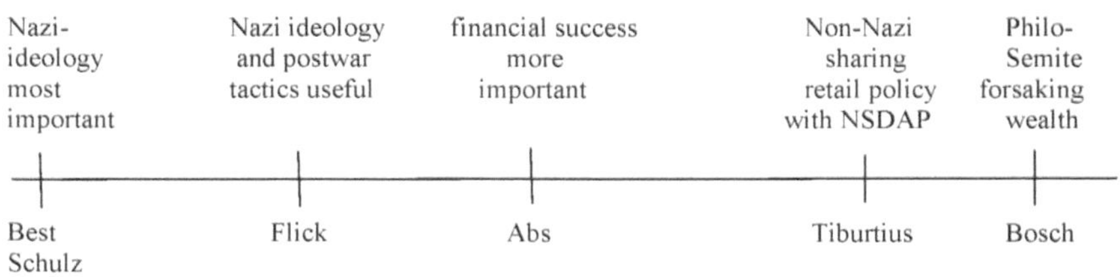

Goldmann affirmed that department stores, large banks and industrial cartels were merely the result of "modern economic development" and therefore had nothing to do with religious preferences. Although the article's author was a Rabbi in Leipzig, rather than an economist or businessman, he maintained that the economic trend had adversely affected the Jewish middle class more than the Gentile competition. Jewish business culture had supported the perspective that a small business owner had a greater earning potential, than a white-collar employee in the same sector. But after World War I, the small Jewish private banker was the first entrepreneur to observe the tendency that his stand-alone bank was purchased by a larger enterprise as one of numerous branches. In order to avoid premature retirement, the former owner of a financial institution discovered that "where he has found a job, he is an officer with strictly prescribed powers and with a modest outlook for the future." Although first witnessed in the banking sector, this progression was also occurring in retail with the result that "the number of economically independent Jews will become ever smaller." The adults within the Centralverein allowed the younger generation to propose solutions to this structural change in the economy in a March 8, 1929 supplement to their newspaper. One of the four young adult respondents suggested that Jews preparing for a profession should consider mid-level civil service, since it was "one of the most solid pillars" of German society.[76]

After mourning that no year since 1923 was as filled with adversity as 1929 had been, Kurt Zielenziger surveyed the disaster in sectors of heavy Jewish involvement, such as the insolvencies of private banks and the permanent closing of doors in the textile and ready-made clothing industries resulting from high taxes, reparations and the lack of capital. The beginning of the new year of 1930 was also an opportune moment to update the verdicts in cases of boycotts against Jewish shops and department stores. The judgments in Bochum, Augsburg, Aachen and Hamm prohibited not only the boycott per se but also appeals for such actions through fliers, placards and newspapers.[77]

But the annual publication of the Centralverein's legal successes against local boycotts did not result in a universal interpretation of the courtroom victories. The front-paged optimism by Ludwig Holländer in the January 2, 1931 edition was followed one week later by Günther Stein's pessimistic perspective. In part, Stein's views were molded by Marxist ideology whereby he claimed that those "who designate today's worldwide economic crisis as the consequence of the war, makes things too easy. We live in a crisis period of capitalism." In addition, he maintained that the fate of Jews would be much worse than non-Jews, since they would clearly suffer higher levels of penury and distress.[78] The Zionists did not accept the Centralverein's program of serving all German-Jews, since they doubted whether the average blue-collar employee would read the detailed essays in the *C.V. Zeitung* and be swayed by logical arguments, rather than the attention-grabbing cartoons of *Der Angriff*.

More fruitful for contemporary research than a Communist interpretation of capitalism is the connection between the banks and the department stores. Max Warburg assessed that the primary event, which derailed Europe and America was the 1931 collapse of Austria's Creditanstalt. The loss of over one billion Schillings was interpreted by the Jewish banker as an alarm for banks throughout the world. As is well-known, less than two months after the bank's collapse, Germany's largest textile company, Norddeutsche Wollkämmerei und Kammgarnspinnerei, failed and the gigantic brewery, Schultheiß-Patzenhofer and also the Darmstädter- and Nationalbank were on the edge of bankruptcy. But one of Warburg's memoir greatest contributions was his correlation of a little-known fact. The non-Jewish Karstadt chain also suffered enormously because of the bank failure.[79] Chapter 5 will expand upon the theme of the interdependency of banks and department stores by detailing how an individual such as Georg Karg was able to enlist the support of a banking consortium to recall a loan, enabling him to purchase the Hermann Tietz conglomerate for a pittance.

NOTES

1. Alfred Marcus, *Die wirtschaftliche Krise des deutschen Juden; Eine soziologische Untersuchung* (Berlin: Verlag von Georg Stilke, 1931), p. v-31.
2. Marcus, *Die wirtschaftliche Krise*, pp. 143–160.
3. Although I accept the explanation that fixed prices and payment in cash were strategic in promoting the growth of Oscar's shop, Kaufhof's official company history rejects the claim that these were "revolutionary" innovations, because they were simultaneously "discovered" by other businessmen and moreover are insufficient to account for the spurt in development. Despite having traced these breakthroughs back to 1852 when the world's first department store was opened by Aristide Boucicaut in Paris, the historians writing Kaufhof's history suggest that flexibility, a readiness to innovate, diligence, farsightedness, and the ability to analyze were the cause for Kaufhof's original growth by Oscar's older brother Leonhard Tietz. See Bernd Heimbüchel, Alexander Kierdorf, Stefan Pohl, and Caludia Teichner, *Erlebniswelt Kaufhof; Ein Warenhaus in Deutschland* (Köln: Wienand Verlag, 2001), p. 9.
4. Georg Tietz, *Hermann Tietz; Geschichte einer Familie und ihrer Warenhäuser* (Stuttgart: Deutsche Verlags-Anstalt, 1965), pp. 19–25.
5. Andreas Wagner, "Martin Mutschmann; Der braune Gaufürst (1935–45)," in Mike Schmeitzner and Andreas Wagner (Eds.), *Von Macht und Ohnmacht; Sächsische Ministerpräsidenten im Zeitalter der Extreme 1919–1952* (Beucha: Sax-Verlag, 2006), pp. 279–281. Also see Agatha Kobuch, "Mutschmann Martin," *Neue Deutsche Bigraphie*. Achtzehnter Band (Berlin: Duncker & Humblot, 1996), p. 659.

6. Tietz, *Hermann Tietz; Geschichte*, pp. 30–33.

7. Tietz, *Hermann Tietz; Geschichte*, pp. 39–40.

8. Unfortunately, Georg Tietz's family memoir merely records that the year-end inventory (in which he was present) occurred on a Sunday. However, the only years on which December 31 fell on a Sunday include three possibilities: 1893, 1899, or 1905. Having been born on January 10, 1889, Georg would not yet have been five years of age in 1893, but would almost have been eleven years old in 1899 and nearly seventeen in 1905. Being a few days shy of his fifth birthday appears too early for his involvement in the store. Working in the store at age eleven appears more reasonable. In addition, Georg's account suggests that Hermann protected Georg during the disturbances. Although Hermann lived until May 3, 1907, and thus the inventory could have been conducted on December 31, 1905, Georg would have been almost seventeen years old and presumably would have been looking after his sixty-eight-year-old great uncle. Furthermore, Georg's narrative records a department store tax occurring about the same time as the scuffle during inventory. Representative Lutz submitted a petition in 1895 to the Bavarian Parliament, requesting a revision of the May 19, 1881, Tax Code with regarding to department stores and branches of businesses. The first House of the Diet approved the measure on November 15, 1895, with the second Chamber concurring on January 29, 1896. This Bavarian department store tax legislation would support the identification of 1889 as the year in which the melee occurred. See Johannes Wernicke's section "Die gegen die Warenhäuser geforderten Abwehrmittel" in *Kapitalismus und Mittelstandspolitik* (Jena: Verlag von Gustav Fischer, 1907), pp. 628–629.

9. In describing the occasion, in which he was present, Georg Tietz used the expression "Radaubrüder" and not anti-Semite or member of a right-wing political party.

10. The beer garden was founded in 1812, but received its current name in 1880 after Joseph Wagner, the owner of the Augustiner brewery, purchased the garden. It has apparently not changed its layout since 1896, when it apparently contained 5,000 seats.

11. Tietz, *Hermann Tietz; Geschichte*, pp. 44–45.

12. Tietz, *Hermann Tietz; Geschichte*, pp. 16–17, 45–46.

13. Kathleen Canning, *Languages of Labor and Gender: Female Factory Work in Germany, 1850–1914* (Ithaca: University of Michigan Press, 2002).

14. Erich Glier, *Die sächsische Spitzen- und Stickereiindustrie seit 1914. Niedergang und Existenzkampf einer deutschen Mode- und Exportindustrie* (Plauen: Franz Neupert G.m.b.H, 1932), pp. 24–25.

15. Tietz, *Hermann Tietz; Geschichte*, pp. 136–138.

16. Heimbüchel, Kierdorf, Pohl, and Teichner, *Erlebniswelt Kaufhof*, p. 86.

17. J. A. Hill, "Taxes on Department Stores," *The Quarterly Journal of Economics*, Vol. 15, No. 2 (February, 1901), pp. 299–303.

18. In a later decade, when Jewish board members were excluded from Gentile department stores, it was specifically mentioned that Rudolf Karstadt and Thomas Althoff had originated in "old Christian families from Mecklenburg," in "Aufsichtsratsveränderungen bei Karstadt," *Vossische Zeitung* (April 1, 1933), p. 11.

19. Uwe Spiekermann, "Der Mittelstand stirbt! Der Kampf zwischen mittelständischem Einzelhandel und Warenhäusern in Deutschland 1890–1933," in Godela Weiss-Sussex and Ulrike Zitzlsperger (Eds.), *Das Berliner Warenhaus; Geschichte und Diskurse/The Berlin Department Store; History and Discourse* (Frankfurt am Main: Peter Lang GmbH, 2013), p. 43.

20. With the symbol "*M*," I am intending the Goldmark, which was replaced with the Papiermark as Germany left the gold standard on August 4, 1914. By this nomenclature, I intend to address the question of how to assess the value of real estate and buildings constructed with Goldmarks, but later held to be financially vulnerable and seized in hostile takeovers when fixed assets were valued in Reichmarks.

21. Spiekermann, *Berliner Warenhaus*, pp. 61–63.

22. Colze, *Berliner Warenhäuser* (Berlin: Fannei und Walz, 1989), pp. 8–9, 13.

23. *50 Jahre*, p. 106.

24. Johannes Wernicke, "Warenhaus, Industrie und Mittelstand," *Rechts- und Staatswissenschaftliche Studien*, Heft XLIV (1911), p. 17.

25. Hans-Ulrich Wehler, *Deutsche Gesellschaftsgeschichte. Von der "Deutschen Doppelrevolution" bis zum Beginn des Ersten Weltkrieges. 1849–1914* (München: Verlag C.H. Beck, 1995), p. x.

26. The pattern of Germany's three largest banks withdrawing loans previously extended to a Jewish-owned firm in order that the financial institution would earn a commission or become the sole provider of services is central to this inspection's theory of how Aryanizations occurred. In this pre–World War I instance, the Deutsche Bank would have become the depository bank for all shares of Hermann Tietz. Thereby, the financial institution would have been entitled to place one of its executives on the Tietz Supervisory Board and to vote all shares remaining in its vault.

27. Tietz, *Hermann Tietz; Geschichte*, pp. 139–145.

28. Dieter Ziegler, "Die Aufsichtsräte der deutschen Aktiengesellschaften in den zwanziger Jahren. Eine empirische Untersuchung zum Problem der Bankenmacht," *Zeitschrift für Unternehmensgeschichte/Journal of Business History*, Vol. 43, No. 2 (1998), pp. 200–201.

29. Tietz, *Hermann Tietz; Geschichte*, pp. 146–151. Also see Harry Gordon Selfridge, "Selling Selfridge; Some Random Reflections of an American Merchant in London," *The Saturday Evening Post*, Vol. 208, No 10 (September 7, 1935), p. 90.

30. Years after the conclusion of World War I, Selfridge still exuded an international spirit. He confessed in a popular memoir that his cosmopolitan vision had risen when as a junior partner he paid his own way to determine whether Marshall Field's department store could expand to the capitals of Britain, Germany, France, Russia, and Spain. Mr. Fields rejected the proposal to increase his retail scope, which in Selfridge's opinion was due to his unwillingness to incur risks. Selfridge's ambition drove him to sell his share in the partnership and operate the Schlesinger and Mayer store in competition with Marshall Field's for ninety days. He sold his newly acquired business for a quarter of a million dollar profit and two years later contemplated purchasing Marshall Field's. Selfridge approached J.P. Morgan Bank in New York about a loan to fund the cash acquisition, which would include ten million

dollars for goodwill. But Field's sudden death ended Selfridge's plans. The advent of subways and automobiles in England caused Selfridge to challenge "the staid old stores of London." As the building was being erected on Oxford Street, its Greek façade was wryly equated with the British Museum. Selfridge later added that if his enterprise been a financial failure in London, he would have sought retail success in Paris or Berlin. Another illustration of his international perspective was observable in a publicity event four months after his store opened. The French aviator Louis Bleriot was the first to fly across the English Channel in a competition hosted by the *Daily Mail*. Selfridge offered £200 to the newspaper, if the monoplane could be showcased in his building. During the course of the following four days, 120,000 people came to the store to view the airplane. But similar to the opposition faced by the Tietz family in Germany, the smaller shop owners in the Marylebone area "were hostile in the extreme," fearing that "a large new store in their midst would ruin many of them." Selfridge recollected that a British newspaper editor added words reminiscent of opposition in the Reich that the department store was "an impertinent intrusion on honest British shopkeepers who had difficulty enough in making ends meet, without having to face the blatant, bombastic and circuslike methods of an American interloper named Selfridge." See the four-part series: Harry Gordon Selfridge, "Selling Selfridge," pp. 16–53; Vol. 208, No. 6 (August 10, 1935), pp. 18–70, Vol. 208, No. 8 (August 24, 1935), pp. 26–68, and Vol. 208, No. 10 (September 7, 1935), pp. 16–53.

31. Tietz, *Hermann Tietz; Geschichte*, pp. 157–164.

32. Tietz, *Hermann Tietz; Geschichte*, pp. 166–167.

33. Tietz, *Hermann Tietz; Geschichte*, pp. 168–172.

34. Enver Pasha entered World War I on the side of Germany, because of Turkey's traditional animosity with Russia. Britain theorized that it could achieve two goals simultaneously through a massive assault in the Dardanelles. The plan was to eliminate Turkey from the war and resupply Russia. But the British underestimated the fighting power of Turkey in battles at Gallipoli in which the Turks lost 300,000 soldiers and the British lost 265,000. On January 9, 1916, the British completed the evacuation of their small beachhead. The Turkish army continued the Gallipoli victory by repulsing Major General Charles Townshend from Ctesiphon in November 1915 and then forcing him to surrender with 10,000 men on April 29, 1916. A third reverse for the Allies was inflicted in the spring of 1918 upon British General L.C. Dunsterville, when he attempted to deny Baku's oil to Germany and Turkey. Instead, he was driven out by the Turkish army in September 1918. Both Britain and Germany had underrated the Turkish military, leading Georg Tietz and other German businessmen to quickly sell their assets in the Ottoman Empire. See John Keegan, *The First World War* (New York: Alfred A. Knopf, 1999), pp. 234–249, 300–301, and 383–385.

35. Georg Tietz's ill-received attempt to deliver bad news regarding the state of World War I to Kaiser Wilhelm II requires some background information on the monarch's personality. Currently, there are three scholarly perspectives regarding how the Kaiser's difficult personality affected German foreign policy. Professor Emeritus John Röhl of the University of Sussex held that the Kaiser appointed like-minded Conservative officials, who implemented his will. Isabel Hull, Professor at

Cornell University, proposed a more caustic interpretation by concluding that the truth could never be communicated to Wilhelm. It had to be couched in a comforting manner. Wolfgang J. Mommsen, former Director of the German Historical Institute in London, offered a mediating theory that only selected newspaper reports could be delivered to the monarch, but because he wanted to be popular with his subjects, the coverage "carried enormous weight with him." All three academic viewpoints contain the element that the Kaiser did not have any tolerance for foreign policy views conflicting with his own. See Wolfgang J. Mommsen, "Kaiser Wilhelm II and German Politics," *Journal of Contemporary History*, Vol. 25, No. 2/3 (May–June 1990), pp. 295–296.

36. Tietz, *Hermann Tietz; Geschichte*, pp. 177–182.

37. Belinda J. Davis, *Home Fires Burning: Food Politics, and Everyday Life in World War I Berlin* (Chapel Hill: University of North Carolina Press, 2000).

38. Tietz, *Hermann Tietz; Geschichte*, pp. 184–193.

39. See David Oels (Ed.), *Der ganze Verlag ist einfach eine Bonbonniere: Ullstein in der ersten Hälfte des 20. Jahrhundert*s (Berlin: Walter de Gruyter, 2014.)

40. Tietz, *Hermann Tietz; Geschichte*, pp. 194–197.

41. Tietz, *Hermann Tietz; Geschichte*, pp. 198–202.

42. Joerg Baten and Rainer Schulz, "Making profits in wartime: corporate profits, inequality, and GDP in Germany during the First World War," *The Economic History Review*, Vol. 58, No. 1 (February 2005), pp. 35–44.

43. Daniel Siemens, "Die SA und der nationalsozialistische Mythos vom Kampf um Berlin," in Michael Wildt and Christoph Kreutzmüller (Eds.), *Berlin 1933–1945* (München: Siedler Verlag, 2013), pp. 34–38.

44. "Steuerhinterziehungen Berliner Warenhäuser," *Der Angriff*, No. 24 (December 12, 1927).

45. "Tietz muß keine Steuern zahlen," *Der Angriff*, No. 24 (December 12, 1927).

46. "Das Christkind bei Tietz," *Der Angriff*, No. 24 (December 12, 1927).

47. Rare outbursts of an economic nature can be found in Goebbels's December 5, 1925, frenzy in Hamburg: "German industry and the German spirit for business was exploited by Jews." Oddly, there was no further explosion for several years. In fact, the next diary eruption on January 4, 1930, was also occasioned by a prior attack against President Paul von Hindenburg in the December 29, 1929, *Angriff*. However, it is unclear whether Goebbels published comment should be interpreted financially: "Mr. Hindenburg will do here what he has done in similar previous cases through the interventions of his Jewish and Marxist advisors." The third economically oriented diary entry within this fifty-month period occurred on February 10, 1930, when Goebbels ironically appeared to provide a positive retail assessment when the ladies in Melitta Wiedemann's coffee circle proposed establishing a consumer organization and Goebbels was in complete agreement. See Ralf Georg Reuth, *Joseph Goebbels Tagebücher 1924–1945*. Band I. Erweiterte Sonderausgabe, 2. Auflage (München: Piper Verlag GmbH, 2000), p. 209; Band II 441, p. 458.

48. Internal squabbles within the NSDAP received far more attention in the private sphere of Goebbels diary. In the same fifty-month period, Goebbels maintained in his December 18, 1925, diary entry that Gregor Straßer's plan was inadequate and Gau leaders meeting in Bamberg concurred by rejecting Straßer's socialism in favor of Hitler's plan of leaving private property in the hands of business owners. Similarly, Goebbels confided in his February 24, 1926, entry that the camarilla around Hitler in Munich would diligently agitate, forcing Goebbels to submit to Hitler's concessions to Straßer on August 25, 1926. Nevertheless, by September 23, 1926, Straßer had become "excessively jealous" of Goebbels. By June 22, 1928, Goebbels had concluded that Otto Straßer was the Satan of the National Socialist movement and must be destroyed at any cost. He had become a "rotten capitalist" and his "star was fading." On August 24, 1928, Goebbels acknowledged that he had many enemies in Munich and by December 6, 1928, perceived that Otto Straßer hated him. He therefore evinced no sympathy on August 28, 1929, when Straßer was sentenced to six months imprisonment. Goebbels himself appeared to summarize the numerous diary entries by commenting on October 16, 1929, that he had been maintaining for years that Straßer was a "traitor." Earlier on June 12, 1926, the focus of Goebbels's criticism had expanded to Karl Kaufmann's laziness, which caused the Gau of Berlin to become a pigpen. This required Goebbels to assumed responsibility for Berlin on a temporary basis on August 27, 1926. Walther Stennes joined the list of competing Nazi officials, who incurred Goebbels's wrath in the confidentiality of his diary. On November 5, 1929, he disclosed that Stennes's rebellion must be "eradicated" and within a few weeks that Heinrich Himmler was "fickle" and that Alfred Rosenberg was behind the plot to make *Der Angriff* a poor copy of the *Völkische Beobachter.* Even Hitler was not exempt from Goebbels's private criticism, being accused on January 29, 1930, of indecisiveness with regard to Goebbels's media battle with the Straßers. By February 16, 1930, Goebbels lamented that Hitler's inability to make a decision had led to anarchy. After the appearance of Straßer's newspaper in Berlin on March 1, 1930, Goebbels resigned, provoking Hitler's fury. On March 5, 1930, Goebbels bemoaned: "If only we had a goal-oriented, strict leadership! But instead? Poor Hitler!" See Reuth, *Joseph Goebbels,* Band I. 212, 228, 253, 272–273, 278, 301, 303, 307, 314, 339, 399, 415, 423, 428; Band II 452, 459, 465–467.

49. The caption to a cartoon in the interior of the December 12, 1927, edition of *Der Angriff* claimed: "Der Christus ans Kreuz schlagen ließ, macht heute mit dem Christfest seinen Reibach!" The massive German dictionary directed the reader from "Reibach" to "Rebbach," where the reader was instructed that the word originated in the Yiddish language. See Gerhard Wahrig, *Deutsches Worterbuch.* Völlig überarbeitete Neuausgabe (München: Mosaik Verlag, 1984), p. 3006. This is confirmed in the Yiddish language, where "revekh" means "profit." See Uriel Weinreich, *Modern English-Yiddish / Yiddish-English Dictionary* (New York: Schocken Books, 1977), 408.

50. Reuth, *Joseph Goebbels*, pp. 284–285, 291–292, 295.

51. Admittedly, these circulation figures might have been exaggerated in Goebbels's September 23 and September 25, 1928, diary entries and they also refer to the special Dawes Plan edition of *Der Angriff.* In contrast, the admission of only 200

paid subscriptions in the November 4, 1928, entry seems small. See Reuth, *Joseph Goebbels*, pp. 319–320, 330.

52. Oscar Tietz founded the Verband Deutscher Waren- und Kaufhäuser as a professional association for department store owners in 1903. This book will use the translation of "Association," in order to differentiate it from a second organization, which Oscar played a role in initiating, namely the Hauptgemeinschaft des Deutschen Einzelhandels. The second organization was much larger, representing even the smallest of retailers. Ironically, the Hauptgemeinschaft turned against the department stores, a theme addressed in the conclusion of this chapter and the beginning of chapter 5.

53. "Kriminalbeamte als Weinachtsengel," *Der Angriff*, Number 26 (December 26, 1927). "Kampf gegen Unmoral – 'grober Unfug'," *Der Angriff*, Number 26 (December 26, 1927); "Der Staatsanwalt für Tietz A.G.," *Der Angriff* (February 20, 1928).

54. "Die Selbstverurteilung der Rassenjustiz," *Der Angriff* (June 11, 1928).

55. Reuth, *Joseph Goebbels*, 296, 300, 307, 332. As frequently as the volume's pages appear to indicate Goebbels's need for legal protection, based on his Reichstag immunity, they fail to indicate that other NSDAP Members of Parliament required protection due to their illicit behavior far more frequently. Thus, the Centralverein deutscher Staatsbürger jüdischen Glaubens newspaper reported: "There are 209 pending criminal proceedings against National Socialist Representatives in the Reichstag. In the majority of cases it concerns public defamations in rallies or in the press. At the forefront is the Editor of the *Völkischen Beobachter* Representative [Walter] Buch against whom 36 proceedings are pending. Gregor Straßer 27 proceedings for offences against the Law for the Protection of the Republic; Ludwig Münchmeyer 24 trials; and Erich Koch fron Königsberg 23; Joseph Goebbels 16; and against Gottfried Feder 12." "Der Mißbrauch der Pressefreiheit; Zum Vorgehen des Reichstages," *C.V. Zeitung*, Vol. X, No. 7 (February 13, 1931), p. 70.

56. "Dem Warenhaus keinen Pfennig!" *Der Angriff* (December 3, 1928); and "Das Weihnachtsgeschäft der Warenhäuser," *Der Angriff* (December 10, 1928).

57. "Ochse, siehste Wertheim nicht?" *Der Angriff* (December 12, 1927).

58. "Warenhäusler versklaven deutsche Arbeitskraft," *Der Angriff* (February 20, 1928).

59. "Sechs Millionen Reichsmark Dividende!" *Der Angriff* (June 11, 1928), p. 1.

60. "Sechs Millionen Reichsmark Dividende!" and "Warenhaus und Bankpalast," *Der Angriff* (June 11, 1928).

61. "Was macht Herr Schacht mit dem Geld?" *Der Angriff* (December 10, 1928).

62. "Ritualmord! Warenhäuser und Großbanken schächten das deutsche Wirtschaftsleben," *Der Angriff* (March 18, 1929).

63. "Kinder fronen im Warenhaus," *Der Angriff* (December 24, 1930), p. 1. For the feudal understanding of "Frondienst," see Wahrig, *Worterbuch*, 1386. Also see "Warenhäuser werden Besteuert. Braunschweig voran!," *Der Angriff* (December 27, 1930).

64. Joachim Tiburtius, "Grundlagen zur Unterrichtung über den deutschen Einzelhandel," in BA R 43 II/370, 2.

65. "Blendwerk," *Der Angriff*, Number 8 (February 20, 1928), p. 1. "Deutsche Kaufmann! Das Warenhaus ruiniert Dich!" *Der Angriff*, Number 24 (June 11, 1928), p. 1. "Mittelstandsgroschen bauen Paläste des Warenhauskapitals," *Der Angriff*, Number 11 (March 18, 1929).

66. BA R 43 II/370.

67. "Dem Warenhaus keinen Pfennig!," *Der Angriff*, Number 49 (December 3, 1928).

68. BA R 43 II/370, p. 3.

69. "Warenhaus—Allerlei," *Der Angriff*, Number 50 (December 10, 1928).

70. BA R 43 II/370, p. 3.

71. "Der Staatsanwalt für Tietz A.G.," *Der Angriff*, Number 8 (February 20, 1928), p. 1.

72. Kurt Zielenziger, "Der Untergang des jüdischen Mittelstandes," *C.V. Zeitung*, Vol. IV, No. 46 (November 13, 1925), p. 729.

73. Kurt Zielenziger, "Die reichsten Leute der Welt; Schwerindustire und Großgrundbesitzer," *C.V. Zeitung*, Vol. IV, No. 50 (December 11, 1925), p. 784.

74. Kurt Zielenziger, "Das Warenhaus," *C.V. Zeitung*, Vol. VII, No. 50 (December 14, 1928), p. 701.

75. Zielenziger, Das Warenhaus, pp. 701–702.

76. Felix Goldmann, "Das Warenhaus; Was wird aus dem jüdischen Mittelstand?" *C.V. Zeitung*, Vol. VIII, No. 1 (January 4, 1929), pp. 5–6. Ernst Wolff, "Ueberwindung der Berufsnot," *Von deutsch-jüdischer Jugend*, Vol. 5, No. 3 (March 8, 1929).

77. Kurt Zielenziger, "Bilanz der Wirtschaft," *C.V. Zeitung*, Vol. IX, No. 1 (January 3, 1930), pp. 1–2. Also see "Wichtige Entscheidungen zum Kampf gegen den Wirtschaftsboycott," *C.V. Zeitung*, Vol. IX, No. 3 (January 17, 1930), p. 26; and "Wichtige Entscheidung im Kampf gegen den Wirtschaftsboycott," *C.V. Zeitung*, Vol. IX, No. 6 (February 7, 1930), p. 63.

78. Compare Ludwig Holländer, "Täuschungen und Entäuschungen," *C.V. Zeitung*, Vol. X, No. 1 (January 2, 1931), p. 1 with Günther Stein, "Wege aus der Krise?; Die Arbeitslosigkeit und das Schicksal der Juden," *C.V. Zeitung*, Vol. A, No. 2 (January 9, 1931), pp. 9–10.

79. Max Warburg, *Aus meinen Aufzeichnungen* (Glückstadt: J.J. Augustin, 1952), p. 142.

Chapter 5

Aryanization of Hermann Tietz

A. SUPPORTING STRANDS OF EVIDENCE FOR HERMANN TIETZ'S ARYANIZATION

In the previous chapter, agreement was demonstrated between the Hauptgemeinschaft and Goebbels's *Der Angriff* during the period from December 1928 through December 1930. A similar anti-department store sentiment is evident through the liberal *Vossische Zeitung*'s coverage of the smaller retailers during the timeframe from November 1932 through May 1933. By examining the fear of large enterprises by middle-class shopkeepers in the *Vossische Zeitung*, conservative religious views of the economy can be separated from Goebbels's anti-Semitism.

As early as November 2, 1932, the liberal newspaper warned that in the coming days, the Hauptgemeinschaft would be expressing opinions regarding the "battle between large and small companies, which had split the profession into two hostile camps." The broadsheet forecast that if the November 15 General Assembly excluded department stores from its membership, the organization would lose its supervisory character and would be transformed into an alliance fighting for the middle class. But the newspaper was not hopeful that reason would prevail over southern German retailers, whose combative mood primarily arose from competition caused by consumers' declining purchasing power as well as the explosion in new outlets typified by one Ruhr chain, which expanded from 3 to 165 branches in the preceding six years. The newspaper expressed hope in Wendelin Hecht's study about small independent shops uniting to share the costs of purchasing and advertising. With uniform accounting, banks would lend to such alliances more readily. By November 8, the General Assembly's Agenda had been fixed with the morning being a closed session and the afternoon entailing a speech by Minister of the Economy Hermann Warmbold and the concluding address by Board Member Joachim Tiburtius. Days before the Assembly, efforts were underway to avoid either the resignation or exclusion of the large companies. However, it was recognized that regional retail societies were more influenced by politics than the larger nationwide organization.[1]

"An astonishing majority" of mid- and small-sized retailers balloted in the November 15 closed session in support of shoe stores' proposal for a special tax on large companies. Feelings of ill-will, caused by the 134 to 71 vote, occasioned an immediate meeting of the Presidency of the Association of Department Stores (Verband Deutscher Waren- und Kaufhäuser) although no final decision was reached. Instead, a committee from within the Hauptgemeinschaft was entrusted with drafting a new constitution before the next General Assembly in the beginning of 1933.[2]

Finance Minister Warmbold represented conservative Elbian agricultural interests and was not a NSDAP member. His afternoon address attempted to mollify the smaller retailers' combative spirit by declaring that the economic crisis had begun to brighten. He affirmed that an increase in the bond rates was an essential sign of the recovery of German capital market. He appealed to retailers to comply with the government's stimulation program and thereby to counteract declining sales. He declared that small bank loans had recently become more resilient than loans to big businesses. The newspaper depicted Joachim Tiburtius's final oration as a "captivating appeal" in which he portrayed the creation of retail laws as an "historical task." He pled for "trustful cooperation" in unraveling the tensions. But hopes for reconciliation were dashed as hours later the department store coalition communicated to the Haupgemeinschaft that the "gross injury" committed in the Assembly no longer made "fruitful cooperation" possible.[3] One of the cofounders of the Hauptgemeinschaft was Heinrich Grünfeld,[4] who shortly thereafter announced that he would not run for another term because of declining health. But this rationale was a polite way of expressing his lack of physical strength to oppose the belligerent members from southern Germany. The newspaper inferred that "recent events in the Hauptgemeinschaft were especially painful." This conclusion coincided with an understanding that anti-modernism within Warmbold's agrarian perspective and religious views of a cooperative economy within Tiburtius' viewpoint had become insufficient to contentious members of the Hauptgemeinschaft. This interpretation is supported by the quick succession of Hauptgemeinschaft Directors from Grünfeld to Tiburtius to Paul Hilland within the span of months from the end of 1932 through the beginning of 1933. Older conservative morality-based executives, such as Grünfeld and Tiburtius, were unable to coexist with radical regional members demanding a new constitution, such as Hilland.[5]

Formulating a new constitution must have entailed new stresses after the departure of the Association of Department Stores as well as the Association of Food Chains, because four drafts were required following the General Assembly in November. Nevertheless, the centralization of power was clear as the number of executive members was reduced from six to four.[6]

Retailers' opposition to department stores was one factor enabling Georg Karg to acquire the Hermann Tietz department store chain. In addition to further newspaper articles, there are four other strands of evidence, which indicate how Georg Karg, a non-anti-Semitic colleague acquired the firm. The documentation regarding the Aryanization, which occurred in early July of 1933 includes the June 23, 1933 Cabinet debate regarding a failed loan attempt to aid the Tietz Company; the Deutsche Bank and M. M. Warburg Bank's notes regarding the extending of the private sector's Loan I for 5,758,000 RM and Loan II for 8,742,000 RM effective July 15, 1933, which enabled the Aryanization; the Centralverein's legal attempts to reinstate terminated Tietz employees and the later oral testimony by the son of one of the Jewish partners.

It is ironic that Adolf Hitler came to power in part through the enfeeblement of the Weimar Republic, caused by bickering political parties incapable of forming compromises. Yet, the first strand of evidence commences with a summary of the June 23, 1933 meeting at the Reich Chancellery[7] involving an unresolved dispute between Wolfgang Reichardt, a director in the Ministry of the Economy and Hjalmar Schacht, president of the Reichbank, documenting a failed loan attempting to assist the Tietz chain.[8] In a non-agenda item, Reichardt raised the issue of a financial intervention on behalf of the Hermann Tietz Department Store Conglomerate, which had fallen into "financial difficulty" due to strongly declining sales. On the basis of its 17,450 employees and having paid 12.5 million RM in taxes in addition to 2 million in social welfare benefits, the Ministry of the Economy called for a bailout. Debts to suppliers could not be paid nor had new orders been placed with industry. Nevertheless, Reichardt had evaluated that the firm was financially sound with assets exceeding liabilities and the situation being a temporary problem in which an 11 million RM loan was needed to pay for the merchandise. Reichardt claimed that the Akzeptbank was prepared to organize a private consortium of banks, if the Reichsbank would approve. Thus, he implied that the Reichsbank apparently wanted to know if the government was in agreement.

Perhaps as either an added inducement or an indication of how paltry Tietz's need was, Reichardt added that the indebtedness of other department stores to the banks totaled 750 million RM, which provided employment to an estimated 60,000 to 70,000 people. He further conjectured that if Tietz was allowed to enter bankruptcy, then there existed the danger that other chains would follow suit occasioning the destruction of large fortunes. Thus, he held it as a requisite that the government consented to the loan of 11 million RM, for which there would be sufficient Tietz collateral. But the government would need to declare that its intent was not "to smash department stores to pieces."

It must have taken either great courage or extreme folly to speak for the ambitious Reichbank's president during an official cabinet meeting in which he was present.[9] Hjalmar Schacht retorted that he was unaware that the Bank had approved the loan. He not only would be unable to take a position on the extension of credit until after the department store question had been settled, but he also doubted that the requested loan would be assured.

Minister of the Economy Alfred Hugenberg attempted to restore amiable relations by observing that in the interests of the middle class, an expansion of department stores had to be prevented, although the destruction of existing business concerns would be disadvantageous for the overall German economy.

Although the archival document from the cabinet meeting specified the following as a statement of the Chancellor, perhaps it was understood that Hitler's spokesman had expressed it since this utterance did not end all discussion.[10] In contrast, any statement by Hitler would have brought immediate resolution to the Reichardt versus Schacht disagreement. The chancellor's representative expressed that the department stores' heavy indebtedness of 750 million had existed for a year and thus he came to the conclusion that they were not viable. In the long run, they were not capable of being renovated. If one were to help at the present time, then the same emergency could reoccur in six months or a year. In addition, Dr. Reichardt's reference to the situation of the department stores within the German economy would not change anything. All interventions would merely postpone the catastrophe.

Viewing the previous paragraph as the utterance of either Rudolf Heß or Hans Lammers, instead of Adolf Hitler, makes Schacht's rejoinder that the department store problem should have been resolved a long time ago easier to comprehend. Even as few as five months after Hitler's ascension, it appears inconceivable that Schacht would have corrected Hitler's "error," that the difficulty in the department stores had existed for eighteen months, rather than the actual six. Hjalmar concluded that he was not in a position to decide on Tietz's fate during the cabinet meeting, whereupon Heß or Lammers retorted that what was being decided was the consequences of a possible financial collapse, since the previous government should have conducted a proper economic policy. The banks would have extended large loans from an improper economic basis. The minutes concluded that no decision was reached, but an addendum requested that objections be submitted within twenty-four hours.[11]

That very evening Schacht penned his opposition to Hans Lammers, State Secretary in the Chancellery, stating that the granting of a loan in support of Tietz was secondary to resolving the middle-class issue of department stores, which had become bound up with the völkisch point of view. The Ministry of the Economy was responsible for allowing this topic to come to a crisis, by not solving it in the last year and a half. An assured economic foundation had to be established before loans could be granted. However, the central government in Berlin appeared reticent to adopt any decisive action with regard to the department store, which paralleled its refusal to adopt any tax on department stores or other large retailers,[12] although it allowed each individual state to double its tax on such sales chains.[13]

The Reich Chancellery's hesitance to take action against Jewish-owned department stores was due to the existing unemployment of 4.8 million Germans. Schacht's protest to Lammers regarding the Akzeptbank's and Reichbank's intent to approve an 11 million RM loan provided a brief window of opportunity for Georg Karg. Simultaneous with his employment with Tietz, he developed a secret association with Helmut Friedel of the Dresdner Bank's subsidiary, Bankhaus Hardy. By July 15, 1933, Karg had implemented a solution to the central government's impasse. Instead of an 11 million loan endorsed by the Akzeptbank and the Reichbank, Karg had arranged a "reorganization" of Hermann Tietz's management. In this "win-win" situation, the Berlin government would benefit through an Aryanization without incurring any financial burden. Instead Karg's employment with Bankhaus Hardy had led to Loan I of 5,758,000 RM and Loan II of 8,742,000 RM to stabilize the department store chain as it became a non-Jewish company. The banking consortium granting Loan I and II was benefited by consolidating existing lines of credit as well as earning new commissions and fees. In addition, the financial institutions curried favor with the government by preserving jobs while transforming a Jewish firm into an Aryan company. Karg prospered by becoming a Tietz partner by investing only 50,000 RM of his own funds. Hugo Zwillenberg was immediately terminated as one of the partners, the Tietz brothers were coerced to assume all liabilities and soon thereafter Karg became the sole owner of the conglomerate. The central government, the banks and Karg had all benefited at the Tietz's expense.

Six articles published by the *Vossische Zeitung* from July 15–29, 1933, indicate that although the public might not have known of the cabinet's failed June 23 attempt to provide an 11 million RM loan to assist the Tietz stores, it was aware that by July 15 a banking consortium had provided an amount between 13 and 14.5 million RM to Aryanize the company. The newspaper extolled the banks for exercising financial acumen in preserving jobs and outstanding loans by "reorganizing" the Tietz Company under non-Jewish management. The Saturday morning edition of July 15 presented the situation as a fait accompli in which a "reorganization, assured the continuation of the business on a more economic basis." The evening edition used the term "modification," and reported that the negotiations had been "protracted," with corporate banks, private banks, mortgage institutions and especially the large circle of merchandisers extending credit. Thereafter, the broadsheet mentioned the theme of preserving 15,000 employee jobs and the short-term credit of nearly 20,000 merchandisers. Had the Tietz takeover been unsuccessful, the paper was concerned that hundreds of small- to mid-sized suppliers would have been in trouble. The publication notified the public by July 15 that this was an Aryanization since some representatives of the lenders would become partners in the company, notably with special voting rights. The Garantie- und Akzeptbank had organized the private banks and mortgage institutions to raise a loan of approximately 13 million RM on the basis that non-Jews would direct Hermann Tietz.

Within days, the *Vossische Zeitung* added statistics from Gustav Stolper's *Deutsche Volkswirt* regarding the decline in Tietz sales. The data appears beyond reproach, since not only was Stolper a Jewish economist, but his publication attracted contributions from such notable financial forecasters as Joseph Schumpeter and Friedrich August von Hayek. The *Voss* cited Stolper as reporting that Tietz had its highest sales of 300 million in 1923, but a decade later had only half the revenues. In 1932, the department store had ordered only 91.54 million RM from industry and merely 40.28 million RM from agriculture. Moreover, acquiring the Jandorf stores brought mortgage debt to approximately 100 million RM.[14] However, the reader should be cautioned that the *Vossische Zeitung* was receiving much of its information from the journal produced by the Reichsverband der Mittel- und Großbetriebe des Deutschen Einzelhandels, one of the department stores chief adversaries. More significantly, the reader is left uncertain how to interpret the data since the key factor of the correlation between a store's purchases and its sales is unknown. If the Hermann Tietz's mark-up had been 10 percent, then 1932 sales would have been 145 million RM with a gross profit of 13.18 million RM. Additionally, the reader faced the additional problem of not being informed of Tietz's operating costs in order to subtract them from gross profits to determine net profitability.

Post–World War II access to private Tietz accounting records in the Bundesarchiv provides insider information unavailable to the Vossische Zeitung's readership in 1933. A translated July 15, 1933 Profit and Loss Statement is provided in Table 5.1, indicating that the imagined profit margin of 10 percent was too high. After subtracting Tietz's operating costs of payroll, rent, taxes, and write-downs of 29.0 million RM, the net profit was 2.6 million RM.

Simone Ladwig-Winters interpreted the demise of Jewish ownership of Hermann Tietz as a result of too hasty expansion in the number of branches.

Table 5.1 Hermann Tietz Profit and Loss Statement, July 15, 1933

Debits		*Credits*	
Salaries and hourly wages	12,407,249.52	Profit from inventory	25,329,279.86
Social benefits	913,554.54	Profit from exchanging foreign currency	6,345,412.55
Write-downs on plant	566,116.08		
Other write-downs	867,178.82		
Provision for pensions and other responsibilities	400,000.00		
Interest owed	1,621,625.38		
Taxes	1,757,606.52		
Rent	4,457,805.24		
All other costs	6,046,020.62		
Net profit	2,637,535.69		
Total	**31,674,692.41**	**Gross profit**	**31,674,692.41**

Note: I have translated the accounting terms from the Bundesarchiv's document R8119F 15211, Microfiche 6, Document #199.

But contrasting the Tietz brothers' modest profit with the situation of wholesalers in related markets indicates that the Jewish owners' positive returns was very favorable in a German market in which costs had exceeded sales for five years. For Georg and Martin Tietz, to share a 2.6 million RM profit with Hugo Zwillenberg would not make any of the three Jewish co-owners wealthy enough to join the twelve most financially endowed Prussians in Table 4.1 of this investigation. Nevertheless, German wholesalers, carrying the same categories of merchandise as department stores, had been unable to earn a profit for years (Table 5.2).

Although many of the insider details are not reported in the *Vossische Zeitung*, it did specify that at the time of the variously announced 13 to 14.5 million RM loan, personnel changes were initiated. First and foremost, the family-owned and operated company was transformed into a limited

Table 5.2 1932 German Wholesalers' Circumstances in Contrast with 1928

Wholesale Industry	*Sales (%)*	*Costs (%)*	*Level of Inventory (%)*
Food	86.3	84.2	63.5
Tobacco	76.0	83.4	67.0
Textiles	45.0	65.0	40.0
Fabric for clothing	29.5	42.9	27.8
Tailors' products	45.0	78.0	55–60
Yarn	15.0	27.0	12.0
Bicycle and automobile needs	75.0	90.0	80.0
Pharmaceuticals	62.1	67.1	50.0

Source: I translated the newspaper article "Elastischer Großhandel; Eine Fünf-Jahres-Bilanz," from Page 11 of the morning edition of the *Vossische Zeitung*.

liability company, to be known as Hermann Tietz and Company. This signified that the new non-Jewish owners would not be responsible for the company's debts. Second, one of the three personally liable Jewish partners, Dr. Hugo Zwillenberg, was retired immediately. He was being replaced on the Board by the managing director of the newly created Hertie Department Stores as well as a trustee of the financial institutions. Although mentioning Zwillenberg by name, neither the identities of the new managing director nor the new trustee were specified in the newspaper, a pattern of secrecy maintained even decades later during Germany's postwar economic recovery. There appeared to be a cover-up surrounding the new ownership. Fortunately, the correspondence behind the negotiations has preserved the identity of the non-Jewish Director as Georg Karg and the Trustee as Trabant Reichsfreiherr von und zu der Tann-Rathsamhausen. Third, the broadsheet mentioned that Hertie was assured the decisive influence in Hermann Tietz, as well as the cooperation of the retained "Aryan professionals" in the company.[15] Georg Karg's simultaneous employment with both Tietz and Bankhaus Hardy had long preceded the *Voss*'s July 15 announcement of the Aryanization. The financial and personnel arrangements must have been negotiated prior to mid-July. It is possible that the sudden retirement of Hugo Zwillenberg on July 15 should be linked with the previous terminations of Hans Apfel and other Tietz employees, discussed in section E of this chapter. Karg's cost-savings benefited from NSBO opposition to Jewish employees in Tietz.

During the period of the hostile takeover of Hermann Tietz, Walter Spiecker, president of the Reichverband der deutschen Mittel- und Großbetriebe des deutschen Einzelhandels, often tried to urge the government to speedier and more extreme measures against department stores. Reich Commissar for the Economy Otto Wagener had called for the closure of all semi-autonomous craft operations in department stores by October 1, 1933. However, he allowed for extensions as well as exceptions. Mid-sized and large retailers in the private sector were ahead of the central Nazi government in their opposition to department stores and their use of subcontractors. The professional organization was dissatisfied that the government measure would not be effective in June 1933. Thus, Spiecker was forced to plead with Reichverband Members in their publication *Überblick* to comply with the government's proposals and he was compelled to explain that the closures would affect only those craftsmen producing new items and not those making repairs. Spiecker sought to reassure members that the planned sales tax would not affect them, but on the other hand a proposed tax of up to 10 percent of department stores' sales would be an impossible burden since leading department stores in a good year showed net profits of less than 4 percent.[16] Such a tax proposed from the retail sector would have a "strangling effect" on department stores and already it was obvious that the mere prospect brought the larger retail chains insecurity. In addition, a comprehensive special tax could lead to price increases necessitating a restriction on consumption by 90 percent of consumers, which would void the mid-sized and large retailers' victory over department stores. Thus, lawmakers decided in June 1933 to delay the implementation of a department store tax.[17]

However, the government's attempt to postpone the restriction of special services within department stores as well as the special tax on such large retailers succumbed to pressure from the private sector long before the lawmakers' target date of October 1. Both the sales tax and dispensing of prepared food already crept back into the public debate by July 15. An amendment was made to the May 12, 1933 Law for the Protection of the Retail Trade, whereby regional officials were empowered to withdraw permission to dispense alcoholic beverages or prepared foods, which would have been enjoyed in the premises of a department store. The action was granted, if the liquor and food "needs were no longer present" and with their exclusion, the business as a whole would not be endangered. On the same day, it was reported that if regional taxes were being increased, then local administrators were also authorized to increase department stores' taxes, up to a maximum of twice the then current amount. Later in July, when the legislation was published, it was announced that the new government impositions on department stores would be retroactive to April 1.[18] Hermann Tietz's cash flow would have been adversely affected by the doubling of its taxes, based on the amount of its sales.

In July when Minister of the Economy Kurt Schmitt returned to the issue of independent subcontractors practicing their craft within department stores, he cast a broad sweep on artisanal products including bread, baked goods, pastries, upholstery, wallpaper, shoe repair, eyeglasses, furs, furniture, watch repair, automobile repair, bicycle repair and hair styling. The cutoff point was moved earlier from October 1 to September 1. But because every job was important in the combat against unemployment, the newspaper editorialized that no one was considering destroying department stores, although such establishments had lost some of their financial advantage against other retailers. However, the newspaper commented that the actions at Hermann Tietz clearly showed that the department stores' situation had become difficult during the crisis years. The publication assessed that the large chains were no longer able to exist without outside assistance, but nevertheless they were not left to their fate. Legal measures had hindered provinces and communities from taxing them to such an extent that their continued existence would be endangered. The paper surmised that the present tax could at a maximum be doubled and although the effect would be noticeable, it would not be fatal. The Law for the Protection of the Retail Trade may well have limited department stores' expansion, but the newspaper conjectured that without the branches, they would continue to exist. The article moralized that in the future, these large retailers should offer no more competition to small, stand-alone artisans by eliminating their in-house butchers, bakers, repair service experts, hair stylists and photographers. The editorial had mentioned that department stores had numerous enemies, but had the *Vossische Zeitung* become one of them? Had the *Voss* lost its role as the gem within the Ullstein Publishing House's unbiased reporting as early as July 1933? Enduring the greater tax, while losing the numerous crafts within its facilities was a two-fold blow against Hermann Tietz's cash flow.[19]

In contrast, the publication appeared to boast about the performance of smaller specialty shops in comparison with the department stores. The article's subtitle praised that there was a "shift in sales," whereby Table 5.3 indicated less of a decline among smaller shops.

Although Table 5.3 indicated that the rate of sales in department stores was declining faster than for other retailers in 1933, prior newspaper coverage had made two caveats. First, the years of crisis had inflicted wounds on smaller retailers, which possessed limited financial strength. To add inventory, both small and large merchants were reliant on outside capital. Second, since credit worthiness had improved, the number of small retailers' insolvencies had diminished with a peak of more than 500 per month in 1931 being reduced to approximately 150 at the beginning of 1933. In addition, the number of settlement procedures with creditors had been reduced from more than 400 to far below 100.[20] Thus, the claim that protective measures had brought a shift in sales from department stores to smaller specialty shops must be tempered by the decline in small retail competition.

Although Goebbels had allowed the *Vossische Zeitung* to continue publication, because of its large foreign readership, perhaps this indicates that the editors had to phrase the truth very cautiously to avoid complete censorship. What had not been explicitly stated was that retailers' slower declining sales rates, than those of department stores, had been achieved at the expense of hundreds of small businesses becoming bankrupt. Only by combining this positive interpretation from July with a negative February dispatch does an accurate picture emerge. There had been 40,000 German retailers who discontinued payments during the 1928 through 1931 period. Even in such a

Table 5.3 Reduction in Sales for January–May 1933 Compared to 1932

	Total Retail (%)	*Department Stores (%)*
Total sales	10.5	16.7
Groceries	7.5	19.5
Textiles and clothing	10.3	15.7

Source: I translated the article "Konsolidierung im Einzelhandel; Preis—Tiefstand überwunden—Verlagerung der Umsätze," from Page 9 of the evening edition of the July 20, 1933, *Vossische Zeitung*.

bleak public pronouncement that there had been 5,300 insolvencies in 1928 and approximately 10,000 in 1931, the fact that the number had fallen to 8,700 in 1932 was construed to mean that "overall in Germany the crisis has burned itself out."[21]

In the face of high unemployment, job creation was the federal government's primary concern. Weakening department store sales enabled local governments to maintain the majority of tens of thousands of positions in the Jewish concerns, with the majority of the large retailers reducing their staff by only 4–10 percent. Simultaneously, the central government aided the middle class by adding thousands of employment opportunities.[22] The loss of 140 positions in the largest of retail chains was more than compensated by creating tens of thousands of jobs. Two strands of evidence support this elucidation. First, the tax on department stores became the responsibility of state governments with Hesse implementing the measure, but the larger state of Prussia declined to authorize any legislation. Second, the formation of employment opportunities had already been a massive public program during the Republic. On December 15, 1932, President Paul von Hindenburg had authorized 500 million RM for the inception of new business positions. In addition, Chancellor Heinrich Brüning had recognized the need for the state to fund commercial shipbuilding and had made 12 million RM available. Director Franz Stapelfeldt of the Deutsche Schiff- und Maschinenbau AG intended to add to the workforce by modernizing the merchant marine through a reduced interest loan from abroad. Erwin Fuchs, the Head of the Civil Engineering Department for the City of Berlin, issued an extensive job creation program to keep 20,000 civil engineering workers employed for years building streets, bridges and water works. In addition, the federal government had decided to extend the weekly unemployment allowances beyond April 1, 1933, until further notice. Large sums were also expended on rearmament as evidenced by President Paul von Hindenburg's April 1, 1933 congratulatory telegram to Hermann von Fischel, Captain of the recently constructed battleship "Deutschland." German unemployment had been so successfully combated that tax vouchers, which had been granted to companies via a September 4, 1932 Ordinance to stimulate additional hiring, were suspended by new legislation on April 7, 1933.[23]

One might have expected that seasonal employment due to Christmas, the end of winter season closeout sale, or the linen week sale, would have diminished unemployment. However, such retail factors appeared to have no effect on those needing jobs. Nevertheless, an overall declining trend in German unemployment appeared as shown in Table 5.4.

When June 1933 department store data became available via the Reichsverband der Mittel- und Großbetriebe des deutschen Einzelhandels, the theme of sales shifting from department stores to specialty shops was

Table 5.4 Declining Trend in German Unemployment

Date	*Total Unemployment*
October 1932	5,109,000
November 1932	5,358,000
December 1932	5,773,000
January 1933	6,014,000
February 1933	6,001,000
March 1933	5,598,000
April 1933	5,331,000
May 1933	5,000,000
June 1933	4,850,000

Source: I translated the article "Weitere Entlastung des Arbeitsmarktes; Von Mitte bis Ende Juni 121000 Arbeitslose weniger," from Page 3 of the morning edition of the July 3, 1933, *Vossische Zeitung*.

emphasized by the *Voss* in an extensive article. For ease of understanding, the data is summarized in Table 5.5. There were several factors contributing to the continued decline in department store sales, including the ongoing boycott, the closure of refreshment rooms and the elimination of crafts and repairs. But the volatile issue of a special department store tax, which had been postponed in June of 1933 was adopted by some states in August for firms with sales greater than 400,000 RM.[24]

One must now ask the question regarding how well the newspaper's data on department stores coincided with Hermann Tietz's internal accounting. At the time of the hostile takeover, Georg Tietz along with his brother Martin and brother-in-law Hugo Zwillenberg were required to produce a July 15, 1933, Balance Sheet and a Profit and Loss Statement. A translation into English of the assets and liabilities reveals some issues (see Table 5.6).

Table 5.5 Transfer of Sales from Department Stores to Specialty Stores, June 1933

	June 1933 Decline from 1932 (%)	*May 1933 Decline from 1932 (%)*	*Specialty Store Change from 1932 (%)*
Textiles and clothing	19.8	18.3	1.8 (increase)
Haberdashery	23.2	3.5	
Shoes	20.2	25.7	
Women's clothing	6.0	16.6	
Men's clothing	9.3	17.5	
Groceries	28.0	25.9	3.1 (decrease)
Household goods	25.3	10.8	
Total sales in RM	22.2	19.7	
Number of transactions	15.6		
Incoming merchandise	18.3	9.5	

Source: I translated the article "Warenhausumsatz im Juni; 22.2 v.H. unter Vorjahrshöhe," from page 11 of the morning edition of the August 5, 1933, issue of the *Vossische Zeitung*.

Table 5.6 Balance Sheet Prepared by Jewish Partners, July 15, 1933

Assets in RM		*Liabilities in RM*	
Property, plant, equipment	16,880,000.00	Withholding, including taxes	2,679,185.37
Conglomerate equity	18,624,899.40	Debt on merchandise	20,302,152.61
Property interests	10,000.00	Liabilities to subsidiaries	18,084,076.69
Merchandise	24,300,000.00	Other accounts payable	4,936,844.61
Stocks and bonds	1,655,756.72	Bills of exchange payable	761,887.97
Active mortgages	697,606.77	Bank debts	46,933,574.27
Mortgage custodian account	21,350,000.00	Open obligations	1,913,992.42
Accounts receivable	2,789,469.78	Owner's equity: Martin Tietz	516,311.77
Accounts receivable to corporate subsidiaries	7,490,509.95	Owner's equity: Georg Tietz	100,000.00
Cash	872,038.79	Owner's equity: Hugo Zwillenberg	108,253.82
Banks and post office checking accounts	501,256.63	Owner's equity: Betty Tietz	643,617.04
Prepaid accruals	1,808,358.53	Eventual obligations from guarantees (not in total)	55,000,000.00
Right of recourse from guarantees (not in total)	55,000,000.00	Eventual obligations from exchange (not in total)	225,000.00
Right of recourse from exchange obligations (not in total)	225,000.00		
Total	**96,979,896.57**	**Total**	**96,979,896.57**

Source: I have translated the accounting terminology in the Bundesarchiv financial statement R8119F 15211, Microfiche #6, Document #201.

Three aspects of the Balance Sheet immediately demand attention. First, the "Right of Recourse" in the Asset side of the ledger is not a customary accounting term, so its meaning is unclear. It is also exactly balanced by the "Eventual Obligations" in the liability side, which is also unusual. But since these figures are not included in the 96.9 million RM total, it does not appear to be a means of subterfuge although it is certainly a non-standard bookkeeping practice.

A second observation is the indebtedness to the banks of 46.9 million RM. This indicates that Hermann Tietz had unusually high liabilities in comparison with the size of the company. The unusual factor presumably arose from constructing large facilities on choice real estate in the downtown areas of Berlin, Munich, Hamburg, Stuttgart, Karlsruhe, and other metropolitan areas. But a compensating factor was that Hermann Tietz had 21.3 million RM in a custodian account, specifically to pay for the mortgages and these were presumably to be repaid only during the course of twenty years. However, at the beginning of this chapter, it was noted that the *Vossische Zeitung* had reported that Tietz's mortgage debt had been about 100 million RM in 1926, when it had acquired the Jandorf chain. It is inconceivable that Tietz could have repaid 53 million RM in mortgage debt in seven years, thus the high level of indebtedness claimed by the newspaper is rejected.

Third, obligations of 20.3 million RM for merchandise appear disconcerting, despite the existence of a merchandise account for 24.3 million RM to offset this debt. The reason for the anxiety is that the Christmas 1932 sale as well as the January 1933 end-of-season sale and the February 1933 white sale would have all transpired, leaving Hermann Tietz with 24.3 million RM in cash to pay for merchandise costing 20.3 million. Subtracting the two line items would have left the department store with only 4 million to purchase merchandise for the upcoming Christmas 1933 sale. Since Christmas was by far the largest retail transaction of the year, this results in the conclusion that Hermann Tietz was lacking in liquidity. The chain's new management would have required the large Loan I and Loan II from the private financial institutions to purchase holiday merchandise. Without the new loans, the reorganized conglomerate would have been vulnerable.

Since there is a direct correlation between net profit and the purchase price of a company, a presentation of the Profit and Loss Statement will await discussion of the new non-Jewish director, Georg Karg. From the current focus on internal weaknesses, the assessment will shift its concern to external problems.

B. MARCH 1933 ATTACK ON THE DEPARTMENT STORE ASSOCIATION

In the days leading up to the March 5, 1933, Reichstag election, Hermann Göring made the ridiculous claim that Germany's Communist Party had formed a team of up to 200 terrorists. Disguised by wearing SA uniforms, their task was allegedly to carry out "attacks on cars, department stores and shops." This distortion was insufficient to camouflage the ensuing offensive against the large retailers, especially since the police on occasion assisted the locally organized SA. On March 7, the police in Duisburg closed Leonhard Tietz's single-price store as well as the Woolworth. The central government in Berlin was being informed by the Chamber of Commerce and Industry that one could not count on the stores in the Essen area being reopened any time soon. In neighboring Bottrop, the local SA closed all Jewish stores on March 8 and about 5:00 p.m. the same activity occurred in Mühlheim. In contrast with these independently minded SA actions, the Gau leadership in Dusseldorf immediately took steps to prohibit the unauthorized events against department stores and single-price retailers. But in Magdeburg, the intervening police were too few in number and were pushed aside. Shots were fired in the Karstadt-owned Epa single-price store and in the ensuing hustle women and children were trampled to the ground. Criminal complaints were filed against four of the perpetrators. Some Berlin department stores and single-price stores were confronted with SA accosting customers, whereas others were forced to close. The police intervened on numerous occasions, in order to allow this category of large retailers to remain open.[25]

However in Göring's March 10 speech in Essen, he posed the rhetorical question: "When they say the populace is terribly inflamed because Jewish department stores are temporarily closed, is it not natural when Germans finally declare: 'Don't buy from Jews, rather from Germans!'" He concluded that he would "ruthlessly" employ the police, when the German people were harmed, but he rejected the notion that the police were "a protective force of Jewish department stores." The statement drew thunderous applause and may have encouraged civil disobedience in Hamburg, where the chief of police closed all department stores and single-price establishments because under the circumstances, he was unable to maintain law and order. In contrast, police in Leipzig guarded department stores and single-price establishments with rifles, although the display window of one department store was smashed. The most unusual situation transpired in a Gotha single-price store, where protesters suddenly began destroying merchandise and furnishings, although several perpetrators were arrested by the police. Hitler redirected his second-in-command and the SA by uniting two themes in a March 12 radio address. To calm SA violence, President von Hindenburg allowed the swastika flag to fly alongside the German flag on public buildings for three days. Hitler employed this concession as a symbol of the NSDAP victory and thus commanded all individual acts by the SA against businesses to cease.[26]

Gera was the town where Oscar and Hermann opened their first shop. It was also the location, where the reaction to the thriving Jewish retailers commenced. The Gera Retail Association voted to exclude all Jewish firms from its membership on March 21, 1933. In offering an explanation for the action, it was claimed that it was not due to the desire to exclude competition, but rather "the German middle class was defending itself against foreigners." On the following day, the Presidency of the Association of German Department Stores resigned and the new management was commissioned. One of the three new non-Jewish executives was Adolf Feldmann, the owner of a clothing store in Gotha, sixty miles west of Gera. He was joined by Fritz Jacobsen of Kiel, who was the proprietor of two department stores in Kiel and Dr. Willy Baier of Cologne.

The motive in forming a new Board was to wrest ownership not only of the Hermann Tietz stores from Georg Tietz and the Leonhard Tietz chain from Alfred Tietz, but also from other entrepreneurs including Salman Schocken and Moritz Ury. As both a member of the old and new Presidency, Jacobsen was able to coerce the other members to "submit to the decisions of the new management." By May 27, 1933, the new directorate had been expanded to six individuals. Jacobsen was demoted to Deputy President, allowing Walter Spiecker to wield the chief authority and Hans Krüger also to join the Board. Characteristically, Spiecker was later able to "purchase" Kaufhaus Landauer in Stuttgart.[27] The changing membership of the Department Store Association in March 1933 was followed by declining inventory in July 1933. SA violence perpetrated in March 1933 was restrained in July. Rather than being destroyed in the Spring of 1933, department stores were weakened enabling conservative businessmen to collaborate with conservative banks in assuming ownership of these giant retailers.

The financial frailty can be traced in the amount of Tietz funds available for marketing campaigns. The department store tried to counteract a decline in its customer base by attempting to coax consumers by means of large expenditures in display ads. In relation to other chains, Tietz may have spent less. Nevertheless, the promotional campaigns still allowed for entire pages in the newspapers.

C. TIETZ'S ADVERTISING AS AN INDICATOR OF RELATIVE FINANCIAL INSTABILITY

Hermann Tietz's advertising in the *Vossische Zeitung* implies a relative weakness in its cash flow vis-à-vis other chains. The *Vossische Zeitung* was Germany's oldest newspaper and held a literary, left-of-center editorial stance, somewhat akin to the *New York Times* or the *Washington Post* in the United States today. Unlike the *Times* or the *Post*, the German newspaper was in financial difficulties and heavily dependent on the display ads purchased by the department store chains. In fact, no other combination of companies including the car manufacturers Mercedes and Opel as well as the tire manufacturers such as Dunlop and Continental in addition to the electrical company AEG together advertised as heavily as one of the Berlin department stores such as Hermann Tietz, KaDeWe, Karstadt, Wertheim, Nathan Israel, or Leopold Gadiel. In an article referring to KaDeWe's innovation of adding a recipe to its announcement, the broadsheet acknowledged that department stores ran grocery advertisements every Friday. Although KaDeWe was the flagship store owned by Hermann Tietz, its marketing approach remained distinct from the parent company. In the ten Fridays between November 4, 1932, and January 6, 1933, Hermann Tietz did not employ any funds to market food, whereas KaDeWe paid for six ads and both the Karstadt and Wertheim department store chains purchased such marketing devices on all ten Fridays.[28]

The lack of financial outlays for merchandizing in the newspaper could be due to Tietz's problems in cash flow or else its concentration on the large sales of Christmas and January inventory closeouts. Thus, Tietz invested in four large Christmas ads between December 4 and 18, 1932, and KaDeWe purchased three, whereas rivaling department store Wertheim bought two and Karstadt only one. Even greater marketing expenditures were made for the inventory sales in which Hermann Tietz acquired the most newspaper exposure with four full pages on Sunday January 1 and one additional full page on January 8, 1933. Of all the other department stores, only Wertheim attempted to match such a capital outlay with two full pages on January 1 and one added page the following Sunday.

However enticing the department stores' marketing may have been, German consumers did not spend their scarce Reichmarks as heavily as the chains required in order to be financially solid. But to gain a better perspective on department stores' financial predicament, the newspaper observed that the entire ready-made clothing sector lamented that "despite initially favorable sales," transactions for non-custom-tailored clothing during the winter ended on "a discordant note." With inventory clothing sales not meeting department store expectation, the *Vossische Zeitung* reported that department stores were putting all their hopes on the February linen sales. Germans called it "white week." Another indication that the customer base had declined was the fact that "white week" extended from January 30 until as late as February 12, 1933. Not knowing the prices for different sized display ads, it is difficult to know whether Hermann Tietz outspent rival Wertheim. Wertheim began with presale advertisements on both January 27 and 28 followed by a full-paged promotion on January 29. In contrast, Hermann Tietz purchased no announcements prior to its two full pages on January 29. Tietz paid for three subsequent notices in a short February 1–5 time span, whereas Wertheim's budget allowed for four notices over the longer January 31–February 9 timeframe, with Nathan Israel being the sole department store seeking to squeeze final sales as late as February 12, 1933.

Both Tietz and Wertheim were featured in an article regarding "white week" in which it was reported that to keep from being blinded by the large quantities of white fabric, Tietz was also offering linens in delicate pink, lilac and blue. Adding to Tietz's stimulus for Berlin housewives to buy were the smooth tulle and glowing balls, hanging in the atrium, which the marketing executives hoped would inspire a true fairy tale aura. The newspaper concluded that stacks of every conceivable type of merchandise "enticed," prompting the rhetorical question of whether every woman would discover something "adorable" in Hermann Tietz. The following day, Tietz's premium store KaDeWe was featured in an article indicating that this business deviated from the traditionally promoted sheets, tablecloths and towels by offering children's underwear, women's lingerie, professional clothing and silk fabrics. Apparently, the departure from custom was effective, since the newspaper reported the strong crowds during the first morning of the sale. The departure from traditional sale merchandise was another tactic for the department store to woo customers back from specialty shops.

Although German economic histories typically portray the country as starting to climb out of the Great Depression before Hitler's ascension at the end of January 1933, the Reich Association of Men's and Children's Clothing lamented in February 1933 that members' sales for 1932 had decreased on average by 21.81 percent from 1931. Since the mainstays of the department stores were clothing, linens and groceries, one might have concluded that Hermann Tietz and the other Berlin department stores outperformed their retail competitors. This assessment is substantiated by the fact that declining sales occurred despite the fact that 94 percent of the smaller retailers allowed consumers to buy clothing on credit of between 6 percent and 30 percent. In contrast with the double-digit retail decline reported by the newspaper, entire department stores' sales for December 1932 lagged the prior December by only 9.9 percent and the November 1932 purchases declined from the previous year's sales by 9.3 percent.

The decrease was attributed to poor Christmas sales, but the newspaper analyzed that if sales were viewed by volume, rather than revenue, then the number of purchases could have been higher than the prior year since clothing prices were reduced by 16 percent and food by 12 percent.[29] Clothing wholesalers were worried about profitability, since:

> despite a substantive reduction in insolvency losses, the financial statements show that the leading men's and women's clothing businesses had unsatisfactory outcomes in the last year. As it is unanimously reported, the successful large businesses hardly earned more than business expenses, taxes and assessments for health benefits. The building of reserves . . . was not possible anywhere.[30]

Prices were a principal part of department store strategy. An analysis of Hermann Tietz prices over the period of time in which control of the company was lost indicates an upward trend, designed to offset the declining number of customers. For this investigation, I chose a basket of twelve grocery items, intentionally avoiding fruits and vegetables for which prices and availability would be affected by the season. In the first fourteen weeks, the most conspicuous factor is the consistent lack of prices for five or more items. This could reflect the fact that food wholesalers were unwilling to extend any further short-term credit to Hermann Tietz for grocery purchases. This would coincide with evidence from the balance sheet indicating that there was only 4 million RM in cash available for merchandise in all departments of every branch. Perhaps grocery wholesalers were unwilling to extend as much on credit as they had done in prior business years. Of the twelve items in Table 5.7, seven

Table 5.7 Hermann Tietz's Prices (in RM) Under Jewish Ownership

	Dates													
	2/17	*2/24*	*3/10*	*3/17*	*3/24*	*3/31*	*4/7*	*4/13*	*4/21*	*4/28*	*5/5*	*5/12*	*5/19*	*5/26*
Coffee/lb	1.90	1.90	1.90	1.90		1.90	1.90	1.90	1.90	1.90	1.90	1.90	1.90	1.90
Pork loin	0.66	0.72	0.68	0.68	0.68	0.68	0.72	0.70	0.68	0.68	0.72	0.70	0.70	0.64
Live carp	0.58	0.58	0.58	0.60	0.58	0.58	0.58	0.55	0.62	0.60	0.62	0.62	0.62	—
Roast beef	—	0.98	0.98	—	0.98	—	—	1.08	—	—	—	—	—	—
Pork belly	0.64	0.66	0.68	0.64	0.62	0.62	0.60	0.60	0.60	0.58	0.58	0.58	0.60	—
Beef roll	0.78	0.82	0.82	0.82	0.80	—	0.84	0.84	0.84	0.88	0.88	—	—	—
Veal club	0.56	0.64	0.56	0.54	0.58	0.68	0.68	0.70	0.64	0.64	0.64	0.64	0.68	0.68
Prosciutto	1.20	1.25	1.25	1.25	—	—	—	—	—	—	—	—	—	—
Kippers	0.17	0.17	0.16	0.18	0.18	—	0.24	—	—	—	—	—	—	0.22
Gouda	—	—	—	—	—	—	—	—	—	—	—	—	—	—
Cider/5 lt	3.00	—		3.00	—	—	—	—	—	—	—	—	3.00	—
Butter	1.12	1.12	1.14	1.12	1.12	1.12	1.12	—	1.14	1.16	1.16	1.28	1.48	1.48

Source: I have assembled price information from the February 17 through May 26, 1933, advertisements in the *Vossische Zeitung*.

components rise in price, including live carp, roast beef, beef roll, veal, prosciutto, kippers and butter.

Table 5.8 discloses two aspects of Georg Karg's marketing strategy. With the 14.5 million RM loan, he was able to procure prosciutto and kippers from prior vendors as well as introducing gouda and cider. However, the tactic of raising prices was maintained. The introduction of gouda and cider in these fourteen weeks may indicate the confluence of Hitler's ending of the revolution in July 1933 with the new non-Jewish director's assuaging of the anger of the SA. "Brown shirts" may no longer have prevented customers from entering the Aryan-managed Tietz stores.

In an attempt to halt the violence of the SA negatively affecting the German economy, Hitler started a massive public relations campaign. The Liberal *Vossische Zeitung* printed seven front-page articles in the period July 10–July 23, 1933, to declare that the revolution was completed and that unauthorized actions of the SA in the economy would be viewed as sabotage. But the Führer's marketing offensive was far more subtle than the June 30, 1934 Night of the Long Knives. Often it directly confronted only SA-appointed Commissars or NSBO shop stewards. On July 9, Hitler addressed 70,000 SA members in Dortmund and proclaimed that the political parties had been defeated. But he appealed to the SA to conduct itself with "iron discipline" so that two tasks could be accomplished: the training of the German people to become the bearers of new government reforms and to battle unemployment.

However, the specification of the SA's responsibilities in achieving these two goals remained for Hitler's subordinates to delineate. Interior Minister Wilhelm Frick stipulated in a newsletter to all Reich governors and state governments that Hitler's speech to the SA meant that the revolution was completed and had "entered its normal lawful construction phase." This stage would be endangered by a second revolution and anyone speaking in such terms "rebelled against the Führer." Such speech was "sabotage" against the government's solution of the unemployment problem and thereby harmed the German people. "Sabotage" was identified as "unauthorized interventions in the economy." Only the implementation of explicit decrees would be tolerated. Otherwise it was claimed that Communists might attempt to "sneak into" the NSBO or the Nazi labor union or some other organization and disturb the German economy.

Hitler must have recognized the magnitude of reining in the violence of the SA, because on July 12, 1933, he gave a second two-and-a-half-hour address in the Chancellery to the Gau leaders, Labor Trustees and Shop Stewards of the NSBO. Hitler affirmed that National Socialism "had conquered the land, but now it had to be cultivated in peace." The next speech in the daily campaign to end unauthorized acts of violence against the economy came from Minister of the Economy Kurt Schmitt on July 12. In addressing state

Table 5.8 Hermann Tietz Prices in Period of Hostile Takeover

	Dates													
	6/9	*6/16*	*6/23*	*6/30*	*7/7*	*7/14*	*7/21*	*7/28*	*8/4*	*8/11*	*8/18*	*8/25*	*9/1*	*9/8*
Coffee/lb	1.90	1.90	1.90	1.90	1.90	5 type	5 type	1.90	1.90	1.90	1.80	1.76	1.80	1.80
Pork loin	0.68	0.68	—	0.58	0.66	0.62	0.68	—	0.78	0.78	—	0.78	0.76	0.74
Live carp	—	—	—	—	—	—		—	—	—	—	—	—	—
Roast beef	0.98	—	—	—	—	0.98		—	—	—	—	—	—	—
Pork belly	0.60	0.58	0.58	0.48	0.60	0.58	0.60	0.66	0.68	0.70	0.68	0.68	0.68	0.68
Beef roll	—	—	—	—	—	—		—	—	—	—	—	—	0.88
Veal club	0.64	0.66	0.58	0.58	0.64	0.58	0.58	0.58	0.64	0.68	0.72	0.68	0.68	0.68
Prosciutto	1.24	1.24	1.18	1.18	1.18	1.18	1.18	1.18	1.20	1.20	1.20	1.25	1.25	1.28
Kippers	—	—	0.32	—	0.48	0.35	0.30	0.24	0.26	0.26	0.28	0.28	0.26	0.26
Gouda	—	0.70	0.70	0.70	0.72	0.72	0.72	0.72	0.72	0.72	0.72	0.72	0.78	0.74
Cider/5 lt	3.00	—	3.00	3.00	3.00	3.00	3.00	3.00	—	3.00	3.00	3.00	3.00	3.00
Butter	1.36	1.36	1.36	1.36	1.36	1.36	1.38	1.40	1.44	1.46	1.48	1.48	1.48	1.50

Source: I have compiled prices from the June 9 through the September 8, 1933, editions of the *Vossische Zeitung*.

economic officials, Schmitt affirmed that "order and the security of law were the indispensable conditions" for a thriving economy. The next subordinate to emphasize Hitler's insistence of the end to violence was Prussian Minister of Justice Hanns Kerrl, who made it compulsory for state institutions of justice to combat every act of sabotage with great severity. Such acts were identified as "unauthorized interference in the economy" and punishable by imprisonment or in certain circumstances with the death penalty. Economic commissars and NSBO shop stewards had previously been addressed as possible perpetrators. But for the first time the most likely suspects were pinpointed as the SA by means of the referral to "provocateurs wearing uniforms." Hermann Göring was the next minion to support Hitler's turn to support peaceful stimuli to the economy. Göring issued a circular in which the activities of commissars, appointed by the SA leadership, were to be completed and for those few exceptions a report on their operations and who employed them was to be submitted by August 1, 1933. Göring pursued the issue on July 24 in a meeting with the Prussian Council of Ministers in which he reiterated that the revolution had ended and henceforth the focus was directed to the expansion and construction of the state.[31]

Returning to the topic of grocery advertisements, it is noticeable that another marketing tactic employed was to introduce five different types of coffees, with the four new varieties selling from 2.20 RM per pound to 3.20 RM, significantly more expensive than the 1.90 RM in Table 5.7. As is well-known, merchandise at the top end of a category usually sells at a significantly higher profit margin. The introduction of high-end specialty items might have been an attempt to demonstrate to Freiherr von Tann-Rathsamhausen and the banking consortium that Georg Karg sought a profit to repay the banks for their loan.

D. GEORG KARG'S EXPERIENCE WITH JANDORF LED TO OWNERSHIP OF TIETZ

The conservative businessmen, who appropriated the Jewish firms, were often executives within the companies. Although this demonstrated an incredible lack of loyalty to the Jewish owners, the large German bankers undoubtedly viewed the insider knowledge of merchandise, suppliers, marketing strategies and profit margins to take enormous benefit in any hostile buyout. Such was the case with Georg Karg, who in 1908 moved from the world of an apprenticeship in Meseritz to becoming employed by Tietz's competitor, Jandorf in Berlin. Although earning only 75 RM per month in the six-store chain, known as "cheap Jacob," by 1913 Karg used his knowledge of textiles and his extraordinary retention of details to become the manager of the second-largest Jandorf department store on the Wilmersdorfer Straße. In 1926, Adolf Jandorf sold his chain, including the renowned Kaufhaus des Westens (aka "KaDeWe") to the brothers Georg and Martin Tietz and their brother-in-law, Dr. Hugo Zwillenberg. Karg became the manager for the centralized purchasing of textiles in the expanded Hermann Tietz chain and was so confident in his future with Tietz that he rejected a 500,000 RM annual salary to become a Board Member for another competitor, Karstadt.[32]

As the Jewish owners of Hermann Tietz displayed their trust in Karg, he secretly began simultaneous employment with Bankhaus Hardy, one of the department store's lending institutions. There he not only obtained an insider perspective on the Tietz Conglomerate's financial situation, but he also established a strong working relationship with Helmut Friedel. Friedel was not the only new business partner, whom Karg cultivated. It appears that the financial institutions extending Loan I and Loan II to Hermann Tietz were concerned about the Conglomerate's profitability in light of the ongoing boycotts. They also desired to develop a good connection with the new regime. As a non-Jew, Karg was able to convince the bankers about the security of their loans by formulating an Aryanization strategy. Although neither Karg nor the five investment leaders were members of the NSDAP, the security of their assets and reassurance of greater profitability were of enormous significance. Thus, Karg built alliances with Emil Ebeling of the Deutsche Bank und Disconto-Gesellschaft, who extended 1,138,300 RM in founding capital; Reinhold Quaatz of the Dresdner Bank, who provided 914,615 RM; Rudolf Löb of Mendelssohn & Company; Charley Hartung of Hardy, who supplied 323,085 RM; and Kurt Hamann of Viktoria Versicherungs-Gesellschaft. By July 25, 1933, all plans made during the prior months were already in place and it was time for Karg to wrest control of Hermann Tietz from the unsuspecting owners. On that fateful day, Karg and Friedel each deposited 50,000 RM and before a notary at the Hardy Bank, they inaugurated the Hertie Kaufhaus Beteiligungs Gesellschaft mit beschränkter Haftung. Two key factors become immediately apparent from the new company name. First, Karg felt confident of emerging victorious because he would remove all associations with the Jewish owners as demonstrated by changing the name from Hermann Tietz to Hertie. Second, Karg changed the image of the retailer from a despised Warenhaus to a more reputable Kaufhaus. Through these measures Karg intended to assuage all criticism, which had supported the boycott and adversely affected sales. Karg immediately earned the trust of the banks through a contract that he forced the Tietz family to sign on July 29, 1933.[33]

Karg sought to end the boycott by the terms of the contract, which stipulated that Hugo Zwillenberg was immediately dismissed from all ownership rights in the Conglomerate.[34] Rather than presenting more prices in a third table, I think that the new owner's marketing strategy will become evident by examining five of his display advertisements commencing with the August 25, 1933 edition of the *Vossische Zeitung*. In this Friday announcement, the traditional rectangle bearing the company name was replaced with a trapezoid with the interim firm's name Hermann Tietz and Company. The designation benefited from the thousands of customers' loyalty to the brand, but simultaneously informed the public that there were new co-owners. Maintaining suppliers and customers, while solving the accounting puzzle of determining where all the conglomerate's assets lay, would require many months. Thus, the Aryanization could not be instantaneous. Nevertheless, a change in ownership had begun in July 1933. Another alteration in the company's advertisements was the replacement of the printed word "groceries" below the firm's name for the phrase "inexpensive groceries" in script. Georg Karg was thereby announcing the business's new ownership. In case the new chain's name was too subtle for the casual shopper, the September 15, 1933, issue of the newspaper not only continued the new company's logo but added the rhyme: "German housewives, don't forget German fruits and vegetables at any meal!" Rather than being written in a Latin alphabet, it was written in the Gothic style preferred by National Socialism. In addition, another section of the promotion bore the political message: "Support German winegrowers! Drink nature-pure wine!"

Kippers had customarily been featured in the Hermann Tietz notices. But in addition to the new company name, the slogan of eating German fruit and drinking German wine, the September 22, 1933 ad also proclaimed: "The good German [underscored in the original] kippers are here!" By September 29, not only were these headings written in Fraktur but also were all the food items. The Latin alphabet had completely disappeared. The merchandising campaign to end the ongoing SA boycott against Hermann Tietz had intensified.

Georg Karg began experimenting with other marketing tactics. Alongside the groceries, he began advertising October 2–4 fashion shows to stimulate women's clothing purchases on the traditionally slow shopping days of Monday through Wednesday. Free tickets were available to view the couture at both the Leipzigerstraße and Alexanderplatz mega-stores in morning and afternoon presentations. After running display advertisements entirely in Gothic for three consecutive weeks, the announcements abruptly returned to an entirely Latin alphabet. A novel notice regarding presenting a coupon before the purchase of reduced-price margarine appears to elucidate that by the October 20, 1933, advertisement, Georg Karg had proved to the NSDAP that Hermann Tietz's new management had wrested decision-making from the Jewish brothers and should therefore benefit from being allowed to redeem government food coupons. Ration cards for margarine were important since a comparison of Table 5.7 with 5.8 indicates that the price of butter had soared from 1.12 RM on February 17 to 1.50 RM on September 8 and by

October 20, the price of one pound would stabilize at 1.58 RM. This inflated price was excessive for many Germans, requiring government intervention.

A company's value far exceeds the worth of its buildings and inventory, because of the importance of name recognition by the thousands of customers. Brand recognition requires many years of convincing consumers of the high quality being offered at inexpensive prices. There would have been no point in rejecting thousands of interested buyers, so the formerly Jewish firm's designation was gradually changed from Hermann Tietz to Hermann Tietz and Company to Hertie, which was an abbreviation of Hermann Tietz.

By October 27, Karg felt sufficiently secure with the Party that he could appeal to both SA extremists and the customary German consumers. On the one hand, the cheese section of the promotion was labeled "for the cheese propaganda week," whereas the fish and seafood section observed the Catholic prohibition of eating meat on Fridays by noting, "Friday is the fish day for Berliners." For Karg, the ideology of the consumer was immaterial. As a non-NSDAP Party member, he merely wanted to maximize profits by increasing sales.

Why had businessmen such as Walter Spiecker and Georg Karg been so eager to acquire a department store? A re-examination of Hermann Tietz's Profit and Loss Statement from July 15, 1933 will quickly answer this rhetorical question. The net profit after paying all wages, benefits, and other expenses was only 2.6 million RM, which according to generally accepted accounting practices in twenty-first-century America is not a large amount for such an extensive conglomerate. Nevertheless, two significant statements must be asserted. In a period of 5 million unemployed Germans, for Georg Tietz to annually pay down 2.3 million of his indebtedness to the banks while splitting 300,000 RM with his brother and brother-in-law as a yearly salary was an enviable financial position. It is unclear how Germans of the 1930s made purchasing decisions. But the generally accepted practice in twenty-first-century America is to buy a company for three to five times its net profit. Had Georg Karg and the banks made a fair purchase offer to the Tietz family, Karg and Freiherr von Tann-Rathsamhausen would have extended between 7.8 million RM and 13 million RM. But Karg had no funds for a down payment and furthermore Georg and Martin Tietz were burdened with all the liabilities. Georg Karg's unfriendly acquisition of the department store chain had deleterious effects not only on the Tietz brothers but also on their employees.

E. KARG'S TERMINATIONS EXCEEDED THE LAW

Not only had the new Gentile owner of the department store not paid the former owners anything for the company but he also sought to overcome the detrimental effects of the boycott by terminating numerous Jewish employees.

The Gestapo confiscated Centralverein deutscher Staatsbürger jüdischen Glaubens's records in November 1938 and it was feared by historians that these records had become lost. But in February 1990, *Isvestiya* disclosed that the secret Osobyi Archives in Moscow held German records. In October 1992, Avraham Barkai discovered 4,371 files from the CV's headquarters. The Conference on Jewish Material Claims against Germany made funds available to photograph the CV files, resulting in over 350,000 frames of microfilm.[35] I have analyzed 275 frames of the microfilm referring to Hermann Tietz, between the years 1933 and 1935.

The Tietz microfilm focuses on the theme of Jewish salespeople being dismissed because of Nazi pressure and also as a cost-saving measure by Georg Karg. In addition, the microfilm highlights the CV's legal attempts to have Tietz employees reinstated or else compensated. Of special note is the large percentage of terminated staff, who had been frontline soldiers during World War I and thus supposedly protected by President Paul von Hindenburg's amendment to the April 7, 1933 Law for the Restoration of the Professional Civil Service.

The microfilm commences with Hans Apfel, who had been a frontline soldier for the German army from March 1917 until the end of the war. From August 3, 1919 until March 1920, he served as a volunteer with the Officer Company in the Tiergarten, a unit within the Greater Berlin Rifle Regiment. Seeking a return to civilian life, Apfel found employment in one of the Berlin branches of the Hermann Tietz Department Store chain, rising to the status of sales manager for the garment warehouse. However, his employment ended abruptly, when he was placed on leave of absence and escorted out of the store on March 30, 1933. The situation intensified on April 29 with his status being downgraded due to his "membership in Judaism." His termination became effective on May 31, 1933.

Mr. Birnbaum, the personnel manager, advised Apfel to lodge an appeal with the NSBO's work council, which was rejected by May 4, 1933. During the appeal process, it was divulged that Apfel had previously terminated employees, who were National Socialists. But in his unsuccessful defense, Apfel maintained that the subordinates had committed misdemeanors during work hours. The memo containing these details was forwarded to Wolf Simon Matzdorff in order that the various Centralverein attorneys could consult with each other before advising Apfel about the suggested course of action.[36]

This was by no means the only early example of action against Jewish employees of Hermann Tietz by the NSBO. Centralverein Attorney Alfred Gerstel met with Mr. Stein the Personnel Manager of a second Hermann

Tietz flagship in Berlin the Kaufhaus des Westens (KaDeWe) on behalf of Mr. B. This Jewish employee had been warned on Tuesday April 4 to leave his worksite and he had never returned. Mr. Stein advised attorney Gerstel to negotiate with Director Müller at the Tietz Headquarters in the Leipzigerstraße facility in Berlin. Müller articulated that from the beginning of April 1933 the NSBO had demanded that "Jewish propagandists" were not allowed in the Berlin stores, thereby ensuring that Nazis would maintain their employment in Hermann Tietz. Although Gerstel of the Centralverein knew Müller from Tietz "very well," Gerstel concluded in his May 12, 1933 memo that Müller would be unable to provide anything for Mr. B, who had already been unemployed for more than five weeks. Apparently out of fear of the NSBO, the Tietz director requested that the Centralverein attorney keep all details of the discussion confidential.[37]

By the beginning of April 1933, the NSBO was so firmly entrenched in Hermann Tietz that it was able to restrict Jewish salespeople from entering into the stores and thereby to completely safeguard the employment of its own members. In contrast with the NSBO's vigorous activity, actions by Centralverein attorneys merely assumed that the strength of Germany as a legal state was sufficient to overcome the power of the NSBO. This trust in the power of law in the early days of the Third Reich was reflected in Hans Reichmann's June 21, 1933 response to Heinz Binder. Reichmann had been an attorney for the CV from 1922 through 1926 at which time he became the regional director of the Centralverein in Berlin.[38] In the letter, he merely reviewed the now-meaningless statutes that Jewish employees had five days within the notification of a dismissal in which to lodge an appeal with the work council and thereafter the council had a further seven days to make a determination.[39] In contrast with the Centralverein's legal activities, it already appears as though notification of termination for a Jewish employee signified a fait accompli.

Hans Guggenheimer of the Centralverein in Munich attempted to inform Alfred Wiener at the CV's headquarters in Berlin that termination of Tietz employees occurred in Munich earlier than in the capital. Twelve Jewish employees had already been dismissed from the Munich store. Being a journalist Guggenheimer phrased it profoundly:

> There is probably no example within the dark history of our oppression that Jewish employees had to be dismissed from a Jewish business simply because they were Jews. . . . An expedited intervention from your [the Centralverein Headquarters in Berlin] law office to the relevant official agencies is even more necessary, because if the various decrees of the central economic organizations against Jews are not permissible, then you should intervene here! . . . I did not want to burden your attorney Dr. Werner Cahnmann in this matter, since the

local [Munich] branch of the Centralverein is still dissolved. Nevertheless, there must still be authoritative bodies there in Berlin which will in due time acknowledge that such injustices will not be permitted even in Munich.[40]

Werner Cahnmann recorded the attack against Tietz's next-largest competitor in Munich, Max Uhlfelder's department store.[41] Long before the November 9, 1938, Kristallnacht, the display windows of the Uhlfelder store were smashed on March 10, 1933. Cahnmann's judicial counterpart, Michael Siegel, went to Munich's central police station to commence a legal proceeding. Rather than handle this in a courtroom, the SS beat him so severely that several teeth were knocked out and his ear drum was ruptured. Then the legs of his trousers were cut off, a sign was hung about his neck with an inscription and he was forced to march barefoot from the Ettstraße to the central train station. The photo recording the incident was published on the front page of the March 23, 1933 edition of the *Washington Times*, transforming it into a world-recognized icon. Cahnmann analyzed the anti-department store situation in Munich by concluding: "At this time, it was surely too late for confrontational tactics."[42]

The Munich chapter of the NSBO insisted that even long-term Jewish employees of the Tietz Company had to be terminated, effective July 1, 1933. During a June 29, 1933 meeting, the management of the Munich store announced that they were attempting to keep the number of dismissed employees to a minimum, but pressure from the NSBO would result in heads of households being terminated. Knowledge from the Tietz meeting was shared with the businessmen's committee of Munich's Jewish congregation. It was reported that the NSBO headquarters had issued instructions to the local branch not to interfere with personnel issues and that dismissed Jewish employees were to be given the full protection of §84 of the Work Council Law. Not only did Jewish representatives have false hopes that the responsible operating council would recognize the appeals of the terminated Tietz employees as legitimate, but the Jewish emissaries failed to recognize that the Munich NSBO refused to heed Berlin's directives.[43]

On June 30, 1933, Cahnmann warned that in the course of resolving the financial difficulties of the Hermann Tietz Company, that the lending banks would wrench ownership away from Georg and Martin Tietz and transform the firm into a joint stock company. Furthermore, the banks would demand that "the Jewish employees or else a considerable part of them will be dismissed." He further cautioned: "There's a great danger that the Karstadt case will be repeated with the Tietz Company. Experience shows that mass dismissals of Jewish employees can hardly be overturned once they occur."[44] Karstadt AG terminated 830 Jewish employees, including four Board members and forty-seven branch managers.

Attorney David Krombach informed Wolf Simon Matzdorff, a Centralverein lawyer, of terminations at the Kaufhaus des Westens with July 8 data supplied by Mr. Tichauer, a sales manager, who had not only been fired but had also had his appeal rejected by the Work's Council. Tichauer noted that an additional twenty to thirty Jewish sales managers had suffered his fate in addition to an unknown number of Jewish sales personnel and trainees. In contradicting management's claims that the Tietz actions were merely the consequences of cost-cutting, Tichauer maintained that only Aryans earning two salaries or those in discontinued departments were dismissed.[45]

Munich's July 12, 1933 memo to Berlin requested that the CV headquarters meet with the main office of the NSBO and ask that "detailed instruction" be sent to local NSBO chapters that Jewish employees should remain unmolested and that veterans and their family members not be treated worse than the Civil Service Law intended. Munich's rationale to the central CV office was an astonishing disclosure of the plight of the Jewish workforce early in the Third Reich: "because Jewish employees are still employed in non-Jewish companies only in rare cases."[46]

Less than two weeks later, Werner Cahnmann followed up the memo with the disturbing detail that the NSBO had demanded that Jewish employees within Tietz would be limited to 1.8 percent of the workforce as well as excluding Jews from positions as buyers or any other elevated position. In the July 21 communication, the regional office of the Centralverein in Munich expressed the hope that veterans and their family members should not be included by the NSBO in the 1.8 percent ceiling.[47] Further dismissals of the Jewish staff of Hermann Tietz were an ongoing concern for the Munich branch of the CV not only expressed by their July 28 report of further Jewish terminations[48] but also through the firing of World War I soldiers, such as Siegfried "Fred" Bickart from the Karlsruhe store.

Bickart had volunteered for the German army at age 16½, been wounded at the front and earned the Iron Cross Second Class. Since September 8, 1930, he had been employed by the Karlsruhe branch of Tietz as a buyer and division manager for gloves, stockings, knitted fabrics and woolens. In addition, Bickart had been an instructor for the training of the entire personnel. But because of the "synchronization" with National Socialism, he was forced to give up his position. Despite the regret of the Karlsruhe store and despite his wartime exploits, his termination would be carried out as soon as a replacement could be found.[49] Bickart must have been exasperated by the CV, since both the July 27 letter of recommendation from the Karlsruhe store and his July 30 letter to the Centralverein in Berlin mentioned the reason for his termination was the department store chain's synchronization into the Nazi economy. In addition, Bickart had mentioned that the store was searching for a qualified individual to assume his responsibilities. Nevertheless,

Hans Reichmann, who had been an attorney for the CV in Berlin since 1927, apparently accepted the new management's excuse by lamely responding on August 3, 1933, that Bickart had been fired because of necessary cost savings.[50]

Despite having a copy of the July 30, 1933, newspaper article "The Reorganization of Hermann Tietz" in CV headquarters' files, neither Reichmann nor any of the other executives appear to have understood what was happening to Tietz employees. The *Berliner Morgenpost* summarized that Hermann Tietz and Company had received a 14.5 million RM loan and that Hugo Zwillenberg was eliminated from the firm. The chief executive officer (CEO) of Hertie had arisen as the new proprietor.[51] Nevertheless Reichmann offered the platitude that up until now, it had not been possible to obtain a statement regarding Jewish employees from the company management.[52]

Georg Karg's role in the termination of Jewish employees also aroused interest with regard to the appeal made by Albert Schloss. Schloss had worked for the Tietz store in Stuttgart for approximately three years before receiving a notification of termination on August 17, 1933. He filed an appeal on August 23 on the basis of undue hardship, which was denied by the Works Council. But Schloss maintained that his appeal was rejected without further ado on the orders of Director Karg, rather than being examined on its merits.

Bruno Weil, the Attorney for the Wurttemberg regional office, asked the CV headquarters for its input on the merits of the Claim for Redress.[53] Berthold Weinberg responded on June 6, 1934 to the Wurttemberg request by noting several laws, including the previously mentioned November 24, 1933 Decree by Franz Seldte against the dismissal of non-Aryan employees. Nevertheless, Weinberg did concede that the labor court in Berlin had disregarded these legal precedents in their January 25, 1934 decision against an Action for Damages filed by the CV against a Works Council. Astonishingly the CV lacked the funds to file an appeal against the January 25 decision.[54]

In lieu of an assertive legal defense of fired Tietz employees, the Centralverein attorneys meekly requested that Devaux re-examine a series of cases beginning with a review of Helene Moses' (unrelated to Oskar Moses) September 30, 1933 notification of dismissal. In Munich, the NSBO had insisted as early as July 1933 that even long-term Jewish employees had to be let go. This practice was adopted in Berlin as Miss Moses was notified in the Fall, after nine years of service with the troubleshooting team from the Leipzigerstraßer headquarters.

A third dismissed veteran to appeal for assistance from the Centralverein was J. Schloss from Plauen. His August 8, 1933 appeal to the CV was met with the response that the use of frontline service argument had been rejected by employers as insignificant.[55] Such bleak prospects for Jewish veterans of

World War I was only momentarily broken, when Fred Bickart communicated on August 15 that his announced termination was for the moment not implemented because of his status as a frontline soldier.[56]

Attorney Alfred Gerstel met Baron von der Tann on Saturday, November 25, after seven Jewish employees had been dismissed from the department store's central office. Von der Tann claimed that "because of the stubborn refusal of the previous owners to fire Jewish employees, which was expressed until the Summer of 1933, there was in the NSBO cells of all Tietz operations an unprecedented bitterness against the Jewish employees."

By the Fall of 1933, the number of Jews employed by Hermann Tietz was no more than 7 percent of the Conglomerate's many divisions. Easily replaced Jewish employees had already been eliminated, whereas those in higher-ranking positions had not been affected as much. The result was that although Jews composed approximately 7 percent of the workforce, their wages substantially exceeded 7 percent of the Conglomerate's salaries. Thus, in the Baron's opinion, managers and executives would have to be terminated, although for the present time, Tann was unable to find suitable Aryan replacements as department managers and buyers in the fabric and clothing divisions. Second, withdrawal of dismissals from earlier in 1933 would unfortunately not be possible, since in order to maintain the percentage, Tann would need to terminate some other Jewish employees for every possible reinstatement.

As Alfred Gerstel was leaving the November 25 meeting with the Baron, he coincidentally met Martin Tietz. Martin claimed that approximately two-thirds of the Jews originally employed were still on the payroll, but this figure could not be maintained if the boycott against the Tietz companies continued. Although most scholars understand the April 1, 1933 boycott to have lasted merely one day, Martin's statement was corroborated by the prior discussion of Hitler's speeches seeking to end unauthorized activities by the SA. In section B of this chapter, the pre-April boycotts in Duisburg, Essen, Bottrop, Mühlheim and Magdeburg were mentioned. The reader will recall that it was uncertain when larger retailers would be allowed to resume business in Essen.[57]

Gerstel requested to make the details of the discussion with Tann available to Tietz employees. The recommendation was accepted and implemented in the December 5, 1933 letter to Frieda Schmidt.[58]

Either enormous pressure was exerted upon Baron von der Tann by the NSBO to fire Jewish buyers or managers or else his ability to find suitable Aryan replacements dramatically changed between his November 25 meeting with Alfred Gerstel and the end of 1933. Oskar Moses had been a buyer for Tietz's knitwear, woolens, gloves and stocking departments since July 1929. Despite von der Tann's admission that he had been unable to find replacements for Jewish buyers, Moses was terminated on December 30, 1933. Since his voluntary enlistment for service in World War I on August 24, 1914 and since his service on the foremost front with the infantry for four years beginning with the October 1914 Battle of the Yser Canal were well-known to Hermann Tietz, he was astonished that his dismissal could not be prevented based on an analogy with the April 7 Civil Service Law. Moses cited Minister Wilhelm Frick's position in the *Deutsche Juristen-Zeitung* that indiscriminate terminations of employees, simply because they were Jewish, were unacceptable. This was especially the case, if those potentially being terminated were frontline soldiers and the Interior Minister specifically implied department store employees. Moses did not perceive that he would be able to obtain another source of employment in the foreseeable future and thus he sent his appeal to the Work Council by registered mail on January 4, 1934.[59]

Perhaps because the Centralverein was so inundated by the termination of Jewish employees, the organization appears to have begun sending form letters citing the old details from Baron von der Tann. Thus, Hans Reichmann committed the error of responding to Oskar's dismissed daughter, rather than to Moses himself.[60]

The Christmas–New Year's dismissals were not limited to Berlin. At the insistence of Attorneys Rudolf Samson and Dr. Guckenheimer, the Hamburg-Altona regional branch of the CV informed headquarters that six Jewish employees at Hermann Tietz had received notification of termination on January 1, 1934. Although the department store's rationale was allegedly based on operational cutbacks, no Aryans were affected. On the basis of Kurt Schmitt's well-known decrees as Minister of the Economy, Samson and Guckenheimer were requesting that the central office intervene in order that a rescission of the dismissals might be possible.[61]

Retired Captain Devaux had replaced Mr. Birnbaum as the personnel director in the Leipzigerstraße headquarters of Hermann Tietz. As the Wilmersdorferstraße branch manager, Mr. Levy had been able to keep the apprentice Mr. Behrend on the staff after his apprenticeship ended on November 15, 1933. However as Jewish managers and executives were laid off by the bank-led new owners, Mr. Levy's Aryan replacement dismissed Mr. Behrend. Baron von der Tann's postponement of firing Jewish executives and managers apparently lasted only until December 1933 or January 1934. At that time, the banking consortium was able to insist that Mr. Birnbaum and Mr. Levy both be replaced.

Louis Meyer's daughter Elisabeth maintained that the statistics office in which she worked accomplished good work for Tietz, but could barely keep up with the workload. In addition, her father had been a frontline soldier in World War I for three years. Furthermore, she petitioned on the basis of Interior Minister Wilhelm Frick's article "Racial Questions in German Legislation" in the most recent edition of the *Deutsche Juristen-Zeitung*.[62] After the young clerk in the statistics office had filed her appeal with the Works Council, the Centralverein's headquarters complied with Hamburg's request through a January 9, 1934 letter to Hermann Tietz's management. In the correspondence, the company's executives were reminded of Kurt Schmitt's September 8, 1933 communication to the Chamber of Commerce and Industry in which the minister of the economy opposed the differentiation between Aryans and Jews in the economy and especially objected to the boycotting of non-Aryan companies.[63]

Louis Meyer wrote on behalf of his twenty-year-old daughter, who had worked for Tietz in Hamburg for nearly four years. By the time of the January 11 correspondence seeking assistance from the Centralverein, the appeal by Meyer's daughter had already been rejected by Tietz and two Aryans had been hired in her place as temporary help. Louis indicated that the Hamburg action in various departments of the Tietz store contradicted an article in the latest edition of the *C.V. Zeitung* as well as opposed the desires of the German government.[64] On January 16, the Hamburg-Altona regional office added that all six appeals were declined and so a petition was filed with the trustee as well as a legal action in the labor court.[65] That same day, Reichmann meekly suggested that Louis Meyer establish contact with the CV attorneys in Hamburg.[66]

The Hamburg regional office of the CV conducted a lengthy discussion with Mr. Pohl, the Aryan personnel director for the local Tietz store, who was unable to assist. Similarly Mr. J. Hesslein, the first Jewish director of the Hamburg branch, was unable to intervene. But the dismissed employees were attempting a new approach by seeking compensation from the department store through the labor court as well as any recourse against the operating council.[67] Retired Judge Otto Seligmann filed the legal action on a pro bono basis and at the end of January, the six dismissed employees awaited the hearing.[68] However at the February 2 hearing, the former Tietz employees withdrew their lawsuit after the judge pointed out the hopelessness of the situation.[69]

By January 24, Hans Reichmann's strategy was to remind Tietz executives of Wilhelm Frick's pronouncements in the *Deutsche Juristen-Zeitung* and so he requested a second meeting with Baron von der Tann.[70] Apparently, the firing of Jewish employees in the department store had been so extensive that they had reduced the number of Jews to less than the 7 percent mentioned by Tann to CV Attorney Alfred Gerstel in their November 25 meeting. When no second meeting with Tann appeared forthcoming, Reichmann's ineptitude drove him to seek the number of Jewish employees and their percentage of the entire Tietz workforce from Hugo Zwillenberg,[71] despite the fact that Zwillenberg had himself been fired seven months earlier! Zwillenberg arranged for CV Attorney Berthold Weinberg to meet with the department stores' Personnel Manager, retired Captain Devaux in order to obtain accurate numbers.[72] The department store's delay until February 10 in responding to Reichmann's January 24 request for a second meeting with Baron von der Tann resulted in Reichmann's introduction to Georg Karg.[73]

Before the Hitler Oath of August 2, 1934, there had been an Oath to the People and the Fatherland, which had been required of civil servants and the military. Such an Oath may have been a requirement by the new owner of the department store chain in February 1934. When Martin Wolff allegedly made subversive statements during his affidavit, he was handed over to the Gestapo. The Secret State Police held him for five days, but after he was released, he was terminated without notice. Personnel Manager Devaux emphasized that a reinstatement of this dimension was completely out-of-the-question.[74]

On May 28, 1934, Martin Wolff provided his side of the story. A lady had claimed to witness Wolff gathering a financial collection for two colleagues Mr. Dobermann and Mr. Thiele, who were in the concentration camp. But Wolff claimed that he neither knew anything about a collection nor donated anything. In addition, the building supervisor claimed that Wolff had said: "If things had occurred differently [under the Communists in Berlin], the outcome [in Germany] would have been different." Wolff denied ever having made such a remark. But the building supervisor retorted that Mr. Liese heard Wolff make this remark, which Mr. Liese denied. Nevertheless, the supervisor claimed that it had been proven that Wolff made the remark. As Wolff was about to leave the Berlin store that evening, he was arrested and taken to the police station. After Wolff was released, the supervisor dismissed him without giving notice. Wolff maintained that he had never been involved in any political activity. In addition, he noted that he had served on the front during World War I for 3½ years.[75]

A summary of Georg Karg's dismissal of fifteen Hermann Tietz employees, supposedly protected by Hindenburg's stipulation to the Civil Service Law, is provided in Table 5.10. Table 5.10 assists in eliciting conclusions regarding the attempted defense by Centralverein attorneys on behalf of Hermann Tietz's terminated employees. Recall that Table 5.9 had indicated that the largest single expenditure in the July 15, 1933 Profit and Loss Statement had been 12,407,249 RM for salaries and wages. But six months later, the line item had been reduced to 11,601,776 RM. The reduction of 805,473 RM paid to employees underscores that the fifteen Jewish employees in Table 5.10 merely represent the few individuals represented by Centralverein attorneys and not the complete number who had been terminated.

Georg Karg's weekly cash report #4 from August 30, 1933 confirms the interpretation that the CV represented only a few of the terminated Tietz

Table 5.9 The Smoking Gun Revealed in a Profit and Loss Statement

Debits		*Credits*	
Salaries and hourly wages	12,407,249.52	Profit from inventory	25,329,279.86
Social benefits	913,554.54	Profit from exchanging foreign currency	6,345,412.55
Write-downs on plant	566,116.08		
Other write-downs	867,178.82		
Provision for pensions and other responsibilities	400,000.00		
Interest owed	1,621,625.38		
Taxes	1,757,606.52		
Rent	4,457,805.24		
All other costs	6,046,020.62		
Net profit	2,637,535.69		
Total	**31,674,692.41**	**Gross profit**	**31,674,692.41**

Source: Table 5.1 has been reproduced here as Table 5.9 for purposes of the renewed discussion. Recall that it is preserved in the Bundesarchiv as R8119F 15211, Microfiche #6, Document #199.

employees. The weekly report noted that "approximately 500 non-Aryan white-collar employees had been fired."[76] Nevertheless, the KaDeWe, Leipzigerstraße and Alexanderplatz stores in Berlin along with the Munich and Hamburg branches represented the largest facilities in the nineteen-branch Tietz chain and in their branches the CV had attempted to exert the little influence it had.

Current scholarship on the end of the Weimar Republic understands a nuanced approach to Gentile-Jewish relationships in Germany. For example, Cornelia Hecht's 2003 volume on Weimar anti-Semitism examined Ludwig Holländer's January 10, 1930 feature in the *CV Zeitung*. She interpreted Holländer's thesis was not that the German populace was anti-Semitic, but rather that the government, the republican parties and the public lacked the moral courage to take a stand against the defamation campaigns by the NSDAP.[77]

A nuanced interpretation of the role of anti-Semitism in the economy is also required in the time period following that assessed in this research. Saul Friedländer analyzed the SD Reports for 1937 and noticed that the Nazi Party organization affirmed that both the Catholic and Protestant Confessing Churches "strengthen[ed] the opposition to National Socialism, [by] try[ing] to hamper the work of the Reich with regard to Jewry." Friedländer explained church member actions in the SD Report as: "anti-Semitism was apparently not becoming an *active* force within the overall population."[78]

The recently discovered Osobyi Archive files regarding the Centralverein's attempted defense of terminated Tietz employees has been interpreted as Karg's method of alleviating local NSBO frustration and obtaining the end of boycott actions against the department store. Karg's primary motivation has not been

Table 5.10 Terminated Tietz Employees

Name	*Years of Duty on Front*	*Tietz Location*	*Years of Tietz Employment*	*Position in Tietz*	*Firing Date*
Hans Apfel	1 year 8 months	Berlin	13 years	Sales Manager	3/30/1933
Mr. "B"	?	Berlin	?	?	4/4/1933
Mr. Tichauer	?	Munich	?	Sales Manager	before 7/8/1933
Siegfried Bickart	Wounded	Karlsruhe	2 years 10 months	Division Manager	before 7/21/1933
Albert Schloss	1 year 6 months	Stuttgart	3 years	Sales Manager	8/17/1933
Helene Moses	No	Berlin	9 years	Trouble-Shooter	9/30/1933
J. Schloss	Yes	Berlin?	?	?	?
Frieda Schmidt	No	Berlin	?	?	?
Oskar Moses	4 years 6 months	Berlin?	4 years 5 months	Buyer	12/30/1933
Mr. Birnbaum	?	Berlin	?	Personnel Director	12/1933–1/1934
Mr. Levy	?	Berlin	?	Branch Manager	12/1933–1/1934
Elisabeth Meyer	Father for 3 years	Hamburg	nearly 4 years	Statistician	1/1/1934
Walter Hermann	Wounded	Berlin	9 years	Linen Salesman	
Philipp Berliner	Wounded	Berlin	3 years	Carpet Salesman	1/30/1934
Martin Wolff	3 years 6 months	Berlin			2/1/1934

Source: This table summarizes approximately one hundred Centralverein documents, comprising CAHJP microfilm copies #96-219, taken by the Gestapo from the Centralverein and after the war brought to Moscow by the Soviet Army.

viewed as anti-Semitism, on the basis that no evidence exists for his völkisch ideology during the Weimar Republic. In addition, nothing exists to attest to his prior membership in the Deutschnationale Handlungsgehilfenverband. Although he reduced his payroll expense to offset dwindling revenue, no source ever claimed that he joined the NSDAP either out of ideological conviction or to enhance the sales of his recently acquired firm.

In contrast with this threefold absence of any confirmation of Karg's racial Weltanschauung, German historians and Holocaust scholars have minimized the ability of a theory of anti-Semitism to explicate either German history or the Shoah. Thirty-five years ago, Ian Kershaw non-equivocally affirmed:

> Germans seldom had Jews on their mind. The constant barrage of [Nazi] propaganda failed to make the Jews the prime target of hatred for most Germans, simply because the issue seemed largely abstract, academic, and unrelated to their own problems. The result was, for the most part, widespread disinterest in the Jewish Question.[79]

Referring to an earlier period in the aftermath of the 1912 Reichstag elections, which marked the temporary cessation of anti-Semitic parties, Saul Friedländer limited the utility of anti-Semitism as an explanatory theory: "the majority of the voters did not manifestly harbor intense anti-Jewish feelings."[80] Cornelia Hecht's most recent German volume on anti-Semitism modified Friedländer's differentiation between an earlier traditional religious-based and later racial-based anti-Semitism. The more nuanced view evaluated public responses to acts of violence: "Large sections of the public as well as Federal and State Governments and even anti-Semitic parties, such as the DNVP, viewed 'ruffian anti-Semitism' unfavorably." In contrast Hecht averred that there was no opposition to anti-Jewish propaganda.[81]

The Tietz family had struggled financially with customers' shopping in specialty stores, rather than the department stores. The family attempted to offset their resulting declining profits by increasing prices. Georg Karg used his concealed relationship with Helmut Friedel of Bankhaus Hardy to form a consortium, including the Deutsche and Dresdner Banks. The consortium's Loan I and II were not offered to assist the Tietz family to overcome their poor cash flow. The credit was extended to enable Karg to reorganize the management of the conglomerate. Success was the primary goal for Karg. In addition to continuing the Tietz strategy of raising prices, Karg terminated hundreds of Jewish employees. Karg's tactic reduced the chain's expenses by nearly one million RM as well as attempting to end SA actions against the stores. Karg's game plan paid off because it not only coincided with Hitler's July 1933 politics of ending the Nazi revolution but also because it was consistent with the banks' policies of obtaining additional commissions and fees from new loans.

F. SUMMARY OF KARG'S ECONOMIZING MEASURES

Whether it had been Rudolf Heß or Hans Lammers, who had represented Adolf Hitler at the June 23, 1933 cabinet meeting, his assessment that it would be impossible to renovate the department stores was not accurate. In the hostile takeover of Hermann Tietz, this chapter has surveyed several different tactics employed by Georg Karg in overcoming the added tax on department stores in some states along with their simultaneous loss of craft repair departments as he became the executive managing the conglomerate. In surveying the increasing prices of groceries, it was observed how Karg negotiated to obtain new funding from the Akzeptbank-led consortium of financial institutions. In turn, this allowed him to purchase grocery items, which had been unavailable for many weeks. In addition, the Profit and Loss Statement was utilized to indicate that Karg should have paid a multiple of the net profit to the Jewish partners. Instead, the new owner not only fired Hugo Zwillenberg but also Jewish employees in Berlin, Munich, Karlsruhe, Stuttgart and Hamburg branches.

Despite all these cost-saving tactics, comparing Table 5.11 with the prior balance statement (Table 5.6) reveals that six months later, Karg was still confronted by depressed sales as consumers had not returned from the specialty shops.

Comparing the July 15, 1933 Balance Statement, preserved in the Deutsche Bank files in the Bundesarchiv (Table 5.6) with the January 31, 1934 statement, maintained in the Ministry of Finance files in Berlin (Table 5.11) immediately reveals that Karg not only stripped Hugo Zwillenberg of his role as a Partner in Hermann Tietz, but also eliminated 892,695 RM from what had been the Tietz family's cash investment in the firm. In addition, it is uncertain whether the new owner viewed the remaining 475,487 RM as his own property, instead of the lifelong contribution of Betty Tietz and her two sons. Although Karg had closed the unprofitable branch in Dresden and fired Jewish employees from flagship stores in Berlin as well as Munich and Hamburg, Table 5.11 clearly indicates that he still suffered the loss of 409,460 RM in his first six months of controlling the company. A second new line item in the assets side of the ledger is the intangible assets. Although no payment had been made to the Jewish family, the new proprietor recognized that the Tietz name had a value in selling merchandise, which he evaluated to be worth 4,914,000 RM.[82]

Although Karg was paid 60,000 RM per year and Freiherr von der Tann received 66,000 RM, Georg and Martin Tietz's monthly remuneration of 5,000 RM was to be further reduced by half. There is a third new line item in the assets side itemized as "Personal and Travel Advances." Previously Karg's expertise had been in making textile purchases for Jansdorf. Now

Table 5.11 Trial Balance Statement, January 31, 1934

Assets in RM		*Liabilities in RM*	
Intangible assets, goodwill	4,914,400	Debt on merchandise (incl. foreign)	22,029,322.24
Prop, plant, equip (incl. 719,239 depreciation)	11,260,000.00	Debts on own property	6,168,339.44
Conglomerate equity	17,808,103.20	Other accounts payable	4,783,081.31
Property interests	3,900.00	Bills of exchange payable	316,373.15
Merchandise	23,863,370.00	Bank debt (incl. consortium 14,406,780)	57,728,010.45
Material	299,600.00	Tax withholding	787,523.81
Stocks and bonds	1,432,885.72	Prepaid expenses	1,459,674.67
Tax credit	57,716.00	Other withholding	1,006,260.00
Active mortgages	637,606.77	Owner's equity	475,487.33
Mortgage custodian account	21,350,000.00		
Accounts receivable	2,502,185.01		
Personal and travel advances	101,642.56		
Accounts receivable to corporate subsidiaries	8,410,523.29		
Stock in consortium account	61,973.14		
Cash	678,071.68		
Post office checking accounts	15,719.12		
Bank credit	93,787.62		
Exchangeable stock	30,533.94		
Interest reserve	18,330.00		
Prepaid accruals	573,264.84		
Right of recourse from tax authorities	231,000.00		
Loss from July 16, 1933–January 31, 1934	409,460.51		
Total	**94,754,072.40**	**Total**	**94,754,072.40**

Source: I have translated accounting terminology from Bundesarchiv document R2/57.689 Microfiche #3, Document $50.

he had personal oversight of buying merchandise in all departments. If this required airplane or train tickets, overnight hotel accommodations and meals, he suddenly had Board approval to spend 101,642 RM to satisfy these needs, although this may have reimbursed other Tietz buyers as well. A fourth novelty was the inclusion of the 14.4 million RM loan in the liabilities side of the ledger. Although Karg had received these funds six months earlier, he had incurred far more merchandise than what Loan I and Loan II had enabled. This is evident by noticing the 1,727,000 RM increase in indebtedness for merchandise between Tables 5.6 and 5.11. A fifth new line item was the 57,716 RM, which the new Aryan owner had allocated in advance for taxes. It is difficult to assess whether Karg wanted to reduce the amount of his property tax obligation or whether he may have desired to impress the Berlin government with his exactitude in meeting his obligations to the Reich, so that further approval might have been extended had Loans I and Loan II been insufficient.[83]

The Deutsche Bank, as one of the largest contributors of Loan I and Loan II began receiving weekly reports on the progress Georg Karg made with regard to transforming the Jewish-owned company into a German firm. Fortunately, the Deutsche Bank records have been preserved in the Bundesarchiv[84] and thereby supplement the *Vossische Zeitung*'s articles and advertisements by Hermann Tietz. One of the chief items in the announcements by Karg is the weekly cash receipts. Although not precisely in agreement with the *Voss*, the general trend reported by both sources is the same. Those receiving the weekly depictions were executives from the financial institutions granting the 14.5 million RM loan. They included Director Fritz Wintermantel of the Deutsche Bank, Dr. Hans Paschke Head of the Deutsche Bank's Legal Department, Dr. Mankiewicz,[85] Director Alfred Hölling of the Dresdner Bank, Attorney Dr. Dresel of Mendelssohn & Company, Dr. Charley Hartung a Jewish Partner in the Hardy Bank, Director Hans Pilder of the Dresdner Bank and Dr. Hamann of the Victoria Insurance Company. These bankers had enabled Karg to take ownership of Hermann Tietz away from the Jewish family by refusing to extend merchandise credits to their former client, but granting a 14.5 million RM loan enabling the Aryanization. The repeated theme that neither Karg nor other businessmen were members of the NSDAP, but mainly self-seeking profit-minded individuals, is supported by the signature block concluding weekly disclosures, which have been previously mentioned in section F of this chapter. Rather than signing the weekly reports to the lending institutions "with a German greeting" or the more explicit "Heil Hitler," Karg concluded with the pre–Third Reich salutation of "with the highest respect." The reader should recall that these weekly announcements were sent to the Dresdner Bank, the financial institution preferred by the SS. Had these documents merely appeared in July 1933, perhaps a current historian might have speculated that the NSDAP or the SS might have tolerated such a lapse in respect to the Führer early in the Third Reich. However, the practice continued from Communication #22 on January 3, 1934, through and including #76 on January 23, 1935.[86] Communicating publicly in such a fashion carried a risk, which a businessman sympathetic to the Nazis would have avoided. Karg's motive in assuming the ownership of the department store chain was not ideological, but rather self-interest. He merely exploited the opportunities presented by anti-Semitism existing in Weimar conservatives.

Both contemporary sources, such as Victor Klemperer and current Holocaust scholars, such as Andrew Bergerson and Peter Fritzsche, agree that refusing to perform the Hitler salute and failing to sign a public document with the Hitler salutation brought the possibility of reprisals early in the Third Reich.

Ian Kershaw depicted four appearances of opposition by Socialists and Communists to the Nazi regime as late as the period from August 1934 through January 1936. In Munich's Secret State Archive, he noted documents recording refusal to provide the Hitler greeting as a gesture of resistance against wages below unemployment benefits in the glass blowing industry and low wages for road construction workers, which would not reimburse the cost of food and clothing. In addition, he discovered hostility because of the withholding of bonuses for working far from home and inadequate structures for temporarily housing construction crews. With as many as 13,000 workers on the Autobahn, their numbers allowed them to complain about the Nazi economy and to refuse to give the Hitler greeting or salute. Since Dachau was founded in 1933 for political prisoners, it provided the Nazis with a means to coerce these Bavarians into compliance. Although both Georg Karg and these southern German proletarians refused the Hitler greeting due to ideology, the Bavarian workers enjoyed a small measure of protection, due to their anonymity in numbers.[87]

Andrew Bergerson observed how in 1930 folklorist Karl Prause had discovered sufficient variations of German greetings to be able to compose a 250-page book mentioning the distinct forms of "good day."[88] But on July 13, 1933, Wilhelm Frick required that all non-Party members greet with "Heil Hitler" during the singing of the national anthem. In conducting postwar interviews with members of the small city of Hildesheim, Bergerson learned that Gustav Hoppe was terminated in March 1936 for failing to give the "Heil Hitler" greeting at the conclusion of a factory celebration. After surveying Talcott Parsons, Michael Balfour and William Sheridan Allen's 1954–1992 interpretations of the significance of uttering "Heil Hitler," Bergerson specified that the new form of address enabled ordinary Germans to assist in transforming civil society into a Volksgemeinschaft, because the greeting identified "political persuasions" to conversation partners. In the Weimar Republic salutations had erased differences, but in the Third Reich, "Heil Hitler" emphasized conflict. Instead of demonstrating civility, the Hitler greeting "now invaded the local public sphere.[89]

Peter Fritzsche is a second Twenty-First Century Holocaust scholar, who emphasized what it would have signified by withholding the Nazi expression: "A few months after January 1933, there was hardly a single person who had not on occasion raised the right arm and exclaimed 'Heil Hitler!' Most people did so several times every day."[90]

Perhaps Victor Klemperer has been unable to resolve English-speaking historians' doubts regarding the repercussions of not employing the Hitler salutation because the English translation of his diary is an abridgment. The omissions from his July 20, 1933 entry is crucial for the present discussion: "The command was given to all civil servants (including me) to use the 'German Hitler Greeting' during duty and in the Department. Interpretation: 'It is expected that an individual will use this greeting, if he wishes to avoid the suspicion of deliberately rejecting the new system of government.' When Klemperer recorded the same warning regarding the necessity of employing the Hitler salutation eight days later, the English translation included it, but omitted the explanation that Miss Mey had informed the professors that "the employees rigorously performed the Hitler salute among themselves."[91]

It took time for Karg's cost-saving measures to have a noticeable effect in offsetting declining sales. Thus, Karg and von der Tann initiated additional measures. Weekly cash receipts in 1933 fell behind their performance in 1932, despite several measures, which Georg Karg had implemented during the summer. The first of the measures entailed an August 3, 1933 memo, which Abraham Frowein[92] wrote after meeting with the new Hermann Tietz executives. As chair for the Trustees of the German Textile Industry, Frowein had been informed by Karg and von der Tann that a substantial part of the overdue claims to textile manufacturers had been made good and the remainder would be settled in a short period of time. In response, Frowein expressed to all members gratitude to the banking consortium for reestablishing loans for the delivery of merchandise. Karg assessed that this open letter would "contribute without doubt to a reassurance of the creditors" (Table 5.12).

Freiherr von der Tann met with Minister of the Economy Kurt Schmitt during the first days of August to enlist his aid and to request that Party newspapers report the conversion of Hermann Tietz from a Jewish to a German enterprise. Schmitt's assistance reversed the closure of the refreshment room in the Munich branch. Furthermore 10.5 million of the 14.5 million RM Loan I and Loan II had been used to repay arrears from June, which had allowed installment payments to repay some of the larger liabilities. Tann achieved a third success, when the August 20, 1933 edition of southern Germany's Nazi newspaper, the *Völkischen Beobachter*, carried a notice of the successful synchronization of the Tietz Conglomerate in the Third Reich's economy.

Table 5.12 Lag Time before Karg's Measures Cause Sales Decline to Cease

Dates													
7/30	*8/5*	*8/12*	*8/19*	*8/26*	*9/2*	*9/9*	*9/16*	*9/23*	*9/30*	*10/7*	*10/14*	*10/21*	*10/28*
33.9	29.0	30.4	28.1	22.1	33.2	2.9	28.4	26.4	28.7	35.2	26.2	23.8	25.9

Source: I have compiled data from the July 30 through October 28, 1933, editions of the *Vossische Zeitung*.

This sparked the hope that other Nazi publications would begin accepting advertisements. A fourth tactic, suggested by the business manager, was to limit employee salaries to 2,500 per month, which Karg anticipated would save 250,000 RM per year. Continued terminations would further cut labor costs.

In discussing the work of Centralverein deutscher Staatsbürger jüdischen Glaubens' attorneys on behalf of fired Jewish employees, it was noted that only a few of those losing their positions attempted to oppose their job loss. Karg's weekly reports to the Hertie Board support this interpretation. By August 1, 1933, there were only 1,000 Jewish employees remaining in the service of Hermann Tietz, since Karg informed the Board that 500 had already been terminated and in some cases replaced by SA members. Examples were provided in which the Jewish manager of the Munich store was retiring as of October 1, 1933 and being replaced by an "Aryan" from the Magdeburg branch. The same thing occurred in the Leipzigerstraße store in Berlin. A further measure being considered was replacement of full-time employees with part-time staff. In addition, the handling of data was being transformed so that costs could be better understood as well as using tax credits to cover upcoming government assessments.

On September 1, 1933, the Ministry of the Economy gave to the department store chain the coveted "German store" posters and Tietz's own vocational school was closed two weeks later, with the expectation that by having staff attend the public schools, 90,000 RM would be saved per year.

The Dresden store was considered unprofitable and thus a liquidation sale had been planned for October 1, 1933. It was postponed until January 2, 1934, out of consideration that Christmas sales would greatly reduce inventory. The elimination of 880,000 RM worth of Dresden's merchandise resulted in a respectable 586,000 RM increase in cash. Additionally, Karg not only spun off the ineffective Magdeburg branch, but employed this tactic for Berlin's three most unproductive sites: Andreasstraße, Kottbusser Damm, and Brunnenstraße. Furthermore, he sold buildings in Weimar, Dresden and Stuttgart not utilized in the nineteen-store chain and thereby receipted nearly 250,000 RM. Not only was Georg Karg an experienced businessman, but the banking executives within his Hertie Advisory Board may have prompted him to introduce other cost-saving measures. By reducing expenses, financial institutions would have safeguarded the repayment of Loan I and Loan II used to purchase new merchandise in Karg's Aryanization operation. The Deutsche Bank, the Dresdner Bank and their partners would have guaranteed the repayment of existing mortgage loans, which they had deferred until March 31, 1935.[93] In addition the financial institutions would have safeguarded the repayment of new credit with interest as well as earning their Aryanization fees.

By the beginning of November, a further 1.3 million RM from Loan I and Loan II was used, leaving a balance of only 200,000 RM remaining from the banking consortium. The last mentioned cost-cutting measure employed by Karg before the dramatic sales results of December 1933 was the elimination of the Jewish business manager in Weimar. Taken together, the measures described earlier depict sustained revenues from continuing declining sales, which in general stabilized the firm. Despite introducing cost-saving measures, sales did not increase, but relative profitability of the company improved (Table 5.13).

Adding to the relative slowdown in the decline of cash receipts from 1932 was the negotiation with finance officials. Deliberations by Freiherr von der Tann resulted in 516,000 RM in taxes for the period from 1930 to 1932 no longer being demanded as well as a reduction of 520,000 RM in 1933 taxes for the company. However due to the central government's concession that the states could double the department store tax, 1933, taxes in Berlin rose by only 7.4 percent in contrast with the provincial increase of 18.1 percent. Current oral accounts archived in the USC Shoah Foundation supplement Tietz accounting data preserved in Berlin's Bundesarchiv.

Hugo Zwillenberg's son Lutz was interviewed by Uri Strauss in Bern, Switzerland on November 9, 1997. Fortunately, Steven Spielberg's Shoah Foundation has acquired a copy of this interview in German in which the details stretched as far back as 1918 or 1919 when his father had acquired a farm in the Mark Brandenburg, which supplied their food requirements after Hugo's financial interests in Hermann Tietz were lost. A second fortunate pre-1933 investment by Zwillenberg was depositing funds in a private Jewish bank in Amsterdam. Lutz recalled that on April 1, 1933, the boycott had forced the family "to their knees," since they were required to pay employee costs, despite customers being prohibited from entering Tietz stores. Lutz remembered that the boycott was not a one-day enactment, but had lasted for weeks, if not months,[94] during which time the chain's Jewish management was prohibited from firing any employees. Lutz also recollected the crucial factor that the boycott had forced the company partners to seek loans from the banks, which were refused.[95] His father was the first to be eliminated, but the same action occurred to brothers Georg and Martin in 1934 after Georg Karg became more firmly entrenched.[96]

Table 5.13 Karg's Savings at Jewish Expense Led to Greater Tietz Stability

Dates			
12/10	*12/17*	*12/24*	*12/30*
15.3%	12.1%	3.6%	16.2%

Source: The table summarizes information gleaned from newspaper articles and documents in the Bundesarchiv.

Various strands of evidence were examined for the "Aryanization" of the nineteen branches of the Hermann Tietz chain, including the *Vossische Zeitung* articles and advertisements, the rediscovered Centralverein legal defense of terminated Tietz employees, the weekly reports by Georg Karg to Board Members from the banking consortium as well as the oral testimony of Lutz Zwillenberg, the son of one of the three Jewish partners. All sources have their problems evidenced by the bankers expressing their concern about Freiherr von der Tann's presentation of the Tietz financial data. Tann attempted to defend his interpretation of the cash receipts by maintaining that there had been a 10 percent increase for the two months of July and August 1934, whereas a mere 0.5 percent for February through June of the same year. But the Deutsche Bank representatives on the Board rejected this explanation, viewing it as an error on Tann's part and not a confusion regarding what time-frame was being considered. Tann was dismissed and Karg became the sole executive. Scholars must be cautious in expounding on the sources, which were written to best represent the interests of the authors.[97]

The point is equally true for oral sources. Lutz Zwillenberg was born in Charlottenburg on December 9, 1925 and was a child when the Aryanization of Hermann Tietz occurred in 1933 and 1934. As a boy he had little interest in the Fasanenstraße synagogue services, which may well have also been true of his father's activity in the Hermann Tietz enterprise. In addition, his father did not disclose the details of his imprisonment in Sachsenhausen after the Kristallnacht in November 1938. The reticence to discuss such personal matters to his son probably also affected the son's knowledge of the Hermann Tietz Company. Furthermore, Lutz's interviewer unwittingly distorted the information by asking about the abbreviation of the Jewish company's name to "Hertie" as though the firm had not been seized, but merely had its name changed.

Nevertheless, all sources support the broad outline that Hermann Tietz was in financial difficulty in part due to a long-lasting boycott. When funds were sought to acquire new merchandise, the friendly business association with financial institutions broke down. The funding requested by the Tietz brothers was rejected, but Loan I and Loan II were offered, which enabled Georg Karg to Aryanize the company. Georg Karg was allowed to acquire the firm at no expense to him. Tann helped manage the company as the representative of the banking consortium. His frayed relationships with the banks led to his departure, leaving Karg as the sole proprietor. One of Germany's largest Jewish firms had been seized by a non-Nazi businessman early in 1933–1934.

Early Aryamizers were not necessarily Nazis. Demonstrating rationales for Aryanizers' actions beyond anti-Semitism enriches the academic understanding of how and why Jewish companies were cheaply purchased.

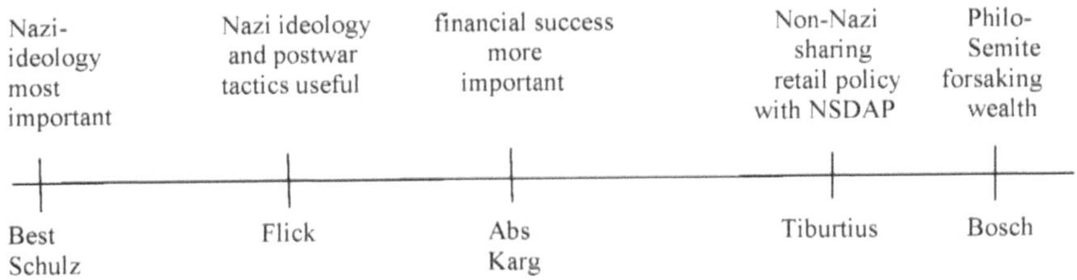

German people were motivated to actions against Jewish people due to various influences. Neither the sole incentive nor the primary incentive in such acts was anti-Semitism. The refusal to join the NSDAP or offer the Hitler salute in public or signing correspondence were indications of inducements from non-NSDAP ideological views.

Holocaust scholar Michael Wildt supported the interpretation that various forces operated behind racial actions. He asserted that in public punishment for a racial offense, the motives were diverse: "The different motives might have been completely variable: greed, jealousy, and malevolence might have animated the actors just as much as an explicit enmity towards Jews."[98]

Anti-Semitism in Weimar conservatives enabled a businessman to collude with banks to wrest ownership from the Jewish company owners. Conservative judges were also influenced in an anti-Semitic environment and were thus unwilling to overturn the economically coerced contracts. Is this a unique example of conservative businessmen being supported by conservative bankers and judges or did this occur to other large Jewish-owned businesses, which were opposed by anti-Semitism in the beginning of the Third Reich? The following chapter will investigate other examples of opportunistic non-Nazi businessmen exploiting anti-Semitism for personal financial enrichment by means of financial assistance from Germany's largest banks.

NOTES

1. "Gemeinschafts-Arbeit in Gefahr; Verständigungs-Versuche im Einzelhandel," *Vossische Zeitung*, morning edition (November 2, 1932), p. 13. Also see "Warmbold vor dem Einzelhandel," *Vossische Zeitung*, evening edition (November 8, 1932), p. 9. Furthermore "Reform statt Spaltung; Vor dem Endkampf im Einzelhandel," *Vossische Zeitung*, morning edition (November 12, 1932), p. 9.

2. "Teilsieg der Warenhäuser; Aber Hauptgemeinschaft für Sondersteuer," *Vossische Zeitung*, evening edition (November 15, 1932), p. 9.

3. "Spaltung des Einzelhandels; Warenhäuser scheiden aus," *Vossische Zeitung*, morning edition (November 16, 1932), p. 10.

4. The reader will recall Georg Tietz's father-in-law Ludwig Grünfeld of F. V. Grünfeld Landeshuter Leinen und Gebildweberei was mentioned on Chapter 4 Section B of this text. The Heinrich Grünfeld, whose Constitution for the Hauptgemeinschaft was validated in March 1919, was a member of this family-owned linen company. Thus, the Tietz and Grünfeld families were united by marriage Fritz V. Grünfeld and Stefi Jersch-Wenzel, *Das Leinenhaus Grünfeld: Erinnerungen und Dokumente* (Berlin: Duncker & Humblot, 1967), p. 78. Heinrich strove for fair representation in the Hauptgemeinschaft, despite his loyalties to Georg Tietz. When the Association of Department Stores left the Hauptgemeinschaft, the remaining retailers lost much of their funding for the umbrella organization Detlef Briesen, *Warenhaus, Massenkonsum und Sozialmoral: zur Geschichte der Konsumkritik im 20. Jahrhundert* (Frankfurt am Main: Campus, 2001), pp. 168–170.

5. "Umbau der Hauptgemeinschaft," *Vossische Zeitung*, evening edition (December 14, 1932), p. 10. Also see Tiburtius' farewell tribute to Grünfeld in "Der Führer des Einzelhandels; Heinrich Grünfeld und die Hauptgemeinschaft," *Vossische Zeitung*, morning edition (December 31, 1932), p. 9.

6. "Umbau im Einzelhandel; Die neue Verfassung der Hauptgemeinschaft," *Vossische Zeitung*, morning edition (February 21, 1933), p. 9.

7. BA R43 II/369.

8. The reader should be advised that the June 23, 1933, minutes from the Reich Chancellery in the Bundesarchiv frequently used the titles of chancellor, minister of the economy, and president of the Reichsbank, rather than personal names since all present would have known the individual meant. For ease of understanding, I have identified the individuals, although the title "Chancellor," probably implies his spokesman Rudolf Heß or State Secretary Hans Lammers rather than interpreting that Hitler was present but unable to reach a decision.

9. After Reichsbank President Rudolf Havenstein died on November 30, 1923, Max Warburg confided in his private papers that both the Board of Directors and the Central Committee of Germany's central bank held that Hjalmar Schacht was unsuitable as a successor, since he had been a partner in the Darmstädter und Nationalbank. But since Carl Helfferich was such an ambitious representative of the nationalistic reaction as well as heavy industry chauvinism, Schacht was chosen as the lesser of two evils. In the ensuing years, Warburg disclosed off-the-record that Schacht lacked any measure of goodwill as well as "suffering from an immeasurable over-estimation of himself." By March 1930, Warburg's tolerance for Schacht's personality as well as his whimsical policies with regard to the currency had evaporated. Warburg called for the convening of the Reichbank's Board to ask for Schacht's dismissal. See Warburg, *Aufzeichnungen*, pp. 121–141.

10. Placing confidence in Heinrich Uhlig's work on the department stores had led Avraham Barkai and Saul Friedländer astray. Without any evidence, Uhlig claimed that because Hermann Tietz had "persistently declined" Aryanizations, the Nazi boycott measures severely affected the chain. Additionally, he maintained that at the end of June 1933, the "Conglomerate faced the alternative of either a re-organization or liquidation." A third speculation was that although Kurt Schmitt had only been the Reich Minister of the Economy since June 29, 1933, he "used the issue of re-organization as a

precedent for the department store problem and personally lectured Hitler [!]" Schmitt allegedly argued that it was absolutely crucial to raise funds for the reorganization. "Naturally, Hitler indignantly rejected the re-organization of a non-Aryan department store by means of a Reich loan." However "after two hours of agitated argument, Hitler capitulated [!]" The result was the paradox that despite the Party's promise of the immediate liquidation of large department stores, "the Führer personally lent his hand to preserve one of the largest of these companies, which . . . was still under Jewish management." On July 7, 1933, Rudolf Heß issued an edict extending tolerance to the department stores and prohibiting any further boycotts or aggressive measures. Uhlig's hypothesis maintained: "The substantive and chronological connection between Hitler's decision in favor of the loan and Rudolf Heß's prohibition of a boycott is so evident that it requires no other proof." Uhlig's evidence for Kurt Schmitt winning a two hour argument with Hitler is not much stronger. Dr. E Michel, a councillor in the Ministry of the Economy apparently mentioned this to Uhlig more than twenty years later Heinrich Uhlig, *Die Warenhäuser im Dritten Reich* [Köln: Westdeutscher Verlag, 1956], pp. 115–117). Fortunately, Avraham Barkai did not accept the more conjectural aspects of Schmitt being verbally victorious over Hitler. Nevertheless, Barkai cited Uhlig as the source for Hitler's personal involvement in providing the Jewish owners of the Tietz chain with a "consolidation loan." Barkai did not recognize the loan to Georg Karg as a means to Aryanize the company Barkai, *Boycott,* p. 17, 72, 191. Friedländer is dependent on Barkai's view on Tietz Friedländer, *Nazi Germany*, p. 24, 340.

11. BA R 43 II/369. Document Number 18–20.

12. Although the February 24, 1920, Nazi Party platform had specifically been opposed to department stores, no unified economic statement was ever developed. Thus, Goebbels expressed outrage in his March 16, 1931, diary entry that Konstantin Hierl and Otto Wagener had submitted a draft economic policy in which none of Goebbels socialistic views were represented. See Reuth, *Joseph Goebbels*, Band 2, 567.

13. BA R 43 II/369. Document Number 15–16, 21–22.

14. "Erfolgreiche Verhandlungen bei Hermann Tietz," *Vossische Zeitung*, morning edition (July15, 1933), p. 9. "Der Umbau von Hermann Tietz; Schutz der Gläubiger und Angestellten–13 Mill. Neue Mittel, *Vossiche Zeitung*, evening edition (July 15, 1933), p. 9. "Das Warenhaus in der Wirtschaft," *Vossische Zeitung*, evening edition (July 21, 1933), p. 11. "Die künftige Organisation der Firma Hermann Tietz," *Vossische Zeitung*, morning edition (July 27, 1933), p. 11.

15. "Der Umbau bei Hermann Tietz; 14.5 Mill RM neue Mittel," *Vossische Zeitung*, evening edition (July 29, 1933), p. 9.

16. Walter Spiecker's remark would indicate that 1932 had been a relatively good year for Hermann Tietz, since section A of this chapter noted that 91.54 million RM in merchandise had been ordered from industry and 40.28 million RM from agriculture. From sales of the 131.82 million RM in goods, Table 5.1 noted a net profit of 2.64 million RM. This would represent a 2 percent profit, somewhat approximating Spiecker's less than 4 percent level.

17. "Warenhaussteuer vertagt; Verbandserklärung der Großbetriebe," *Vossische Zeitung*, evening edition (June 12, 1933), p. 9.

18. "Zum Schutze des Einzelhandels," *Vossische Zeitung* morning edition (July 15, 1933), p. 4; "Regelung der Warenhaus- und Filialsteuer," *Vossische Zeitung* evening edition (July 15, 1933), p. 1. "Die Neuregelung der Warenhaussteuer," *Vossische Zeitung*, morning edition (July 21, 1933), p. 3.

19. "Handwerk im Warenhaus," *Vossische Zeitung*, evening edition (July 18, 1933), p. 3. "Wie wir es sehen; Warenhaus und gewerblicher Mittelstand," *Vossische Zeitung* evening edition (July 19, 1933), p. 3.

20. "Konsolidierung im Einzelhandel; Preis–Tiefstand überwunden–Verlagerung der Umsätze," *Vossische Zeitung* evening edition (July 20, 1933), p. 9.

21. "Krisenverluste des Einzelhandels; Eine Denkschrift der Hauptgemeinschaft," *Vossische Zeitung*, morning edition (February 28, 1933), p. 9.

22. "Das Warenhaus in der Krise," *Vossische Zeitung* (March 2, 1933), p. 11.

23. "Die Neuordnung der Arbeitsbeschaffung," *Vossische Zeitung* (July 27, 1933), p. 3; Edmund Delmonte, "Arbeit für die Werften," *Vossische Zeitung*, morning edition (March 23, 1933), p. 9; "Dauerbeschäftigung für Berlins Tiefbauarbeiter; Die Stadt als Arbeitsgeber," *Vossische Zeitung*, morning edition (March 30, 1933), p. 5; "Arbeitslosenzulagen verlängert," *Vossische Zeitung* (March 30, 1933), p. 2; "Der neue Reichswirtschaftsrat," *Vossische Zeitung*, morning edition (March 31, 1933), p. 1; "Der Reichspräsident an das Panzerschiff 'Deutschland,'" *Vossische Zeitung* (April 2, 1933), p. 6; "Keine Lohnprämien mehr," *Vossische Zeitung* (April 12, 1933), p. 3.

24. "Neue Durchführungsverordnung zur Warenhaus-Filialsteuer," *Vossische Zeitung* evening edition (August 8, 1933), p. 11.

25. "Göring begründet die Notverordnung; Mitteilungen über die kommunistischeGefahr," *Vossische Zeitung* (March 2, 1933), p. 1; "Einheitspreisgeschäfte polizeilich geschlossen," *Vossische Zeitung* (March 8, 1933), p. 6; "Schließung jüdischer Geschäfte; S.A.-Aktion im Rheinland," *Vossische Zeitung* (March 9, 1933), p. 3; "Tumulte vor Geschäten," *Vossische Zeitung* (March 10, 1933), p. 5; and "Polizei greift ein; Zur Offenhaltung der Geschäfte," *Vossische Zeitung* (March 11, 1933), p. 5.

26. "Eine scharfe Rede Görings; Nationalsozialistische Kundgebung in Essen," *Vossische Zeitung* (March 11, 1933), p. 1; "Polizei sichert den Geschäftsverkehr; Warenhausschließungen in Hamburg," *Vossische Zeitung* (March 12, 1933), p. 5; and "Hitlers Rundfunk-Manifest," *Vossische Zeitung* (March 13, 1933), p. 2.

27. "Ausschluß-Beschluß im Gerarer Einzelhandels-Verband," *Vossische Zeitung* (March 22, 1933), p. 2; "Präsidialwechsel beim Warenhausverband," *Vossische Zeitung* (March 23, 1933), p. 9; "Umbau im Warenhausverband; Zusammenschluß aller Einzelhandels-Großbetriebe," *Vossische Zeitung* (May 27, 1933), p. 9.

28. "Da kann man nur guten Appetit wünschen!," *Vossische Zeitung* (January 5, 1933), p. 6.

29. "Reiseerfolge der Konfektion; Auch hier Qualitäts-Umstellung," *Vossische Zeitung* (January 26, 1933), p. 9. "Weiße Woche," *Vossische Zeitung* (January 29, 1933), p. 7. "Was die Geschäfte zeigen. Die Weiße Woche," *Vossische Zeitung* (January 30, 1933), p. 11. "Was die Geschäfte zeigen. Die Weiße Woche." *Vossische Zeitung* (January 31, 1933), p. 6. "21pCt. Weniger Herrenkonfektionsumsatz,"

Vossische Zeitung (February 2, 1933), p. 11. "Geringere Warenhaus-Umsätze. Jahresbilanz 1931," *Vossische Zeitung* (February 4, 1933), p. 11.

30. "Rentabilitäts-Sorgen der Konfektion," *Vossische Zeitung* (February 10, 1933), p. 9.

31. "Hitler an die SA; Ein Appell zu eiserner Disziplin," *Vossische Zeitung* evening edition (July 10, 1933), p. 2; "Abschluß der Revolution; Ein Rundschreiben des Reichsinnenministers an die Statthalter und Landesregierungen," *Vossische Zeitung*, evening edition (July 11, 1933), p. 1; "Die Leistung–einziger Maßstab; Der Reichskanzler vor den Gauleitern und Treuhändern," *Vossische Zeitung* evening edition (July 13, 1933), p. 1; "Rechtssicherheit der Wirtschaft; Dr. Schmitt vor den Länderministern," *Vossische Zeitung* morning edition (July 13, 1933), p. 1; "Bekämpfung von Sabotage; Scharfe Erlasse des preußischen Justizministers," *Vossische Zeitung* morning edition, July 14, 1933, p. 1; "Verwaltung ohne Kommissare; Ein Runderlaßdes Ministerpräsidenten Göring," Vossische Zeitung evening edition (July 18, 1933), p. 1; and "Todesstrafe für Saboteure; Maßnahmen der preußischen Regierung–Ein Reichsgesetz zur Gewährleistung des Rechtsfriedens beantraft," *Vossische Zeitung* morning edition (July 23, 1933), p. 1.

32. Hans Otto Eglau, Der Herr von Hertie," *Die Zeit* (November 27, 1970). Friedrich W. Köhler, *Zur Geschichte der Warenhäuser. Seenot und Untergang des Hertie-Konzerns* (Frankfurt am Main: Haag und Herchen, 1997), p. 26.

33. Simone Ladwig-Winters, *Wertheim–ein Warenhausunternehmen und seine Eigentümer' Ein Beitrag der Entwicklung der Berliner Warenhäuser bis zur 'Arisierung*.' (Münster: LIT, 1997), pp. 152–154.

34. BA R8127 15214.

35. Avraham Barkai, "The C.V. and its Archives, A Reassessment," *Leo Baeck Institute Yearbook*, XLV (2000), pp. 175–177. Also note Avraham Barkai, *"Wehr Dich!" Der Centralverein deutscher Staatsbürger jüdischen Glaubens 1893–1938* (München: C.H. Beck, 2002), pp. 8–9.

36. CAHJP #217-218.

37. CAHJP, #219.

38. Joseph Walk, *Kurzbiographien zur Geschichte der Juden* (München: K G Saur, 1988).

39. CAHJP, #212.

40. CAHJP, #209.

41. Recall Wolfram Selig's discussion of the Uhlfelder department store in this study's review of scholarship in Chapter Two.

42. Werner J. Cahnmann, "The Jews of Munich: 1918-43," in Joseph B. Maier, Judith Marcus, and Zoltán Tarr (Eds.), *German Jewry; Its History and Sociology. Selected Essays by Werner J. Cahnmann* (New Brunswick: Transaction Publishers, 1989), p. 116.

43. CAHJP, #208.

44. CAHJP, #205.

45. CAHJP, #199.

46. CAHJP, #197.

47. CAHJP, #194.

48. CAHJP, #192.
49. CAHJP, #190, #189.
50. CAHJP, #187.
51. CAHJP, #191.
52. CAHJP, #186a.
53. CAHJP, #93.
54. CAHJP, #91-90.
55. CAHJP, #181.
56. CAHJP, #179.
57. CAHJP, #177, #176.
58. CAHJP, #168.
59. CAHJP, #149-148.
60. CAHJP, #146.
61. CAHJP, #165.
62. CAHJP, #161.
63. CAHJP, #162.
64. CAHJP, #160.
65. CAHJP, #158.
66. CAHJP, #157-156.
67. CAHJP, #152.
68. CAHJP, #139.
69. CAHJP, #135.
70. CAHJP, #144.
71. CAHJP, #140.
72. CAHJP, #138.
73. CAHJP, #129.
74. CAHJP, #130.
75. CAHJP, #97-96.
76. BA R8119 15218, Microfiche #1, Document #10.
77. Cornelia Hecht, *Deutsche Juden und Antisemitismus in der Weimarer Republik* (Bonn: Verlag J.H.W. Dietz Nachfolger, GmbH, 2003), pp. 394–395.
78. Friedländer, *Nazi Germany*, p. 235.
79. Ian Kershaw, *Popular Opinion & Political Dissent in the Third Reich*; Bavaria 1933–1945 (Oxford: Clarendon Press, 1983), pp. 274–275.
80. Friedländer, *Nazi Germany*, pp. 75–76.
81. Hecht, *Deutsche Juden*, p. 402.
82. The inconsistency in applying the former appellation "Hermann Tietz" is evident in Abraham Frowein's August 3, 1933, newsletter to other Association members of the German textile industry. Frowein identified his circular letter as concerning the family-owned "Hermann Tietz," but it mentioned the new "expanded management" from the Limited Liability Company. A similar deviation is found in the March 7, 1934, Weekly Cash Report typed on Hertie Kaufhaus Beteiligungs GmbH letterhead, but which has a Hermann Tietz & Company attachment depicting the change in inventory from August 1 to August 15, 1933. See BA R8119F 15218, Microfiche #1, Documents #3 and #51.

83. Documents preserved in the Reich Ministry of Finance may indicate this as an attempt to pay real estate taxes based on an assessment made during the Depression. The Attorney Richard Carl Wolff wrote an April 30, 1934, application to the Reich Minister of Finance Lutz Graf Schwerin von Krosigk on the basis of a consultation he had with Trabart Arthur Rudolf Georg Freiherr von und zu der Tann-Rathsamhausen regarding the possibility of paying an estimated lump sum tax on all real estate holdings. The estimate was complicated by three factors. First, taxes of all department store branches would normally have been paid based on the purchase price. However, nothing had been paid to acquire the chain and thus Hertie Kaufhaus Beteiligungs GmbH was proposing to discount the 1931 property tax by 20 percent to estimate the proposed liability. This appears to be another attempt at a windfall profit, since tax assessments made during 1931 would have been conducted during the Great Depression. By 1934, the property value would have grown significantly. Second, Oscar Tietz's widow Betty held some real estate parcels as private property, which Hertie was claiming as part of the business. These lots included the 350,000 RM property on Legienstraße in Altona and the 276,000 RM property on Krausenstraße in Berlin. Third, Tietz family members controlled some plots, such as Georg's villa on the Königsallee, which Hertie acknowledged were personal possessions. See BA R2 57689, Microfiche #1.

84. BA R8119F 15218 Microfiche #1, Numbers 2–29.

85. Along with Dr. Hölling of the Dresdner Bank, this individual is mentioned in both the September 6, 1933, and January 3, 1934, weekly reports from Georg Karg as having submitted profitability forecasts for the Hertie Kaufhaus Beteiligungs GmbH Advisory Council. As minutes became available for Hertie's Advisory Council for the February 20, 1934, meeting, his surname is listed but neither his first name nor the financial institution he represents. But this individual should not be confused with Paul Mankiewitz, the Deutsche Bank's Spokesman from 1919 to 1923 since this Jewish financier passed away on June 22, 1924. Note BA R8119F 15218, Microfiche #1, Documents #15 and #39.

86. BA R8119F 15218 fiche 1 and 2.

87. Kershaw, *Popular*, pp. 80–84.

88. Andrew Stuart Bergerson, *Ordinary Germans in Extraordinary Times; The Nazi Revolution in Hildesheim* (Bloomington: Indiana University Press, 2004), p. 15.

89. Bergerson, *Ordinary*, pp. 146–152.

90. Peter Fritzsche, *Life and Death in the Third Reich* (Cambridge: The Belknap Press of Harvard University Press, 2008), p. 20.

91. Victor Klemperer, *Ich will Zeugnis ablegen bis zum letzten. Tagebücher 1933–1941* (Berlin: Aufbau-Verlag GmbH, 1997), p. 42, 44.

92. Ironically, Abraham Frowein was not a newcomer to business takeovers. Walter and Lebrecht Stein had moved from Langenberg to Osterath, where they purchased a real estate plot on November 28, 1889. In the following year, they purchased a steam engine and began weaving on March 1, 1891. By 1908, their mill employed a staff of 174 and by 1911, they expanded their facility (See Peter Dohms, *Meerbusch; Die Geschichte der Stadt und der Altgemeinden von den Ursprüngen bis zur Gegenwart* [Meerbusch: Stadt Meerbusch, 1991], p. 466). Abraham Frowein started

a competitive operation in Elberfeld on November 30, 1927. Frowein's textile operation grew from 6 looms in 1927 to 140 in 1930 and 330 in 1932. In 1936, Frowein purchased the Walter & Lebrecht Stein company for an undisclosed sum (See Edmund Sturtz, *175 Jahre Abr. Frowein jun., Abr. & Gebr. Frowein* [Düsseldorf: A Bagel, 1938], pp. 79–81).

93. BA R8127 15215, Document #56.

94. Recall the pre-April boycotts of Tietz stores in Duisburg, Essen, Bottrop, Mühlheim, Magdeburg and Essen mentioned in section B of this chapter.

95. This further supports this exploration's interpretation that the 14.5 million RM Loan I and Loan II by the consortium were never intended as a bailout. These loans were provided as a means whereby Georg Karg could Aryanize the firm.

96. Zwillenberg, Lutz. Interview #36276. Segment 1. Visual History Archive, USC Shoah Foundation, 1997. (Accessed February 14–15, 2017).

97. In a December 2, 1933, letter to Hitler's Economic Advisor Wilhelm Keppler, the Deutsche Treuhand-Aktiengesellschaft für Warenverkehr noted that Trabart Arthur Rudolf Georg Freiherr von und zu der Tann- Rathsamhausen had obtained his position in the beginning of August 1933 as the decisive vote in the Hertie Advisory Board. Tann's annual salary was 66,000 RM for replacing the Jewish Director Löwenberger, who had only been paid 40,000 RM. Nevertheless, the Baron was unsatisfied with this remuneration and became involved in other Aryanizations. For example, Philipp Rosenthal was a world-famous porcelain manufacturer in Selb. But his Board of Directors and Supervisory Board decided to expel him from the firm he founded by electing Karl Krämer of the Bayerischen Hypotheken- und Wechselbank to the Supervisory Board on August 14, 1933. With Krämer's collaboration, the Supervisory Board sold stock to individuals such as Baron von der Tann, who did not think well of Rosenthal. It appears that Tann financially benefited from the Aryanization of other Jewish companies as well. Compare BA R8119F 15211, Microfiche #5, Documents #163-164 with Jürgen Lillteicher, *Raub, Recht und Restitution; Die Rückerstattung jüdischen Eigentums in der frühen Bundesrepublik* (Göttingen: Wallstein Verlag, 2007), pp. 181–182.

98. Michael Wildt, *Hitler's Volksgemeinschaft and the Dynamics of Racial Exclusion; Violence against Jews in Provincial Germany, 1919–1939* (New York: Berghahn Books, 2012), p. 280.

Chapter 6

Early Aryanizations Confirming the Hermann Tietz Paradigm

A. ARYANIZATION OF LEONHARD TIETZ

1. Incorporation of the Leonhard Tietz Department Store Chain

Between the large expenditures required for the grand opening of the expanded, block-long Hohe Straße flagship on December 6, 1902 in Cologne and his desire to compete for Berlin's consumer, Leonhard Tietz must have come to the realization that greater sources of capital were required than what his personal funds would supply. Leonhard supplied 6 million RM in equity from the surplus remaining after 11 million in the firm's liabilities were subtracted from 21 million in assets. This sum was supplemented by two brothers-in-law, Max and Sally (diminutive for Salomon) Baumann, who became limited partners by means of contributing one million apiece from the excess. The cousin, Louis Schloß, provided one million after having managed the branch in Koblenz for years and similarly the cousin, Willy Pintus, added 1 million to the owners' equity after directing the Mainz store for numerous years. Thus, after establishing branches in Bonn (1901), Krefeld (1904) and Mayen (1905), the five partners met the notary Wilhelm Reichner Maria Weisweiler on March 17, 1905, to transform the department stores chain from a privately owned company to a public corporation. The largest in-kind contribution came from the Hohe Straße store valued at 5.5 million RM. At the time of incorporation, the chain consisted of sixteen stores, 2,400 employees and annual sales of 24 million RM.[1]

Eugen Schmalenbach, professor of economics in Cologne's College of Commerce, was responsible for assessing the value of Leonhard Tietz assets before the privately owned company could be allowed to sell stock as a corporation. The flagship store on Cologne's "Miracle Mile," was appraised at

5.5 million RM of the total 13,150,000 million RM in real estate. The edifices in Krefeld, Elberfeld and Dusseldorf fluctuated in value between 1.0 and 1.8 million RM for each. The two other branches in Cologne as well as the three stores in Mainz, Koblenz and Bonn were each appraised between 0.5 and 0.7 million RM, whereas the store in Stralsund was valued at 290,000 RM and the small shop in Düren at 200,000 RM. Furnishings and other assets were valued at 8.6 million RM.[2]

By 1907, the chain's capital had expanded to 12.5 million RM. The further increases in equity to 17.5 million RM in 1911; 25.2 million in 1925; 29.7 million in 1927, and 37.2 in 1928 reflect the boom years during the 1920s, which would enable further expansion in the number of stores.[3] With the potential for increased construction funds through the sale of corporate stock, Leonhard Tietz transformed a purchasing office to the third largest of his seventeen stores in Berlin.[4]

Leonhard established a daughter corporation in Belgium, the *Grands Magasins L. Tietz*. The stock was sold on the Brussels Stock Exchange and quickly increased in value from 6 million Belgium Francs to 9 million. With the added influx in capital, the Antwerp store, which had existed since 1900, was expanded in 1908 as well as the three new stores in Mecheln, St. Niklas and Brügge all being opened while the Antwerp facility was being enlarged. Leonhard's market share was increased through the erection of the Rue Neuve store in 1910, which required a staff of 1,000. Nevertheless, the foreign operations did not preclude further development in Germany, where a new store on the Königsallee became operational in Dusseldorf in 1909. That year, Leonhard's oldest son Alfred Leonhard not only was selected to manage this facility with 4,546 m^2 of sales floor and served by a staff of 1,100, but he also married Margarete Dzialoszynski. In the following year, Alfred Leonhard became a member of the Board of Directors. The Elberfeld store was expanded and the new branch in Chemnitz also held its grand opening in 1910.[5]

By offering new shares of stocks, German banks played a major role in the publicly traded department store chain, Leonhard Tietz. Shortly after the death of Leonhard, Max Grünbaum was promoted from an authorized signatory of the company to a member of the Board. As the financial genius behind the firm, he had assisted Professor Eugen Schmalenbach in appraising the value of the firm's real estate prior to its becoming a corporation. Meetings of the shareholders needed to be called more frequently in order to respond to inflation. Representing the corporation's best understanding of finances, Grünbaum advised both the Board and stockholders in the 1919 and 1920 supplements to the standard annual meetings regarding the need to increase equity. The requirement for greater capital led to the appointment of Walter Seidel from the Dresdner Bank to the Supervisory Board.[6]

The costs of World War I imposed by the Versailles Treaty had emptied German financial institutions of capital, making it difficult to implement American retail innovations for both the privately owned Hermann Tietz and the publicly traded Leonhard Tietz companies. In 1925, members of the Leonhard Tietz Board of Directors returned to the United States in order to negotiate an influx of dollars from prospective American investors. Essential to their success was a thorough audit by Price Waterhouse, which resulted in funding from Lehmann Brothers. Previously in 1906, Lehmann Brothers in conjunction with Goldman, Sachs & Company assisted Sears Roebuck and Company in becoming a publicly traded firm. Lehmann enriched their investment expertise in department stores by funding during the following two decades: F.W. Woolworth Company, May Department Stores Company, Gimbel Brothers, and R.H. Macy & Company. Ernst Baumann traveled to the United States on three occasions before personally signing thousands of shares for Wall Street backed by Lehmann Brothers. Not only did Leonhard Tietz receive 4 million dollars in 1925–1926, but also additional funds were invested in the retail corporation in 1928 and 1929.[7]

A marketing novelty, not introduced by the large American department store chains, was the German retailers' development of a wholly owned single price chain. Sears, Gimbel, and Macy did not have a subsidiary, similar to the Woolworth model.

2. Single Price Stores Developed by Leonhard Tietz

The Leonhard Tietz chain was more successful in imitating America's single price stores than Georg was in the Hermann Tietz Company. Julius Schloß had been impressed by the chain of Woolworth stores, which he had analyzed in his trip to America and knew of their intent to introduce their 5¢ and 10¢ stores in Germany. Fortified with cash from Lehmann Brothers, Leonhard Tietz duplicated the Woolworth concept of selling in only a few price categories in a simple, self-service environment by establishing the Ehape Single Price Stores (Einheitspreis-Handelsgesellschaft mbH). Although Ehape only opened on October 19, 1925, in the following 1926–1927 fiscal year, the new Leonhard Tietz subsidiary had sales of 9.2 million RM and opened twenty-one branches. The enterprise was so successful that it became incorporated on August 1, 1927, with a founding capital of 3 million RM and in the 1927–1928 business year, an additional thirty branches opened and sales rose to 25.8 million RM. Success continued in the 1928–1929 year with the establishment of eleven main stores and thirty-seven small shops with sales rising to 42.1 million RM. The growth in stores began to slow in 1929–1930 with only nine main and nine small stores, but sales nevertheless soared to 59.2 million RM. The slowing trend in expansion continued in 1929–1930 with a total of seventy-three main stores with annual sales of 71 million RM, undoubtedly impacted by the stock market crash and the onset of the Great Depression.[8]

German department stores catered to the middle class and thus neglected cheaper merchandise. In addition, only limited floor space could be allotted to small everyday items. Neither fact was neglected by another department store chain, namely Karstadt. The second 5¢ and 10¢ chain, called Epa (Einheitspreis-Aktiengesellschaft) was inaugurated in response to Leonhard Tietz as a corporation on July 17, 1926, with starting capital of 250,000 RM, although only 62,500 RM was deposited in cash. Its first branch in Bremen was opened on November 25, 1926. In contrast with its slightly earlier competitor Ehape, which focused in the south and west of Germany, Epa concentrated its branches in the north and east of Germany, including Berlin. Perhaps, the key location in the capital was one factor responsible for the fact that Epa became the largest of all German single price chains both in terms of the number of branches as well as sales. A second factor was Ehape's self-imposed restriction to twenty-five and fifty Pfennig merchandise in locations with Leonhard Tietz stores since the chain observed that both stores selling merchandise costing 1 Mark provoked undesirable competition. In contrast, from its inception, Epa had extended its merchandise to the 1 Mark level, even though it enjoyed a close association with its related department store chain. Despite the small initial investment, Epa's growth in branches and sales was astronomical.

By 1931, there were a total of about fifteen different single price companies and associations with approximately 400 stores. The wealth drew the attention of Erich Niemann,[9] who obtained his position as a managing director of the Dresdner Bank on July 1, 1933, because he had been a former pilot with Hermann Göring. Before pressure from Wilhelm Keppler and the NSBO brought Niemann's dismissal, he was placed in charge of the "uncouth" work of Aryanizing Karstadt's Epa single price chain. Before his replacement by Keppler's cousin, Emil Meyer, Niemann used his influence as a Supervisory Board Member to also assist in the Aryanization of the railway car manufacturer Orenstein & Koppel AG.[10]

However, the overheated competition stemming from the rapid expansion of Karstadt's Epa, Leonhard Tietz's Ehape, and Woolworth combined with the Hauptgemeinschaft's pressure on government to levy special taxes and issue moratoriums on the large chains contributed to financial difficulties in 1932 and 1933. A moratorium on new retail construction in cities with more than 100,000 inhabitants took place, as previously noted indicating the continuity of anti-department store legislation in the Weimar Republic and the Third Reich.[11] But December 1932 amendments extended the moratorium to all cities and towns. In addition, single price stores were prohibited from expanding their existing sales capacity and moving to a new location in order to change customers' impression of the store's character. Also, prior legislation had allowed a transitional period of nine weeks to compensate for expansions in which a rental contract had already been signed or builders were in the process of launching new construction. But time to segue now vanished and damages would not be compensated by the federal or state government. Furthermore, the number of allowable price levels was restricted to ten and the quantity of items bundled together could not be shifted from the customary dozen to a more unusual amount, such as ten. The new provisions were specifically intended to close the final loophole in order to prevent single price stores from increasing their market share in the retail trade.[12] As troublesome as these anti-free trade measures might have been, the larger problem for single price chains would have been the five to six million unemployed during the period of October 1932 to April 1933,[13] who undoubtedly conserved cash for the essential categories of food, heat and rent.

After Ehape's Board of Directors accepted the 1931–1932 final balance statement, Leonhard Tietz reported to the press a net profit of a mere 750,000 RM. To maintain good investor relations and a high value of the share price, Ehape issued a 6 percent dividend although the broadsheet contrasted it with the prior year's return to investors of 8 percent. Additional gloomy news included the fact that only 250,000 RM could be placed in a reserve account and simply 68,580 RM was carried forward into the 1932–1933 budget. The Ehape sales decline from April to June 1932 temporarily improved in July–September 1932. This may best be explained through seasonal employment during the summer of 1932. Table 5.4 had chronicled the ebb and flow of German unemployment from October 1932 through June 1933. But if additional data is supplied, it will be observed that a 1932 nadir in unemployment was experienced (see Table 6.1). A comparison of Table 5.4 with Table 6.1 indicates that the momentary decline in unemployment

Table 6.1 Antecedents to Table 5.4 on German Unemployment

Date	*Unemployment*
January 1932	6,042,000
February 1932	6,128,000
March 1932	6,034,000
June 1932	5,476,000
August 1932	5,224,000
September 1932	5,103,000
October 1932	5,109,000

Source: The information is contained in the article "Weitere," which was published on page 3 of the morning edition of the July 8, 1933, *Vossische Zeitung*.

from June through October 1932 prompted Ehape's July–September increased sales. The comparison also demonstrates that no period replicated the low levels of unemployment in June–October 1932 until May and June 1933.[14]

Although no forecast was immediately offered for the 1932–1933 fiscal year by the newspaper, in the 1931–1932 balance statement there was a reassuring decrease in the inventory, but an increase in liquid assets caused by a considerable restructuring in the liabilities. A first budget item noticed was the decrease in inventory from 6.73 million RM to 5.26 million RM, which caused a decrease in merchandising debt from 5.72 to 4.54 million RM. A second factor was a small increase in wages and salaries, promoted by a limited expansion of the chain. A third aspect was the designation of 900,000 RM for rented buildings, since new construction was prohibited. A further sign of financial strength was the assignment of 1.69 million RM in depreciation from current revenues, rather than raising new capital. Nevertheless, short-term bank debt rose from 5.19 million RM to 5.72 and long-term bank liabilities appeared for the first time in the amount of 2.56 million RM. The newspaper surmised that the new loans apparently served to cover mortgages. A final circumstance was that total liabilities amounted to 17 million RM partially offset by 6 million RM invested in shares of company stock and 1 million in the reserve fund, with a gross profit of 750,000 RM from sales of 16.13 million RM.[15]

The size of the Cologne-based Leonhard Tietz department store chain and its associated Ehape chain can be appreciated by examining it from the perspective of the city's tax register. There were 5,268 merchandising firms, which were required to pay taxes in 1914. However, the number of tiny shops in Cologne eking out an existence for the owner's family far exceeded the number of tax payers. Such was the case for the city, which the 1931 edition of Germany's most famous encyclopedia described as "the number one location for trade in western Germany."[16]

The preceding analysis of the 1931–1932 balance sheet, produced at the end of December 1932, provides a good understanding of the value of the firm in the spring of 1933. The annual profit was 750,000 RM and the bank balances had soared from 150,000 RM in 1930–1931 to 2,225,000 RM in 1931–1932. In chapter 5, section D, the generally accepted rule of thumb in assessing the value of a firm was given as three to five times the annual net profit. Had German banks offered a fair price for the Ehape chain in the spring of 1933, the financial institutions should have extended between 2,250,000 RM and 3,750,000 RM. The weakened condition of Leonhard Tietz manifested by the marginal profit of an incorporated company led to the appointment of bank executives as Tietz Board members.

3. Banks Pay Tietz 800,000 RM for 24 Million in Tietz Stock

Small retailers felt their existence threatened by department stores as well as labor unions, which had formed consumer associations. This competition could be quite extensive. For example, the Free Union's retail alliance included 40,000 members covering a swath of the Rhineland 150 kilometers long and 45 kilometers wide, serving 46 communities. Additional threats stemmed from the chains of 5¢ and 10¢ stores in which the culture of self-service and the inexpensive prices was despised by small merchants. Further perils were perceived from private monopolies in which department stores not only sold but also produced their own merchandise. Leonhard Tietz practiced such vertical integration by manufacturing its own stockings in Bitburg as well as linens in Vogtland. NSDAP Members added anti-Semitism to the imagined menace through its depiction of Jewish department stores as being part of the global conspiracy of non-productive capitalism attempting to dominate the world.[17]

In April and May 1933, there were repeated attacks against Jewish businesses, disruptions of shareholder meetings by the SA and NSBO, temporary occupation of offices as well as arbitrary appointments of Commissars for firms viewed as Jewish. Nevertheless, it was the behind-the-scenes activities of banks and not the public disruptions by SA and NSBO, which determined the fate of Leonhard Tietz and other Jewish corporations. In fact, when the violence in the streets did not cease by June 1933, Hitler declared before party officials in the beginning of July that the Nazi revolution was finished and within a few days Interior Minister Wilhelm Frick underscored the point with a Decree. By mid-July, Otto Wagener was deposed from his position as Commissar for the Economy and the NSBO was prohibited from accepting new members. In addition, NSDAP leadership arrested dissatisfied SA and excluded them from the organization.[18]

In contrast, the Deutsche Bank, Dresdner Bank and Commerzbank's most effective weapon against Leonhard Tietz and other stock-issuing companies was the posting of a bank representative on the Jewish firm's Supervisory Board. There were two aspects of this strategy quite foreign to American financial institutions. First the United States has only a Board of Directors and not an additional Board. Second in Germany prior to the Reform of 1937, a custodian bank could not only vote the shares of its member on the Supervisory Board but also for a depositor who did not vote. Before the Reform, the bank as safe-guarder of the stock did not even need to notify a client that it had voted in the shareholder's place. In addition, if the new non-Jewish owner transferred a large block of stock to another bank after an Aryanization, the new custodian could displace a competitor from the Supervisory Board and thus gain important information on the internal operations of the company. Seldom did such displacements occur without consequences in lending relationships. Such activities transpired in the Spring and Summer of 1933 despite the Dresdner Bank having a larger number of Jews sitting on their Boards and presiding over branches other than their large financial institutions.[19]

As the son of a founder of the corporation, Julius Schloß became Vice President of Sales in 1920. In October 1942, Julius reflected back on the pinnacle of the firm, which had been reached at the time of the fiftieth anniversary in February 1930. At that time, the business had forty-one department stores and seventy-five single price stores in the Ehape subsidiary. With sales of approximately 350 million RM, employing more than 20,000 people of whom 1,500 were Jewish, the firm was the second-largest retailer in Germany.

On the eve of the April 1 Boycott, Alfred Tietz took the evening train from Cologne on March 29, 1933, in order to join Franz Levy in consultation with bankers and government leaders, while Gerhard Tietz, Franz Baumann and Schloß decided to close all branches before the Nazi action. One of the decisions made in Berlin was to appoint Abraham Frowein, President of the International Chamber of Commerce (ICC) to become the new Tietz Board Chair.[20] Frowein's influence as Chair for the Trustees of the German Textile Industry has already been seen in his communication with Georg Karg during the Aryanization of Hermann Tietz in chapter 5, section F. However, his power as president over 100 chapters of the ICC in fifty countries was more pronounced in his direct remarks to Prime Minister Édouard Herriot. In a December 1, 1932 speech in Paris, Frowein boldly reminded the French statesman of his summer statement at the Lausanne Conference that economic competition required new methods and processes. Thereby, Frowein positioned the ICC to play a role in new business developments. Three months later, this forceful personality restructured Leonhard Tietz.[21]

After informing Tietz Board Members in the Commerzbank in Cologne regarding the Berlin decisions, Gerhard Tietz fled to Holland, whereas Frowein came to Cologne and "suggested that all Jewish officers and also the Jewish Board Members should resign." During the April 3 meeting, conducted in the Deutsche Bank, all Jewish executives resigned and with the exception of Frowein, all new Board members were bankers. Within two days, the same information had been published in the newspapers: the Jewish partners Alfred Leonhard Tietz, Julius Schloß, Franz Levy, Franz Baumann and Gerhard Tietz as well as various members of the Supervisory Board had all "retired" and been replaced by Abraham Frowein, Friedrich Reinhart Board Chairman of the Commerzbank, Dr. Bayer and Christian Rensing.[22]

In 1930, Tietz shares were sold at three times their nominal value, whereas by 1933, the value had dropped to 10 percent. Julius Schloß had interpreted this loss in equity as the result of Point 16 of Hitler's February 24, 1920

NSDAP Program, without addressing the inconsistency of why the share price had been 155 RM on January 6, 1930, but had increased to 160.75 RM on June 2, 1930. Schloß also did not utilize his insider knowledge of the department store chain to elucidate why there had been a thirteen-year gap between the 1933 effect and the alleged 1920 cause. Schloß encountered a similar difficulty in maintaining that sales had fallen by more than half. He attributed the drop in revenue as attributable to the Boycott, which began on April 1, 1933. Although this may be accurate, it does not elucidate why the share price made small recoveries in April and June, before hitting rock bottom at the end of July 1933. Perhaps a closer analysis of the stock price will help elucidate how the Jewish-owned firm was acquired by Germany's largest banks. Of the 31 million RM in the firm's equity 16.3 million RM was owned by the extended family, but the Commerzbank, Deutsche Bank and Dresdner Bank paid the former Jewish owners a fraction of the stock's value.[23]

The public announcement of the dismissal of Jewish executives in April coincided with the spring of 1933 decline in value of Leonhard Tietz shares as demonstrated in Tables 6.2 and 6.3. In order to distinguish investors' responses to internal company activities from external market forces, such as the Reichbank's prime interest rate or the value of the German Mark vis-à-vis foreign currencies, I have conducted a longitudinal study comparing the value of Tietz stock with six other publicly traded firms. It is unclear what factors caused Tietz stock to peak in January 1933. Two of the other incorporated companies examined here were also Jewish-owned, namely the Engelhardt brewery and the Orenstein & Koppel railroad car manufacturer.[24] After Hitler's January 31, 1933 appointment as Chancellor, investors were nervous in February about Engelhardt, but not about Orenstein.

Although the daily Leonhard Tietz volatility remained, a downward spiral in the value of the stock developed in March through May as investors became informed of measures taken against the department store. In contrast, the Jewish-owned Engelhardt brewery rebounded, whereas the Jewish-owned Orenstein & Koppel railway car manufacturer joined the Gentile industrialists such as Daimler-Benz, I.G. Farben and Mannesmann in soaring stock prices.

The adverse effects of the April 1, 1933 boycott are supported by the dwindling Leonhard Tietz stock price. The share price hit a low of 24.00 RM on March 31 and by April 3 had temporarily rebounded to 29.00 RM. By the middle to end of May, shares had plummeted. They were consistently trading at or below 20 RM. Low stock valuation was not the sole bad news facing shareholders. Another issue was the June 18, 1933 newspaper reportage that unlike the 6 percent dividend given in the 1931–1932 fiscal year based on a net profit of 2.3 million RM, no dividend would be provided to investors in the 1932–1933 year due to the net profit being a mere 88,476 RM. Instead

Table 6.2 Normal Volatility in the Price of Leonhard Tietz Stock

	1/2	*1/9*	*1/16*	*1/23*	*1/30*	*2/1*	*2/6*	*2/13*	*2/20*
Leonhard Tietz	39.25	40.75	45.38	43.88	42.50	38.50	36.25	38.00	36.50
AEG	30.63	31.88	29.25	29.63	30.00	27.50	26.63	27.38	26.13
Daimler	19.88	23.38	21.00	22.13	20.25	23.38	20.25	24.00	24.13
Engelhardt	100.00	100.00	100.00	99.00	98.75	95.00	94.75	90.00	88.00
IG Farben	96.75	107.00	102.00	103.75	104.13	107.50	103.35	109.38	109.63
Mannesmann	62.75	62.63	62.63	62.50	59.63	64.88	68.25	62.00	60.75
Orenstein & Koppel	42.50	43.75	42.50	42.00	40.00	44.50	40.00	42.25	41.26

Source: This material was assembled from daily stock quotations in the January 2–February 20, 1933, editions of the *Vossische Zeitung*.

Table 6.3 Loss of Value as Reflected in Leonhard Tietz Stock Price

	3/27	*3/31*	*4/4*	*4/11*	*4/21*	*5/2*	*5/13*	*5/26*	*5/30*
Leonhard Tietz	34.00	24.00	28.00	30.00	29.00	26.00	19.50	20.13	19.75
AEG	36.75	28.00	29.25	30.25	32.00	29.25	26.13	25.00	24.25
Daimler	32.00	27.75	29.75	36.38	37.00	35.00	30.38	30.00	31.13
Engelhardt	98.00	90.00	93.50	92.50	98.00	128.00	118.00	116.75	114.23
IG Farben	137.25	120.00	126.50	128.63	143.13	143.63	127.25	130.00	131.00
Mannesmann	75.38	61.50	67.13	69.75	76.50	81.63	75.50	70.13	69.00
Orenstein & Koppel	63.75	46.00	46.25	48.00	51.00	53.13	49.50	50.50	49.00

Source: This financial data was compiled from daily stock quotations published in the March 27–May 30, 1933, editions of the *Vossische Zeitung*.

7.02 million RM had been paid in taxes with 5.49 million for interest and 4.88 million in write-downs. Department store sales, which did not include the Ehape single price stores, further declined from 178.6 million RM to 147 million, providing a net profit of the aforementioned 88,476 RM. Similar to the Hermann Tietz strategy depicted in Tables 5.7 and 5.8 in chapter 5, section C, the broadsheet observed that the Leonhard Tietz chain had increased the prices of merchandise in an attempt to offset the declines in revenue. The newspaper confirmed the decline in the value of investors' equity previously provided in Julius Schloß's memoir as 31.2 million RM but noted a reserve fund of 6.58 million RM.[25]

At the July 11, 1933 annual shareholders meeting, 22,845,500 RM in common shares and 200,000 RM in preferred shares were represented. Supervisory Board Chair Fritz Andreae, representing the Hardy Bank, was pleased that the government was not intent on destroying department stores.[26] He estimated the value of this sector in the retail market at 1 billion RM. He maintained that despite the decrease in sales from 178.6 million to 147.0 million RM, there would have been a dividend had it not been for the 5.9 percent increase in taxes and social welfare payments. This was particularly true of the recently implemented increases in the department store tax. In Andreae's opinion, this demonstrated the wisdom of the firm's management. The new Board Director Dr. Otto Baier recommended that the stockholders change the name of the company to Westdeutsche Kaufhof A.G., so that newspapers would no longer be pressured to decline printing of the chain's advertisements. Also voted on was the acceptance of Mr. Bjornson-Sonaar from Berlin to the Kaufhof Supervisory Board. Newspaper coverage provided conflicting reports on whether Commerzbank director Friedrich Reinhardt also joined the Board or whether he merely wanted to continue his April 3, 1933 activity in the Financial Committee since he had already reached the maximum number of seats he was allowed to hold.[27]

Supervisory Board Chair Andreae corrected Julius Schloß's later memoir that the Boycott had cut Tietz sales by 50 percent, when as mentioned in the prior paragraph, the decline was 17.7 percent from 178.6 to 147 million RM. However, Andreae's attribution of the special tax on department stores as wielding decisive influence is rejected by business historians, who maintain that the special taxes did not inflict serious damage on the department stores.[28] In place of Andreae's emphasis on the role of state-imposed taxes, the following table will introduce an analysis of the banks' role in Aryanization based upon their own financial statement.

Tables 6.2–6.4 demonstrates that although Leonhard Tietz share prices declined during the Weimar Republic, the nadir was reached only after the bankers wrested ownership from the Jewish entrepreneurs. Combining data from stock prices with annual balance statements, a clearer financial

Table 6.4 Collapse in the Price of Leonhard Tietz Stock

	6/2	*6/9*	*6/16*	*6/23*	*6/30*	*7/7*	*7/14*	*7/21*	*7/28*
Leonhard Tietz	20.50	25.50	25.00	20.75	18.00	15.63	17.00	17.00	15.63
AEG	25.63	24.75	24.63	21.75	23.25	22.63	21.50	21.75	20.00
Daimler	32.38	31.50	30.13	27.00	29.88	28.75	29.75	29.60	29.25
Engelhardt	116.50	114.00	118.00	112.00	108.00	106.00	104.00	108.00	105.35
IG Farben	135.00	138.50	134.25	126.13	129.25	129.00	133.00	130.63	130.75
Mannesmann	71.50	70.73	66.25	60.00	64.38	61.25	62.00	63.75	62.00
Orenstein & Koppel	51.63	48.50	47.63	40.25	44.00	42.00	37.88	36.00	35.13

Source: These stock quotations were published in the June 2–July 28, 1933, editions of the *Vossische Zeitung*.

picture emerges regarding the period from the end of the founders' ownership through the beginning of the banks' possession. In order to include January inventory sales in the annual financial document, Tietz's fiscal year ran from February 1 through January 31. For the year ending January 31, 1932, Tietz had given a 6 percent dividend totaling 1.86 million RM, based on a net profit of 2,262,478 RM. However the June 19, 1933 announcement reported that no dividend would be offered for the year concluding on January 31, 1933, since the net profit had only been 88,476 RM. But the financial instrument conceded that not only had the regularly scheduled depreciations been met, but also "it was held to be essential to carry out special depreciations in the real estate account." This special write-down was not implemented in the year ending January 1932, but the line item was 1,130,252 RM for the year ending January 1933. This was not a legally required expense and would have been sufficient for a 3.6 percent dividend in 1933. Although the record was prepared in mid-June for the July 11, 1933 annual shareholders meeting, any dividend would have enriched those holding stocks on January 31, 1933. It appears reasonable to conclude that the bankers sought a method whereby the company could be strengthened at the original owners' further expense.[29] This conclusion might seem speculative until the balance statement's accommodation to the new political system is read:

> In an already difficult economic period, an unusual decline in sales arose, which had to be offset as soon as possible to avoid financial weakening of our company. Therefore, we began a concerted effort through the preparation of certain adjustments and a new orientation of our business and personnel policies to accommodate the existing opposition. Thereby we want to create the prerequisites for an egalitarian integration of our company into the new German economy.[30]

A second example whereby the bankers could claim that they had made "Westdeutsche Kaufhof" more profitable was by means of the devaluation of the dollar. Prior to the currency fluctuation, the department store chain had acquired loans in the United States for 6.018 million dollars. When the dollar decreased in value, more than 9 million RM could be written into a currency adjustment account as a windfall profit. If the new Supervisory Board members could repay the American bondholders before January 31, 1935, they could legally claim the amount as a legitimate profit.[31] Not possessing the merchandising capabilities of the Tietz family members, it appears that the Commerzbank, Deutsche Bank and Dresdner Bank directors attempted to enhance the company's value through accounting stratagems as well as adapting to the new regime.

Perpetrators such as Georg Karg, Baron von der Tann and Abraham Frowein would reappear in the acquisition of other Jewish-owned companies if time permitted their inclusion in this monograph. Once such businessmen had gained experience in the methods whereby a large firm could be acquired in the period 1933–1935, the quest for enhanced wealth provoked individuals to later repeat the process. The next example of the Mosse advertising and publishing agency is included primarily because the role of Max Winkler is so clear in both Mosse and its competitor Ullstein.

B. MOSSE VERLAG'S LACK OF LIQUIDITY SIMPLIFIED ARYANIZATION FOR WINKLER

1. Lachmann-Mosse's Ineptitude or Wolff's Political Inflexibility?

Rudolf Mosse was not a passionate journalist. He founded the *Berliner Tageblatt* in January 1872 due to his anger over Carl Robert Lessing's intransigence in refusing to offer Mosse a reduced price for the large quantities of advertisements, which he had hitherto placed in the *Vossische Zeitung*. As an advertising platform, the *Tageblatt* catered to Berlin's business world. However, its character began to change at the turn of the Century when Editor-in-Chief Theodor Wolff began to give the broadsheet a definite political perspective. The strength of Mosse's capital was not reinvested in the enterprise, as it was in the Scherl publishing house and Ullstein publishing house, but instead formed the basis of Rudolf's private wealth. Within six months, the number of employees expanded from 20 to approximately 1,500, achieving annual sales by the outbreak of World War I of 20 million RM. In 1911, Mosse's adopted daughter Felicia married Hans Lachmann, a metal wholesaler. Mosse did not view him as his successor, but transferred to him only 50 percent ownership of the *Berliner Tageblatt* and left the management of his publishing firm to Martin (Cohn) Carbe, the son of his partner, Emil Cohn. Although Carbe was "level-headed, capable and prudent," it was Theodor Wolff, who personified the Left-Liberal spirit of the newspaper.[32] Mosse sent Wolff to Paris for twelve years as a correspondent, during which time he gained a stockpile of experiences of the world, before Mosse selected him as the Editor-in-Chief of the *Tageblatt* in 1906. For twenty-seven years, his editorials were a national institution, elevating a business publication to international recognition and making Wolff the nation's most important journalist. His centrality to the business has been explicitly affirmed both before and after the owner's death on September 8, 1920: "What Rudolf Mosse bequeathed to his heirs, he inherited from Theodor Wolf."[33]

Rudolf had been taught to use wealth "to protect the legal status of the [Jewish] community and its members and to decidedly oppose slanders, attacks and discrimination."[34] Alongside the art Rudolf collected, he utilized his wealth for philanthropic purposes. In his January 1920 Last Will and Testament, he bequeathed 100,000 RM for the Reform Congregation to freely dispose of as they saw best.[35]

Rudolf's son-in-law, Hans Lachmann-Mosse pursued the advertising and publishing empire without either the cautious editorial policy or the decisive publishing characteristics of the founder. Nevertheless, he was bound in a common business destiny with his two nephews and cousin, namely Managing Director Anselm Hartog, Publishing Director Martin (Cohn) Carbe and Editor-in-Chief Theodor Wolff. As previously discussed in this text, the foreign advertising offices "devoured cash." In addition to adding to his inherited art collection, Lachmann-Mosse "strained the liquid reserves" by purchasing the *8-Uhr-Abendblatt* in 1928. He granted longer payment schedules to advertising customers than what he had been allowed by the newspapers, meaning that Lachmann-Mosse was financing other private companies' advertising campaigns.

In the midst of these poor business decisions, the Zurich advertising office under the direction of Alfred Schwabacher was required to transfer 6 percent of its sales revenue as an annuity for Hans and Felicia Lachmann-Mosse's personal use. This occurred at a time when Zurich was the sole location where financial institutions were willing to extend loans to Mosse and thus jeopardized the company's ability to secure additional short-term credit.[36]

Frequent disagreements between Carbe and Lachmann-Mosse from 1920 onward made management of the business impossible, for which de Mendelssohn holds Lachmann-Mosse chiefly responsible: "He was ambitious and adventurous, without possessing a vision of publishing" and thereby felt disabled by Carbe, who was operating in the spirit of the deceased founder. At every turn, Lachmann-Mosse's plans were opposed by the more prudent Carbe with the result that the two could scarcely work together. Following the demise of the firm's mastermind, there were large financial reserves and the advertisements earned millions. Both the *Berliner Tageblatt*'s circulation and reputation grew, chiefly due to Theodor Wolff's personality and ability to recruit new editors. But he too had difficulties coexisting with Lachmann-Mosse, especially as profits were squandered in establishing branches of the advertising agency in New York, London, Paris, Milan, Barcelona, Amsterdam and other metropoles.[37] Lachmann-Mosse invested in two additional risky speculations: the *Acht-Uhr-Abendblatt* for 4 million RM, when the economy was already declining, and the development of the Lehniner Platz through the construction of Berlin's largest movie theater in 1928.[38]

Most historians as well as professionals within the *Berliner Tageblatt* noted that Wolff blamed the demise on Lachmann-Mosse's lack of political concern coupled with an excessive use of company funds for personal enjoyment. However, a few scholars of modern history suggest that Wolff bore the responsibility for failing to observe how his politics increasingly differed with the views of ever-larger numbers of prior subscribers.[39]

In 1930, the U.S. government wanted to purchase Hans Lachmann-Mosse's Leizigerstraße palace for use as its embassy. Hans declined the offer of 5 million RM, imagining that if so much were proffered, he could obtain even more. Instead the Nazis later acquired it for Hans Frank's Academy of German Law for a quarter of the amount. In addition, he spent 5 million RM of the company's funds on renovating his private estate at Schenkendorf. Furthermore, he purchased large real estate plots on the Hohenzollerndamm and the Lehniner Platz in Berlin and engaged the expensive architect Erich Mendelssohn to draw blueprints. Another speculative investment was his financial support of the Cabaret of Comedians.[40]

Historians later recorded that on December 31, 1930, Carbe sold his shares to Lachmann-Mosse and left the company as a broken man. The first of four reasons why Carbe left was Hans's "unbelievably brutal, antisocial attitude," which stood in complete contradiction to the company founder and the stance of the newspaper. Whereas Carbe maintained that social responsibilities were part of the firm's core values, Hans insisted that such attitudes represented a prewar mentality. In response Carbe retorted: "The pre-war mentality was asocial."

A second indication of Hans Lachmann's deviation from the company's corporate culture was his acceptance of smut advertisements. Lachmann must have considered such small anonymous ads as a source of revenue, but other in-house executives perceived them as dishonoring the name of Rudolf Mosse. Although the government concluded that soliciting of sex had not been formally interpreted as a press offense, theoretically, it could be viewed as aiding and abetting of prostitution. Police Vice President Bernhard Weiss disclosed to Carbe that the publishing house was warned of the possible violation of §184 number 4, but prosecution was not to be expected. In addition, when Feder mentioned to Lachmann-Mosse that the Cabinet had also been occupied with the matter, he responded that Theodor Wolff had already informed him that Chancellor Brüning had also complained about the ads.

A third rationale for Carbe's departure was Lachmann's attempt to influence the newspaper's political perspective by diminishing support for the Republic and lessening criticism of individuals such as Alfred Hugenberg and Wilhelm Frick. Thereby, Lachmann expected to broaden the range of readers and thus expand the possibility of advertisers. Carbe's final motive in leaving Mosse employment was due to the literary level to which the *Berliner*

Tageblatt had alarmingly sunk. Feder lamented the newspaper's decline and Carbe's immanent departure to Weiss, who responded that "we republicans could pack up." Carbe held that Lachmann's financial ineptness was driving the firm toward bankruptcy.[41]

By September 1931, it was clear to the Association of German Newspaper Publishers that Mosse was collecting payments for placing advertisements in various publications in a haphazard fashion. By printing ads before collecting payments, the firm was frequently not receiving any compensation.[42] The general public often mistakenly viewed the Mosse Company as having "gone bankrupt" before Hitler's ascension to power. Elisabeth Kraus corrected this misunderstanding by referring to the July 21, 1933, edition of *Der deutsche Oekonomist*. The publication observed that the firm had ceased payments in June 1933, due to a lack of cash assets, not because of over-indebtedness. The Balance Sheet recorded assets of 14.98 million RM with only 11.31 million RM in liabilities. Either new cash had to be procured or employee dismissals had to produce cash savings.[43] Lachmann's attempt to bring fiscal matters under control by broadening the appeal to right-of-center advertisers through the termination of Jewish employees in the political section of the publication not only adversely affected the publication's left-of-center reputation but also destroyed relationships with highly skilled staff.

2. Lachmann-Mosse's Firing of Jewish Employees

Some historians have concluded that in his private life, Lachmann-Mosse was humble, but in his inherited firm, he ruthlessly introduced economizing measures and thereby destroyed the editorial and operational staffs' trust, which nearly provoked anarchy. It is recorded that terminations rained down, especially on Jewish employees, in order to relax the Nazi boycott against the Mosse's core business of advertising.[44] Ernst Feder's diary recorded that Hans had introduced cost-saving measures in 1929, which had saved 500,000 RM in the *Berliner Tageblatt*. In an October 22, 1930, meeting with the editorial staff, he produced a plan to save a further 600,000 RM in 1930. His strategy was to terminate a list of employees, which he shared allowing the *Tageblatt* editors to make substitutions. The firings were mainly to be conducted in the political section of the newspaper, since Lachmann-Mosse held that the business and feuilleton sections were in good working order.[45]

In disgust, Feder walked out of Lachmann-Mosse's meeting with his editorial staff. He was confronted by a series of employees, whom he was unable to assist. In contrast, Hans Goslar magnanimously approached him with the request that his position be given to an older, Jewish head of a household, since Goslar was young and unmarried. Feder was not the first newspaper executive, who made the decision to leave the publishing empire. Martin

(Cohn) Carbe arranged his severance pay with the owner on December 11, 1930, due to Lachmann-Mosse's "unbelievably brutal, anti-social attitude." In addition, the proprietor's acceptance of smut advertisement exerted an influence on the reportage, leading to an "alarming" reduction in the quality of the newspaper, which occurred before the Nazis came to power.[46]

Before Carbe's planned January 1, 1931 departure, Lachmann-Mosse threatened him with legal action, if he did not terminate Ernst Feder. Thus, on Saturday December 13, 1930, Carbe fired Feder effective from June 30, 1931. When Feder asked for the reasons for his dismissal, Carbe responded "nothing special, [just] cost-saving measures." Lachmann-Mosse must have discussed Feder's removal before December 13, because when Editor-in-Chief Theodor Wolff learned about the action, he furiously stormed into the owner's office maintaining that the owner had broken his promise. In Carbe's presence, Lachmann-Mosse retracted Feder's firing and allowed the reinstated editor to choose his own departure date by April 1, 1931. Wolff confided to Feder on that fateful December day that Carbe and Feder were not the sole executives planning on leaving. The Editor-in-Chief had already discussed his resignation with his wife, due to the inability to "tolerate" the owner's policies.[47]

Lachmann-Mosse's acceptance of smut advertisements was a troublesome action, which repeatedly drew opposition. When Feder raised the issue on December 16, 1930, the proprietor's rejoinder was that Max Urbanski, editor of the local section of the *Berliner Tageblatt*, had been informed by police of what was allowed. It is highly unusual that the owner did not seek a legal opinion from either Feder or Rudolf Olden, both of whom were highly regarded attorneys on his staff. Chancellor Heinrich Brüning's complaint to Theodor Wolff about the advertisements underscored the seriousness of the advertisements. In addition, Feder informed the owner that the Cabinet had discussed the matter and his local dentist had circulated a list of subscribers willing to cancel their subscriptions due to the announcements in the newspapers. Furthermore, on April 24, 1931, University of Berlin Professor of Journalism Emil Dovifat sounded the alarm that Catholic associations were pressuring Prussian Minister of Justice Hermann Schmidt to intervene.

By December 19, 1930, Feder had dictated his letter of resignation since the proprietor did not appreciate his eleven years of activity in defense of the Republic. The dismissal drove Carbe to the competing Ullstein publishing house on January 27, 1931.[48]

Carbe was not the sole editor, who left the *Berliner Tageblatt* because of Lachmann-Mosse and joined the Ullstein competitor. On March 7, 1931, Felix Pinner gave his notice to become the editor of the *Vossische Zeitung*'s business section. Rather than displaying regret, the proprietor immediately went to the composing room and demanded that Pinner's name be withdrawn from the masthead. The witticism circulated that Ullstein should now be called the "Mosseleum."[49]

Lachmann-Mosse introduced further cost-saving measures on April 13, 1931. In response, Theodor Wolff blamed the owner's introduction of costly supplements to the *Berliner Tageblatt* as the cause of cost overruns. In addition, he held that the methods of restricting expenses were ineffective. Furthermore, in May 1931, he fumed that the brunt of the excessive expenditures was borne by the political section of the newspaper, which now had to share correspondents with the *Frankfurter Zeitung*. After nearly twenty-four years of service to Mosse, Wolff was unwilling to endure limits to his freedom as Editor-in-Chief.[50]

The readership noticed the absence of some of the leading *Berliner Tageblatt* personalities. By July 14, 1931, Munich Professor Lujo Brentano was saddened by Feder's departure and fearful that he would have no activity to occupy his time. Therefore, Brentano sent him Daniel Halévy's book *Décadence de la liberté* and suggested that Feder write a similar work about Germany.[51]

Lachmann-Mosse's domestic politics differed from the editors and the journalists. In firing Feder, Carbe had mentioned that the owner held that a political article every eight days was sufficient. Hans's actual statement exceeded this depiction: "It is sufficient when we support Brüning's Cabinet with two lines." In Feder's letter, he affirmed: "opposing me is an owner who does not appreciate my service . . . although the Editor-in-Chief informed me that he sees in me the weight-bearing pillar of the Political Editorial Staff." The departure from Rudolf Mosse's support for the Republic was also noticed by the Jewish community. The Centralverein had been guaranteed a 4 ½ page advertisement to express its programmatic political statement. However, by August 21, 1931, Lachmann-Mosse had incurred the anger of the Jewish umbrella organization by reducing the amount of promised space to only two pages. Similarly, Attorney Ludwig Pickardt, who was defending a Communist in the Felsenecke Trial, complained on May 14, 1932, that the *Berliner Tageblatt* did not fight National Socialism more vigorously.[52]

Perhaps another illustration of Lachmann-Mosse's lack of support for the Republic and its Jewish minority is evidenced in his lack of coverage of the death of Jewish philanthropist James Simon. Feder acknowledged his respects in the *Frankfurter Zeitung*, but neither the *Berliner Tageblatt* nor the *Vossische Zeitung* acknowledged the death. In contrast, Bernhard Kahn, the Berlin Director of the American Joint Distribution Committee, attended the May 26, 1932 funeral services. By October 4, 1932, the *Vossische Zeitung*'s political editor was recorded as observing that the public held that the *Berliner Tageblatt* had lost its featherweight status and the *Voss* had forfeited its heavyweight position.[53]

On the other hand, Elisabeth Kraus claimed this perspective on Lachmann-Mosse did "not corresponding with reality." Based on records from 1928–1930 which Alfred Schwabacher used in order to raise loans from Swiss banks, she interpreted that the Mosse publishing house applied for bank credit on the basis of advertising and not the newspapers. She perceived that there was not much room to maneuver since the *Berliner Tageblatt* had suffered losses since 1930. Thus, it was not "absurd," but rather entirely logical that Lachmann-Mosse, in an attempt to save what was salvageable, made the financial cuts primarily with the *Berliner Tageblatt*. In fact, she speculated that before the economizing efforts, Martin Carbe had steered the newspaper toward the right side of the political spectrum.[54] Decades later, Lachmann-Mosse's son became an historian at the University of Wisconsin at Madison and contended that in postwar accounts, the responsibility for the demise of the family's publishing house had all been shifted to his father:

> When these editors wrote their autobiographies after the war, a very one-sided portrait was bound to emerge. Only hostile voices were heard, and they blamed my father for all the financial difficulties the firm experienced in the years before the Nazi takeover, disregarding the havoc wrought by ever-increasing right-wing pressure. The rumors about the firm's supposed bankruptcy, spread at the time and taken up again by journalists after the war, would have collapsed upon closer examination. The vast real-estate holdings of the family alone more than matched outstanding debts.[55]

George Mosse's assertion that memory deteriorates with time is certainly true. This factor may accurately depict the case in Margret Boveri's 1965 recollections. However, Mosse's analysis is inapplicable to the cited October 1930–October 1932 references from Ernst Feder's diary. In addition, before his death in 1963 Fred Hildenbrandt emphatically repeated in his memoir that Lachmann-Mosse had ruined the company before Hitler came to power: "To this day, my unshaken conviction is that the Rudolf Mosse Publishing House did not perish because of Hitler. . . . Its demise could be anticipated from the moment that Hans Lachmann-Mosse made the decision to exercise control, I believe one-and-a-half years before Hitler."[56] Furthermore, the statements from editors Ernst Feder, Martin Carbe and Theodor Wolff never discount financial reverses stemming from anti-Semitic pressure to avoid placing advertisements through Mosse. However, Mosse's non-liquid wealth in villas and paintings had value, only if a buyer could have been located. Lachmann-Mosse was a victim. George Mosse admirably defended his childhood memory of his father. However older relatives, such as Ernst Feder and Martin (Cohn) Carbe, who had been executives in the company, had opposite opinions and substantiated their thoughts with documentation from the time.

Lachmann-Mosse's interests lay in the arts, especially music. He displayed little regard for business, let alone political developments. The public viewed the *Berliner Tageblatt* as the spearhead of Left-Liberal politics. By either firing key Jewish and Gentile intellectuals or pressuring them to leave, Mosse-Lachmann brought the firm to political self-paralysis at a time when stalwart defense of democracy was required. In fostering a hostile work environment for pivotal editors and journalists, he sacrificed ideology to obtain an improved cash flow, which he hoped right-wing readers might have been able to provide.[57]

George Mosse was between ten and fifteen years old, when Mosse publishing house's business decisions were made at the end of the Weimar Republic. It is admirable that in his memoir he defended his father and felt that company executives had shifted all the blame on him. However, it appears that not selling the family palace, when offered cash by the U.S. Embassy, spending scarce cash on additional art for personal pleasure, making risky investments in theaters and demanding cash from the Swiss office for his own financial security were all actions, which jeopardized the company's liquidity for his own benefit.

Memory definitely deteriorates with time. Nevertheless, the statements from editors Ernst Feder, Martin Carbe and Theodor Wolff never discount the financial reverses stemming from anti-Semitic pressure not to place advertisements through Mosse. However, Mosse's non-liquid wealth in villas and paintings had value, only if a buyer could have been located (Table 6.5).

It would seem that one could practically compose an intellectual history of the Weimar Republic from the list of *Berliner Tageblatt* employees terminated by Hans Lachmann-Mosse.[58] But the dramatic change in the lives of terminated newspaper employees was also experienced by the owner and his wife. By the Sunday April 5, 1933 edition of the *Tageblatt*, other newspapers began reporting about Hans Lachmann-Mosse's resignation. Hans and his wife had attempted to preserve family ownership of the company by donating the "surplus" to World War I veterans for fifteen years.[59]

Table 6.5 Key Terminated *Berliner-Tageblatt* Professionals

Name	*Position*	*Jewish?*	*World War I Veteran?*	*Date of Planned Resignation or Dismissal*
Martin Carbe	Executive Manager	Yes		12/12/1930
Theodor Wolff	Editor in Chief	Yes		12/13/1930
Felix Pinner	Business	Yes		3/7/1931
Ernst Feder	Domestic Politics	Yes		6/30/1931
Fred Hildenbrandt	Feuilleton Editor	No	Yes	1932

Source: Material gleaned from memories published in Ernst Feder's *Heute sprach ich mit* and Fred Hildenbrandt's *Ich soll dich grüssen*.

3. Weakness of Mosse Verlag-Enabled Winkler's Aryanization

Feder, Boveri, Köhler and Sösemann have held Hans Lachmann-Mosse as being unsuited for the demands of operating a European-wide advertising agency and a chain of German newspapers, whereas the historians Mosse and Kraus affirm that the responsibility for the financial woes belongs elsewhere. The best resolution of this dilemma appears to be that although Lachmann-Mosse was ill-suited to manage a business, he possessed assets to avert a bankruptcy and the banking industry offered a purchase price far in excess of what Aryanizer Max Winkler offered.

Winkler was placed on the Graudenz city payroll in 1914 and later was elected as the liberal Deutsche Demokratische Party's candidate to the position of Deputy Mayor. By 1919, he became a representative for the West Prussian community in the State Assembly. When the region was incorporated into Poland, he moved to Berlin in order to lobby for the welfare of Germans living under Polish dominion. By 1920, he was appointed Reich Trustee and Economic Adviser for the former German territories. The Reich Chancellery and the Ministry of the Interior approved a plan drafted by Winkler, whereby the Weimar Government supplied immediate aid in the amount of 116 million RM. Approximately half of the sum was conferred to German bank and industry stock in companies located in the area ceded to Poland. The remainder was under the control of Winkler for covert support of the German press and under the direction of Attorney Erich Krahmer-Möllenberg for the encouragement of German-speaking schools. To maintain the clandestine nature of their activities, Winkler chose the public limited liability structure which did not require the publication of balance statements nor mandate the sources of their funding.[60]

Comprehending Winkler's financial transactions is made more difficult not only because documentation for secret transactions is scarce, but also because in tandem with Krahmer-Möllenberg, he founded numerous firms to conceal the identity of those supplying the capital. In June 1925, the Hollandsche Buitenland Bank was created in the Hague, which by September 1925 had distributed 11.8 million RM for German minorities in Poland, the Baltic states and Yugoslavia. Similarly, the Ossa Vermittlungs- und Handelsgesellschaft was established in March 1926 granting 30 million RM to ethnic German farmers in Posen, West Prussia, the Baltic states and the Volga Republic. To avoid public debates, these activities were ironically not made known to either the Nazi or Communist Parties.[61]

Winkler also founded the Cautio Trust Company as a front organization on January 14, 1929, whereby German banks transferred to his firm millions of Reichsmarks from the state in order to prevent farms and businesses from being sold to Poles. By 1933, he was the Trustee for nineteen enterprises as well as providing financial support for a dozen German-language newspapers promoting the culture of the Fatherland. Although he received 7 million RM to encourage the democratic political parties backing Paul von Hindenburg in the 1932 elections, he became indispensable to the National Socialists in 1933 thanks to his ease in adapting to the changing political times. Winkler had begun the consolidation of the German press during the Weimar Republic through his administration of Prussian newspapers.[62]

While Winkler's power was ascending, the Mosse Verlag's strength was decreasing. This is clear, despite most of the evidence surrounding Winkler and many documents from Mosse having been destroyed during the war. Thus, prior research has often been forced to rely upon Winkler's biased confession during the postwar August 7, 13, and September interrogations from the Nuremberg Trial. On the other hand, from Mosse's Leipzig branch, it became clear that Lachmann-Mosse applied for bankruptcy protection with the court in Berlin-Charlottenburg in September 1932. The Rudolf Mosse Foundation was established on April 8, 1933, with 100,000 RM in capital, with the net profits from publishing to be distributed exclusively "for charitable purposes." A decade later the Nazi government viewed this action as a maneuver whereby Lachmann-Mosse could transfer wealth abroad. However, in the postwar restitution process, it was maintained that this procedure was a means of limiting the cash flow and slowly rebuilding value in order to overcome the financial difficulties.

On the basis of a 1933 audit by the Dresdner Bank regarding Mosse's excess of 8 million RM in assets over liabilities, the bank was prepared to loan the publishing house between 2 and 2.5 million RM. Therefore, the firm's Chief Counsel confidently corresponded with the Chancellery on June 30, 1933, that a financial reorganization by the Reich was possible without any risk. However, the government refused to participate. The publishing house stopped making all payments on July 12, yet non-Mosse newspapers reported that the publishing house's assets far exceeded the liabilities. The correct understanding of the Mosse bankruptcy is that the firm possessed large amounts of fixed assets, but few cash instruments. Bankruptcy protection would have been sought by Mosse due to poor cash flow, forcing him to sell some fixed assets.

In early summer of 1933, the Prussian Minister of Culture Bernhard Rust was asked whether Berlin's National Gallery was interested in acquiring the entire Mosse art collection. The Museum deceitfully responded that negotiations for two pieces by Wilhelm Leibl (1844–1900) and Hans Thoma (1839–1924) should be conducted in such a fashion that the paintings would be acquired for free. The publishing house ceased payments on July 12, 1933 and similarly the Foundation discontinued paying creditors two months later. The newspaper provided the significant detail that Lachmann-Mosse planned to use private assets to pay for the company's outstanding debts. When the gallery refused to pay for any of the Mosse's art, this shattered Hans's hopes of paying all creditors. Settlement procedures regarding the firm's assets began in Charlottenburg on September 13, 1933 and concluded on February 9, 1934. As part of Lachmann-Mosse's original expectations, the auditor Dr. I Semler had planned to completely reimburse creditors owed less than 500 RM within a month after the settlement hearing; creditors owed between 500 and 1,000 RM within six months and creditors owed over 1,000 RM within a year. Semler anticipated paying creditors on the basis of unencumbered real estate worth 1.78 million RM, a further 1 million RM in the company's real estate and 600,000 RM from the Mosse art collection. The auditor's plan was promoted on the premise that the business would continue, since Semler's May 31, 1933 balance statement had indicated that the 14.98 million RM in assets outweighed the 11.31 million in liabilities. The largest obligations of 1.7 million RM were owed to the Dresdner Bank and a further 3.6 million RM to the pension fund. Lachmann had invested the 3.6 million in a real estate gamble on the Lehniner Platz.[63] This gambit, and the criticism to which it had been subjected by Wolff and Boveri in section B1 of this chapter, partially validates the editors' disapproval of Lachmann's risky investments. Nevertheless, the endorsement by his son George Mosse that personally owned real estate could cover all speculative financial ventures is accurate, despite the fact that the Wohnhaus-Grundstücksverwertungs A.G. was a significant cause for the publishing house's financial difficulties.[64]

With no cash being raised through the sale of private art, the Dresdner Bank, two mortgage institutions and the pension fund were faced with the possibility of receiving only 30 percent of what they were owed. The Treuhand-Verwaltung GmbH was established as the Trustee in the Spring of 1934 with operating capital of 20,000 RM and on behalf of the personnel continued publishing the *Berliner Tageblatt* under the direction of the Settlement Administrator Walter Haupt. After the war, Haupt and Max Winkler provided conflicting sworn testimony. Nevertheless, Kraus has determined that Winkler established the Cautio GmbH in 1929 in order to acquire press and film companies and Bedo Panner of the Dresdner Bank had gratuitously transferred 20,000 RM to Winkler to invest in the Treuhand. The Reich Ministry of Finance expended 3.3 million RM in Treasury Bonds to secure loans granted by the Dresdner Bank. Peter de Mendelssohn observed that Max Winkler's Cautio had access to a 30 million RM advance from the government. By the end of 1934, Cautio had acquired the largest building between the Jerusalemer, Schützen, and Zimmerstraße as well as the publishing house and all publishing rights for only 4.5 million of the available 30 million RM. The extension of 30 million RM to Winkler diminishes the significance of Feder's claim that Mosse's building plot was unusable and with the exception of the Reich Address Book, the publishing rights entailed hardly any value. Feder also considered that in comparison with the Ullstein printing presses, the Mosse machinery was obsolete. Feder's assessment may safely be rejected on the basis that a banking consortium under the leadership of the Dresdner and Hardy Banks viewed the financial situation quite differently in taking over the firm and installing both Winkler and his business manager, Julius Mundhenke, on the new Supervisory Board.[65]

In contrast with the traditional academic view that claimed that the Mosse publishing house did not need to be Aryanized, because it went into bankruptcy, this depiction indicates that Max Winckler and the Dresdner Bank gladly assumed the firm because the value of the assets far exceeded the liabilities. An instant profit of 3.6 million RM was made, especially since pension liabilities would only have to be paid out over the following two decades.

C. MAX WINKLER'S ARYANIZATION OF ULLSTEIN

Whereas creativity among Mosse editors led to conflicts with the fiscally irresponsible owner, business innovations among the five Ullstein brothers brought about a stronger newspaper publishing house. The dissension among Mosse executives led to a takeover by Max Winkler, whereas the squabbles among the Ullstein siblings entailed a temporary respite under Hans Schaeffer's leadership before Winkler was able to wrench ownership from the Jewish proprietors.

For modern printing presses to be worth the high cost of investment, Leopold Ullstein needed to run the machines throughout the day and thus the existing *Berliner Zeitung* was printed during the night for distribution to the capital the following morning. The *Berliner Abendzeitung* was produced during the afternoon for distribution in the provinces. The second-oldest son Louis conceived of reducing the time it required to reach its readership by forgoing the post office and taking the broadsheet directly to the trains. Vertical integration ensued as a network of branches was established for the anticipated three newspapers, suppliers were included in the chain and a news agency provided non-competing local papers with information. Although the evening paper first appeared on September 1, 1887, it quickly achieved a circulation of 70,000 a number not reached by Mosse's rival *Berliner Tageblatt* until 1900. By January 1889 as the combined circulation of the two Ullstein broadsheets surpassed 100,000 copies, the two oldest sons Hans and Louis had become partners. After seventy-three-year-old Leopold passed away on December 4, 1899, Franz, Rudolf and Hermann became partners and faced the problem of lack of space. The five brothers tore down the Kochstraße edifice, although built only fifteen years previously, bought an adjacent parcel

and constructed a 1,313 square meter facility in time to commemorate the firm's twenty-fifth anniversary on October 3, 1902.

Berlin police had been concerned that hawking newspapers on the streets would impede the flow of traffic. So the appearance of an afternoon edition waited until the law had been overturned. A marketing innovation included the relinquishing of paid subscriptions and the introduction of newsboys, dressed in uniform. The new noontime audience included businessmen interested in the stock market, urban men consumed by sports and women interested in fashion. The brainchild of Louis was inaugurated on October 22, 1904 and was known by its abbreviation *B.Z.* Financial support by means of advertisement came from automobile manufacturers, fashion designers, cosmetic producers and restaurants. The publication soon eclipsed both the morning and evening editions, reaching its zenith of 203,000 copies in October 1929.[66]

Youngest son Hermann Ullstein's greatest success resulted from the innovation of Kodak's instantaneous photography as well as his appointment of Kurt Korff as editor of the *Berliner Illustrierte.* Korff had an amazing insight into politics, science and art as well as an ability to recount the news via photographs.[67] Although the profit per copy was merely one pfennig, by 1933 the circulation rose to two million. Of greater significance than the 20,000 RM profit per issue was the 150,000 RM earned from advertisements for the weekly publication, which yielded an annual profit of 8.8 million RM.[68]

Prior to his entry as a partner in the family-owned company, Louis had experience in business, so he thought that he should enjoy a certain pre-eminence in the firm, a thought which infuriated Franz the middle child. In contrast, Rudolf embodied the technical expertise and always pressed for a larger budget in his domain of the printing presses. Franz manifested a flair for critical thinking, whereas Hermann viewed his expertise in the realm of publicity and marketing. With the advent of the third generation of Ullsteins into the firm at the end of the 1920s, a mediator was required to resolve family disputes. Opposed to this relatively minor tension between family members, there suddenly occurred a "spectacular conflict [which] culminated in the Summer 1930 dismissal of Franz Ullstein as the Chairman of the Board of Directors" and temporarily restored Louis from the Chair of the Supervisory Board to the pinnacle of the company.[69]

George Mosse's desire to shield his father Hans Lachmann-Mosse from criticism that he ill-advisedly invested in the Lehniner Platz and sought advertising revenue over journalistic perspectives was presented in section B1 of this chapter. Hermann Ullstein's memoir is similar to George Mosse's recollections in aspiring to protect the family's reputation. However, other sources are more forthright. Arthur Koestler, who had been Ullstein's science editor since 1930, revealed in his memoir that Franz Ullstein was an outstandingly intelligent, humorous and charming individual. But he maintained that his brothers possessed none of these qualities. The historian Erhard Schütz added some of the scandalous details of the five brothers' "furious arguments." Franz intended to marry Rosalie Gräfenberg, the daughter of the banker Max Goldschmidt. Since she regularly wrote for Ullstein newspapers, the brothers feared that Franz would gain even more strength in the struggle for power. In addition, Georg Bernhard, the long-time editor of the *Vossische Zeitung*, feared that his position could be taken by her. In December 1929, Joseph Matthes wrote an extortion letter to Franz claiming to have photographs indicating that Gräfenberg had been a German-French double agent during World War I. A press representative in Paris paid 500 RM for the dubious material, which was confidentially shared with Bernhard in April 1930. Although the data appeared spurious, the publicized family debate was used to fend off Franz's efforts to assume the firm's leadership. Because of lack of evidence, the judge found Rosie innocent on March 29, 1931. After the verdict, Franz was reinstated and Bernhard became the business manager of the Association of Berlin Department Stores after being dismissed from Ullstein. However, after Franz's restoration, Carl von Ossietzky described him as a "weary man" and analyzed the publishing house as having descended from a liberal democratic niveau to yellow journalism.[70]

The five brothers first sought the editorial prowess of Martin Carbe and when that proved insufficient the siblings later hired the financial expertise and wealth of acquaintances of Hans Schäffer in order that their five attorneys would not consume the Ullstein's assets. As early as December 12, 1930, Carbe had mentioned to Ernst Feder that he was leaving Mosse for its larger rival Ullstein, although he had perhaps not mentioned that the scope of his responsibilities would extend beyond that of being merely the political editor. But by January 27, 1931, Feder was aware of Carbe's brighter prospects with the more prosperous competitor: "Carbe has gone to the Ullstein Publishing House, apparently to represent the claims of the three brothers Hans, Louis and Rudolf against Franz." The *Vossische Zeitung* political editor Carl Misch confirmed that Carbe had an office in the Ullstein publishing house and reaffirmed that he was defending three brothers' interests against Franz.

As previously noted in chapter 5, section C, any one of the Jewish-owned department stores advertised far more extensively in Ullstein's *Vossische Zeitung* than car manufacturers, tire makers and electricity producers combined. But the intertwined financial plight of Jewish-owned newspapers with Jewish-owned department stores became evident in Feder's February 9, 1931 diary entry in observing another aspect of Carbe's activities with Ullstein. He was negotiating with Georg Bernhard, the former Editor-in-Chief of the *Vossische Zeitung*, who now represented the Executive Committee for the Association of Department Stores for cheaper advertising rates on the behalf of the frequently advertising chains. A second linkage between the Ullstein publishing house and the department store chains arose when Hermann purchased a woman's magazine from the Verlag Friedrich Schirmer in 1905. Rather than offering housekeeping advice, Hermann determined to make fashion its foundation. He established a tailor shop with fifty seamstresses and produced paper patterns, allowing women to easily sew their own cloths. Not only did readership quickly escalate from 30,000 to 500,000 but department stores in Hannover, Breslau and Frankfurt am Main requested to become vendors of the patterns. Ullstein sold 2,000 different patterns to the chains annually. The large retailers added value to the novelty by selling the item below cost, so that the ladies would be induced to purchase cloth and other accessories in their stores.[71]

But Carbe's diplomatic competence did not allow his Ullstein career to endure for even eighteen months, because by May 23, 1932, Professor Julius Hirsch lamented that Carbe no longer had the "necessary vigor" for the position. The Ullstein brothers shifted their expectations for resolving the sibling rivalry to Hans Schäffer's financial acumen.[72]

The Ullsteins knew of Hans's aptitude as the State Secretary in the Reich Ministry of Finance as well as his arbitration skills in helping to resolve the 1931 family dispute over Rosalie. Hans was ready for a career change, having mused with Chancellor Heinrich Brüning whether he should seek a diplomatic post in the gorgeous city of Bern, join the weak banking industry or return to his prewar profession as an attorney. But the Ullstein-owned *Propyläen World History* had caught the attention of Brüning. Hans also referred to the appeal of four additional in-house publications: the *Berliner Morgenpost*, *Tempo*, the *Grünen Post*, and the *Vossische Zeitung*. But he confessed that after focusing on the question of postwar German reparations for twelve years, it was not easy to leave the Ministry and thus left it to the Chancellor's discretion when he should retire.[73] Schäffer intended to gloss over his growing alienation with Brüning and retire on the grounds of being unable to bear the responsibility for the Treasury.[74]

Brüning suggested a face-saving solution. He remarked that someone needed to personally promote Germany's cause in the United States and Schäffer had the feeling that the Chancellor wanted to send him to America for a few weeks, so that his disappearance from the government would appear to be justified.[75]

In becoming Ullstein's chief executive for the turbulent nine months from June 6, 1932 to March 10, 1933, Schäffer repeatedly availed himself of his ability to speak unequivocally, but succinctly. This was essential not only with regard to the editorial staff, but also to the Ullstein family owners. His interpersonal skill was required in the *Vossische Zeitung*'s editorial staff, which included such left-wing proponents as Carl Misch, Moritz Goldstein and Heinz Pol. They increasingly lost influence to right-wing adherents Hans Zehrer, Wilhelm von Oertzen and Sven von Müller. Fortunately, moderate voices also operated within the *Voss's* executives, including Julius Elbau, Max Reiner and Albrecht von Montgelas.[76]

While Hermann's memoir placed the cause of the five siblings' dispute in the arena of an organizational battle for authority in the family concern, Hans's diary also implied ideological differences among the clan members. On August 15, 1932, Schäffer ate dinner with Louis Ullstein's son, Heinz, and Otto Straßer during which Straßer drew a parallel between the three inconclusive military offensives in 1918 and Hitler's gradual victories during the three elections of 1932. To oppose Hitler's successes, Straßer suggested to Heinz that he wanted to sign a contract to use the Ullstein printing presses to produce a newspaper to support the Schwarze Front's attempt to bring National Socialists back to an anti-capitalistic viewpoint. Straßer offered that Franz could assume the newspaper after six months, but would be required to maintain the editorial staff for three years. In Straßer's mind, the mutual benefit was the elimination of Adolf Hitler.[77] Schäffer had grave misgivings about the proposed contract, viewing it as a ruse, which would not end well. In addition, he contended that the publishing house had a worldview, but no political goals. He concluded that this would be a good opportunity for the Social Democrat Party, but not for Ullstein. Astonishingly, Heinz held that his personal worldview did not greatly deviate from Straßer's. Heinz was interested in the publishing possibilities of a new newspaper, but thought the collaboration was only conceivable if Straßer renounced his political career in favor of remaining a journalist. Schäffer was concerned that Straßer differentiated between Germans and Jews, to which Straßer responded that the Jewish people separated themselves by their lifestyle. Schäffer rejected that claim and insisted that his coreligionists desired to be Germans. Those who disputed this view, robbed Jews of their Fatherland, where they had lived for centuries. Schäffer emphasized that affiliation in a nation was a matter of intent and not blood. Although Straβer agreed, he insisted that the Jewish people needed to be open to the possibility of marrying non-Jews. Schäffer mentioned that he would bring the contract offer to Franz Ullstein's attention, but did not want to raise any expectations with Straßer.[78]

A second proposition in which Heinz and Straßer were in agreement concerned the unsuitability of the German people for democracy. Schäffer retorted that all German people felt comfortable with democracy, including Scandinavians and Swiss. Dictatorships were a form of government adopted by Roman and Oriental peoples. Straßer attempted to clarify that he was recommending an "authoritative democracy." Three weeks later, Heinz returned to his right-leaning political view, although he was more democratically oriented, than republican. He contended that Germany needed a type of democracy, which differed from other Western countries. Germany required its own form of democracy. Once again Schäffer objected that the Weimar Constitution had endured ten years of foreign political difficulties, a severe economic crisis and an enormous inflation. He insisted that no other constitution would have survived.[79]

On a third occasion, Heinz emphasized his position that due to the Germanic Volk's distinct characteristics, it required a different form of democracy from all other peoples. He concluded that perhaps all foreign political problems and the economic crises were occasioned solely by the Weimar Constitution.[80] Perhaps Heinz's contentious political opinions had been formed during childhood and adolescence, since his father Louis also displayed a controversial perspective. Louis contended that Paul von Hindenburg should retire and recommend his successor as president, rather than allowing Germans to choose his replacement in an election.[81]

Louis's younger brother Hermann attempted to take a more neutral position. He broached the topic of whether the *B.Z am Mittag* had gone too far in welcoming the Deutschnationale Volkspartei's (DVNP) right-wing Stahlhelm and queried whether the Social Democrat Party's Reichsbanner was annoyed by the greeting. In contrast, Hermann observed that Ullstein newspapers had always been restrained with regard to the SDP's paramilitary organization. He reminded newspaper executives that the Stahlhelm was a non-Republican organization and that a bad impression would be created, if the Ullstein newspapers were viewed on its side. Whereas Heinz surmised that the publishing house had not treated the Catholic Center Party poorly, Hermann considered that a union between the Center Party and the Nazi Party guaranteed the constitution.[82]

To the previously mentioned innovations of high-speed printing presses, direct delivery to trains, distribution on the streets by newsboys, instantly developed photographs, another novelty was the imitation of the flamboyant American journalism of the tabloid. Ullstein's contribution to titillating news was entitled *Tempo*, which means "speed" and it was intended to offset the financial losses of the outmoded *Vossische Zeitung*.

Alfred Hugenberg's *Berliner Nachtausgabe* and Lachmann-Mosse's *8-Uhr Abendblatt* had proven to be highly successful evening newspapers since the mid-1920s. However, Ullstein had missed the development of the tabloid and according to Editor Felix von Eckardt, the company did not start recruiting an editorial staff until March 1928. Gustav Kauder became the Editor-in-Chief of the new publication and although he did not have the international reputation of Georg Bernhard or Theodor Wolff, he was one of Berlin's most celebrated journalists. According to the *Vossische Zeitung*'s art critic Max Osborn, *Tempo* was meant to incorporate the Weimar Republic's new feelings of life. *Tempo*'s target audience was the young middle class, especially white-collar workers and employed women. Women were a majority of the population after the casualties endured in World War I and the birth-years from 1900 to 1910 were the largest in German history. Ullstein attempted to compensate for its late entry into the market by boasting that its newspaper knew "how to adjust to the special needs and nerves of a changed time."

The publishing house's support for the Liberal DDP political party was explicitly associated with consumerism. The legal age to vote had been lowered from twenty-five to twenty and the origin of the publication may be associated with the absence of 4 million first-time voters among the pro-Republican parties during the May 1928 elections. Two months after the tabloid's inauguration, an article contrasted Germany's higher form of government with dictatorships in Portugal, Spain and Russia. It emphasized Germany's higher quality of life as evidenced by advertisements for refrigerators, cars and summer vacations in exotic distant lands.

Tempo differentiated itself from the competition in a few important aspects especially with regard to its appearance: *Tempo* had more pictures than previous German dailies. In contrast with the *B.Z. am Mittag*, which had the highest street sales, the *BZ* had no front-page photos, whereas the first edition of *Tempo* had four photos, which nearly filled the front page. *Tempo* reported the news through text and vivid photos. In 1931, the editorial staff of *Tempo* spent 102,599 RM for illustrations, whereas the *B.Z. am Mittag* spent only 70,728 RM during the same period.[83]

Hermann Ullstein thought that *Tempo*'s financial difficulties did not arise from expensive use of photography. He placed the blame on the layout of small German Fraktur print set in narrow columns. Nevertheless, neither the newly minted *Tempo* nor the 227-year-old *Vossische Zeitung*, which the tabloid was meant to rescue financially, was abandoned despite the annual loss of 2 million RM by the prestigious broadsheet. Between January 1931 and January 1933, the circulation of the *Voss* and *Tempo* declined by one-third; the *Berliner Morgenpost* by one-fourth; the *B.Z. am Mittag* by one-fifth and the *Berliner Illustrierte Zeitung* by one-seventh. Reduction in the number of sold copies did not reduce fixed costs, but adversely affected profits, which necessitated cost-saving measures in the variable costs.[84] As the Mosse publishing house and Ullstein publishing house chased funding from advertisers, they abandoned their liberal and left-of-center views. The result was a decline in subscriptions from disillusioned readers (Table 6.6).

Reconstructing the events whereby the Ullstein publishing house was Aryanized is made difficult because many of the details of the secret negotiations were withheld from the Jewish owners.[85] Postwar statements made by perpetrators such as Max Winkler of the Cura Trustee and Auditing Company or Ferdinand Bausback of the Deutsche Bank were whitewashed accounts to exculpate them from any punishment. Statements by company executives

Table 6.6 Declining Ullstein Newspaper Circulations

	7/1929	*4/1930*	*1/1931*	*4/1931*	*4/1932*	*7/1932*	*1/1933*	*4/1933*
Voss	70,960	72,380	81,000	73,970	57,480	56,700	53,500	57,000
Tempo	100,940	139,110	145,450	124,650	103,320	112,400	96,920	104,060
Morgenpost	615,730	623,010	591,940	572,770	513,780	487,190	449,710	454,730
BZ am Mittag	192,130	170,440	175,170	159,220	149,140	155,380	139,390	146,160
Illustrierte	1,883,010	1,851,690	1,753,580	1,819,130	1,617,160	1,603,220	1,502,090	1,469,810

Source: Material provided in Modris Ekstein's, *The Limits of Reason*.

in denazification hearings were probably enhanced in the expectation that absolving the perpetrators from jail sentences would lead to the return of some of the Jewish assets. The following narrative relies heavily on Hans Schäffer's diary, Oron Hale's interrogations on behalf of the U.S. military and company executives' accounts in the hundredth anniversary volumes.

Max Winkler did not join the NSDAP until 1937, although he appeared to have no ideological compunctions restraining his shift from being a nationalist in January 1933 to a mild supporter of the Nazis in the following few days.

Winkler had obtained funding from right-wing sources for his newspapers throughout the Weimar era, supporting German nationalists living in Baltic countries. Continued financial support was the means whereby he bribed editors to adhere to right-wing views in areas that had been part of the Reich prior to World War I. Paul Schiemann had written five editorials critical of the NSDAP for the völkisch newspaper *Rigasche Rundschau*'s November 9 and 23, 1932 issues as well as the December 6, 13, and 20 editions. Although Schiemann did not think that National Socialism was out-of-the-question, his editorials rebuked the deprivation of foreign-born and minority rights, as well as theories of racial struggle and contempt for non-Nordic-looking people. In addition, he maintained that Adolf Hitler had destroyed national feelings of community with his unambiguous anti-Semitism. As the Reich Trustee and majority shareholder of the Latvian newspaper, Max Winkler wrote Editor-in-Chief Schiemann on February 4, 1933, requesting him to take into account the new political circumstances. In his February 9 response, the editor acknowledged that the newspaper's restraint had been viewed as objectionable by NSDAP fanatics residing in Latvia. Winkler demanded the immediate dismissal of Foreign Affairs Editor Hans von Rimscha. Although there is no explicit confirmation of a direct confrontation between Winkler and Schiemann, the Editor left Riga for exile in the Viennese suburbs at the end of March, privately stepped down from his office on June 30 and publicly announced his resignation in the July 8, 1933 edition. At a time when Mosse and Ullstein were struggling for advertising revenue, Winkler had the finances necessary to guarantee that the fifty-five-year-old editor and his wife would be taken care of for the remainder of their lives.[86]

On February 12, 1933, Schäffer made a presentation at the Friedrich List Society Conference in Oeynhausen, which was monitored by National Socialist observers. On February 17, the publication of *Tempo* was prohibited for a week and the constitutionally guaranteed freedom for editors and reporters was threatened by the February 28 Reichstag Fire Ordinance. Heinz Ullstein was arrested by a band of seven SA men during the night of March 5–6, 1933.[87] After his release, Heinz affirmed that he would not play the martyr for publishing house beliefs, which he had previously unsuccessfully opposed. Schäffer also confided in his March 6 diary entry that Waldemar Bonsel requested to be discharged from his contract with Ullstein and Carl Zuckmayer's serialized novel in the *Berliner Illustrierte* had to be discontinued. Ullstein's financial difficulties could be attributed to the inability to publish works for which rights had been purchased. Kleist prize recipient Alfred Neumann was an example of an author, who had been paid an advance, but the prior payment of 56,427 RM had to be taken as a loss in 1934.[88]

By March 6, 1933, Schäffer already realized that the former Stuttgart branch manager of the Deutsche Bank and current chair of the Supervisory Board Ferdinand Bausback was coveting his position as Director. Two days later, Bausback reported that he had learned that the government wanted to notify the publishing company that a "Galician Jew" (i.e., Schäffer) had to be sacrificed namely Schäffer. Hans asked him what would happen, if a SA troop broke into the Ullstein complex and demanded that the swastika flag be hoisted as was done at Mosse's *Berliner Tageblatt.* Bausback disingenuously responded that the Ullstein firm would prohibit the action and call the police, although no force should be exerted by the thousands of company employees. When Louis Ullstein repeated the question of raising the swastika flag during the impending commemoration of those killed in World War I, Schäffer responded that it should be taken down during the night. But Gustav Willner, Chief of Accounting and Finance, rejoined that such action would invite the building's occupation by the SA.[89]

On March 6, Richard A. Müller replaced Hans as the Chairman of the Ullstein Board. Eduard Stadtler was hired as the "political director" to ensure improved relations with the NSDAP, although his contacts with Party leadership were modest. Supervisory Board Chair Bausback had previously attempted to redevelop the Ufa Film Company and by means of a play on his German name had earned the nickname of "Dismantler."[90] Stadtler and Müller terminated Jewish white-collar employees from the payroll in April 1933 in order to make the firm more appealing to a new owner.

Before the publishing house was prepared for non-Jewish ownership through terminations, the number of third-generation Ullstein sons, daughters, and in-laws in executive positions outnumbered the five brothers. Karl Ullstein, who was Hans's oldest son, and Fritz Ross, who was Hans's brother-in-law, had been Members of the Board of Directors. Franz's daughter Elisabeth had married Kurt Saalfeld, who also had been a Board Member. Gertrud Engelmann, Käthe Ullstein's daughter, married Arthur Hess, who was a personnel manager. Fritz Koch was the son of Käthe Ullstein's sister Else. Both Fritz and Louis's son Heinz were Members of the Supervisory Board. Eduard Benfey was married to Lotte Fleischmann, one of Leopold's granddaughters. Benfey also had a vote on the Supervisory Board. To the list of seven Ullstein Board Members from the third generation, the names of two other Jewish executives may be added: Emil Herz and Kurt Szafranski. But of these nine Jewish executives, some were excluded as early as Hans Schäffer in March 1933. As of November 1933, only Franz represented the five brothers and only Karl Ullstein and Fritz Ross embodied the third generation as executives in the Ullstein publishing house.[91]

Former Reich Finance Minister Hermann Dietrich suggested to Franz Ullstein that the company should meet with Max Winkler. Winkler had Max Weißner prepare a thorough financial analysis on the publishing company, but nevertheless feigned a lack of interest, when Franz met with him in his Brückenallee apartment. Thereafter, the Ullstein brothers gave Ludwig Ruge power of attorney to find a new non-Jewish proprietor. Ruge first met with Max Winkler on May 17, 1934. Winkler claimed that he was merely acting as a Trustee for clients, whose names he was not empowered to disclose. In addition, he was unable to offer a purchase price higher than the par value of the stock, but did threaten that in case the negotiations broke down, the publishing house and its shareholders would have to face the NSDAP's coercive measures. However the extended Ullstein clan had expected the sale to be based on the stock's market value, which was ten times higher than the par value of 6 million RM. Adding to the oddness of the sale was the fact that only a draft contract had been prepared by Max Winkler, Fritz Ross and Ludwig Ruge. Nevertheless, Winkler required confirmation of the Ullstein's acceptance by 6:00 p.m. on June 7, 1934.[92]

Goebbels's April 19, 1934 address on "The Tasks of the German Press in the new Reich" sarcastically directed his comments to those publishers, who quickly joined the Party but did not agree with its ideology. Goebbels mocked their lack of courage and claimed to prefer that such editors should display their true attitudes. The *Grüne Post*'s Editor-in-Chief Ehm Welk naively responded in the entire five-column first page of the April 29, 1934 edition. The first column began by addressing Goebbels's scorn for the uniformity of the press and its renunciation of criticism. In the fourth column, Welk designated Goebbels as a patron of jokes and irony, but such a person was multi-faceted. In contrast, the newspaper's boundaries had become ever-more constricted. Previously the press could utilize humor to test the boundaries of legislative measures and government officials, but with all the Minister of Propaganda's demands, Welk was uncertain.[93]

Welk had uncritically walked into an ambush. The issue was immediately impounded. But those few copies to escape were clandestinely sold for 6 RM apiece. The *Grüne Post* was prohibited for the unusually long period of three months and Ullstein was informed to fire Welk without notice. Welk was sent to the Oranienburg Concentration Camp and the publishing house faced a catastrophic blow. Although the *Grüne Post*'s circulation of approximately 700,000 was smaller than the 1 million copies of the *Berliner Illustrierte*

Zeitung, it far exceeded the combined total of four other Ullstein publications. But after Winkler's purchase of the newspaper company, the *Grüne Post*'s June 10, 1934 edition was published on time, after a lapse of only five weeks. Max Wießner, who clandestinely investigated the firm's financial status, became the new general director.[94]

On July 26, 1934, the *Berliner Börsen-Zeitung* reported that Franz Ullstein, Fritz Ross and others had retired from the Ullstein Supervisory Board. The last members of three generations of the Ullstein clan had been dismissed.[95]

Well-known German companies had paid Winkler 6,095,000 RM in advance for advertisements. The cash enabled him to purchase the Ullstein stock, which he deposited with the Deutsche Bank. The bank had previously served as the chief lending institution of the publisher, but now took care of the stock transfer. Between 1934 and 1937, the government's commercial registry in the Berlin suburb of Charlottenburg listed the Deutsche Bank and Winkler's Cautio Treuhand as holders of 3.9 million RM worth of Ullstein stock. An additional 1.5 million RM was listed as being held by Max Winkler personally. The remaining 600,000 RM was held by Deutsche Bank executive turned Ullstein Supervisory Board Chair Ferdinand Bausback. The Ullstein family forfeited the majority of the sales price through taxes.[96]

Max Winkler and the Deutsche Bank had exploited pressure from the Nazi regime to become the owners of the publishing company. Winkler was also adept at cultivating business contacts, including the publishing magnate Max Amann and the brain behind his Eher Verlag, Rolf Rienhardt. Amann was so motivated by the profit motif, that he strove to keep Gauleiters, other than Goebbels, out of the publishing industry during the Third Reich. However, in the cheap purchase of the private bank Gebrüder Arnhold, the Regional Leader of Saxony played a key role in enabling the Dresdner Bank to acquire a privately owned financial institution at an inexpensive price. In tracing a narrative of early Aryanizations from Hermann Tietz through the Ullstein publishing house to the Arnhold Bank, company insiders or those experienced in the business sector had been able to cheaply acquire a Jewish firm due to assistance from either the Dresdner or Deutsche Banks.

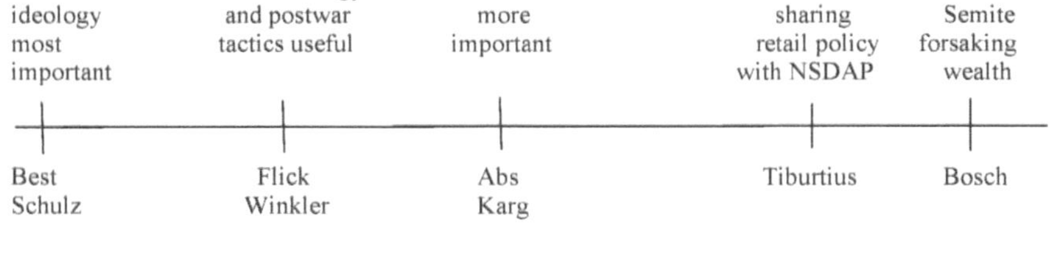

D. ARYANIZATION OF GEBRÜDER ARNHOLD

By the end of the 1920s, there were only four other private banks, which rivaled Gebrüder Arnhold's capital of more than fifty million, namely the M. M. Warburg in Hamburg, Simon Hirschland in Essen, Salomon Oppenheim Jr. and Company in Cologne and Mendelssohn & Company in Berlin. Although incorporated banks with their larger stock-generated capital circumscribed the private banks' sphere of commercial activity, Gebrüder Arnhold was continually able to expand its business connections in commerce and industry. It was the first Saxon bank to establish a presence in the capital. Ironically, the small Berlin branch founded in 1907 survived the early Aryanization of the main Dresden headquarters, which had been established in 1864. Although Adolf Arnhold married the daughter of textile industrialist Georg Marwitz from Dresden and Ella Arnhold married the telephone manufacturer Hans Lewenz, the commercial relationships formed through these weddings were unable to overcome the revenge by a spurned textile manufacturer from Plauen, named Martin Mutschmann. Before that time, the Bank was in a strong financial position, although current scholarship debates whether the success was due to marriages among the banking elite or new strategies of extending loans to mid-sized companies.[97]

The Arnhold Bank withstood the economic and banking crisis relatively unscathed as evidenced in 1932 by its 150 equity investments in other companies and its eighty-five seats on German corporations' Supervisory Boards. Such public recognition of Arnhold Bank executives included the election of Hans Arnhold to the Supervisory Board of the Berlin Lombardkasse A.G. on August 6, 1931; Alfred Meyer's appointment to the Supervisory Board of the Berliner Kassen Vereins Bank on March 4, 1932, and Adolf Arnhold's selection as a Member of the Stock Exchange Board on January 19, 1933. On June 22, 1931, Bankhaus Gebrüder Arnhold and the S. Bleichröder Bank signed a cooperative agreement, in which Arnold extended a 3 million RM assistance loan to Bleichröder.[98] These are four of only thirteen biographical remarks penned in an eighty-five-page handwritten document, which the modern archivist labeled as the *History of the Arnhold Bank: 1864–1936*. Otherwise, the manuscript appears as an annotated accounting record book. This manuscript supplements an excursus on the Arnhold Bank in a four volume, 2,400-page investigation of the Dresdner Bank's involvement during World War II. To its credit, the Dresdner Bank paid 1.6 million euros to a team of ten German historians to analyze twelve kilometers of its files during the Third Reich. Most of the data concerned the bank's beneficial actions for the SS but also documents its interest in cheaply acquiring Jewish-owned companies, including the Arnhold Bank.[99]

Under the influence of Gauleiter Martin Mutschmann, an extraordinarily radical climate of anti-Jewish repression established itself early in Saxony. The measures clearly exceeded the April 1, 1933 boycott. The fact that the Arnhold Bank came into the focus of anti-Semitic attacks was not due to only ideological motives, but should be more specifically ascribed to the private revenge of the Gauleiter. Mutschmann blamed the earlier failure of his textile factory in Plauen during the mid-1920s on the Bank's repeated rejection of his request for a loan. The hostility was intense since he was aware that the bank had extended credit to three other local fabric-making companies including the Tuch-Kunst- Wollwerke Jauche & Company A.G., the Plauen Spitzenfabrik A.G., and the Dresdner Gardinen & Spitzen Manufaktor A.G.[100] The Arnholds were anonymously informed in 1933 that Mutschmann would do anything to force them to leave the country.[101] The family first discussed abandoning the company headquarters in Dresden in the Summer of 1933 and concentrated their activities in the miniature Berlin branch. The first consequences of Nazi pressure in Saxony resulted in Fall 1933 with Adolf Arnhold's and Alfred Meyer's exclusion from company management. They were replaced by the Jewish authorized signatory Fritz Merzbach and the long-term Dresdner Bank Board Member Walther Frisch. Frisch's appointment occurred without a contribution of capital and he entered as the first non-Jewish partner in what had been a family-owned, private bank.[102]

In Köhler's opinion, the circumstances of Walther Frisch's exclusion from the Dresdner Bank and his admission in Gebrüder Arnhold have not been adequately explained and therefore are the subject of "far-reaching speculation."[103] Historians have promoted explanations of Frisch's inclusion as a co-owner, ranging from being a knowledgeable source of industry players to secretly being an agent, whereby Germany's second-largest bank could cheaply acquire the family firm. Theories that include Keith Ulrich's assessment, that Frisch lost his position with the Dresdner Bank because of his alleged Jewish lineage, have been quickly discounted by scholarship. Simone Lässig mentioned a second premise in which Frisch, as an Aryan bank expert, subtly approached the Jewish bankers as a supposed helper, in offering a solution for the difficulties caused by persecution in Dresden. It was maintained that the actual background of Frisch's efforts ushered in a refined long-term initially undetectable Aryanization strategy, whereby the Jewish bank should be prepared for a complete transfer into Aryan hands. Both assumptions are incorrect according to Ingo Köhler. Instead Köhler surmises that the offer for a departing large bank director to enter into a private bank as a partner was attractive from both a financial as well as a social respect. Because Walther Frisch's elimination from the Dresdner Board presumably did not occur entirely voluntarily, Köhler interpreted that Frisch probably owed his entrance into Bankhaus Arnhold to a strategic decision of Gebrüder

Arnhold's owners. After the first harassment by the Gauleiter the owners probably sought an expert, who because of his contacts and reputation as an Aryan representative of a large bank would be in a position to resolve the foreseeable problems with Dresden authorities.

At the same time the change in executive personnel served as a visible concession to Mutschmann, bound with the hope of maneuvering the Bank out of the focus of anti-Semitic attacks. What is certain is that the Arnhold family was willing to restrict its public presence in Saxony as far as possible in August 1933. Although Frisch was not appointed until October 1, Köhler speculated that Walther's influence inspired this change in Arnhold behavior. In the face of the Boycott, the Bank registered an increasing number of account closures and the migration of private Aryan and company accounts. This development accompanied the loss of numerous Supervisory Board seats, which weakened the economic position of the Arnhold Bank.

Between 1933 and 1935, the Arnhold family found itself exposed to three accusations of financial crimes. In May 1933, there was a large proceeding concerning the alleged 1923 fraud in acquiring shares of the Aschinger Hotel and Restaurant in Berlin. The plaintiff was the managing director and major shareholder Fritz Aschinger. Shortly after Hitler's ascension, he entered into contract with Wilhelm Keppler. He notified Keppler that ten years ago the Arnholds had in a supposedly fraudulent way acquired 750,000 RM worth of Aschinger shares. Keppler summoned the Jewish bankers to several hours of interrogation. On September 3, 1934, Heinrich Arnhold responded that if someone intended to Aryanize a company, one should honestly say so and not make unjustified allegations.[104]

In January 1934, Dresden's prosecutor undertook a judicial inquiry against Bankhaus Arnhold because of alleged fraud during the reorganization of the Sachsenwerk Licht und Kraft AG in 1930. Although the prosecutor could present no proof for his indictment, the Dresden court instituted criminal proceedings against the owners of the Bank. Unashamedly, the Saxon Minister of the Economy Georg Lenk confessed that the goal of the proceedings could not be a conviction. Rather the Gau leadership advised him to hang the indictment as a sword of Damocles over the Arnholds in order to make them amenable to sell their Dresden firm.[105] In April 1935, the Bank was threatened with the revocation of its rights as a foreign exchange bank, which achieved the actual goal. The Bank owners agreed to the sale of their business. Martin Mutschmann cooperated well with Walther Frisch and the Dresdner Bank in the machinations leading to Aryanization.

However, three factors require deviation from Ingo Köhler's interpretation of the Aryanization of the Arnhold Bank. First, Walther Frisch became a partner in the Jewish-owned company without supplying any of his own funds. Second the period from October 1933 through March 1938 when he was a

Partner in Arnhold overlaps with his April 1937 through June 1944 employment as the managing director of Hardy & Company Bank. Hardy was a formerly Jewish-owned bank purchased by the Dresdner Bank. Frisch thus had no qualms about leading Aryanized firms. Third, Frisch retired at age sixty-five and moved hundreds of miles southwest to Lake Constance, where he became the Honorary Mayor of Lindau in July 1944 and Lord Mayor in December 1945. However, he came out of retirement during the late 1950s to become a Member of the Dresdner Bank's Central Advisory Board, so he maintained good relationships with Germany's second-largest bank. These facts lead to the conclusion that it may be easier for German scholars to expose the anti-Jewish activities of a German institution during a tumultuous war, than to expose the unscrupulous character of a man, who became a Lord Mayor in postwar "repentant" Germany.

Already in April 1934 a stroke prevented senior executive Heinrich Arnhold from directing the daily business of the Bank. On October 10, 1935, at the age of fifty, Heinrich died from a second stroke. A postwar compensation hearing determined the cause of death was the massive psychological stress. Heinrich Arnhold's death was probably the final impetus for the family to accept the Fall 1935 offer of exploratory discussions to sell the Bank. Since 1929, the Dresdner Bank had shown interest in the takeover of Gebrüder Arnhold in order to strengthen their Dresden branch in the profitable mid-sized corporate customer business. Hugo Israel, the former Chief Counsel of the Dresdner Bank, had apparently arranged contact with Gebrüder Arnhold already in October 1935. Whether Israel operated further under contract with the Dresdner Bank, on the basis of his connections with both sides of the negotiation as an independent middleman, cannot be answered with certainty.[106]

The potential for a conflict of interest was not limited to Walther Frisch, since Walther Bernhard had been a Deputy Board Member of the Dresdner Bank until he was dismissed as a non-Aryan in the Fall of 1933. In the beginning of 1934, he assumed the position of legal counsel in the service of Gebrüder Arnhold. In fact, six of the seven negotiators had worked closely together before 1933 as either continuing or former Dresdner Bank executives.[107] Frisch and Bernhard, together with Kurt Arnhold, undertook negotiations with the Dresdner Bank. After the Dresdner Bank Board Member Alfred Busch and the Dresdner Bank Manager Kurt Krahmer presented a concrete takeover bid at the beginning of November 1935, the negotiations were brought to a rapid conclusion. Already in a working committee meeting of the Dresdner Bank's Supervisory Board, Carl Goetz reported on November 26, 1935 regarding the advanced state of the negotiations and gave a detailed overview of the purchased Bankhaus Arnhold. According to Goetz's information, the total assets of only the Arnhold headquarters was approximately 30 million RM. Arnhold's value he estimated at about 21 million payables on the liabilities side and 16 million in accounts receivable; 7 million in securities and investments; as well as real estate with an estimated value of 3 million on the asset side.[108]

The first drafts of the takeover contract were already submitted to the Ministry of the Economy, the Reichsbank and Banking Commissioner Friedrich Ernst for review. After the plans for the transaction had passed the government agencies without objection, the owners of the Arnhold Bank signed the sales contract with the Dresdner Bank on December 2, 1935. The contract also provided for the acquisition of the company buildings and real estate of the Dresden headquarters, whereas other property remained in the family possession. With the takeover, all 225 non-Jewish employees switched to the service of the new Dresdner Bank branch, whereas for the most part Jewish employees were laid off. Only a small number of Jewish employees could transfer to the Bankhaus Arnhold in Berlin. The Dresdner Bank also interceded on behalf of Aryan retirees of the Arnhold Bank for pension benefits, but not for the former Jewish employees.

The financial world would describe the acquisition of the Arnhold Bank as an asset deal, as opposed to a stock deal, in which the Dresdner Bank purchased only the assets, not the liabilities.[109] Goetz's previously mentioned assessment of the assets as 30 million RM is easily substantiated by sixteen investments in government securities entered in the annotated accounting ledger from March 16, 1931 through August 25, 1933. The most frequently repeated financial support was a fourfold investment in public job creation, including 500,000 RM of 65 million RM requested for street construction on August 30, 1932; an additional 500,000 RM on December 15, 1932; a further 333,000 RM for Phase II of a 35 million RM program; and a final 2 million RM in a 40 million RM measure. Perhaps in an attempt to assuage Gauleiter Martin Mutschmann, purchases of local Treasury Bills also were reoccurring entries. For example, participation in Saxony's 20 million RM campaign on March 11, 1931; and 500,000 RM for the City of Dresden on February 1, 1932, as well as 550,000 RM in Saxony's appeal for 10 million RM.[110]

Notations regarding the write-down in value of private corporations' stock values are the predominant element in the archival manuscript, since it mainly records the difficult financial years of 1931–1932. Although the ventures had declined in worth, large assets remained in Arnhold's portfolio. The Arnhold Bank took a particular interest in the brewing industry and thus this sector is most commonly represented by devaluations. Carl Adolf Riebeck's Leipziger Brauerei zu Reudnitz was Germany's fourth-largest producer of beer in which the stock declined in value from 18,610,000 RM to 16,410,000 on April 28, 1932 and deteriorated further to 10,980,000 RM on June 22, 1933. The supporting Bank für Brauindustrie slipped from 11,980,000 RM to 10,000,000 on September 22, 1932 and Karl Fritzer's small brewery Malzfabrik Mellrichstadt fell from 305,000 RM to 205,000 on March 29, 1933. Georg and Karl Ebert's Bayerisch Brauerei Aschaffenburg lost value from 2,005,000 RM to 1,505,000 on May 31, 1933.

These beer producers were not Jewish, nor were Jewish company owners given priority in receiving loans from the Arnhold Bank.[111] Nevertheless, the German business system encouraged a circle of trust by infusing one company's executives into another's Supervisory Board. Thus, the Aryanization of Bankhaus Arnhold must have produced a ripple effect in existing Jewish firms receiving loans. For example, Richard Blumenfeld's company was incorporated in 1905 and became the largest tile and ceramic manufacturer in Velten. He was not only elected to Potsdam's Chamber of Commerce but also became a Supervisory Board Member of Triton Werke Bamberger-Leroi A.G., another endeavor financially supported by Arnhold. Richard suffered a stroke in 1930 and retired. However, after recovering, he attempted to return but was prevented by managing employees who had secretly established a NSBO cell in his company. On August 10, 1932, the value of the Richard Blumenfeld Veltener Ofenfabrik A.G. held by the Arnhold Bank was written down from 1,800,000 RM to 1,507,000 and further declined to 1,007,500 RM on August 15, 1933. On August 15, the firm was Aryanized and the name was changed to Veltener Ofen- und Keramik.

Another Jewish client of the Arnhold Bank was Heinrich Roß, who established the Rotophot A.G. für graphische Industrie in 1912 and became the leader of postcards bearing the photos of film stars. In addition to being the proprietor of the publishing house, he was the Chair of the Jewish Brotherhood in the Neukölln suburb of Berlin from 1922 to 1934. On October 28, 1931, the value of his issued shares held by the Arnhold Bank declined from 650,000 RM to 300,000, which further declined to 50,000 RM on September 26, 1933.[112]

Another extreme devaluation in share price occurred with Max Roesler in the Feinstein Gutfabrik A.G. When the value of its stock held by the Arnhold Bank plummeted from 1,075,000 RM to 215,000 on May 31, 1933, the company became the property of the Arnhold Bank. It too was later Aryanized.[113]

Although trumped up charges against the Arnhold Bank concluded in acquittals, the pressure caused Heinrich Arnhold to die from stress induced strokes. The Dresdner Bank had long been interested in acquiring the family-held institution in order to expand its influence in mid-sized corporations. Negotiators with a conflict of interest were utilized to arrange an inexpensive purchase. After a number of write-downs, the Dresdner Bank still acquired 30 million RM in assets. Although one might have imagined that Germany's second-largest financial institution would have been satisfied with such a

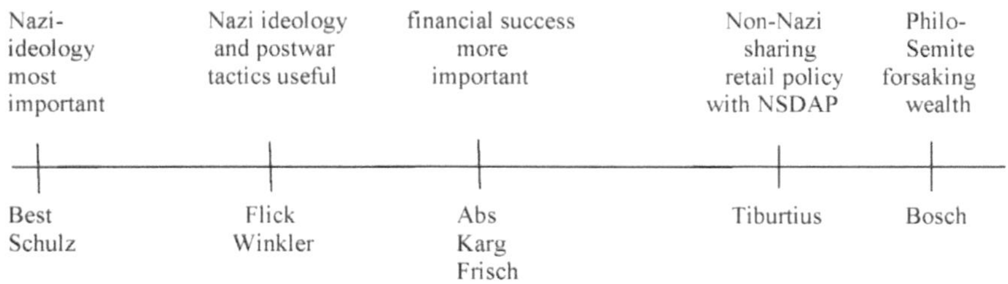

boost in equity, this was not the case. Christopher Kopper concluded: "This can be judged as an unfair treatment by the Dresdner Bank." Nevertheless, in a subsequent June 10, 1936 arbitration proceeding, the Dresdner Bank compelled a 75,000 RM additional payment from the Arnhold family. In addition, only fifteen Jewish employees were transferred to the Berlin residue and the former headquarters was continued with non-Jewish employees as the Waisenhausstraße branch of the Dresdner Bank.[114]

Negotiators with divided loyalties, such as Walther Frisch, sided with the Dresdner Bank. Even after obtaining Arnhold assets worth 30 million RM, the Dresdner Bank was unsatisfied and coerced an additional concession. Frisch's postwar renewed loyalty to the Dresdner Bank does not justify any position on the graph to the left of center. Having examined Bankhaus Arnhold's large investments in the beer industry, the Aryanization of Germany's largest brewery will now be examined.

E. THE ENGELHARDT BREWERY

German breweries were concerned that pasteurizing their beer would negatively affect its quality. But Ignatz Nacher was a businessman not a brew master and thus he was ready to adopt this French innovation, when he bought Ernst Engelhardt's brewery in 1901. The preservation of the beverage was a decisive factor in the firm's growth by allowing transport and storage. By 1907, an expansion of the facility was required, necessitating the sale of one million RM in stock, the majority of which Nacher himself owned. By the end of World War I, he had acquired four breweries in Berlin and one in Königsberg, paid for with Engelhardt stock. During the postwar inflation, he further flourished through vertical integration, by establishing his own malt house, trading in hops and purchasing a factory for producing crates for the bottles. By the end of the 1920s, his stock was valued at twelve million RM, but owning the majority of shares caused problems of liquidity.[115]

As a member of the Engelhardt's Supervisory Board, Siegmund Bodenheimer was able to facilitate loans for the brewery's expansion from the Darmstädter Bank für Handel und Industrie as early as 1904. Bodenheimer's allegiance shifted from one lender to another as the Darmstädter was acquired by the Danat Bank, which, in turn, was purchased by the Dresdner Bank.[116]

The jewel, but also the source of the attacks on Nacher's conglomerate, was a hotel service on Berlin's downtown Alexanderplatz. Since the mid-1920s, rumors had spread that the city wanted to purchase the prime real estate to construct a new subway. By 1927, speculators had offered Nacher up to ten million RM, which represented a multiple of the actual market value. In 1930, the city's Berolina real estate company purchased the site for 8,990,000 RM. Further, 120,000 RM, which Nacher had included for "political purposes," was later viewed as a bribe to Walter Golde, the negotiator for Berlin's real estate department.[117]

As the first seeds to justify an Aryanization proposal were sown, another source of dissension became visible. This second conflict arose after the Dresdner Bank acquired the Danat Bank. Siegmund Bodenheimer was given less freedom to maneuver as the Chair of Engelhardt's Supervisory Board under the Dresdner Bank than he had previously been provided with the Danat Bank. He was expected to reduce Engelhardt's indebtedness with the Dresdner Bank. However, according to a new provision in the beer law, Engelhardt would obtain a large reduction in its taxes, if it could be shown that a holding company owned 26 percent share of its provincial breweries. To obtain this reduction in government obligations, Nacher expected an additional loan of 1.6 million RM from the Dresdner Bank in the fall of 1932.

A third fount of hostility lay in Nacher's intention to give a 5 percent dividend for the fiscal year ending on September 30, 1932. This decision was the prerogative of the Supervisory Board, but no date had been scheduled for the annual shareholders' meeting. Instead, Bodenheimer had arranged for an audit by an independent accounting firm. Nacher viewed this ploy as a means whereby the Dresdner Bank could prevent a dividend and force Engelhardt to reduce its ten million RM indebtedness with the financial institution.[118]

On December 6, 1932, newspapers announced that the date on which stockholders could examine the 1931–1932 balance statement would be December 15. Since beer sales had been good during August and September and since a dividend had been provided in the prior year ending in September 1931, a similar positive result was expected. The same publication reported the good news on December 15, 1932, that a distribution of between 4 percent and 5 percent was expected for those holding the twelve million RM worth of stock, but the bad news was that Siegmund Bodenheimer of the Dresdner Bank had resigned as the chair of Engelhardt's Supervisory Board due to "personal reasons."[119]

Although the public was curious about Bodenheimer's resignation and the Alexanderplatz property, Engelhardt kept most details regarding those circumstances away from the newspapers' scrutiny. But what continued to be examined before Hitler's assumption to power in January 1933 was the disseminated balance statement. Engelhardt had sufficient annual sales in order to afford 2.8 million in depreciations during the 1931–1932 fiscal year. But revenue of 20.81 million RM had allowed an 8 percent dividend for the 1930–1931 business year, whereas in the 1931–1932 year, the revenue of 12.88 million RM enabled only a 5 percent distribution. Separate accounting for the parent company and each subsidiary allowed Engelhardt to provide a dividend from each firm (Table 6.7).

Nacher had clashed with Bodenheimer of the Dresdner Bank, whether his financial institution would lend an additional 1.6 million RM loan, so that Engelhardt could have taken advantage of a Fall 1932 amendment to the beer tax law. But months later, Edmund Delmonte emphasized in an editorial that financial stability would not be restored to the brewing industry by means of tax reductions alone. Instead, a revival of the business sector would only be achieved by means of a revival in the German economy. As evidence for this statement, Dr. Delmonte indicated that of the nation's 306 breweries, only 119 provided a dividend in 1932. In addition to this troublesome state of affairs, he added that those making a distribution of cash had done so due to interest on unused cash reserves or rent. As Table 6.8 implied, shareholders received a return on their investment based on something other than the year's net profit. Engelhardt's return to investors could demonstrate the firm's strength or the generosity of Nacher's marketing strategy to attract new assetholders or satisfy existing investors. Delmonte's concern about investing in breweries could be depicted as shown in Table 6.8.

Delmonte indicated the symbiotic relationship between breweries, restaurants and banks. Perhaps the largest customer for German breweries was the

Table 6.7 Comparison of Engelhardt Annual Dividends

Company Name	*Profit for Year Ending 9/30/1931*	*Dividend for 1931*	*Profit for Year Ending 9/30/1932*	*Dividend for 1932*
Engelhardt Brauerei	1.27 million RM	8%	850,000 RM	5%
E. Greifswald	22,625 RM	6%	21,763 RM	6%
E. Weißwasser	24,875 RM	6%	21,924 RM	6%
E. Königsberg	24,924 RM	8%	26,251 RM	8%
E. Rathenow			30,066 RM	6%
E. Schlesische			32,109 RM	

Source: I translated the following three *Vossische Zeitung* articles to compile this table: "Gesunde Engelhardt-Brauerei; Doppelter Kapitalbetrag in 8 Jahren aus Gewinnen abgeschrieben—Kapazität nur zu 40 Prozent ausgenutzt—Unkosten angepaßt," *Vossische Zeitung*, evening edition, January 16, 1933, p. 9. "Günstige Abschlüsse im Engelhardt-Konzern," *Vossische Zeitung*, morning edition, January 22, 1933, p. 25. "Schlesische Engelhardt-Brauerei zufrieden," *Vossische Zeitung*, evening edition, February 3, 1933, p. 10.

Table 6.8 Edmund Delmonte's Survey of German Brewery Dividends, 1932

Type of Dividend Given in 1932	*Number of Corporations*
Increased dividend	11
Unchanged dividend vis-à-vis 1931	41
Reduced dividend vis-à-vis 1931	55
No dividend for 1932	42
Number of incorporated breweries responding in 1933	149 (i.e., 48.7% response rate)

Source: I translated Edmund Delmonte's article "Brauereien unter Druck; Fast 400 Millionen Außenstände," which appeared in the February 11, 1933, morning edition of the *Vossische Zeitung* on Page 10.

restaurant business sector and thus it was estimated that restaurants owed breweries between 300 and 400 million RM. Because of the existing government laws, breweries were able to pass along much of the estimated 1932 beer tax of 277 million RM to restaurants. Not only did banks provide loans to breweries, but they also viewed the breweries' financing of restaurants as a profitable investment for financial institutions. But the issuing of dividends and the 300 to 400 million RM in accounts receivable owed to the breweries could not hide from Delmonte the dramatic decline in the quantity of beer produced in Germany (Table 6.9). The volume of beer brewed in Germany between 1929 and 1933 had decreased by nearly half, resulting in fixed costs increasing from 1.25 RM to 1.50 RM per hectoliter (26.4 gallons). The nation had also lost its first-place position in exporting beer. In 1913, the Reich had delivered 26.4 million gallons abroad, but the volume had dwindled to 6.6 million gallons in 1932. England had become the world's largest supplier. Under such financial circumstances, Edmund Delmonte questioned whether it was wise for German breweries to distribute their scarce cash in dividends.

Outgoing Supervisory Board Chair Siegmund Bodenheimer warned Engelhardt's Deputy Board Chair Joseph Koeth to oppose the proposed dividend, a position endorsed by the Chair of the Dresdner Bank. To counteract this position, Nacher planned to have Herbert von Breska elected to Engelhardt's Supervisory Board. As a representative of the Berliner Handels-Gesellschaft, Breska's selection would have meant that for the first time since 1907, a competing large bank would have had influence on the

Table 6.9 Decline in German Beer Production

Year	*Production in Gallons*
Prewar	1.823 billion
1929–1930	1.532 billion
1931–1932	977 million
1932–1933	<792 million

Source: The data was published in Edmund Delmonte's February 11, 1933, *Vossische Zeitung* "Brauereien unter Druck" article.

brewery. Nacher had scored a temporary victory at the expense of alienating his decade-long support from his main financial backer. The Dresdner Bank stopped its opposition to the issuing of a dividend, despite the scathing results of the independent audit.[120]

A second mistake occurred in the beginning of March 1933 as NSDAP Member Rudolf Luedtke was suddenly appointed to the Board. Nacher deluded himself by imagining that Luedtke's influence was sufficient to stop the Nazi boycott, since a party member was on the Board. In addition, Nacher alienated the new Supervisory Board Chair as well as the Board of Directors with his unilateral appointment. After Hitler's March 5, 1933 election victory, a Nazi Commissar was forced on the company, who caused Jewish employees to be dismissed. Nacher was outraged by such interference in the personnel of his company. He requested that Koeth convene a Supervisory Board meeting to deal with Commissar Petersen. But in his April 10, 1933 letter to Nacher, Koeth contended that such concessions prevented NSDAP encroachments into Engelhardt's management. But far more serious than Commissar Petersen was the spying performed by Engelhardt authorized signatory Lothar Schütt. Schütt informed Deputy Gau Leader Artur Görlitzer about Nacher's 1930 bribe of 120,000 RM to the city's negotiator Walter Golde.[121]

On May 18, 1933, the Berlin Magistrate Ludwig Steeg attempted to warn Engelhardt's management that Nacher's expectation of merely being fined 20,000 RM did not perceive how seriously the city was taking the matter. Instead Berlin was demanding a 2.5 million RM stock packet held by Engelhardt's holding company. Nacher controlled only 6.37 million RM of the conglomerate's 12 million capital. By personally depositing the 2.5 million worth of shares in a blocked account for Lord Mayor Julius Lippert, Nacher would lose control of his empire. The only apparent recourse consisted of Nacher's right to repurchase the shares for 3 million RM within two years. However, in the May 19, 1956, restitution process, both sides recalled that Nacher could only exercise that right if a Lippert designated Trustee ensured that the stock would be resold to an impeccable Aryan business.[122]

Continual demands by Berlin officials produced resistance by Engelhardt executives. One day after the extortion of the 2.5 million RM, Lothar Schütt demanded to be included on the Board for his industrial spying and Lippert wanted Ludwig Steeg to be included as well. In response, Joseph Koeth declared in a June 8, 1933 meeting that he was not prepared to yield to any further demands by Lippert. Koeth affirmed that Lippert's dictates violated the May agreements and in addition, it was unclear whether the Gauleiter had the right to represent the City of Berlin in the alleged overpayment of the Alexanderplatz real estate parcel. Instead, the Board desired to deal with Lord Mayor Heinrich Sahm and City Treasurer Karl

Steiniger. But Koeth also maintained that Nacher should compensate the conglomerate, since only 49 percent of the stock deposited in the blocked account personally belonged to him. Ernst Sander, the Dresdner Bank's representative on the Board, concurred with Koeth's insistence that Nacher repay the company.[123]

After the resignations of Joseph Koeth, Ernst Sander and Herbert von Breska from the Supervisory Board, a power vacuum ensued in which Engelhardt's will to resist the City of Berlin collapsed. However, the Dresdner Bank assumed power over the brewery at a September 19, 1934 meeting with Koeth in which the bank agreed to three personnel reconfigurations. The Bank complied with Lippert's demands for a representative on the Supervisory Board; that Lothar Schütt should be rewarded for his spying on the brewery with a seat on the Board of Directors; and that the termination of Jewish employees in Engelhardt should continue. In return for these relatively minor concessions, the Dresdner Bank obtained its major goals. The Berliner Handels-Gesellschaft, a competing bank, was excluded from the Supervisory Board. Also, the Dresdner Bank executive Alfred Hölling became the Deputy Chair of Engelhardt's Supervisory Board. Furthermore, Dresdner Bank industrial advisor Hilarius Giebel served on Engelhardt's Supervisory Board, but was paid at the Board of Director level for all the time he devoted to brewery activities. The City of Berlin guaranteed the Dresdner Bank a free hand in all company matters.[124]

As far back as 1932, Nacher had considered Giebel for the Board, but he was forced to change his mind after threatened resignations by Board Members Hermann Eisner and Gerhard Danziger. Because of this offense, Giebel persecuted Nacher and Engelhardt's Board. As Dieter Ziegler concluded, "If the Dresdner Bank had the goal of successfully bringing the Aryanization of the Engelhardt Brewery to a conclusion, Giebel was a good choice."[125]

Ignatz suffered a nervous breakdown in the beginning of November 1933 and on the advice of his physician went to a sanatorium in Garmisch-Partenkirchen. But rather than finding rest, he was arrested there on charges of bribery on November 17 and transported back to Berlin. The trial began in the beginning of January 1934, but a legal expert demonstrated that the sales price was not excessive. The financial specialist compared three other Alexanderplatz properties and determined that the city had paid a greater price per square meter for other properties than it did for the Engelhardt acquisition. Nacher's 2,700 square meter building cost about 9 million RM or 3,500 RM per square meter. In contrast, the Aschinger structure of 2,300 square meters amounted to 13.3 million RM, which corresponded to 5,850 RM per square meter. The two other edifices cost the city 4,200 RM and 4,800 RM per square meter. Although bribery charges were dropped, Walter Golde was sentenced to six months for embezzlement and Nacher to four months for aiding and abetting. However, the Supreme Court overturned the ruling against Nacher on February 14, 1935.[126]

The Dresdner Bank took advantage of the pressure on Nacher during the criminal trial to strip away his claims on assets from the brewery. Once again, the bank opposed Engelhardt's annual dividend, which would nullify Nacher's bonus for his last year of employment. The lack of a dividend would also negatively impact the profitability of his Borussia firm and the holding company. In addition, investors might sell stock not producing a dividend. The result would be a lower valuation of the shares on the stock exchange. Two weeks before the February 28, 1934 annual shareholders meeting, Dresdner Bank executive Alfred Hölling told Joseph Koeth to combat Nacher's resistance as strenuously as possible. Nacher realized that as long as he refused to meet the Dresdner Bank's demands, it would prevent stockholders from releasing him of his financial responsibility as president of the company. Therefore, Nacher offered three settlement proposals regarding the dissolution of the holding company and the clear separation of his property from company assets. One week before the General Assembly, Nacher made the concessions to Hilarius Giebel, the Dresdner Bank's agent. However, Giebel rejected all three and would not renounce the right to demand compensation from Nacher. The Dresdner Bank's plan to intimidate Nacher and his supporting shareholders was implemented by Giebel's posting of SA guards in the February 28, 1934 Assembly. When Waldemar Koch decried the unfair manner in which Nacher was treated, Koch was publicly beaten up by the SA during the shareholder meeting. Three days later, the last four Jewish employees received notices of termination.[127]

A contemporary would have had to read between the lines of the newspaper to detect what had transpired at Engelhardt's February shareholder meeting. The headline in the financial section on the following day announced: "Agitated General Assembly of the Engelhardt Brewery." The publication blandly reported that the opposition's petition for a postponement was rejected and that the balance statement was approved by 57,659 votes to 50,404 with 336 abstentions. Management had won over the objection by the opposition, representing the interests of the retired company president and major shareholder, Mr. Nacher. Was the discrepancy between the editor's use of the word "agitated" in the headline and the prosaic reportage of a narrow victory sufficient to alert an astute reader that something more violent had occurred? Two pages earlier in the same newspaper, there had appeared a featured article proclaiming the "success" of the Dresdner Bank, although assets had declined by 353 million RM between the end of 1932 and the conclusion of 1933. Although expenses had decreased by only 10 million RM, net profits had increased from 9.48 million in 1932 to 11.56 million RM in 1933. Thirteen months after Hitler's ascension to power, would the discerning reader have understood that the two articles were somehow related and that more was implied than printed? Had the newspaper alluded to a connection between the two lengthy articles or was it merely coincidence that five months after the conclusion of Engelhardt's fiscal year and two months after the end of the Dresdner Bank's year, the newspaper disclosed aspects of both firms' balance statement on the same day? Nearly four weeks later, the broadsheet added the final information regarding Nacher's Borussia Company filing an action to annul the February 28 General Assembly's approval of the Balance and Profit and Loss Statements; to invalidate the discharge of Board of Director as well as Supervisory Board members, and to prohibit use of the net profits. Oral hearings had been scheduled with Berlin's District Court for May 4, 1934.[128] Thereby, Nacher continued the fight to prevent the Dresdner Bank from utilizing Engelhardt profits to pay down its obligations with the lender and from Aryanizing the conglomerate.

Since July 1934 the Dresdner Bank had attempted to purchase the 2.4 million RM packet of shares, which the City of Berlin possessed. But the City would not sell them as long as Nacher held the right of repurchase. The Dresdner Bank needed to find a way whereby it could coerce Nacher to relinquish that right. Part of the Dresdner Bank's strategy was evident through the arrest of Waldemar Koch, based on Giebel's June 12, 1934 written denunciation to the police. The next stage in the strategy was Nacher's arrest on August 28, 1934 at his Bad Tölz manor. Nacher was forced to transfer power of attorney from Waldemar Koch to Albrecht Aschoff. The contract written by Aschoff entailed Nacher's relinquishment of the rights to repurchase stock held by the City of Berlin as well as the sale of 2.6 million RM in shares possessed by Borussia A.G. Thereby the Dresdner Bank became the majority shareholder of the Engelhardt Brewery. To further diminish the financial liability to the bank and secure the position of the bank as the new owner, Nacher had to withdraw his claims for a pension as well as his final bonus. Furthermore, stocks valued at 930,000 RM were taken as a settlement for damages, which Ignatz never admitted. The historian Dieter Ziegler concluded that the Dresdner Bank's agent Hilarius Giebel was responsible for Nacher's arrest. The Dresdner Bank had used its influence with the Berlin Gau Leadership to pressure Ignatz to sell 51 percent of all Engelhardt shares to the company. By owning the majority of shares, the financial institution was able to force other concessions. These September 7, 1934 requirements included that the brewery and all subsidiaries were obligated for five years to seek loans only from the Dresdner Bank and the brewery was obliged to maintain a minimum of a one million RM account balance with the financial institution.[129]

Postwar restitution processes indicated how the end of the Third Reich did not change the intransigence of Dresdner Bank executives in their pursuit of retaining Engelhardt assets at the expense of Ignatz Nacher. New York attorney Max Hirschberg began the first restitution process against the bank and City of Berlin in September 1949. The heirs were not interested in the recovery of the stock at that time, but instead wanted a back payment in DM. Dresdner Bank executive Carl Goetz was allegedly unable to recall anything important in the February 27, 1946 interrogation about the bank's purchase of the second packet of Engelhardt stock during the Summer of 1934. However, in a January 13, 1953 file note, Goetz characterized to Hans-Joachim Laabs, the General Counsel of the Dresdner Bank, that the Aryanization of the brewery's stock was a normal process in the Third Reich, "which was played out daily by a major bank." By 1953, the heirs had changed their minds. They were no longer interested in cash, but wanted a restoration of their property. This was especially important to Hermann Eisner, because only by this means could he regain his position in the company, which he had lost in 1933.[130]

No later than January 1953, the Dresdner Bank began to gather documentation to defend itself against restitution claims. Although the bank assumed that Siegmund Bodenheimer would harbor few friendly feelings toward the financial institution, it nevertheless contacted him in New York. All attempts by the bank to form a united front against the heirs with the Berlin Senate failed, including an appeal in a legal brief by attorney Karl Aden for support. In spite of these adverse circumstances Carl Goetz, Alfred Hölling and Hugo Zinßer, who had all been members of the Dresdner Bank's Board of Directors prior to 1945, all held in principle a negative attitude toward a settlement in the restitution process in June 1955. Hermann Eisner's one trump card, by which he hoped to force the bank to a cooperative attitude, was his alliance with the Schultheiß Brewery in which Schultheiß would acquire more than half of all Engelhardt shares. In return, Schultheiß guaranteed Engelhardt's independence, including Hermann Eisner's ability to resume leading the Engelhardt and Groterjan breweries. The heirs increased their cash offer for the Engelhardt stock from 300,000 DM to 425,000 DM but also stipulated an acceptance deadline by November 15, 1955. In contrast, the bank hoped to wear down the heirs through its delaying strategy. Although the bank recognized that the return of the stock was inevitable, it hoped to further increase the cash settlement offered to it, because it recognized that Schultheiß was in a hurry for the return of the stock. Carl Goetz was willing to extend the process because he claimed that the bank had "behaved completely honorably." Nevertheless, if the city would pay a high indemnification and the brewery was willing to accept a low amount of compensation, with the result that the Dresdner Bank suffered no loss, Goetz was willing to settle by November 1955.[131]

The bank's attorney Hans-Joachim Laabs warned the three Board members Alfred Höling, Carl Schleipen and Hans Rinn not to jeopardize the good relationship with Schultheiß. In addition, Karl-Heinz Lehmann wrote a seven-page December 2, 1955 explanation to Goetz. But the Board decided to extend the legal wrangling to its conclusion, even though the City Counselor Paul Füllsack urged Laabs to settle. But Goetz continued to be completely unamenable. In the beginning of February 1956, Attorney Laabs met with Schultheiß Board Member Hans Sixtus and later with Eisner. Losing the majority of Engelhardt's stock would mean loss of control by the Dresdner Bank over the brewery. But Sixtus suggested that the Dresdner be guaranteed main bank functions in Engelhardt as well as retaining one vote on the Supervisory Board. By mid-March 1956, Senator Haas and Senate President Füllsack had agreed with the bank regarding the amount of back compensation that would be paid. But in the calculation, the city used the ten RM to one DM ratio from the postwar currency reform. Therefore, the city offered to pay the bank 250,000 DM. However, the Dresdner Bank rejected the amount, claiming it should be one million DM, based on the 1956 settlement date for damages, rather than on the 1933 sale date.[132]

The City of Berlin was not prepared to pay more than 500,000 to 600,000 DM. Thus, the bank concluded in May 1956 that negotiations had failed and a mid-October date was scheduled with the Restitution Court. Simultaneously the city claimed that when it purchased Engelhardt's headquarters on the Alexanderplatz in 1930, it had to compensate evicted tenants so it could construct the subway. The city suddenly maintained that these payments should have been deducted from the purchase price given to Engelhardt. However, the city had no evidence for this assertion. The Restitution Court decided in two weeks during October 1956 what the three parties had been unwilling to negotiate in more than a year and a half. The Dresdner Bank had to return to Nacher's heirs the 2.5 million RM worth of Engelhardt shares in return for 600,000 DM.[133] The Aryanization of Engelhardt was rectified.

At the end of December 1956 when all settlement transactions were completed, the Trustee for the brewery was removed. Hermann Eisner was summoned to the Board, pending his confirmation in a Supervisory Board meeting. The conclusion by the contemporary historian Ralf Ahrens that it was "an extremely favorable solution for the Dresdner Bank" appears suspect. The bank only received 600,000 DM for stock, which had a market value of 1 million DM. In addition, the financial institution was required to pay attorney costs of 400,000 DM. Ahrens drew this conclusion on the basis of an accounting profit. Because of the postwar currency reform, the bank had entered the Engelhardt stock in their financial ledgers as being worth merely 212,287.50 DM. So, when the City of Berlin paid the bank 600,000 DM, their profit on paper was nearly 400,000 DM. Of far greater economic significance was the ability of the Dresdner Bank's affiliate, the Bank für Handel und Industrie, to replace the Berliner Bank as the main bank serving

both the Engelhardt and Groterjan breweries.[134] In Ahrens' assessment, Carl Goetz's lack of moral scruples had paid dividends:

> The lack of an awareness of injustice was so embossed in Goetz, that he could not imagine that a German court would be able to come to any other assessment. He twisted the Aryanization policies of the Dresdner Bank during the 1930s into the entirely normal events of daily bank business.[135]

The model proposed in this exploration revolves around a German businessman obtaining financial support from one of the nation's three largest banks to Aryanize a profitable Jewish-owned firm during the 1933 to 1935 time period. In the example of the Engelhardt Brewery, the Dresdner Bank became the major shareholder. In the following example of the Simson weapons manufacturer, there was also a deviation from the paradigm. The Jewish company was twice offered a to Gentile industrialist before the shares left the possession of the Trustee and ultimately became a "foundation."

F. ARYANIZATION OF SIMSON GUN MANUFACTURERS

Several members of the Inter-Allied Military Commission of Control (IMCC) were Jewish and therefore it was rumored that Arthur and Julius Simson's gun factory had been provided a 1925 contract by coreligionists to supply the German infantry with weapons. The hearsay may be completely unfounded since there were logical reasons why the Allies would have preferred Simson being awarded the contract. One explanation would have been the French and British desire to punish the firms enabling the Reich to initiate World War I. The Simon Wiesenthal Center in Vienna assisted Simson's nephew Ewald Mayer to discover a second interpretation. The Allies desired to slow production of weapons by awarding the contract to such a small company, that it would be unable to satisfy the Defense Ministry's requirements.[136]

From an accounting perspective, a further basis was that a large manufacturing facility would have incurred great fixed costs in producing small quantities.

A contemporary National Socialist source noted gunsmith Rudolf Reger's lament in the April 1926 edition of the newspaper *Fredericus* that factories such as the Mauserwerke in Oberndorf, the Deutsche Waffen- und Munitionsfabriken and the Sauer und Sohn were all eliminated from military production. Party Members in Suhl began grousing in 1927 that the Jewish firm was deceiving the Allies' Control Commission. They claimed that when inspection teams from the German Army came to examine the plant, manufacturing temporarily shifted from the private production of bicycle parts to automatic weapons and some of the mechanisms were scrapped. This was nothing more than malicious speculation. One would certainly think that military rifles and pistols would require a high grade of steel to withstand the heat of repeatedly firing a weapon. In contrast, cheap aluminum would be sufficient material for a bicycle. In addition, machinery required to meet the exact specifications of a weapon would need to be far more exacting than those for a bicycle. A rifle might not fire, if the variation of a part was more than one millimeter, but it would seem that a bicycle would operate with a part differing from the ideal by five millimeters. Furthermore, the training to manufacture rifle components probably required a highly skilled machinist, but one would have the impression that nearly any blue-collar worker could assemble a bicycle.[137]

Apparently, the state provided cost recovery of 12 million RM for Simson to purchase equipment to fabricate infantry rifles, which promoted jealousy from other potential manufacturers. A secret February 21, 1932 report spying on the firm for the National Socialist Gau in Thuringia noted that the state-approved prices were "very adequate." It observed that a prewar infantry rifle had cost 68 RM, but in 1932 sold for 187 RM and a machine gun valued at approximately 900 RM before the war now fetched 3,400 RM.[138] The sole source manufacturing required that a competing Sauer firm dismiss a large part of its staff, leaving no more than 100 employees. Ostensibly Simson was striving for the elimination of its competitors, even pushing Sauer und Sohn from the hunting rifle market, where the difference in price for one model was 100 dollars. A Nazi newspaper editorialized that since the state subsidy to Simson was three times as high as previously, it ought to have prevented the Jewish-owned firm from selling hunting rifles at giveaway prices.[139]

After Fritz Sauckel became the leader of the Nazi Gau in Thuringia in August 1927 he made the Simson monopoly of infantry weapons a personal vendetta. Using Party Member Erich Sack's testimony, an article appeared in Fritz Sauckel's newspaper *Der Nationalsozialist*. In a second September

27, 1927 inspection by the German Army of Simson's recently subsidized facility, it was claimed that only a part of the bicycle parts was concealed, since the investigators appeared on Saturday at 10:00 a.m. Although Sauckel repeatedly filed complaints with Thuringia's Interior Minister, they were disregarded. Wilhelm Frick's comments on the Simson activities during the Weimar era were also dismissed as maneuvers on the behalf of competing firms. Even when Fritz Sauckel became Thuringia's Minister of the Interior on August 26, 1932, National Socialists considered that their accusations were not receiving proper attention.

Arthur and Julius Simson shrewdly devised plans to counteract any opposition prior to Hitler's ascension to power. On January 8, 1933, Julius informed his attorney that the contracts making the firm acceptable to a future Nazi economy had been completed. However, the plans did not include any option to sell the family business, since the exclusive contract with the German Army made the brothers feel protected. Nevertheless, they considered it necessary to delete the family name from the company's designation. It was changed to the Weapons and Vehicle Factory in Suhl. A second step in their accommodation to an immanent Nazi regime was to formally split the civilian bicycle and motorcycle production from military manufacturing. Civilian construction was planned to be leased to an Aryan consortium, composed of Simson family partners. A third step was the formulation of a declaration affirming that staff would increase by 45 percent. New employees would include 180 SA members, 20 SS, 18 Stahlhelm members and 14 World War I veterans.[140]

But with Hitler's ascension, Nazis viewed it as time to begin a legal investigation of Simson's pursuits. On March 29, 1933, Hellmuth Gommlich, Superintendent of Police in Zella-Mehlis, began an examination of the Simson factory in which he systematically intimidated the employees. People in the small town of Suhl held that the time was right to affirm their National Socialist convictions by denouncing the Simsons. People who had never been on the Simson payroll reported about "irregularities," which had lasted for years, including supplying foreign governments with blueprints of German Army weapons. A Nazi brochure claimed that Gommlich had apparently compared more than 52,000 invoices and interrogated hundreds of witnesses in a fourteen-month inquiry. It was maintained that despite financial records being "destroyed" and only family members having an overall perspective, Gommlich was able to determine that profits were one-third of gross sales. National Socialists contended that this would have been inconceivable for any other firm. However historians affirm that the audit of various armament companies' records between 1928 and 1933 revealed considerable profit. Scholars concluded that none of the sole contract firms, including Simson, was guilty of fraud.[141]

Out of jealousy with the Jewish family's gun monopoly, Fritz Walther of the Association of Zella-Mehlis Gun Manufacturers complained to Hitler in March 1933 that the sole source contract was driving Gentile companies into bankruptcy. The German military was convinced that the accusations were without foundation and could be traced back to jealousy. Nevertheless, Lt. General Alfred von Vollard-Bockelberg accepted Sauckel's suggestion of filing a criminal complaint against Arthur Simson and his top managers, regarding allegations of giving themselves exorbitant salaries.[142]

The seriousness of the accusations intensified. A February 21, 1932 report to the Gau had made the superficial complaint that the workforce was composed of Socialists and Communists. By May 5, 1933, the issue against the Simson brothers was focused on the more serious charge of fraud (Table 6.10).

Since Criminal Commissar Boening reported in such detail, the accusation bore the appearance of plausibility. However, Leopold Schwarzschild's contemporary emigré publication from Paris indicated why the charges against the Simson plant in Suhl had to be false:

> prices and profits of the factory in Suhl were regulated by the War Department, exercising a stringent control over the plant in Suhl if only because the firm had had a monopoly for all legal army supplied since the signature of the Versailles Treaty. The War Department was to be blamed for [any alleged] excessive prices and excessively high profits.[143]

German exiles clearly perceived that all billing for weapons and services was under the watchful scrutiny of the Army Munitions Office, since the Inter-Allied Military Commission of Control was monitoring German military procurement in accordance with post–World War I peace provisions. The army could not bear to receive less than that for which it had paid.

Nevertheless, Lieutenant General Alfred von Vollard-Bockelberg adopted Gauleiter Sauckel's suggestion of filing a criminal complaint against Arthur Simson and his managers on the grounds of inflated salaries. Simson's

Table 6.10 Criminal Commissar Wilhelm Boening's Evidence for "Fraud"

Rifle Part	*Quantity*	*Simson Price*	*Others Price*
Gun chamber		94.44 RM	27.00 RM
Extractor (expels spent shell casing out of chamber)	2,000	8.94 RM	3.75 RM
Firing pin	2,700	8.64 RM	2.35 RM
Gun hammer	3,000	18.23 RM	6.75 RM
Bushing	800	4.25 RM	1.00 RM

Source: Accusation contained in a court record cited by Ulrike Schulz entitled, "Ermittlungsbericht des Kriminalkommissars Boening gegen die Firma Simson & Co. vom 5. Mai 1933, in welchem er angebliche Betrügereien der Firma und überteuerte Kieferungen an das Reichswehrministerium auflistet."

Technical Director Walter Baetz was arrested in the beginning of September 1933 on charges of having bribed two state officials. Arthur and Julius felt they were no longer able to oppose synchronization and founded the Limited Partnership, Berlin-Suhler Waffen und Fahrzeugwerke Simson on September 19, 1933 as an interim solution, in which Dr. Herbert Hoffmann was appointed as a Trustee to decide all controversies. However, the selection of Hoffmann proved to be extremely unwise, since he demonstrated himself to be disloyal to the Simson family. In addition, he lacked the necessary technical competencies. On December 15, 1933, Arthur Simson was ordered to appear for an interrogation, which astonishingly was led by Hoffmann. The "Trustee" urged a restructuring, but Arthur made no concessions at that time, since his attorney was not present. But by January 4, 1934, Arthur agreed to Hoffmann's request to become the business manager. The daily operation of the firm was given to him, whereas Arthur and Julius were prohibited from entering the factory. Not only was the new situation detrimental to the Jewish family, but also to the army, which was committed to continuing arms purchases.[144]

By June 1934 the Simsons wanted to fire Hoffmann because of his continual contract violations. The army initially agreed, since they desired that the position of Trustee be separated from the business manager and a technically trained executive be hired. Thus, on June 28, 1934, Hoffmann was given notice of his termination. However, since the negotiations concerning the future of the company dragged on through the Fall of 1934, it allowed Hoffmann time to consolidate his position (Table 6.11).[145]

The army also maneuvered for power, whereas the Jewish attempt to oust Hoffmann and regain control over the firm became less possible. The Aryanization of the Simson's business was already evident. Thus, Julius Simson moved to Davos, Switzerland, in the beginning of October 1934, whereas Arthur spent most of his time in San Remo, Italy. On the other hand, Major General Kurt Liese had gained more authority over the firm by allowing Hoffmann to remain. By October 6, the Army Weapons Office had made

Table 6.11 New Aryan Management Team for Simson

Name	*Position*	*Post-War Fate*
Herbert Hoffmann	Managing director	
Werner Heynen	CEO	Fled to southern Germany on June 23, 1945
Jürgen Freiherr von Orgies-Rutenberg	Personnel director	
Karl Beckurts	Operations manager	
Otto Eberhardt	Chairman, Board of Directors	Lost without a trace

Source: Material published in Siegfried Schütt's *Die Simson-Legende*.

a first offer to sell Simson to the Flick Company. However, Friedrich Flick had mixed thoughts regarding the acquisition. The purchase had financial benefits, if he could integrate the Jewish firm with his Maxhütte steel pipe business. However, the integration into his business empire would require investment and the army was not interested in supplying start-up funding as it had previously done for Simson. Instead, the military expected a nine million RM purchase price as well as an investment of approximately twenty million RM by Flick. Friedrich's reticence to invest such great amounts of capital led to the demise of this first offer to him. At that time, Arthur Simson would certainly have rejected such a low bid.[146]

Attorney Hans Koch assisted in the family attempt to regain control over the firm, but he was coerced to abandon his endeavor, when he was brought into "protective custody." Periodically, Arthur traveled from San Remo to Berlin in order to resolve company problems. On April 11, 1935, he was imprisoned in Berlin for alleged treason. Fourteen days later, this provided the army with a convenient opportunity to extend a second sales offer to Friedrick Flick. Arthur was not released until August 8. Although he was set free, he was not authorized to leave the greater Berlin area nor permitted to enter his former office. In addition, he was not allowed to correspond with his brother and his passport was confiscated.[147]

The Deutsche Revisions- und Treuhand AG was tasked with discovering fraudulent accounting practices, in order to "legally" appropriate the Jewish-owned firm after two failed attempts to sell it to Friedrich Flick. The Trust company renewed the old fraud claims in their audit of August 1935. They estimated that the family had made an excessive profit of 23.2 million RM between the years 1924 and 1933. This extraordinary amount could have only been the gross profit before taxes, salaries and other expenses were deducted. Another egregious accounting offense for the Trustee agency was the establishment of the company's value at eight million RM, far below the fair valuation of nineteen million RM. On November 23, 1935, Arthur was forced to recognize his alleged guilt by signing a contract in the amount of 9.75 million RM. Subtracting the worth of the business of eight million from the debt owed, left a remaining obligation of 1.75 million RM. The Simson family not only did not receive any payment for their company, but they were required to pay nearly two million RM.[148]

In contrast with previously discussed coerced sales of large Jewish-owned department stores, newspaper publishers and a private bank, it was the breach of the army's contract with the Simsons, rather than the banks' withdrawal of loans, which economically allowed for the expropriation of the munitions firm. Another difference was that although the army intended to sell the weapons' manufacturer to Flick, the Trustee Herbert Hoffmann held all the company shares after two failed sales attempts in 1934–1935. Fritz Sauckel made the symbolic gesture in the *Völkische Beobachter* that the Simson factory was Hitler's 1935 Christmas present. In response, Arthur camouflaged his February 9, 1936 emigration to Switzerland as a skiing vacation. More than forty European and American newspapers carried reports on the fate of the Jewish rifle manufacturer. But the majority of Paris, London and Prague journalists did not accept the claim that the Simsons had obtained excessive profits. Arthur and Julius' nephew, Ewald Mayer, traveled to the border in the same train compartment as a Hohenzollern princess and Hjalmar Schacht, so the cursory examination of his passport allowed his escape.[149]

Herbert Hoffmann did not remain loyal to his Jewish employers, but became the chief shareholder after two failed sales attempts to Friedrich Flick during the 1934 to 1935 timeframe. Only thereafter did the Jewish-owned company become a "foundation."

G. REPEATED MOTIFS IN THE ARYANIZATION OF JEWISH COMPANIES

Two advantages of the company-focused methodology as contrasted with scholarship's customary city-focused structure have become apparent from this chapter. The first is the business relationships between Jewish-owned companies became immediately transparent. For example, the grocery advertisements as well as the full-page announcements of annual sales demonstrated the interdependence of Hermann Tietz, Leonhard Tietz and other department stores with the Mosse and Ullstein newspapers. A second example of this phenomenon was the downfall of other small- and mid-sized industrial companies, when the Arnhold Bank was Aryanized.

The role of the non-Jewish, banking giants such as the Deutsche and Dresdner Banks in the Aryanization of large Jewish-owned firms was another of the many motifs made visible by concentrating on companies, instead of cities. This was first apparent in the Dresdner Bank's recall of existing loans to Hermann Tietz and its inclusion in a consortium to support Georg Karg's takeover. The Dresdner Bank also provided capital to Max Winkler in his quest to obtain ownership of both the Mosse publishing house and the Ullstein publishing house. Not only Winkler but also Deutsche Bank executive Ferdinand Bausback became the owner of an enormous block of Ullstein stock.

A corollary of this pattern was the sudden inclusion of a Dresdner Bank executive in the Supervisory Board. The reader will recall Walter Seidel's admission to the Leonhard Tietz Board as well as Dresdner Bank executive Alfred Hölling and Dresdner consultant Hilarius Giebel inclusions in the Engelhardt Board. Since a Supervisory Board is unknown to American businesses, it bears to be reminded that an appointment would entail inside knowledge of the Jewish-owned company as well as shareholder voting rights and the ability to influence the firm's decisions.

On occasion, the Dresdner Bank's activities went far beyond avarice. According to a July 8, 1949 note in the Dresdner Bank files, British investigators understood that the Bank had arranged Kurt's arrest in order to force the Arnhold Bank to a quick sale. The arrest induced the Jewish financial institution to drop their central demand to have the sale proceeds transferred to a foreign country.[150] In a second Aryanization, the Bank provoked the physical assault on Waldemar Koch and not only induced his arrest but also the arrest of Engelhardt's president, Ignatz Nacher.

Breaking of trust was an additional recurring element. Georg Karg had been a trusted manager in Hermann Tietz, before arranging to acquire his employer's firm. Such behavior reached its zenith in the large number of Arnhold Bank executives, who failed to recuse themselves as former Dresdner Bank managers in the acquisition of Arnhold by the non-Jewish financial institution.

There were three incidents, which may have supported the mistaken interpretation of a top-down takeover by Nazi elite. Thus, the Saxon Gauleiter Martin Mutschmann was involved in the acquisition of Arnhold Bank; the Thuringian Gauleiter Fritz Sauckel participated in the cheap purchase of Simson; and Berlin Lord Mayor Julius Lippert temporarily held authority over a large packet of Engelhardt stock. However, Mutschmann's role may better be interpreted as a desire for vengeance when his lace factory in Plauen went into bankruptcy after he was unable to obtain a loan from the Arnholds. Correspondingly, the City of Berlin continually hesitated to illegally sell Engelhardt shares to the Dresdner Bank, when Ignatz Nacher held repurchase rights. Similarly, the Army Weapons Office appears to have been the key participant in playing off Sauckel against Arthur Simson in its attempt to either sell the gun manufacturer to Friedrich Flick or gain as much influence over the Jewish firm as possible.

Profit at any price by the Dresdner Bank also characterized Alfred Hölling's vision to intimidate Ignatz Nacher and Hilarius Giebel's utilization of the SA in the Engelhardt stockholders' annual meeting. Those who were the beneficiaries of the brewery's demise were not the SA, but rather Hölling, who became deputy chair of the Supervisory Board, and Lothar Schütt, whose spying on Engelhardt was rewarded by a seat on its Board. Furthermore, the Dresdner Bank was able to force the brewery to only use their financial services as well as maintaining an account of at least one million RM in the company.

Those who early seized profitable Jewish-owned firms often had experience in the same business sector. Georg Karg had been a buyer for Hermann

Nazi-ideology most important	Nazi ideology and postwar tactics useful	financial success more important	Non-Nazi sharing retail policy with NSDAP	Philo-Semite forsaking wealth
Best Schulz	Flick Winkler	Abs Karg Frisch Goetz Hoffmann	Tiburtius	Bosch

Tietz. Max Winkler had financially supported newspapers in those parts of Germany, which the Versailles Treaty had separated from the nation. As the country's second-largest financial institution, the Dresdner Bank not only had experience in monetary matters but would immediately benefit as well from broadening its reach into mid-sized business lending.

Interest in Aryanization has not diminished over the decades since the end of World War II. Perhaps this concern will inaugurate a greater investigation of the individual perpetrators.

NOTES

1. Peter Fuchs, *100 Jahre Kaufhof Köln, 1891–1991* (Köln: asmuth satz & druck, 1991), pp. 58–59.

2. Heimbüchel, Kierdorf, Pohl, and Teichner, *Erlebniswelt Kaufhof*, pp. 41–47. Both Fuchs and Heimbüchel agree that the corporation's starting capital was based on real estate and not cash and both concluded that this amount was 10 million marks, although Heimbühel supplied the more exact figures of 11.75 million in liabilities was subtracted from 13.15 million in real estate and 8.6 million in furnishings to achieve the result.

3. Heidrun Homburg, "Warenhausunternehmen," in Gerald F. Feldman (Ed.), *Industrie und Inflation. Studien und Dokumente zur Politik der deutschen Unternehmer 1916–1923* (Hamburg: Hoffmann und Campe, 1977).

4. Fuchs, *100 Jahre*, p. 61.

5. Fuchs, *100 Jahre*, pp. 60–61. Also see Heimbüchel, Kierdorf, Pohl, and Teichner, *Erlebniswelt Kaufhof*, 68.

6. Banks played a crucial role in the growth and maintenance of large German companies as evidenced in both the Hermann Tietz and Leonhard Tietz department store chains. Following World War I, bankers stressed the stabilization of the currency, whereas heavy industrialists desired to exploit inflation by purchasing plants and equipment at inexpensive prices as well as rebuild foreign market share with cheap finished products. Although Leonhard Tietz also raised funds through the sale of stock, it was always strapped for cash. In contrast, after the war and inflation, there

were eight German industrial firms possessing more cash than the Deutsche Bank. See Feldman, *Industrie*, p. 185, 200.

7. Heimbüchel, Kierdorf, Pohl, and Teichner, *Erlebniswelt Kaufhof*, pp. 77–78.

8. Horst Richard Mutz, *Das Einheitspreisgeschäft als neuzeitliche Betriebsform im deutschen Einzelhandel* (Berlin: Industrieverlag Spaeth & Linde, 1932), pp. 29, 40–42. Heimbüchel, Kierdorf, Pohl, and Teichner, *Erlebniswelt Kaufhof*, pp. 78–80.

9. Erich Niemann's role in the Aryanization of Orenstein & Koppel will be addressed in chapter 7.

10. Dieter Ziegler, "Entjudung und Nazifizierung 1933–1937," in Johannes Bähr (Ed.), *Die Dresdner Bank in der Wirtschaft des Dritten Reichs* (München: R. Oldenbourg Verlag, 2006), pp. 90–93. Dieter Ziegler, *Die Dresdner Bank und die deutschen Juden* (München: R. Oldenbourg Verlag, 2006), p. 222.

11. See above Chapter Four, Section B5.

12. "Einheitspreis-Sperre; Neugründungen allgemein verboten–selbst Geschäftsverlegung untersagt," *Vossische Zeitung* (December 28, 1932), p. 12.

13. Recall table 5.3.

14. Scholars such as Theo Balderston, Knut Borchardt, Carl-Ludwig Holtfrerich, and Harold James have debated the causes of Weimar unemployment for decades, without reaching a consensus. A recent, more sophisticated investigation than that presented here concluded: "During the Great Depression there was a negative demand shock, which was communicated to the labor market by nominal inertia. On the supply side the effect of the rising real tariff wage was partly offset by the decline in the replacement ratio. In the recovery, the labor market benefited from a positive demand shock." As mathematically advanced as this research is, it may still have difficulties elucidating the monthly ebbs and flows attempted here. To view the numerous equations, see Nicholas H. Dimsdale, Nicholas Horsewood, and Arthur van Riel, "Unemployment in Interwar Germany: An Analysis of the Labor Market, 1927–1936," *The Journal of Economic History*, Vol. 66, No. 3 (September, 2006), pp. 778–808.

15. Compare "Weiter rückläufiger Ehape-Umsatz," *Vossische Zeitung*, morning edition (December 23, 1932), p. 11 with "Hohe Ehape-Bankguthaben," *Vossische Zeitung* (December 28, 1932), p. 12.

16. Hermann Kellenbenz (Ed.), *Zwei Jahrtausende Kölner Wirtschaft*. Band 2: Vom 18. Jahrhundert bis zur Gegenwart (Köln: Greven Verlag, 1975), p. 413.

17. Kellenbenz, *Zwei Jahrtausende*, p. 416.

18. To the seven front-page articles attempting to forestall a second Nazi revolution, previously mentioned in chapter 5, section D, the reader should also note the following newspaper reportage: "Hitler gegen jede Störung der Ordnung; Rüksichtslos gegen die sogenannte zweite Revolution," *Berliner Börsen-Zeitung* (July 3, 1933); "Einzelaktionen gegen Konsumvereine strengstens untersagt; Dr. Ley kündigt scharfe Maßnahmen an," *Berliner Börsen-Zeitung* (July 5, 1933); "Sperre für SA, SS und Stahlhelm," *Vossische Zeitung* (July 6, 1933), p. 2; "Hitler: Nun Evolution!; Der Reichskanzler gegen unsachliche Eingriffe in die Wirtschaft.–Alle Macht liegt bei der Reichsgewalt!" *Berliner Börsen-Zeitung*, Evening Edition (July 7, 1933), p. 1; "Aktionen gegen Warenhäser vorläufig untersagt; Ein Erlaß der NS-Parteileitung,"

Berliner *Börsen-Zeitung* (July 8, 1933); "Aktionen gegen Warenhäuser untersagt," *Vossische Zeitung* (July 8, 1933), p. 3; "Große Kanzlerrede vor dem Treuhändern der Arbeit. Die politische Macht erobert man in einem Zuge. Für die Wirtschaft gelten andere Gesetze," *Berliner Börsen-Zeitung* (July 13, 1933), p. 1; "Eingreifen des Kampfbundes untersagt," *Vossische Zeitung* (July 15, 1933), p. 4.

19. Ziegler, *Dresdner Bank*, pp. 214–215.

20. The role of the Deutsche Bank and Dresdner Bank in the Aryanization of large Jewish-owned companies is central to this assessment. Thus, the question arises of whether the Abraham Frowein associated with the takeover of Leonhard Tietz is related to Robert Frowein, who joined the NSDAP in 1936 He had been the Frankfurt branch manager of the Deutsche Bank since 1938 and was added to the Board after the Party began attacking the Catholic Board Members in May 1943. If Abraham and Robert were related, then this might suggest Deutsche Bank influence in the takeover of Leonhard Tietz. See Harold James, "The Deutsche Bank and the Dictatorship 1933–1945," in Lothar Gall (Ed.), *The Deutsche Bank 1870–1995*. pp. 342–343.

21. Recall chapter 5, section F, and see "Froweins Appell an Herriot," *Vossische Zeitung* evening edition (December 1, 1932), p. 9.

22. Compare Julian Castle Stanford [aka Julius Schloß], *Reflections; The Diary of a German-Jew in Hiding* (Oakland: Judah L. Magnus Memorial Museum, 1965), pp. 1–6 with "Neues Handelskammer-Präsidium; Der Personal-Umbau der Wirtschaft," *Berliner Morgenpost* (April 6, 1933) and "Neue Vorstandsmitglieder der Leonhard Tietz," *Vossische Zeitung* (April 5, 1933), p. 13.

23. Stanford, *Reflections*, pp. 6–7.

24. The share prices of these Jewish-owned corporations are intentionally analyzed as a basis for discussing Engelhardt section E of this chapter, and Orenstein and Kopple in chapter 7.

25. "Kleiner Gewinn Leonhard Tietz; Nach höheren Abschreibungen–Betriebsumstellung zur Umsatzstürtzung," *Vossische Zeitung* (June 18, 1933), p. 13; "Die Anschlußverträge der Tietz A.G.," *Vossische Zeitung* (June 19, 1933), 9; and "Leonhard Tietz," *Berliner Börsen-Zeitung* (June 19, 1933).

26. Recall that the issue arose during the June 23, 1933, cabinet meeting, which was discussed with regard to Hermann Tietz's fate in chapter 5, section A.

27. Compare "Neues Handelskammer-Präsidium; Der Peronal-Umbau der Wirtschaft," *Berliner Morgenpost* (April 6, 1933), p. 8 with "Leonhard Tietz A.G. Generalversammlung," *Berliner Börsen-Zeitung* (July 12, 1933), p. 10.

28. Hartmut Berghoff, *Moderne Unternehmensgeschichte; Eine themen- und theorieorientierte Einführung* (Paderborn: Ferdinand Schöningh, 2004), p. 345.

29. "Kleiner Gewinn Leonhard Tietz; Nach höheren Abschreibungen–Betriebsumstellung zur Umsatzstützung," *Vosssische Zeitung* morning edition (June 18, 1933), p. 13; and "Leonhard Tietz Aktien-Gesselschaft; Bilanz für den 31. January 1933," *Berliner Börsen-Zeitung* (July 14, 1933), p. 6.

30. "Leonhard Tietz," *Berliner Börsen-Zeitung* (June 19, 1933), p. 1.

31. "9 Mill. Währungsreserve der Westdeutsche Kaufhof A.-G.," *Vossische Zeitung* (December 10, 1933), p. 20.

32. Elisabeth Kraus, *Die Familie Mosse; Deutsch-jüdisches Bürgertum im 19. Und 20. Jahrhundert* (München: Verlag C.H. Beck, 1999), p. 494.

33. Peter de Mendelssohn, *Zeitungsstadt Berlin.* Überarbeitete und erweiterte Auflage (Frankfurt am Main: Verlag Ullstein GmbH, 1982), pp. 96, 157, 180–181, 225, 313.

34. Elisabeth Kraus, *Die Familie Mosse; Deutsch-jüdisches Bürgertum im 19. Und 20. Jahrhundert* (München: Verlag C.H. Beck, 1999), p. 397.

35. Kraus, *Die Familie Mosse*, pp. 407–408.

36. Kraus, *Die Familie Mosse*, pp. 492–499.

37. Kraus maintained that it was still unclear whether the foreign advertising agencies were a wise investment or not, although she did admit that they devoured large amounts of the scarce, necessary cash. Kraus, *Die Familie Mosse*, p. 496.

38. de Mendelssohn, *Zeitungsstadt*, pp. 398–399. Within a few years of its establishment, the New York branch required nearly 2 million RM according to "Rudolf Mosse will weiterarbeiten; Aktiver Status–Moratorium als Vergleichsvorschlag–8,8 Millionen ungedeckte Schulden," *Vossische Zeitung* (July 14, 1933), p. 9.

39. Bernd Sösemann, *Theodor Wolff; Ein Leben mit der Zeitung* (Stuttgart: Franz Steiner Verlag, 2012), p. 195.

40. Margret Boveri, *Wir lügen alle; Eine Hauptstadtzeitung unter Hitler* (Olten: Walter-Verlag, 1965), p. 32.

41. Ernst Feder, *Heute sprach ich mit . . . Tagebücher eines Berliner Publizisten 1926–1932* (Stuttgart: Deutsche Verlags-Anstalt, 1971), pp. 277–280.

42. de Mendelssohn, *Zeitungsstadt*, p. 400.

43. Kraus, *Die Familie Mosse*, p. 498.

44. Wolfram Köhler, *Der Chef-Redakteur Theodor Wolff: Ein Leben in Europa 1868–1943* (Düsseldorf: Droste, 1978), p. 264.

45. Ernst Feder, *Heute sprach ich mit . . . Tagebücher eines Berliner Publizisten 1926–1932* (Stuttgart: Deutsche Verlags-Anstalt, 1971), p. 275.

46. Feder, *Heute*, pp. 276–278.

47. Feder, *Heute*, p. 279.

48. Compare Wolfram Köhler, *Der Chef-Redakteur Theodor Wolff; Ein Leben in Europa 1868–1943* (Düssseldorf: Droste Verlag, 1978), p. 141 with Feder, *Heute*, pp. 280–286.

49. Feder, *Heute*, pp. 286–287.

50. Feder, *Heute*, pp. 293–294.

51. Feder, *Heute*, p. 299.

52. Feder, *Heute*, pp. 275–280, 305.

53. Feder, *Heute*, pp. 309–310, 316. I have included Elisabeth Kraus's German history of the Mosse family in order to present a balanced assessment of the publishing house. Although it is the most recent scholarly biography, I am attributing a higher value to the contemporary diary written by the insider, Ernst Feder.

54. Contrast Köhler, Boveri and Sösemann with Kraus, *Die Familie Mosse*, pp. 510–511.

55. George L. Mosse, *Confronting History; A Memoir* (Madison: The University of Wisconsin Press, 2000), 43.

56. Fred Hildenbrandt *Ich soll dich grüssen von Berlin, 1922–1932; Berliner Erinnerungen ganz und gar unpolitisch Post mortem herausgegeben von zwei Freunden* (München: Franz Ehrenwirth Verlag, 1966), pp. 11–12.

57. Kraus, *Die Familie Mosse*, pp. 492–493; and Köhler, *Chef*, p. 204.

58. Kraus depicted the ninety member staff of the newspaper as a veritable *Who's Who* of serious journalism, representing the "elite troops" supporting the Weimar Republic. Kraus, *Die Familie Mosse*, p. 495.

59. "Veränderungen beim 'Berliner Tageblatt' und in der 'Kölnischen Volkszeitung,'" *Vossische Zeitung* (April 9, 1933), p. 3.

60. Bernhard Rosenköter, *Treuhandpolitik; Die Haupttreuhandstelle Ost und der Raub polnischer Vermögen 1939–1945* (Essen: Klartext Verlag, 2003), pp. 27–33.

61. Rosenköter, *Treuhandpolitik,* pp. 51–57.

62. Oron J. Hale, *The Captive Press in the Third Reich* (Princeton: Princeton University Press, 1964), pp. 127–128. Thomas Tavernaro, *Der Verlag Hitlers und der NSDAP. Die Franz Eher Nachfolger GmbH* (Wien: Verlag für Literatur- und Sprachwissenschaft, 2004), p. 52.

63. Compare Kraus, *Die Familie Mosse*, p. 520 with "Finanzielle Neuordnung bei Rudolf Mosse," *Vossische Zeitung* (July 13, 1933), p. 3 and "Rudolf Mosse will weiterarbeiten; Aktiver Status–Moratorium als Vergleichsvorschlag–8,8 Millionen ungedeckte Schulden," *Vossische Zeitung* (July 14, 1933), p. 9.

64. Contrast Wolff's and Boveri's correct assessment in section B of this chapter with George Mosse's over-estimation of the value of family real estate.

65. Kraus, *Familie Mosse*, pp. 519–523. Rosenkötter, *Treuhandpolitik,* p. 63.

66. Peter de Mendelssohn, "Die Anfänge," in W. Joachim Freyburg and Hans Wallenberg (Eds.), *Hundert Jahre Ullstein 1877–1977* (Berlin: Ullstein Verlag, 1977), pp. 69–71, 78–81. Hermann Ullstein, *The Rise and Fall of the House of Ullstein* (New York: Simon and Schuster, 1943), pp. 92–94.

67. The impact of Korff's ideas were not restricted to Germany. Korff and Kurt Safransky met with Henry Luce in the United States and suggested that he duplicate their *Berliner Ilustrierte Zeitung* concept. The result was *Life Magazine*. See Ullstein, *Rise,* pp. 90–91.

68. Ullstein, *Rise,* pp. 87–88.

69. Compare Ullstein, *Rise,* pp. 64–67, 219–221 with Martin Münzel, *Die jüdischen Mitglieder der deutschen Wirtschaftselite 1927–1955. Verdrängung–Emigration–Rückkeht* (Paderborn: Ferdinand Schöningh, 2006), pp. 395–396.

70. Compare section C of this chapter with Erhard Schütz, "Wir, jawohl wir formen das geistige Antlitz der Nation," in David Oels and Ute Schneider (Eds.), *Der ganze Verlag ist einfach eine Bonbonniere. Ullstein in der ersten Hälfte des 20. Jahrhunderts* (Berlin: Walter de Gruyter GmbH, 2015), pp. 20–22 and Walter F. Peterson, *The Berlin Liberal Press in Exile: A History of the Pariser Tageblatt* (Tübingen: Max Niemeyer Verlag, 1987), pp. 31–32.

71. Hermann Ullstein, "Aus Ullsteins großer Zeit," in W. Joachim Freyburg and Hand Wallenberg (Eds.), *Hundert Jahre Ullstein 1877–1977*. Vol. 1 (Berlin: Ullstein Verlag, 1977), pp. 133–136.

72. Feder, *Heute,* pp. 285–286, 309.

73. Hans Schaeffer papers; AR 7177; Box 9; Folder 17; Leo Baeck Institute, Diary (November 20, 1931); and Diary (November 20, 1931), pp. 1045–1049.

74. Compare Münzel, *Mitglieder*, pp. 101–102 with Hans Schaeffer papers; AR 7177; Box 10; Folder 2; Leo Baeck Institute, Diary (March 21 and 22, 1932), pp. 386, 397.

75. Hans Schaeffer papers; AR 7177; Box 10; Folder 2; Leo Baeck Institute, Diary (March 23, 24 and 29, 1932), Diary (March 23, 24 and 29, 1932), 403, 407, 416.

76. Münzel, *Mitglieder*, Bernd Sösemann, "Im Spiegel der Voß: Der Kampf um die Republik," in W. Joachim Freyburg (Ed.), *Hundert Jahre Ullstein 1877–1977* (Frankfurt am Main: Verlag Ullstein GmbH, 1977), p. 253.

77. If the information about the August 15, 1932, conversation between Heinz Ullstein and Otto Straßer had originated with Straßer, rather than Hans Schäffer's diary, it might have been completely disregarded. Ian Kershaw depicted Otto as "a biased and often unreliable source." But the discussion appears logical in light of Straßer having published the contents of a private meeting, which he held with Hitler in the pamphlet *Ministersessel oder Revolution?* The publication disclosed details of the May 21, 1930, conversation regarding Hitler's offer to buy Otto's Kampfverlag and to promote Straßer as his press chief. By means of this tactic, Hitler wanted to sideline one of his most vocal critics within the NSDAP. A few weeks later, Gregor Straßer observed that his brother's elevation of Socialism over the Führer would make it impossible for him to remain within the Party. Hitler frustrated Goebbels by postponing any action against Straßer, since he needed the votes of Otto's supporters during the June Saxony election. Hitler needlessly awaited an opportunity to strike Straßer, since Otto publicly resigned on July 4, 1930. Having lost his publishing house and any possibility of financial support from the NSDAP, Otto was desperate for a means to publicize his ideology. As Kershaw discerned: "Once outside the NSDAP, he lost all significance." He chose as an unlikely ally a member of the Jewish communication colossus. For details on Otto Straßer, see Ian Kershaw, *Hitler 1889–1936 Hubris* (New York: W.W. Norton, 1999), pp. 241, 325–328.

78. Hans Schaeffer papers; AR 7177; Box 10; Folder 3; Leo Baeck Institute, Diary (August 15, 1932), pp. 748–754

79. Hans Schaeffer papers; AR 7177; Box 10; Folder 3; Leo Baeck Institute, Diary (September 6, 1932), p. 837.

80. Hans Schaeffer papers; AR 7177; Box 10; Folder 3; Leo Baeck Institute, Diary (September 13, 1932), pp. 856–857.

81. Hans Schaeffer papers; AR 7177; Box 10; Folder 3; Leo Baeck Institute, Diary (September 11, 1932), p. 851.

82. Hans Schaeffer papers; AR 7177; Box 10; Folder 3; Leo Baeck Institute, Diary (September 6 and 9, 1932), pp. 836, 842–843.

83. Jochen Hung, "Die Zeitung der Zeit. Die Tageszeitung Tempo und das Ende der Weimarer Republik," in David Oels and Ute Schneider (Eds.), *Der ganze Verlag ist einfach eine Bonbonniere. Ullstein in der ersten Hälfte des 20. Jahrhunderts* (Berlin: Walter de Gruyter GmbH, 2015), pp. 139–146.

84. Ullstein, *Rise*, pp. 245–247, 264. Münzel, *Mitglieder*, p. 396.

85. Wolfgang Wippermann maintained that this claim was merely a strategical ploy utilized as part of Rudolf Ullstein's and Gustav Willner's postwar restitution process. On the basis of Max Amann's 1935 visit to "his new publishing house, it should have been completely clear to the entire workforce and to family members living in Berlin, who the new owner was." Unfortunately, the Berlin historian offered no details of either what was said or done during Amann's visit that would have led to such a conclusion. A tour by numerous dignitaries would not have enabled an individual to conclude which, if any, of the guests had become the new proprietor. See Wolfgang Wippermann, "Eule und Hakenkreuz; Ullstein und Deutscher Verlag im Dritten Reich 1933 bis 1945," in Anne Enderlein and Ulf Geyersbach (Eds.), *Ullstein Chronik 1903–2011* (Berlin: Ullstein Buchverlage GmbH, 2011), p. 210.

86. Helmut Kause, "Der publizistische Widerstand Paul Schiemanns gegen den Nationalsozialismus in den deutschen Volksgruppen," in Michael Garleff (Ed.), *Deutschbalten, Weimar Republik und Drittes Reich* (Köln: Böhlau Verlag, 2001), pp. 201–206.

87. Heinz Ullstein wrote a chapter in his memoir on Georg Bernhard's fall from power as the editor of the Vossische Zeitung in August 1930. Next, he penned a chapter on famous individuals, such as Gottfried Benn, Heinrich, and Thomas Mann, whom he met. This was followed by his rescue from the Rosenstrasse prison by his separated wife Änne in March 1943. However, only Hans Schäffer's diary recorded his March 1933 arrest by the SA and no reason was provided for the action. But other March 1933 arrests of editors are well known, including the March 9th imprisonment of Fritz Gerlach, former editor-in-chief of the *Münchner Neueste Nachrichten*, the March 13th arrest of Fritz Büchner, and the planned March arrest of Ullstein's *Feuilleton* editor Stefan Grossmann. For additional details on Bernhard or the Rosenstrasse arrest, see Heinz Ullstein, *Spielplatz meines Lebens: Erinnerungen* (München: Kindler Verlag, 1962), pp. 314–319, 329–345. For other editors arrests in March 1933, see Peter Langer, "Paul Reusch und die Gleichschaltung der Münchner Neuesten Nachrichten 1933," *Vierteljahrshefte für Zeitgeschichte*, Vol. 53, No. 2 (2005), pp. 210–211. Wippermann provided the example that "at the beginning of March 1933," various Ullstein family members were subject to personal attacks, including Heinz who was assaulted in his Dahlem villa. However, the Berlin professor provided no explanatory details. See Wippermann, *Chronik*, p. 200.

88. Hans Schaeffer papers; AR 7177; Box 10; Folder 4; Leo Baeck Institute, Diary (March 5 and 6, 1933), pp. 1–7. Wippermann, *Chronik,* p. 209.

89. Compare Hans Schaeffer papers; AR 7177; Box 10; Folder 4; Leo Baeck Institute, Diary (March 6, 8 and 9, 1933), pp. 8, 12–14 with Peter de Mendelssohn, "Als die Presse gefesselt war," in W. Joachim Freyburg (Ed.), *Hundert Jahre Ullstein 1877–1977*, p. 229.

90. The German play on words is between his name "Bausback" and a German variation of "dismantler," namely "Abbausback." Compare Hans Schaeffer papers; AR 7177; Box 10; Folder 4; Leo Baeck Institute, Diary (March 6, 1933), pp. 5–8 with Wippermann, *Chronik*, pp. 201–202.

91. Compare Hans Schaeffer papers; AR 7177; Box 10; Folder 4; Leo Baeck Institute, Diary (March 10, 1933), pp. 14–16 with Wippermann, *Chronik*, pp. 202–205 and Münzel, *Mitglieder*, pp. 395–397.

92. de Mendelssohn, *Presse,* pp. 222–224.

93. Compare Thomas Trimm, “Herr Reichsminister–ein Wort bitte!,” *Die Grüne Post*, April 29, 1934, 1 with de Mendelssohn, *Presse*, pp. 214–217.

94. de Mendelssohn, *Presse*, pp. 219–225.

95. “NSBO Ullstein,” *Vossische Zeitung* (July 19, 1933), p. 6; “NSBO Versammlung des Verlages Ullstein,” *Vossische Zeitung* (August 6, 1933), p. 6; de Mendelssohn, *Presse*, pp. 227–228.

96. Tavernaro, *Verlag Hitlers*, p. 55. Wippermann, *Chronik*, pp. 207–208.

97. Contrast Ingo Köhler, “Soziale und wirtschaftliche Vernetzung als Erfolgsfaktor: Das Dresdner Privatbankhaus Grbr. Arnhold (1864–1933),” in Ulrich Heß (Ed.), *Unternehmen im regionalen und lokalen Raum 1750–2000* (Leipzig: Leipziger Universitätsverlag, 2004), pp. 303–308 with Simone Lässig, “Jüdische Privatbanken in Dresden,” *Dresdner Hefte*, Vol. 18, No 61 (2000), p. 94.

98. The reader should recall Fritz Stern, *Bismarck, Bleichröder and the Building of the German Empire* (New York: Vintage Books, 1979).

99. Center for Jewish History, PID: 4413301, *Geschichte des Bankhaus Arnhold: 1864–1936* (June 22, 1931), 39b; (August 6, 1931), 40a; (March 4, 1932), 41a; and (January 19, 1933), 43a. Ingo Köhler, “Die Arisierung jüdischer Privatbanken,” in Dieter Ziegler (Ed.), *Die Dresdner Bank und die deutschen Juden. Die Dresdner Bank im Dritten Reich,* Vol. 2 (München: R. Oldenbourg Verlag, 2006), p. 137.

100. Center for Jewish History, PID: 4413301 (March 17, 1931), 39a; (December 12, 1931), 40b; and (November 29, 1932), 42b.

101. Henry Arnhold provided Simone Lässig insight into the Arnhold Family Archives in which Adolf had written a 1939 manuscript, recalling this incident. See Simone Lässig, “Nationalsozialistische Judenpolitik und jüdische Selbstbehauptung vor dem Novembepogrom: Das Beispiel Bankiersfamilie Arnhold,” in Reiner Pommerin (Ed.), *Dresden unterm Hakenkreuz* (Köln: Böhlau Verlag, 1998), p. 156.

102. Ingo Köhler’s research in the Dresdner Bank’s records clarifies conflicting entries in the Arnhold Bank manuscript. Although the handwritten manuscript resembles a diary, it records Fritz Merbach’s and Walther Frisch’s acceptance as partners as early as October 1, 1933, whereas Adolf Arnhold and Alfred Meyer are not forcibly retired until December 31, 1933. Perhaps this indicated that the former Jewish owners lost their assets in October, but were still obligated for the liabilities in December. Center for Jewish History PID: 4413301, 44a and 44b.

103. Köhler, Die Arisierung, p. 138.

104. Köhler, Die Arisierung, pp. 139–140.

105. Köhler, Die Arisierung, p. 140.

106. Köhler, Die Arisierung, p. 140.

107. Ingo Köhler, *Die Arisierung der Privatbanken im Dritten Reich; Verdrängung, Ausschaltung und die Frage der Wiedergutmachung* (München: C.H. Beck, 2005), p. 219.

108. Köhler, Die Arisierung, pp. 141–142.

109. Dieter Ziegler, “Die Verdrängung der Juden aus der Dresdner Bank,” *Vierteljahrshefte für Zeitgeschichte*, 47 (1999), p. 210.

110. Center for Jewish History, PID: 4413301 (March 11, 1931), 39a; (February 1, 1932), 41a; (May 26, 1932), 41a; (August 30, 1932), 42; (December 15, 1932), 42b; (January 31, 1933), 43a; and (April 24, 1933), 43b.

111. The five largest private banks, including Simon Hirschland in Essen, Mendelssohn & Company in Berlin; Sal. Openheim in Köln, M. Warburg & Company in Hamburg and Gebrüder Arnhold, thought they would be protected by Hjalmar Schacht because between 1933 and 1935, they supplied one-seventh of all import loans to the German economy. Thereby, it is evident that private Jewish financial institutions did not limit their services to Jewish firms. See Lässig, Nationalsozialistische Judenpolitik, p. 146.

112. Center for Jewish History, PID: 4413301 (October 28, 1931), 40b; and (September 26, 1933), 44a.

113. Center for Jewish History, PID: 4413301 (May 31, 1933), 43b.

114. This represents a slight variation from the paradigm of Aryanization presented in this review. The Arnhold family forfeited their invested capital as the Dresden headquarters, investments in numerous industries, and supervisory board seats in these other companies were cheaply acquired by the Dresdner Bank. However, the small Berlin branch continued for a couple years as a small rump of what had been one of Germany's five largest private banks. Also see Kopper, *Zwischen*, 240–241.

115. Dieter Ziegler, "Die Arisierung von Kapitalgesellschaften in Fallstudien," *Die Dresdner Bank und die deutschen Juden* (München: R. Oldenbourg Verlag, 2006), p. 292.

116. Ziegler, Die Arisierung von Kapitalgesellschaften, p. 293.

117. Ziegler, Die Arisierung von Kapitalgesellschaften, p. 294.

118. Ziegler, Die Arisierung von Kapitalgesellschaften, pp. 296–297.

119. See "Engelhardt-Brauerei-Bilanzsitzung am 15. Dezember," *Vossische Zeitung*, morning edition (December 6, 1932), p. 11. "Differenzen im Engelhardt-Aufsichtsrat; Bankdirektor Bodenheimer zurückgetreten," *Vossische Zeitung*, evening edition (December 15, 1932), p. 9.

120. Ziegler, Die Arisierung von Kapitalgesellschaften, pp. 298–299.

121. Ziegler, Die Arisierung von Kapitalgesellschaften, pp. 299–300. Johannes Ludwig, *Boykott, Enteignung Mord. Die Entjudung der deutschen Wirtschaft.* 2. Auflage (Hamburg: FACTA OBLITA Verlag GmbH, 1989), pp. 28–34.

122. Ziegler, Die Arisierung von Kapitalgesellschaften, pp. 301–302.

123. Ziegler, Die Arisierung von Kapitalgesellschaften, p. 303.

124. Ziegler, Die Arisierung von Kapitalgesellschaften, pp. 307–308.

125. Ziegler, Die Arisierung von Kapitalgesellschaften, pp. 308–309. Ludwig, *Boykott*, p. 28.

126. Ziegler, Die Arisierung von Kapitalgesellschaften, pp. 309–310.

127. Ziegler, Die Arisierung von Kapitalgesellschaften, pp. 309–314.

128. "Erregte G.-V. der Engelhadt-Brauerei; Verwaltungsanträge unter Protest genehmigt," *Vossische Zeitung* (March 1, 1934), p. 13. "Konsolidierungserfolge der Dresdner Bank; Gewinnerhöhung um 2 Millionen Mark–Reservestärkung und erhöhte Liquidität," *Vossische Zeitung* (March 1, 1934), p. 11. "Engelhardt Brauerei AG., Berlin," *Vossische Zeitung* (March 28, 1934), p. 12.

129. Ziegler, Die Arisierung von Kapitalgesellschaften, pp. 318–322.
130. Ralf Ahrens, *Die Dresdner Bank 1945–1957; Konsequenzen und Kontinuitäten nach dem Ende des NS-Regimes* (München: R. Oldenbourg Verlag, 2007), pp. 372–373.
131. Ahrens, *Die Dresdner Bank*, pp. 373–375.
132. Ahrens, *Die Dresdner Bank*, pp. 376–378.
133. Ahrens, *Die Dresdner Bank*, pp. 378–379.
134. Ahrens, *Die Dresdner Bank*, p. 380.
135. Ahrens, *Die Dresdner Bank*, p. 381.
136. This is the perspective provided by a historian of Thuringia. See Ulrike Schulz "Kurze Geschichte der Simsonwerke 1856–1935," *Die Enteignung der Firma Simson & Co, Suhl/Thüringen (1927–1935)* (Thüringen: Landeszentrale für politische Bildung, 2011), p. 11 as well as Siegfried Schütt, *Die Simson-Legende; Aus der Geschichte eines Traditionsunternehmens* (Gotha: Druckmedienzentrum Gotha, 2005), pp. 29, 35.
137. Ironically, the Jewish-owned firm was so thoroughly German in spirit that the proprietors were willing to deceive the Inter-Allied Commission of Control to the advantage of the Reich. The German Munitions Office had secretly funneled extra funds to the Jewish owners in order to build a factory larger than that allowed by the Versailles Peace Treaty. Had the owners not been thorough patriots, they could have blown the whistle on confidential rearmament plans. See Schulz, Kurze Geschichte der Simsonwerke, p. 11.
138. "Spitzelbericht des Gaufachberaters der NSDAP vom 21. Februar 1932 über die wirtschaftliche Lage und politische Gesinnung der Mitarbeiter in den Simsonwerken," in Schulz, Kurze Geschichte der Simsonwerke, p. 33.
139. Erich Buchmann, *Von der jüdischen Firma Simson zur Nationalsozialistischen Industriestiftung Gustloff-Werke* (Erfurt: U. Bodung-Verlag, 1944), pp. 5–6.
140. Schulz, Kurze Geschichte der Simsonwerke, 14–15.
141. Compare Schulz, Kurze Geschichte der Simsonwerke, pp. 16–17 with Buchmann, *Firma Simson*, 6–9.
142. Schulz, Kurze Geschichte der Simsonwerke, p. 18. Ed Buffaloe, "The Simson Model 1922 and 1926 Vest Pocket Pistol," unblinking eye.com/Guns/Simson .html.
143. English translation of *Das Neue Tage-Buch*, Jahrgang 4 Heft 28 (July 11, 1936), 654ff provided in Julius Simson Family Collection; AR 11961; Box 1; Folder 3; Item #18; Leo Baeck Institute.
144. Schulz, Kurze Geschichte der Simsonwerke, pp. 19–21.
145. Schulz, Kurze Geschichte der Simsonwerke, pp. 22–23.
146. Schulz, Kurze Geschichte der Simsonwerke, pp. 24–25.
147. Schulz, Kurze Geschichte der Simsonwerke, p. 26.
148. Schulz, Kurze Geschichte der Simsonwerke, pp. 28–29.
149. Compare Fritz Fenthol, "Eidesstattliches Versicherung," (October 23, 1955), p. 3. Julius Simson Family Collection; AR 11961; Box number 1; Folder number 3; Leo Baeck Institute with Buchmann, *Firma Simson*, 10 with Schulz, Kurze Geschichte der Simsonwerke, pp. 30–31 and Schütt, *Die Smson-Legende*, p. 37.
150. Köhler, Die Arisierung, p. 232.

Chapter 7

Conclusion

This volume offers a new paradigm for comprehending how and when the Aryanization of the largest Jewish companies within Germany occurred. Helmut Genschel's pioneering perspective viewed the cheap acquisition of Jewish businesses as an ideologically driven, Nazi Party–inspired process. According to his view, the action began with the boycott in 1933, intensified with the Nuremberg Laws in 1935 and reached its pinnacle with the Kristallnacht in 1938. In this chronologically intensifying outlook, Genschel viewed the frenzy of activity at the time of the November 1938 pogrom without differentiating between which enterprises were purchased and which operations had been allowed to go out-of-business. In addition, the emphasis on NSDAP-inspired actions replaced any need to search for individual perpetrators.

Scholars followed Genschel's initiation with three divergent viewpoints. In the second phase of scholarship, Avraham Barkai showed the necessity of employing Jewish sources. His key idea was the basis for this research's decision to start the investigation from the point-of-view of the Jewish companies and not an external political chronology. In the third stage of academic investigation, Frank Bajohr's framework of analyzing one city led him to correct Genschel's top-down, chronological approach. Instead of a series of events inspired by the NSDAP, Bajohr observed that events against Jewish businesses occurred in local areas prior to Party-inspired national actions. Alex Bruns-Wüstefeld also conducted his research during the third facet of academic inquiry. By distinguishing between an inexpensive Aryanization and the liquidation of Jewish operations, he observed that profitable companies were often purchased in the 1933 through 1935 time period, but mom-and-pop shops were allowed to go out-of-business in 1938. Thereby,

Bruns-Wüstefeld's careful analysis correctly interpreted the frenzy of activity noticed by Genschel.

This review incorporated the key determinations by Barkai, Bajohr, and Bruns-Wüstefeld into a revised model for understanding Aryanization. Following Barkai's research, this inspection commenced with an examination of several of the largest Jewish-owned enterprises, which were cheaply purchased during the period from 1933 through 1935. The feverish activity by Genschel was interpreted in light of Bruns-Wüstefeld as due to the innumerable unprofitable one-person operations that nobody wanted to purchase. They were allowed to go-out-of-business, which pleased German retailers, because of the decline in competition.

The present study has added to the foundation established by three historians by noticing a pattern of a group of four participants during the 1930s. The four involved parties, establishing the structure for a *modified* theory on Aryanization, included Jewish proprietors, German businessmen, banks, and the courts. Large Jewish entrepreneurs felt threatened by the rise of anti-Semitism in the new regime. Conservative, non-Nazi German businessmen, unrestricted by the business ethic of Imperial Germany and the Weimar Republic, sought support from financial institutions to cheaply acquire Jewish firms. The judiciary shared the same conservative mentality as the new Gentile owners and therefore did not respond to the coerced purchases. Both businessmen and banks profited from dispossessing the previous Jewish owners.

Businessmen approached Germany's three largest banks with the proposition of withdrawing existing loans to Jewish firms. The Deutsche Bank, the Dresdner Bank and the Commerzbank agreed to the proposals since they would benefit by earning commissions, by receiving insider information after placing one of their executives on the formerly Jewish-owned company's Supervisory Board and by obtaining all future financial business of the firm's new management.

In chapters 5 through 6, I analyzed seven companies. Hermann Tietz and Leonhard Tietz represented two of the largest regional retailers in the nation. Mosse and Ullstein typified the most sizable advertising and newspaper publishers in the country. The Arnhold Bank headquarters in Dresden was an example of one of the most highly capitalized private financial institutions in the Reich. The Engelhard Brewery was the largest beer producer in the Weimar Republic. The Simson Gun Manufacturer was the sole manufacturer for machine guns, rifles, and pistols after the Versailles Treaty.

Proponents of Genschel's traditional model, utilizing the events stemming from Berlin's Civil Service Law, the Nuremberg Laws and the Kristallnacht might object that I have merely found seven outliers from their framework. Should such hesitancy to my proposed paradigm occur, I would like to briefly mention four of the other massive Jewish firms, which were also acquired by

German businessmen during the 1933–1935 time period. Erich Niemann of the Dresdner Bank was effective in eliminating Benno Orenstein and Arthur Koppel from the railroad car manufacturing company, which bore their surnames.[1] A second example is provided by the Nuremberg branch manager of the Dresdner Bank, Reinhold Freiherr von Lüdinghausen, who assisted Gustav Schickedanz in cheaply acquiring Oskar and Emil Rosenfelder's Vereinigte Papierwerke. Similar to the English word "Kleenex," their trademarked product "Tempo" was commonly used instead of the generic term "facial tissue."[2] A third example of Aryanization entailed the Deutsche Bau- und Bodenbank's support for Walter Schwiering to inexpensively purchase Adolf Sommerfeld's construction company, known as the Allgemeine Häuserbau Aktiengesellschaft (AHAG).[3] A final illustration was Alex Haffner's exclusion of the Sigle family as partners in the Salamander Shoe Company, one of the nation's biggest footwear producers.[4]

How many cases of Aryanization should be provided to demonstrate the validity of a model of cheap purchases by businessmen, supported by banks, during the 1933 to 1935 timeframe? Unfortunately, scholarly knowledge of large German-Jewish firms is limited. Perhaps the foremost English-speaking authority on German companies during the Third Reich is Peter Hayes, based on his 1987 book on I.G. Farben, his 2000 coediting of a volume on Aryanization and his 2004 publication on Degussa. Nevertheless Hayes admitted to me in 2013: "I know of no such list [of the largest 100 Jewish-owned firms in Nazi Germany] and having one would be very helpful."[5] The eleven Jewish companies analyzed in this book would certainly be included in a list of the largest 50 or 100 Jewish operations in the late Weimar Republic. In addition, the eleven firms represented nine different business sectors.

The Jewish companies analyzed in this text were not merely large in comparison with other Jewish businesses, but they were market leaders in their sectors. Many were service-oriented or involved the manufacture of products not requiring massive influxes of capital. Thus, although their staffs were often of the same size as the largest of German industrialists, their amount of share capital was a small percentage of the Ruhr industrialists, such as Krupp and Flick (Table 7.1).

Focusing on the Jewish companies, rather than a politically inspired chronology, leads to the question of who the individual perpetrators were. Georg Karg's activities and character have been examined in chapter 5's "purchase" of the Hermann Tietz chain of stores. Chapter 2 also mentioned his later pursuit of Max Uhlfelder's stand-alone department store in Munich. I conclude that a number of months after Karg was able to stabilize his newly obtained Tietz empire, he sought to expand his realm with an additional facility. Another "ordinary" German businessman, who disregarded any business ethic in order to achieve the "higher" goal of extending his power, was Max

Table 7.1 Summary of Large Jewish-Owned Firms

Name	*Location*	*Business Sector*	*Nominal Value in Million Mk*	*Staff*
Leonhard Tietz	Cologne	Retail	31.2	15,000
Hermann Tietz	Munich	Retail	18.6	17,450
Mosse Verlag	Berlin	Advertising & Publishing		
Ullstein Verlag	Berlin	Publishing	c. 30.0	
Gebrüder Arnhold	Dresden	Banking		
Simson Gun Factory	Suhl	Weapons & Vehicle Manufacturing		
Engelhardt Brewery	Berlin	Beverage	12.0	
Salamander Shoes	Nuremberg	Apparel	32.0	
Adolf Sommerfeld	Berlin	Real Estate Development		
Vereinigte Papierwerke	Nuremberg	Paper		
Orenstein & Koppel	Berlin	Transportation	36.48	8,000

Winkler. His Aryanizing activities were mentioned in chapter 6, sections B and C with regard to both the Mosse and Ullstein publishing houses. However, the chapter's reference to the Aryanization of the Ufa Film Company in Hans Schaeffer's diary did not specify Winkler's role. A third illustration of an Aryanizer's intent on extending the scope of his power was Dresdner Bank executive Erich Niemann. Chapter 6, section A's examination of the demise of the Epa Single-Price chain referred to Niemann's role and the same section of the investigation referred to his role in the Aryanization of the Orenstein & Koppel railway car manufacturer. A fourth depiction of an Aryanizer as an empire builder commenced with chapter 7's reference to Gustav Schickedanz's Aryanization of Oskar and Emil Rosenfelder's Vereinigte Papierwerke.

Eighty years after "purchasing" former Jewish companies, both the Aryanizer and the subsequent proprietors often continued to deny any wrongdoing. Because Genschel's model viewed the top leaders of the Third Reich and the NSDAP as the groups responsible for the transfer of company ownership from Jewish to Gentile businessmen, little research has been conducted on the benefiting individuals. More is known about the enabling financial institutions.

Germany's three largest banks served as the linchpin between eager conservative businessmen and the large Jewish firms. They enabled the cheap "purchases" of Jewish institutions by compiling lists of potential buyers, providing company data to the interested parties and granting loans to the new owners. Of the three, neither the Deutsche Bank nor the Commerzbank had a special department for the Aryanization of Jewish-owned businesses as the Dresdner Bank did. Beginning in 2006, the scholarly team of Johannes Bähr, Dieter Ziegler, Harald Wixforth and Klaus-Dietmar Henke began publishing five volumes, transcending the customary scapegoating by the financial institution of Karl Rasche and Erich Niemann.[6] Instead of focusing solely on Rasch and Niemann, the team of four academicians recently researched a much broader spectrum of bank executives. Their evidence opposed the traditional view by the postwar, conservative judiciary.

A German judge in Wiesbaden's denazification Court opined that the "misdemeanors" committed by a few managers during the Nazi dictatorship could not be blamed on the entire executive staff of the Dresdner Bank. Similarly, the financial institution relativized its responsibility and guilt by heaping all the blame on Rasche and Meyer. In contrast, German historian Harald Wixforth assessed that none of the Dresdner executives had any moral scruples, but all hoped to create a brilliant career with the financial institution. Wixforth objected to the whitewashing of the bank's boards, acknowledging that although there was no doubt that Rasche and Meyer bore special responsibility, the boards were aware of their actions on behalf of the bank and never exercised their right to veto any action. Instead, the Board of Directors and the Supervisory Board viewed it as a great business success, when their Aryanizers outmaneuvered the competition.[7]

For decades, scholarship has viewed Aryanization of Jewish-owned companies as the result of anti-Semitic legislation and actions by the central government or the NSDAP. This has diverted the focus away from perpetrators within the Dresdner Bank, who withdrew lines of credit to Jewish proprietors as well as providing company information and loans to conservative German businessmen. Perhaps a sufficient number of years have transpired for other companies to open their archives to assess their staffs' activities in the expropriation of Jewish wealth. The historian Ralf Ahrens' conclusion: "participation in a National Socialist expropriation and persecution program was no obstacle for a brilliant career" in postwar, Germany appears substantiated by Table 7.2.[8]

To the nonspecialist, it must seem incredible that much research still needs to be conducted eighty years after the Aryanizations. Perhaps the adapted paradigm proposed in this review will spur historians to investigate how other major Jewish-owned firms were taken. The structure of early dispossession entailed four major participants: Jewish proprietors, German businessmen, enabling German bankers and unresponsive German judges. Of the players, the bank executives are the most well-known. It is appropriate to strip away the veil of personal privacy. With the passage of so many decades, the German businessmen who became wealthy at Jewish expense are deceased. Perhaps their descendants will allow scholars to examine company records

Table 7.2 Need for Future Research on Aryanizers

German Businessman	*Name of Jewish-Owned Company*	*Name of Postwar Company*
Georg Karg	Hermann Tietz	Hertie
Trabant Reichsfreiherr von und zu der Tann-Rathsamhausen	Hermann Tietz	Hertie
Abraham Frowein	Leonhard Tietz and Ehape	Westdeutsche Kaufhof
Max Winkler	Ullstein Verlag	Ullstein Verlag
Walther Frisch	Gebrüder Arnhold	Dresdner Bank
Hilarius Giebel	Engelhardt Brewery	Schultheiß Brewery
Herbert Hoffmann	Simson & Company	Gerätewerk Simson Suhl
Alex Haffner	Salamander Shoes	Salamander Shoes
Walter Schwiering	Allgemeine Häuserbau AG (AHAG)	Haus und Heim Wohnungsbau AG (Adolf Sommerfeld)
Gustav Schickedanz	Vereinigte Papierwerke	VP-Schickedanz AG
Erich Niemann	Orenstein & Koppel	Orenstein & Koppel

and may replace self-congratulating company histories. A second avenue of investigation would seek data on the former Jewish firms. Since the original proprietors were unaware of the secret negotiations between the businessmen and the large banks, memoirs and oral histories do not customarily reveal many details of the takeover. In addition, as Jewish owners fled the Reich, they usually were unable to take accounting records with them. However subsequent to the end of the Cold War, it has become known that Jewish records seized by the Gestapo were not destroyed, but instead taken to Moscow by the Red Army. This manuscript utilized such Osobyi records concerning Hermann Tietz veterans, who were dismissed by Georg Karg. Perhaps new documentation awaits discovery regarding other former Jewish-owned firms. However, scholars will need the courage to reveal the activities of businessmen, such as Georg Karg and Gustav Schickedanz, who have been viewed as great entrepreneurs in the postwar revival of the German economy.

NOTES

1. Dieter Ziegler, "Die Nationalsozialisten im Betrieb," in Johannes Bähr (Ed.), *Die Dresdner Bank in der Wirtschaft des Dritten Reichs* (München: R. Oldenbourg Verlag, 2006), pp. 133–140. Dieter Ziegler, "Aryanization and the Role of the German Great Banks, 1933–1938," in Gerald D. Feldman and Wolfgang Seibel (Eds.), *Networks of Nazi Persecution; Bureaucracy, Business and the Organization of the Holocaust* (New York: Berghahn Books, 2005), p. 58.

2. Peter Zinke, "Er drohte wieder mit der Gauleitung. Gustav Schcikedanz und die Arisierung," *nurinst. Beiträge zur deutschen und jüdischen Geschichte*. Vol. 4 (2008), pp. 63–68.

3. Celina Kress, *Adolf Sommerfeld/Andrew Sommerfield Bauen für Berlin 1910–1970* (Berlin: Lukas Verlag für Kunst- und Geistesgeschichte, 2011), pp. 204–227.

4. Petra Bräutigam, *Mittelständische Unternehmer im Nationalsozialismus. Wirtschaftliche Entwicklungen und soziale Verhaltensweisen in der Schuh- und Lederindustrie Badens und Württembergs* (München: R. Oldenbourg Verlag, 1997), pp. 33, 59–64, 253–258. Anne Sudrow, *Der Schuh im Nationalsozialismus: Eine Produktgeschichte im deutsch-britisch-amerikanischen Vergleich* (Göttingen: Wallstein Verlag, 2010), pp. 51, 528–541.

5. Peter Hayes, private email (March 11, 2013).

6. Recall the discussion of Ralf Ahrens' journal article on the scapegoating of Karl Rasche at the end of chapter 2.

7. Wixforth, "Die Dresdner Bank und ihre Expansion in Europe—Bankgeschäfte, Bankenpolitik, Besatzungspolitik," *Die Dresdner Bank im Dritten Reich*. Vol. 3 (München: R. Oldenbourg Verlag, 2006), pp. 177–178, 894, 898–899.

8. Harald Wixforth, "Die Dresdner Bank im Sudetenland und im Protektorate Böhmen und Mähren," in Klaus-Dietmar Henke (Ed.), *Die Dresdner Bank im Dritten Reich*. Vol. 3 (München: R. Oldenbourg Verlag, 2006), p. 61; and Ahrens, *Dresdner Bank*, pp. 127–128.

Bibliography

BUNDESARCHIV, BERLIN

Reichskanzlei

BA R 43 II/369. Document #15–16, 18–22

BA R 43 II/370 Joachim Tiburtius, "Grundlagen zur Unterrichtung über den deutschen Einzelhandel."

Deutsche Bank

BA R8119F 15211, Microfiche #5, Documents #163–164

BA R8119F 15211, Microfiche #6, Document #199–201

BA R8119 15218, Microfiche #1, Document #2–29, #39, #51

Reichsminister der Finanzen

BA R2/57.689 Microfiche #3, Document #50

Berliner Handels-Gesellschaft

BA R8127 15215, Documents #14–339

Zulassungsstelle an der Börse

R3118 1094, 1336

02 4412

CENTRAL ARCHIVES FOR THE HISTORY OF THE JEWISH PEOPLE JERUSALEM

Centralverein deutscher Staatsbürger jüdischen Glaubens

HM2-8693 Documents #90–91, 93, 96–97, 129–130, 135, 138–140, 144, 146, 148–149, 152, 156–158, 160–162, 165, 168, 176–177, 179, 181, 186a, 187, 189, 190, 192, 194, 197, 199, 205, 208–209, 212, 217–219.

Center for Jewish History

PID: 4413301, *Geschichte des Bankhaus Arnhold: 1864–1936.*

Leo Baeck Institute, New York

Hans Schaeffer papers; AR 7177; Box 9; Folder 17; Leo Baeck Institute.

Hans Schaeffer papers; AR 7177; Box 10; Folder 2, 3 and 4; Leo Baeck Institute.

Translation of *Das Neue Tage-Buch*, Jahrgang 4 Heft 28 (July 11, 1936), 654ff in Julius Simson Family Collection; AR 11961; Box 1; Folder 3; Item #18; Leo Baeck Institute.

Fritz Fenthol, "Eidesstattliches Versicherung," (October 23, 1955). 3. Julius Simson Family Collection; AR 11961; Box number 1; Folder number 3; Leo Baeck Institute.

USC Shoah Foundation

Zwillenberg, Lutz. Interview #36276. Segment 1. Visual History Archive, USC Shoah Foundation, 1997. Accessed February 14–15, 2017.

Newspaper Articles

C.V. Zeitung

Unknown author. "Die Neuesten Nachrichten in Zietz," *C.V. Zeitung*, Jahrgang I Nummer 13 (August 3, 1922), 164.

Unknown author. "Deutschnationale Sammlungspolitik," *C.V. Zeitung*, Jahrgang I Nummer 26 (November 2, 1922), 1.

Unknown author. "Gegen Rassenhaß, Klassenhaß und Massenhaß," *C.V. Zeitung*, Jahrgang I Nummer 27 (November 9, 1922), 164.

Kurt Zielenziger, "Der Untergang des jüdischen Mittelstandes," *C.V. Zeitung*, Jahrgang IV Nummer 46 (November 13, 1925), 729.

Kurt Zielenziger, "Die reichsten Leute der Welt; Schwerindustire und Großgrundbesitzer," *C.V. Zeitung*, Jahrgang IV Nummer 50 (December 11, 1925), 784.

Unknown author. "Der Warburg-Fritsch-Prozeß. Vor der Urteilsverkündung in Hamburg," *C.V.Zeitung*, Jahrgang V Nummer 4 (January 22, 1926), 41.

Unknown author. "Der Ausgang des Warburg-Fritsch Prozesses. Fritsch zu 1000 Mark Geldstrafe verurteilt," *C.V.Zeitung*, Jahrgang V Nummer 5 (January 29, 1926), 52.

Michael, Rudolf. "Der Hamburger Prozeß," *C.V.Zeitung*, Jahrgang V Nummer 6 (February 5, 1926), 61.

Unknown author. "Völkischer und jüdischer Boykott," *C.V. Zeitung*, Jahrgang V Nummer 14 (April 1, 1926), 193.

Kurt Zielenziger, "Das Warenhaus," *C.V. Zeitung*, Jahrgang VII Nummer 50 (December 14, 1928), 701–702.

Felix Goldmann, "Das Warenhaus; Was wird aus dem jüdischen Mittelstand?" *C.V. Zeitung* Jahrgang VIII Nummer 1 (January 4, 1929), 5–6.

Unknown author. "Ausschreitungen der Nationalsozialisten in Ostpreußen," *C.V. Zeitung*, Jahrgang VIII Nummer 2 (January 11, 1929), 14.

Unknown author. "Die wahren Verantwortlichen. Gegen Friedhofsschändung und politische Hetze," *C.V. Zeitung*, Jahrgang VIII Nummer 11 (March 15, 1929), 132.

Unknown author. "Der Hieb muß sitzen! Ein werkwürdiger Freispruch," *C.V. Zeitung*, Jahrgang VIII Nummer 20 (May 17, 1929), 260.

Kurt Zielenziger, "Bilanz der Wirtschaft," *C.V. Zeitung*, Jahrgang IX Nummer 1 (January 3, 1930), 1–2.

Unknown author. "Wichtige Entscheidungen zum Kampf gegen den Wirtschaftsboycott," *C.V. Zeitung*, Jahrgang IX Nummer 3 (January 17, 1930), 26.

Unknown author. "Wichtige Entscheidung im Kampf gegen den Wirtschaftsboycott," *C.V. Zeitung*, Jahrgang IX Nummer 6 (February 7, 1930), 63.

Unknown author. "Wieder Friedhofsschändungen in Ostpreußen und Franken," *C.V. Zeitung*, Jahrgang IX Nummer 5 (January 31, 1930), 1.

Ludwig Holländer, "Täuschungen und Entäuschungen," *C.V. Zeitung*, Jahrgang X Nummer 1 (January 2, 1931), 1.

Günther Stein, "Wege aus der Krise?; Die Arbeitslosigkeit und das Schicksal der Juden," *C.V. Zeitung*, Jahrgang X Nummer 2 (January 9, 1931), 9–10.

Unknown author. "Wichtige Entscheidung im Kampf gegen den Wirtschaftsboycott; Boycottsandrohung ist ungehöriger Gewissenszwang," *C.V. Zeitung*, Jahrgang X, Nummer 3 (January 16, 1931), 23.

Unknown author. "Auch Landgericht Memmingen gegen Wirtschaftsboycott," *C.V. Zeitung*, Jahrgang X, Nummer 3 (January 16, 1931), 24.

Unknown author. "Der Mißbrauch der Pressefreiheit; Zum Vorgehen des Reichstages," *C.V. Zeitung*, Jahrgang X Nummer 7 (February 13, 1931), 70.

Unknown author. "Landgericht Koburg verbietet Boykott-Preisausschreiben," *C.V. Zeitung*, Jahrgang X Nummer 11 (March 13, 1931), 121.

Unknown author. "Und die Folgen," *C.V. Zeitung*, Jahrgang 10 Nummer 50 (December 11, 1931), 573.

Von deutsch-jüdischer Jugend

Ernst Wolff. "Ueberwindung der Berufsnot," *Von deutsch-jüdischer Jugend*, Jahrgang 5 Nummer 3 (March 8, 1929).

Vossische Zeitung

Unknown author. "Gemeinschafts-Arbeit in Gefahr; Verständigungs-Versuche im Einzelhandel," *Vossische Zeitung*, morning edition (November 2, 1932), 13.

Unknown author. "Warmbold vor dem Einzelhandel," *Vossische Zeitung*, evening edition (November 8, 1932), 9.

Unknown author. "Reform statt Spaltung; Vor dem Endkampf im Einzelhandel," *Vossische Zeitung*, morning edition (November 12, 1932), 9.

Unknown author. "Teilsieg der Warenhäuser; Aber Hauptgemeinschaft für Sondersteuer," *Vossische Zeitung*, evening edition (November 15, 1932), 9.

Unknown author. "Spaltung des Einzelhandels; Warenhäuser scheiden aus," *Vossische Zeitung*, morning edition (November 16, 1932), 10.

Unknown author. "Froweins Appell an Herriot," *Vossische Zeitung*, evening edition (December 1, 1932), 9.

Unknown author. "Engelhardt-Brauerei-Bilanzsitzung am 15. Dezember," *Vossische Zeitung*, morning edition (December 6, 1932), 11.

Unknown author. "Umbau der Hauptgemeinschaft," *Vossische Zeitung*, evening edition (December 14, 1932), 10.

Unknown author. "Differenzen im Engelhardt-Aufsichtsrat; Bankdirektor Bodenheimer zurückgetreten," *Vossische Zeitung*, evening edition (December 15, 1932), 9.

Unknown author. "Weiter rückläufiger Ehape-Umsatz," *Vossische Zeitung*, morning edition (December 23, 1932), 11

Unknown author. "Hohe Ehape-Bankguthaben," *Vossische Zeitung* (December 28, 1932), 12.

Unknown author. " Einheitspreis-Sperre; Neugründungen allgemein verboten—selbst Geschäftsverlegung untersagt," *Vossische Zeitung* (December 28, 1932), 12.

Unknown author. "Der Führer des Einzelhandels; Heinrich Grünfeld und die Hauptgemeinschaft," *Vossische Zeitung*, morning edition (December 31, 1932), 9.

Unknown author. "Da kann man nur guten Appetit wünschen!," *Vossische Zeitung* (January 5, 1933), 6.

Unknown author. "Gesunde Engelhardt-Brauerei; Doppelter Kapitalbetrag in 8 Jahren aus Gewinnen abgeschrieben—Kapazität nur zu 40 Prozent ausgenutzt—Unkosten angepaßt," *Vossische Zeitung*, evening edition (January 16, 1933), 9.

Unknown author. "Günstige Abschlüsse im Engelhardt-Konzern," *Vossische Zeitung*, morning edition (January 22, 1933), 25.

Unknown author. "Rieseerfolge der Konfektion; Auch hier Qualitäts-Umstellung," *Vossische Zeitung* (January 26, 1933), 9.

Unknown author. "Weiße Woche," *Vossische Zeitung* (January 29, 1933), 7.

Unknown author. "Was die Geschäfte zeigen. Die Weiße Woche," *Vossische Zeitung* (January 30, 1933), 11.

Unknown author. "Was die Geschäfte zeigen. Die Weiße Woche." *Vossische Zeitung* (January 31, 1933), 6.

Unknown author. "21pCt. Weniger Herrenkonfektionsumsatz," *Vossische Zeitung* (February 2, 1933), 11.

Unknown author. "Schlesische Engelhardt-Brauerei zufrieden," *Vossische Zeitung*, evening edition (February 3, 1933), 10.

Unknown author. "Geringere Warenhaus-Umsätze. Jahresbilanz 1931," *Vossische Zeitung* (February 4, 1933), 11.

Unknown author. "Rentabilitäts-Sorgen der Konfektion," *Vossische Zeitung* (February 10, 1933), 9.

Delmonte, Edmund. "Brauereien unter Druck; Fast 400 Millionen Außenstände," *Vossische Zeitung*, morning edition (February 11, 1933), 10.

Unknown author. "Umbau im Einzelhandel; Die neue Verfassung der Hauptgemeinschaft," *Vossische Zeitung*, morning edition (February 21, 1933), 9.

Unknown author. "Krisenverluste des Einzelhandels; Eine Denkschrift der Hauptgemeinschaft," *Vossische Zeitung*, morning edition (February 28, 1933), 9.

Unknown author. "Das Warenhaus in der Krise," *Vossische Zeitung* (March 2, 1933), 11.

Unknown author. "Göring begründet die Notverordnung; Mitteilungen über die kommunistische Gefahr," *Vossische Zeitung* (March 2, 1933), 1.

Unknown author. "Einheitspreisgeschäfte polizeilich geschlossen," *Vossische Zeitung* (March 8, 1933), 6.

Unknown author. "Schließung jüdischer Geschäfte; S. A.-Aktion im Rheinland," *Vossische Zeitung* (March 9, 1933), 3.

Unknown author. "Tumulte vor Geschäten," *Vossische Zeitung* (March 10, 1933), 5.

Unknown author. "Polizei greift ein; Zur Offenhaltung der Geschäfte," *Vossische Zeitung* (March 11, 1933), 5.

Unknown author. "Eine scharfe Rede Görings; Nationalsozialistische Kundgebung in Essen," *Vossische Zeitung* (March 11, 1933), 1.

Unknown author. "Polizei sichert den Geschäftsverkehr; Warenhausschließungen in Hamburg," *Vossische Zeitung* (March 12, 1933), 5.

Unknown author. "Hitlers Rundfunk-Manifest," *Vossische Zeitung* (March 13, 1933), 2.

Unknown author. "Ausschluß-Beschluß im Gerarer Einzelhandels-Verband," *Vossische Zeitung* (March 22, 1933), 2.

Unknown author. "Präsidialwechsel beim Warenhausverband," *Vossische Zeitung* (March 23, 1933), 9.

Edmund Delmonte. "Arbeit für die Werften," *Vossische Zeitung*, morning edition (March 23, 1933), 9.

Unknown author. "Dauerbeschäftigung für Berlins Tiefbauarbeiter; Die Stadt als Arbeitsgeber," *Vossische Zeitung*, morning edition (March 30, 1933), 5.

Unknown author. "Arbeitslosenzulagen verlängert," *Vossische Zeitung* (March 30, 1933), 2.

Unknown author. "Der neue Reichswirtschaftsrat," *Vossische Zeitung*, morning edition (March 31, 1933), 1.

Unknown author. "Der Reichspräsident an das Panzerschiff 'Deutschland,'" *Vossische Zeitung* (April 2, 1933), 6.

Unknown author. "Neue Vorstandsmitglieder der Leonhard Tietz," *Vossische Zeitung* (April 5, 1933), 13.

Unknown author. "Veränderungen beim 'Berliner Tageblatt' und in der 'Kölnischen Volkszeitung,'" *Vossische Zeitung* (April 9, 1933), 3.
Unknown author. "Keine Lohnprämien mehr," *Vossische Zeitung* (April 12, 1933), 3.
Unknown author. "Elastischer Großhandel; Eine Fünf-Jahres-Bilanz," *Vossische Zeitung*, morning edition (May 19, 1933), 11.
Unknown author. "Umbau im Warenhausverband; Zusammenschluß aller Einzelhandels-Groß- betriebe," *Vossische Zeitung* (May 27, 1933), 9.
Unknown author. "Warenhaussteuer vertagt; Verbandserklärung der Großbetriebe," *Vossische Zeitung* (June 12, 1933) evening edition, 9.
Unknown author. "Dresdner Bank—Geschäftsbericht für 1932," *Vossische Zeitung* (June 18, 1933), 15.
Unknown author. "Kleiner Gewinn Leonhard Tietz; Nach höheren Abschreibungen—Betriebsumstellung zur Umsatzstürtzung," *Vossische Zeitung* (June 18, 1933), 13.
Unknown author. "Die Anschlußverträge der Tietz A.G.," *Vossische Zeitung* (June 19, 1933), 9.
Unknown author. "Sperre für SA, SS und Stahlhelm," *Vossische Zeitung* (July 6, 1933), 2.
Unknown author. "Weitere Entlastung des Arbeitsmarktes; Von Mitte bis Ende Juni 121000 Arbeitslose weniger," *Vossische Zeitung,* morning edition (July 8, 1933), 3.
Unknown author. "Aktionen gegen Warenhäuser untersagt," *Vossische Zeitung* (July 8, 1933), 3.
Unknown author. "Hitler an die SA; Ein Appell zu eiserner Disziplin," *Vossische Zeitung*, evening edition (July 10, 1933), 2.
Unknown author. "Abschluß der Revolution; Ein Rundschreiben des Reichsinnenministers an die Statthalter und Landesregierungen," *Vossische Zeitung*, evening edition (July 11, 1933), 1.
Unknown author. "Die Leistung—einziger Maßstab; Der Reichskanzler vor den Gauleitern und Treuhändern," *Vossische Zeitung*, evening edition (July 13, 1933), 1.
Unknown author. "Rechtssicherheit der Wirtschaft; Dr. Schmitt vor den Länderministern," *Vossische Zeitung*, morning edition (July 13, 1933), 1.
Unknown author. "Finanzielle Neuordnung bei Rudolf Mosse," *Vossische Zeitung*, July 13, 1933 p.3.
Unknown author. "Bekämpfung von Sabotage; Scharfe Erlasse des preußischen Justizministers," *Vossische Zeitung*, morning edition (July 14, 1933), 1.
Unknown author. "Rudolf Mosse will weiterarbeiten; Aktiver Status—Moratorium als Vergleichsvorschlag—8,8 Millionen ungedeckte Schulden," *Vossische Zeitung* (July 14, 1933), 9.
Unknown author. "Erfolgreiche Verhandlungen bei Hermann Tietz," *Vossische Zeitung*, morning edition (July 15, 1933), 9.
Unknown author. "Der Umbau von Hermann Tietz; Schutz der Gläubiger und Angestellten—13 Mill. Neue Mittel, *Vossiche Zeitung*, evening edition (July 15, 1933), 9.
Unknown author. "Zum Schutze des Einzelhandels," *Vossische Zeitung*, morning edition (July 15, 1933), 4.

Unknown author. "Regelung der Warenhaus- und Filialsteuer," *Vossische Zeitung*, evening edition (July 15, 1933), 1.
Unknown author. "Eingreifen des Kampfbundes untersagt," *Vossische Zeitung* (July 15, 1933), 4.
Unknown author. "Handwerk im Warenhaus," *Vossische Zeitung*, evening edition (July 18, 1933), 3.
Unknown author. "Verwaltung ohne Kommissare; Ein Runderla ßes Ministerpräsidenten Göring," *Vossische Zeitung*, evening edition (July 18, 1933), 1.
Unknown author. "Wie wir es sehen; Warenhaus und gewerblicher Mittelstand," *Vossische Zeitung*, evening edition (July 19, 1933), 3.
Unknown author. "NSBO Ullstein," *Vossische Zeitung* (July 19, 1933), 6.
Unknown author. "Konsolidierung im Einzelhandel; Preis—Tiefstand überwunden—Verlagerung der Umsätze," *Vossische Zeitung*, evening edition (July 20, 1933), 9.
Unknown author. "Die Neuregelung der Warenhaussteuer," *Vossische Zeitung*, morning edition (July 21, 1933), 3.
Unknown author. "Das Warenhaus in der Wirtschaft," *Vossische Zeitung*, evening edition (July 21, 1933), 11.
Unknown author. "Todesstrafe für Saboteure; Maßnahmen der preußischen Regierung—Ein Reichsgesetz zur Gewährleistung des Rechtsfriedens beantraft," *Vossische Zeitung*, morning edition (July 23, 1933), 1.
Unknown author. "Neue Bilanzkürzung der Großbanken; Eine Folge des weiteren Dollarrückgangs," *Vossische Zeitung*, evening edition (July 26, 1933), 10.
Unknown author. "Die künftige Organisation der Firma Hermann Tietz," *Vossische Zeitung*, morning edition (July 27, 1933), 11.
Unknown author. "Die Neuordnung der Arbeitsbeschaffung," *Vossische Zeitung* (July 27, 1933), 3.
Unknown author. "Der Umbau bei Hermann Tietz; 14.5 Mill RM neue Mittel," *Vossische Zeitung*, evening edition (July 29, 1933), 9.
Unknown author. "Warenhausumsatz im Juni; 22.2 v.H. unter Vorjahrshöhe," *Vossische Zeitung*, morning edition (August 5, 1933), 11.
Unknown author. "NSBO Versammlung des Verlages Ullstein," *Vossische Zeitung* (August 6, 1933), 6.
Unknown author. "Neue Durchführungsverordnung zur Warenhaus-Filialsteuer," *Vossische Zeitung*, evening edition (August 8, 1933), 11.
Unknown author. "9 Mill. Währungsreserve der Westdeutsche Kaufhof A.-G.," *Vossische Zeitung* (December 10, 1933), 20.
Unknown author. "Erregte G.-V. der Engelhadt-Brauerei; Verwaltungsanträge unter Protest genehmigt," *Vossische Zeitung* (March 1, 1934), 13.
Unknown author. "Konsolidierungserfolge der Dresdner Bank; Gewinnerhöhung um 2 Millionen Mark—Reservestärkung und erhöhte Liquidität," *Vossische Zeitung* (March 1, 1934), 11.
Unknown author. "Engelhardt Brauerei AG., Berlin," *Vossische Zeitung* (March 28, 1934), 12.

Der Angriff

Unknown author. "Jüdische Warenhausethik," *Der Angriff*, Number 1 (July 4, 1927).
Unknown author. "Die Warenhaus Pomp," *Der Angriff*, Number 2 (July 11, 1927).
Unknown author. "Warenhausbluff und Justiz," *Der Angriff*, Number 18 (October 31, 1927).
Unknown author. "Steuerhinterziehungen Berliner Warenhäuser," *Der Angriff*, Number 24 (December 12, 1927).
Unknown author. "Tietz muß keine Steuern zahlen," *Der Angriff*, Number 24 (December 12, 1927).
Unknown author. "Das Christkind bei Tietz," *Der Angriff*, Number 24 (December 12, 1927).
Unknown author. "Kriminalbeamte als Weinachtsengel," *Der Angriff*, Number 26 (December 26, 1927).
Unknown author. "Kampf gegen Unmoral—'grober Unfug'," *Der Angriff*, Number 26 (December 26, 1927).
Unknown author. "Der Staatsanwalt für Tietz A.G.," *Der Angriff* (February 20, 1928).
Unknown author. "Die Selbstverurteilung der Rassenjustiz," *Der Angriff* (June 11, 1928).
Unknown author. "Dem Warenhaus keinen Pfennig!" *Der Angriff* (December 3, 1928).
Unknown author. "Das Weihnachtsgeschäft der Warenhäuser," *Der Angriff* (December 10, 1928).
Unknown author. "Ochse, siehste Wertheim nicht?" *Der Angriff* (December 12, 1927).
Unknown author. "Warenhäusler versklaven deutsche Arbeitskraft," *Der Angriff* (February 20, 1928).
Unknown author. "Sechs Millionen Reichsmark Dividende!" *Der Angriff* (June 11, 1928).
Unknown author. "Warenhaus und Bankpalast," *Der Angriff* (June 11, 1928).
Unknown author. "Was macht Herr Schacht mit dem Geld?" *Der Angriff* (December 10, 1928).
Unknown author. "Ritualmord! Warenhäuser und Großbanken schächten das deutsche Wirtschaftsleben," *Der Angriff* (March 18, 1929).
Unknown author. "Kinder fronen im Warenhaus," *Der Angriff* (December 24, 1930), 1.
Unknown author. "Warenhäuser werden Besteuert. Braunschweig voran!," *Der Angriff* (December 27, 1930).
Unknown author. "Mittelstandsgroschen bauen Paläste des Warenhauskapitals," *Der Angriff*, Number 11 (March 18, 1929.)
Unknown author. "Warenhaus—Allerlei," *Der Angriff*, Number 50 (December 10, 1928).
Unknown author. "Der Staatsanwalt für Tietz A.G.," *Der Angriff*, Number 8 (February 20, 1928).

Berliner Börsen-Zeitung

Unknown author. "Leonhard Tietz," *Berliner Börsen-Zeitung* (June 19, 1933).

Unknown author. "Hitler gegen jede Störung der Ordnung; Rüksichtslos gegen die sogenannte zweite Revolution," *Berliner Börsen-Zeitung* (July 3, 1933).

Unknown author. "Einzelaktionen gegen Konsumvereine strengstens untersagt; Dr. Ley kündigt scharfe Maßnahmen an," *Berliner Börsen-Zeitung* (July 5, 1933).

Unknown author. "Hitler: Nun Evolution!; Der Reichskanzler gegen unsachliche Eingriffe in die Wirtschaft.—Alle Macht liegt bei der Reichsgewalt!" *Berliner Börsen-Zeitung*, evening edition (July 7, 1933), 1.

Unknown author. "Aktionen gegen Warenhäser vorläufig untersagt; Ein Erlaß der NS-Parteileitung," Berliner *-Zeitung* (July 8, 1933).

Unknown author. "Leonhard Tietz A.G. Generalversammlung," *Berliner Börsen-Zeitung* (July 12, 1933), 10.

Unknown author. "Große Kanzlerrede vor dem Treuhändern der Arbeit. Die politische Macht erobert man in einem Zuge. Für die Wirtschaft gelten andere Gesetze," *Berliner Börsen-Zeitung* (July 13, 1933), 1.

Unknown author. "Leonhard Tietz Aktien-Gesselschaft; Bilanz für den 31. Januar 1933," *Berliner Börsen-Zeitung* (July 14, 1933), 6.

Berliner Morgenpost

Unknown author. "Neues Handelskammer-Präsidium; Der Personal-Umbau der Wirtschaft," *Berliner Morgenpost* (April 6, 1933), 8.

Magazine Articles

Die Grüne Post

Trimm, Thomas. "Herr Reichsminister—ein Wort bitte!," *Die Grüne Post* (April 29, 1934), 1.

The Saturday Evening Post

Selfridge, Harry Gordon. "Selling Selfridge; Some Random Reflections of an American Merchant in London," *The Saturday Evening Post*, Volume 208 Issue 4 (July 27, 1935), 16–53.

Selfridge, *The Saturday Evening Post*, Volume 208 Issue 6 (August 10, 1935), 18–70.

Selfridge, *The Saturday Evening Post*, Volume 208 Issue 8 (August 24, 1935), 26–68.

Selfridge, *The Saturday Evening Post*, Volume 208 Issue 10 (September 7, 1935), 16–53.

German Radio Transcription

Ziegler, Ulrich. "Joop Snep—Überlebender des KZ Sachsenhausen; Wer hinfiel, bekam einen Genickschuss," *Deutschlandfunk Kultur* Transcript of German radio program (May 2, 2015).

U.S. Court Cases

Ursula Ungaro-Benages, Judge as heir of Lilli Berliner nee Orenstein, Plaintiff-Appellant, v. Dresdner Bank AG, Deutsche Bank AG, Defendants-Appellees. No. 03-11880, United States Court of Appeals, Eleventh Circuit. Decided: August 3, 2004.

SECONDARY LITERATURE

Ahrens, Ralf. "Der Exempelkandidat. Die Dresdner Bank und der Nürnberger Prozess gegen Karl Rasche," *Vierteljahrshefte für Zeitgeschichte*, Vol. 52, No. 4 (October 2004): 637–670.

———. *Die Dresdner Bank 1945–1957; Konsequenzen und Kontinuitäten nach dem Ende des NS-Regimes*. München: R. Oldenbourg Verlag, 2007.

Bähr, Johannes, Axel Drecoll, Bernhard Gotto, Kim C. Priemel and Harald Wixforth. *Der Flick-Konzern im Dritten Reich*. München: R. Oldenbourg Verlag, 2008.

Bajohr, Frank. *Arisierung in Hamburg; Die Verdrängung der jüdischen Unternehmer 1933–1945*. 2. Auflage. Hamburg: Hans Christians Verlag, 1998.

———. "Verfolgung aus gesellschaftsgeschichtlicher Perspektive. Die wirtschaftliche Existenzvernichtung der Juden und die deutsche Gesellschaft," *Geschichte und Gesellschaft*, Vol. 26, No. 4 (2000): 629–652.

Ballensiefen, Heinz. "Frankreichs Schuld: Die inneren Gründe für den Zusammenbruch des französischen Staates," *Zeitschrift für Politik*, Vol. 30 (1940): 261–282.

———. "Das Weltjudentum als politische Macht," *Zeitschrift für Politk*, Vol. 30 (1940): 329–341.

Barkai, Avraham. *From Boycott to Annihilation; The Economic Struggle of German Jews 1933–1943*. Hanover: Brandeis University Press, 1989.

———. "Die deutschen Unternehmer und die Judenpolitik im 'Dritten Reich,'" *Geschichte und Gesellschaft*, Vol. 15, No. 2 (1989): 227–247.

———. "German Interests in the Haavara-Transfer Agreement 1933–1939," *Leo Baeck Institute Year Book*, Vol. 35 (1990): 245–266.

———. "Die 'stillen Teilhaber' des NS-Regime," in Lothar Gall and Manfred Pohl (Eds.), *Unternehmen im Nationalsozialismus*. München: Verlag C.H. Beck, 1998, 117.

———. "The C.V. and its Archives, A Reassessment," *Leo Baeck Institute Yearbook*, XLV (2000): 173–182.

———. *"Wehr Dich!" Der Centralverein deutscher Staatsbürger jüdischen Glaubens 1893–1938*. München: C.H. Beck, 2002.

———. *Erlebtes und Gedachtes; Erinnerungen eines unabhängigen Historikers*. Göttingen: Wallstein Verlag, 2011.

Baten, Joerg and Rainer Schulz. Making profits in wartime: Corporate profits, inequality, and GDP in Germany during the First World War," *The Economic History Review*, Vol. 58, No. 1 (February 2005): 34–56.

Berger, Alfred. "Grundsätzliche Bemerkungen zur jüdischen Wanderfürsorge," *Jüdische Arbeits- und Wanderfürsorge* Heft 1 (1927/1928), 7–11.

Berghoff, Hartmut. *Moderne Unternehmensgeschichte; Eine themen- und theorieorientierte Einführung*. Paderborn: Ferdinand Schöningh, 2004.

Bevers, Jürgen. *Der Mann hinter Adenauer. Hans Globkes Anstieg vom NS-Juristen zur Grauen Eminenz der Bonner Republik*. Berlin: Christoph Links Verlag, 2009.

Bing, Ignaz. *Tales from My Life—Memoirs of a Merchant and Cave Explorer in Germany 1840–1918*. Inspiring Young Minds Publishing, 2013.

Boesler, F. Review of Justus Beyer, *Die Ständeideologien der Systemzeit und ihre Überwindung* in *Finanz Archiv/Public Finance Analysis* Vol. 9, No. 3 (1943): 689–691.

Boveri, Margret. *Wir lügen alle; Eine Hauptstadtzeitung unter Hitler*. Olten: Walter-Verlag, 1965.

Bräutigam, Petra. *Mittelständische Unternehmer im Nationalsozialismus. Wirtschaftliche Entwicklungen und soziale Verhaltensweisen in der Schuh- und Lederindustrie Badens und Württembergs*. München: R. Oldenbourg Verlag, 1997.

Briesen, Detlef. *Warenhaus, Massenkonsum und Sozialmoral: zur Geschichte der Konsumkritik im 20. Jahrhundert*. Frankfurt am Main: Campus, 2001.

Browning, Christopher R. *Ordinary Men; Reserve Police Battalion 101 and the Final Solution in Poland*. New York: HarperPerennial, 1998.

Bruns-Wüstefeld, Alex. *Lohnende Geschäfte; Die Entjudung der Wirtschaft am Beispiel Göttingens*. Hannover: Fackelträger Verlag, 1997.

Buchmann, Erich. *Von der jüdischen Firma Simson zur Nationalsozialistischen Industriestiftung Gustloff-Werke*. Erfurt: U. Bodung-Verlag, 1944.

Buffaloe, Ed. "The Simson Model 1922 and 1926 Vest Pocket Pistol," unblinking eye .com/Guns/Simson.html

Cahnmann, Werner J. "The Jews of Munich: 1918–43," in Joseph B. Maier, Judith Marcus, and Zoltán Tarr (Eds.), *German Jewry; Its History and Sociology. Selected Essays by Werner J. Cahnmann*. New Brunswick: Transaction Publishers, 1989.

Canning, Kathleen. *Language of Labor and Gender: Female Factory Work in Germany, 1850–1914*. Ithica: University of Michigan Press, 2002.

Carsten, Francis Ludwig. *The German Workers and the Nazis*. Aldershot: Scolar Press, 1995.

Castle Stanford, Julian [aka Julius Schloß]. *Reflections; The Diary of a German-Jew in Hiding*. Oakland: Judah L. Magnus Memorial Museum, 1965.

Chernow, Ron. *The Warburgs; The Twentieth-Century Odyssey of a Remarkable Jewish Family*. New York: Random House, 1993.

Childers, Thomas and Jane Caplan (Eds). *Reevaluating the Third Reich*. New York: Holmes & Meier, 1993.

Clark, Christopher and Racheli Edelman, "Helping Hitler: An Exchange," *New York Review of Books*. April 9, 2020.

Davis, Belinda J. *Home Fires Burning: Food Politics, and Everyday Life in World War I Berlin*. Chapel Hill: University of North Carolina Press, 2000.

Dean Martin (Ed.). *Robbery and Restitution; The Conflict over Jewish property in Europe*. New York: Berghahn Books, 2007.

———. *Robbing the Jews; The Confiscation of Jewish Property in the Holocaust, 1933–1945*. Cambridge: Cambridge University Press, 2008.

Depkat, Volker. "The Challenges of Biography: European-American Reflections," *Bulletin of the German Historical Institute*, No. 55 (Fall 2014): 39–45.

Dimsdale, Nicholas H., Nicholas Horsewood, and Arthur van Riel. "Unemployment in Interwar Germany: An Analysis of the Labor Market, 1927–1936," *The Journal of Economic History*, Vol. 66, No. 3 (September 2006): 778–808.

Dohms, Peter. *Meerbusch; Die Geschichte der Stadt und der Altgemeinden von den Ursprüngen bis zur Gegenwart*. Meerbusch: Stadt Meerbusch, 1991.

Ekstein, Modris. *The Limits of Reason; The German Democratic Press and the Collapse of Weimar Democracy*. London: Oxford University Press, 1975.

Enzenberger, Hans Magnus (Ed.). *O.M.G.U.S. Ermittlungen gegen die Deutsche Bank 1946/1947*. Nördlingen: Franz Greno, 1985.

Fälter, Jürgen W. *Hitlers Wähler*. München: Verlag C.H. Beck, 1991.

Feder, Ernst. *Heute sprach ich mit... Tagebücher eines Berliner Publizisten 1926–1932*. Stuttgart: Deutsche Verlags-Anstalt, 1971.

Feldenkirchen, Wilfried. *Siemens; Von der Werkstatt zum Weltunternehmen*. München: Piper Verlag GmbH, 1997.

Feldman, Gerald D. "Wer Spinnt? *German Politics and Society*, Vol 20, No. 3 (Fall 2002): 40–55.

Ferguson, Niall. *The Pity of War. Explaining World War I*. New York: Basic Books, 1999.

Fischer, Eugen. Review of Wilhelm Spengler's and Hans Schwerte's book *Forscher und Wissenschaftler im heutigen Europa* in *Zeitschrift für Morphologie und Anthropologie* Vol. 48, No. 1 (November 1956): 101–102.

Förster, Andreas. "Freundschaftliche Übernahme oder 'Arisierung?' Eine Erbengemeinschaft stellt Antrag auf Rückgabe des Eigentums: Das ungeklärte Ende des Bankhauses Mendelssohn," *Berliner Zeitung*, October 17, 1997.

Frei, Norbert. *Adenauer's Germany and the Nazi Past; The Politics of Amnesty and Integration*. New York: Columbia University Press, 2002.

——— and Ralf Ahrens, Jörg Osterloh and Tim Schanetzky, *Flick. Der Konzern, die Familie, die Macht*. München: Karl Blessing Verlag, 2009.

Friedländer, Saul. *Nazi Germany and the Jews, Volume I: The Years of Persecution, 1933–1939*. New York: HarperCollins Publishers, Inc., 1997.

Friedländer, Vera. *Mann kann nicht eine halbe Jüdin sein* Kiel: Agimos Verlag, 1998.

———. *Ich was Zwangsarbeiterin bei Salamander*. Berlin: Verlag das neue Berlin, 2016.

Fuchs, Peter. *100 Jahre Kaufhof Köln, 1891–1991*. Köln: asmuth satz & druck, 1991.

Gall, Lothar. "A Man for all Seasons? Hermann Josef Abs im Dritten Reich," *Zeitschrift für Unternehmensgeschichte,* Vol. 43, No. 2, 1998, 123–175.

———. *Der Bankier Hermann Josef Abs; Eine Biographie*. München: Verlag C.H. Beck, 2005.

Genschel, Helmut. *Die Verdrängung der Juden aus der Wirtschaft im Dritten Reich*. Göttinger Bausteine zur Geschichtswissenschaft. Göttingen: Musterschmidt Verlag, 1966.

Glier, Erich. *Die sächsische Spitzen- und Stickereiindustrie seit 1914. Niedergang und Existenzkampf einer deutschen Mode- und Exportindustrie*. Plauen: Franz Neupert G.m.b.H, 1932.

Gotto, Klaus (Ed.). *Der Staatssekretär Adenauers. Persönlichkeit und politisches Wirken Hans Globkes*. Stuttgart: Verlagsgemeinschaft Ernst Klett, 1980.

Gräfe, Marlis, Bernhard Post and Andreas Schneider (Eds.). *Die Geheime Staatspolizei im NS-Gau Thüringen 1933–1945*. II Halbband. Erfurt: Landeszentrale für politische Bildung Thüringen, 2009.

Griffith, William E. "Denazification in the United States Zone of Germany," *The Annals of the American Academy of Political and Social Science*, Vol. 267 (January 1950): 68–76.

Grossman, Ron. "Holocaust Suit Raises Foreign Policy Issue," *Chicago Tribune*, July 7, 2003.

Gruchmann, Lothar. *Justiz im Dritten Reich 1933–1940; Anpassung und Unterwerfung in der Ära Gürtner*. München: R. Oldenbourg Verlag, 1988.

Grünfeld, Fritz V. and Stefi Jersch-Wenzel. *Das Leinenhaus Grünfeld: Erinnerungen und Dokumente*. Berlin: Duncker & Humblot, 1967.

Gumbel, Emil Julius. *Vier Jahre politischer Mord*. Berlin: Verlag der neuen Gesellschaft, 1922.

Hachmeister, Lutz. *Der Gegnerforscher: Karriere des SS-Führer Franz Alfred Six*. München: Verlag C.H. Beck, 1998.

Hale, Oron J. *The Captive Press in the Third Reich*. Princeton: Princeton University Press, 1964.

Händler-Lachmann, Barbara and Thomas Werther. *"Vergessene Geschäfte verlorene Geschichte"; Jüdisches Wirtschaftsleben in Marburg und seine Vernichtung im Nationalsozialismus*. Marburg: Hitzeroth, 1992.

Hannover, Heinrich and Elisabeth Hannover-Drück. *Politische Justiz 1918–1933*. Berlin: Metropol Verlag, 2019.

Hayes, Peter. "State Policy and Corporate Involvement in the Holocaust," in Michael Berenbaum (Ed.), *The Holocaust and History; the Known, the Unknown, the Disputed and the Reexamined*. Bloomington: Indiana University Press, 1998.

———. *How was it Possible? A Holocaust Reader*. Lincoln: University of Nebraska Press, 2015.

———. *Why? Explaining the Holocaust*. New York: W.W. Norton & Company, 2017.

Heimbüchel, Bernd, Alexander Kierdorf, Stefan Pohl, and Caludia Teichner. *Erlebniswelt Kaufhof; Ein Warenhaus in Deutschland*. Köln: Wienand Verlag, 2001.

Herbert, Ulrich. *Best. Biographische Studien über Radikalismus, Weltanschauung und Vernunft 1903–1989*. Bonn: Verlag J.H.W. Dietz Nachfolger, 1996.

Herbst, Ludolf and Thomas Weihe (Eds). *Die Commerzbank und die Juden 1933–1945*. München: Verlag C. H. Beck, 2004.

Hett, Benjamin Carter. *Crossing Hitler; The Man Who Put the Nazis on the Witness Stand*. Oxford: Oxford University Press, 2008.

Hildenbrandt, Fred. *Ich soll dich grüssen von Berlin, 1922–1932; Berliner Erinnerungen ganz und gar unpolitisch post mortem herausgebenen von zwei Freunden*. München: Franz Ehrenwirth, 1966.

Hill, J. A. "Taxes on Department Stores," *The Quarterly Journal of Economics*, Vol. 15, No. 2 (February 1901): 299–304.

Hoeppel, Alexander. *NS-Justiz und Rechtsbeugung*. Tübingen: Mohe Siebeck, 2019.

Homburg, Heidrun. "Warenhausunternehmen," in Gerald F. Feldman (Ed.), *Industrie und Inflation. Studien und Dokumente zur Politik der deutschen Unternehmer 1916–1923*. Hoffmann und Campe, 1977.

Hördler, Stefan. "Ideologie, Machinszenierung und Exzess: Taten und Täter der 'Köpenicker Blutwoche,'" in Stefan Hördler (Ed.), *SA-Terror als Herrschaftssicherung. "Köpenicker Blutwoche" und öffentliche Gewalt im Nationalsozialismus*. Berlin: Metropol Verlag, 2013.

———. "Entgrenzung und Eingrenzung der Gewalt. Berliner SA, SS und Polizei (1933—1939) in Michael Wildt and Christoph Kreuzmüller (Eds.), *Berlin 1933—1945*. München: Siedler Verlag, 2013.

Hung, Jochen. "Die Zeitung der Zeit. Die Tageszeitung Tempo und das Ende der Weimarer Republik," in David Oels and Ute Schneider (Eds.), *Der ganze Verlag ist einfach eine Bonbonniere. Ullstein in der ersten Hälfte des 20. Jahrhunderts*. Berlin: Walter de Gruyter GmbH, 2015.

Isaacs, Reginald R. *Walter Gropius; Der Mensch und sein Werk,* Vol. 1. Berlin Gebrüder Mann Verlag, 1983.

James, Harold. "The Deutsche Bank and the Dictatorship 1933–1945," in Lothar Gall et al., (Ed.), *The Deutsche Bank 1870–1995*. London: Weidenfeld & Nicolson, 1995.

———. *The Nazi Dictatorship and the Deutsche Bank*. Cambridge: Cambridge University Press, 2004.

Janetzko, Maren. "Die Arisierung-Vermittlung," in *Die Dresdner Bank im Dritten Reich,* Vol. 2. München: R. Oldenbourg Verlag, 2006.

Jünger, Ernst. *Storm of Steel*. New York: Penguin Random House, 2003.

Kause, Helmut. "Der publizistische Widerstand Paul Schiemanns gegen den Nationalsozialismus in den deutschen Volksgruppen," in Michael Garleff (Ed.), *Deutschbalten, Weimar Republik und Drittes Reich*. Köln: Böhlau Verlag, 2001.

Keegan, John. *The First World War*. New York: Alfred A. Knopf, 1999.

Kellenbenz, Hermann (Ed.). *Zwei Jahrtausende Kölner Wirtschaft*, Vol. 2: Vom 18. Jahrhundert bis zur Gegenwart. Köln: Greven Verlag, 1975.

Kempner, Robert M. W. "The Nuremberg Trials as Sources of Recent German Political and Historical Materials," *The American Political Science Review*, Vol. 44, No. 2 (June 1950): 447–459.

Kershaw, Ian. *Hitler 1889–1936 Hubris*. New York: W.W. Norton, 1999.

———. *The Nazi Dictatorship; Problems and Perspectives of Interpretation*, Fourth Edition. New York: Oxford University Press, 2000.

———. "Biography and the Historian; Opportunities and Constraints," in Volker R. Berghahn and Simone Lässig (Eds.), *Biography between Structure and Agency; Central European Lives in International Historiography*. New York: Berghahn Books, 2008.

———. *To Hell and Back; Europe 1914—1949*. New York: Penguin Random House, 2015.

Klee, Ernst. *Das Personen Lexikon zum Dritten Reich; Wer war was vor und nach 1945*. Hamburg: Nikol Verlagsgesellschaft mbH, 2016.
Kobrak, Christopher. *National Cultures and International Competition; The Experience of Schering AG, 1851–1950*. Cambridge: Cambridge University Press, 2002.
Kobrak, Christopher and Andrea H. Schneider. "Big Business and the Third Reich: An Appraisal of the Historical Arguments," in Dan Stone (Ed.), *The Historiography of the Holocaust*. New York: Palgrave Macmillan, 2005, pp.141–172.
Kobuch, Agatha. „Mutschmann Martin," *Neue Deutsche Biographie*. Achtzehnter Band, Berlin: Duncker & Humblot, 1996.
Kocka, Jürgen and Hannes Siegrist. "Die hundert größten deutschen Industrieunternehmen im späten 19. und frühen 20. Jahrhundert; Expansion, Diversifikation und Integration im internationalen Vergleich," in Norbert Horn and Jürgen Kocka (Eds.), *Recht und Entwicklung der Großunternehmen im 19. und frühen 20. Jahrhundert*. Göttingen: Vandenhoeck & Ruprecht, 1979.
Köhler, Ingo. "Soziale und wirtschaftliche Vernetzung als Erfolgsfaktor: Das Dresdner Privatbankhaus Grbr. Arnhold (1864–1933)," in Ulrich Heß (Ed.), *Unternehmen im regionalen und lokalen Raum 1750–2000*. Leipzig: Leipziger Universitätsverlag, 2004.
———. *Die Arisierung der Privatbanken im Dritten Reich; Verdrängung, Ausschaltung und die Frage der Wiedergutmachung*. München: C.H. Beck, 2005.
———. "Die Arisierung jüdischer Privatbanken," in Dieter Ziegler (Ed.), *Die Dresdner Bank und die deutschen Juden. Die Dresdner Bank im Dritten Reich*, Vol. 2. München: R. Oldenbourg Verlag, 2006.
Köhler, Wolfram. *Der Chef-Redakteur Theodor Wolff: Ein Leben in Europa 1868–1943*. Düsseldorf: Droste, 1978.
Kolbe, Corina. "Die Angst der Getretenen vor dem nächsten, härteren Tritt," *Spiegel Online*, September 2, 2016.
König, Helmut. Wolfgang Kuhlmann and Klaus Schwabe. *Vertuschte Vergangenheit; Der Fall Schwerte und die NS-Vergangenheit der deutschen Hochschulen*. München: C.H. Beck, 1997.
Kopper, Christopher. *Zwischen Marktwirtschaft und Dirigismus; Bankenpolitik im "Dritten Reich" 1933—1939*. Bonn: Bouvier Verlag, 1995.
Koszyk, Kurt. *Deutsche Presse 1914–1945*. Geschichte der deutschen Presse Teil III. Berlin: Colloquium Verlag, 1972.
Kraus, Elisabeth. *Die Familie Mosse; Deutsch-jüdisches Bürgertum im 19. Und 20. Jahrhundert*. Müchen: Verlag C.H. Beck, 1999.
Kreimeier, Klaus. *The Ufa Story; A History of Germany's Greatest Film Company, 1918–1945*. Berkeley: University of California Press, 1999.
Kress, Celina. *Adolf Sommerfeld/Andrew Sommerfield Bauen für Berlin 1910–1970*. Berlin: Lukas Verlag für Kunst- und Geistesgeschichte, 2011.
Kreutzmüller, Christoph. *Final Sale in Berlin. The Destruction of Jewish Commercial Activity 1930–1945*. New York: Berghahn Books, 2015.
Kruse, Falko. "Zweierlei Maß für NS-Täter? Über die Tendenz schichtenspezifischer Privilegierungen in Urteilen gegen nationalsozialistische Gewaltverbrecher," *Kritische Justiz*, Vol. 11, No. 3 (1978): 236–253.

Künzler, Adrian. "Judicial Legitimacy and the Role of Courts: Explaining the Transnational Context of the German Border Guard Cases," *Oxford Journal of Legal Studies*, Vol. 32, No. 2 (Summer 2012).

Ladwig-Winters, Simone. *Wertheim—ein Warenhausunternehmen und seine Eigentümer' Ein Beitrag der Entwicklung der Berliner Warenhäuser bis zur 'Arisierung.'* Münster: LIT, 1997.

Lang, Anne-Sophie. "Blut im Schuh," *Die Zeit*. Nummer 47, November 27, 2014.

Lange, Herbert. *Spaziergänge in Kleinmachnow*. Berlin: Haude & Spenersche Verlagsbuchhandlung GmbH, 1995.

Langer, Peter. "Paul Reusch und die Gleichschaltung der Münchner Neuesten Nachrichten 1933," *Vierteljahrshefte für Zeitgeschichte*, Vol. 53, No. 2 (2005): 203–240.

Lässig, Simone. "Nationalsozialistische Judenpolitik und jüdische Selbstbehauptung vor dem Novembepogrom: Das Beispiel Bankiersfamilie Arnhold," in Reiner Pommerin (Ed.), *Dresden unterm Hakenkreuz*. Köln: Böhlau Verlag, 1998.

———. "Jüdische Privatbanken in Dresden," *Dresdner Hefte*, Vol. 18, No. 61 (2000): 85–97.

Lebermann, Kurt. *Die Konzentration der Bingwerke Nürnberg*. Wirtschafts- und Verwaltungsstudien LXI, Leipzig: A. Deichertsche Verlagsbuchhandlung, 1924.

Leggewie, Claus. *Von Schneider zu Schwerte: Das ungewöhnliche Leben eines Mannes, der aus der Geschichte lernen wollte*. München: Carl Hanser Verlag, 1998.

Lepper, Marcel. "Marbacher Archivnachrichten: Pathogenese der bundesrepublikanischen Germanistik? Zum Nachlass Hans Scherte," *Zeitschrift für Germanistik*, Vol. 17, No.1 (2007): 274–279.

Lillteicher, Jürgen. *Raub, Recht und Restitution; Die Rückerstattung jüdischen Eigentums in der frühen Bundesrepublik*. Göttingen: Wallstein Verlag, 2007.

Loos, Erich. Review of Wilhelm Spengler's and Hans Schwerte's book *Denker und Deuter im heutigen Europa* in *Romanische Forschungen*, Vol. 67, No. 3–4 (1956): 401–404.

Ludwig, Johannes. *Boykott, Enteignung Mord. Die Entjudung der deutschen Wirtschaft*. 2. Auflage, Hamburg: FACTA OBLITA Verlag GmbH, 1989.

Mason, Tim. "The Workers' Opposition in Nazi Germany," *History Workshop*, No. 11 (Spring 1981): 120–137.

Mathes, Susanne. "Unruhe und Unmut wegen NS-Vortrag," *Stuttgarter Zeitung*. de March 24, 2011.

Marcus, Alfred. *Die wirtschaftliche Krise des deutschen Juden; Eine soziologische Untersuchung*. Berlin: Verlag von Georg Stilke, 1931.

Mayer-von Götz, Irene. *Terror im Zentrum der Macht. Die frühen Konzentrationslager in Berlin 1933/34–1936*. Berlin: Metropol Verlag, 2008.

de Mendelssohn, Peter. *S. Fischer und sein Verlag*. Frankfurt am Main: S. Fischer Verlag, 1970.

———. "Die Anfänge," in W. Joachim Freyburg and Hans Wallenberg (Eds.), *Hundert Jahre Ullstein 1877–1977*. Berlin: Ullstein Verlag, 1977.

———. *Zeitungsstadt Berlin*. Frankfurt am Main: Verlag Ullstein GmbH, Überarbeitete und erweiterte Auflage, 1982.

Mierzejewski, Alfred C. *Ludwig Erhard: A Biography*. Chapel Hill: University of North Carolina Press, 2014.

Mommsen, Hans. "Konnten Unternehmer im Nationalsozialismus apolitisch bleiben?" in Lothar Gall and Manfred Pohl (Eds.), *Unternehmen im Nationalsozialismus*. München: Verlag C.H. Beck, 1998.

Mommsen, Wolfgang J. "Kaiser Wilhelm II and German Politics," *Journal of Contemporary History*, Vol. 25, No. 2/3 (May-June 1990): 289–316.

Morris, Douglas G. "Accommodating Nazi Tyranny? The Wrong Turn of the Social Democratic Legal Philosopher Gustav Radbruch After the War," *Law and History Review*, Vol. 34, No 3 (August 2016).

Mosse, George L. *The Culture of Western Europe; The Nineteenth and Twentieth Centuries*. Third Edition. Boulder: Westview Press, 1988.

———. *Confronting History; A Memoir*. Madison: The University of Wisconsin Press. 2000.

Mosse, W. E. *The German-Jewish Economic Élite 1820–1935; A Socio-cultural Profile*. Oxford: Clarendon Press, 1989.

Motadel, David. "What do the Hohenzollerns Deserve?" *New York Review of Books*, March 26, 2020.

Münzel, Martin. *Die jüdischen Mitglieder der deutschen Wirtschaftselite 1927–1955. Verdrängung—Emigration—Rückkehr*. Paderborn: Ferdinand Schöningh, 2006.

Mutz, Horst Richard. *Das Einheitspreisgeschäft als neuzeitliche Betriebsform im deutschen Einzelhandel*. Berlin: Industrieverlag Spaeth & Linde, 1932.

Oels, David (Ed.). *Der ganze Verlag ist einfach eine Bonbonniere: Ullstein in der ersten Hälfte des 20. Jahrhunderts*. Berlin: Walter de Gruyter, 2014.

OMGUS. *Dresdner and Deutsche Banks; Special Report of the Military Governor, U.S. Zone*, 1947.

Overesch, Manfred. *Bosch in Hildesheim 1937—1945*. Göttingen: Vandenhoeck & Ruprecht, 2008.

Panwitz, Sebastian. *Das Haus des Kranichs; Die privatbankiers von Mendelssohn & Co (1795–1938)*. Berlin: Hentrich & Hentrich, 2018.

Paulson, Stanley L. "Lon L. Fuller, Gustav Radbruch, and the 'Positivist' Thesis," *Law and Philosophy*, Vol. 13, No. 3 (August 1994).

———. "Radbruch on Unjust Laws: Competing Earlier and Later Views?" *Oxford Journal of Legal Studies*, Vol. 15, No 3 (Autumn 1995).

———. "On the Background and Significance of Gustav Radbruch's Post-War Papers," *Oxford Journal of Legal Studies*, Vol. 26, No 1 (Spring 2006).

———. "Ein ewiger Mythos: Gustav Radbruch als Rechtspositivist—Teil I," *Juristen Zeitung*, Vol. 63, No. 3 (Februar 2008).

Paxton, Robert O. *Vichy France: Old Guard and New Order 1940—1944*. New York: Columbia University Press, 1972.

Perels, Joachim. *Das juristische Erbe des Dritten Reiches; Beschädigungen der demokratischen Rechtsordnung*. Frankfurt: Campus Verlag, 1999.

Peterson, Walter F. *The Berlin Liberal Press in Exile: A History of the Pariser Tageblatt*. Tübingen: Max Niemeyer Verlag, 1987.

Plischke, Elmer. "Denazification Law and Procedure," *The American Journal of International Law*, Vol. 41, No. 4 (October 1947): 807–827.

Port, Andrew I. "Holocaust Scholarship and Politics in the Public Sphere: Reexamining the Causes, Consequences, and Controversy of the *Historikerstreit* and the Goldhagen debate. A Forum with Gerrit Dworok, Richard J. Evans, Mary Fulbrook, Wendy Lower, A. Dirk Moses, Jeffrey K. Olick, and Timothy D. Snyder," *Central European History*, Vol. 50 (2017): 375–403.

Quint, Peter E. "Judging the Past: The Prosecution of East German Border Guards and the GDR Chain of Command," *The Review of Politics*, Vol. 62, No. 2 (Spring 1999).

———. "The Border Guard Trials and the East German Past-Seven Arguments," *The American Journal of Comparative Law*, Vol. 48, No. 4 (Autumn 2000).

Radbruch, Gustav. *Der Innere Weg; Aufriß meines Lebens*. Göttingen: Vandenhoeck & Ruprecht, 1961.

Rauh-Kühne, Cornelia. "Review of "Robert Bosch und der liberale Widerstand gegen Hitler 1933—1945," *Historische Zeitschrift*, Vol. 274, No. 2 (April 2002): 520–521.

Reichardt, Sven. "Violence and Community: A Micro-Study on Nazi Storm Troopers," *Central European History*, Vol. 46, No. 2 (June 2013): 276–291.

Reuth, Ralf Georg. *Joseph Goebbels Tagebücher 1924–1945*. Band I und II. Erweiterte Sonderausgabe, 2. Auflage, München: Piper Verlag GmbH, 2000.

Richards, Earl Jeffrey. "The Schneider/Schwerte Phenomenon: Falsifying One's Biography and the Role of the Manipulative Character in Education after Auschwitz," *German Politics & Society*, Vol. 17, No. 4 (Winter 1999): 74–98.

Römer, Felix. *Kameraden. Die Wehrmacht von innen*. München: Piper Verlag GmbH, 2012.

Rosenkötter, Bernhard. *Treuhandpolitik; Die Haupttreuhandstelle Ost und der Raub polnischer Vermögen 1939–1945*. Essen: Klartext Verlag, 2003.

Rosenthal, Jacob. *Die Ehre des jüdischen Soldaten. Die Judenzählung im Ersten Weltkrieg und ihre Folgen*. Frankfurt am Main: Campus Verlag GmbH, 2007.

Roth, Karl Heinz. "Das Ende eines Mythos. Ludwig Erhard und der Übergang der deutschen Wirtschaft von der Annexions- zur Nachkriegsplanung (1939 bis 1945) I. Teil: 1939 bis 1943," *Zeitschrift für Sozialgeschichte des 20. Und 21. Jahrhunderts*. Heft 4 (1995): 53–93.

Ryback, Timothy W. *Hitler's First Victims; The Quest for Justice*. New York: Alfred A. Knopf, 2014.

Schmalhausen, Bernd. *"Ich bin doch nur ein Maler"; Max und Martha Liebermann im Dritten Reich*. Hildesheim: Georg Olms Verlag, 1994.

Schoeps, Julius H. "Review of Die Deutsche Bank und die 'Arisierung'," *Shofar*, Vol. 21, No. 1 (Fall 2002): 171–174.

Scholtyseck, Joachim. *Robert Bosch und der liberale Widerstand gegen Hitler 1933–1945*. München: Verlag C.H. Beck, 1999.

Schultz, Bernd (Ed.). *James Simon; Philanthrop und Kunstmäzen*. München: Prestel, 2006

Schulz, Ulrike. "Kurze Geschichte der Simsonwerke 1856–1935," *Die Enteignung der Firma Simson & Co, Suhl/Thüringen (1927–1935)*. Thüringen: Landeszentrale für politische Bildung, 2011.

Schütt, Siegfried. *Die Simson-Legende; Aus der Geschichte eines Traditionsunternehmens*. Gotha: Druckmedienzentrum Gotha, 2005.

Schütz, Erhard. "Wir, jawohl wir formen das geistige Antlitz der Nation," in David Oels and Ute Schneider (Eds.), *Der ganze Verlag ist einfach eine Bonbonniere. Ullstein in der ersten Hälfte des 20. Jahrhunderts*. Berlin: Walter de Gruyter GmbH, 2015.

Schwartz, Thomas Alan. "Die Begnadigung deutscher Kriegsverbrecher," *Vierteljahrshefte für Zeitgeschichte*, Vol. 38, No. 3 (July 1990): 375–414.

Selig, Wolfram. *"Arisierung" in München. Die Vernichtung jüdischer Existenz 1937–1939*. Berlin: Metropol Verlag, 2004.

Siegrist, Hannes. "Deutsche Großunternehmen vom späten 19. Jahrhundert bis zur Weimarer Republik; Integration, Diversifikation und Organisation bei den hundert größten deutschen Industrieunternehmen (1887–1927) in international verglecihender Perspektive," *Geschichte und Gesellschaft*, Vol. 6, No. 1 (1980): 60–102.

Siemens, Daniel. "Die SA und der nationalsozialistische Mythos vom Kampf um Berlin," in Michael Wildt and Christoph Kreutzmüller (Eds.), *Berlin 1933–1945*. München: Siedler Verlag, 2013.

Simpson, Christopher. *War Crimes of the Deutsche Bank and the Dresdner Bank; Office of Military Government (U.S.) Reports*. New York: Holmes & Meier, 2002.

Sösemann, Bernd. "Im Spiegel der Voß: Der Kampf um die Republik," in W. Joachim Freyburg (Ed.), *Hundert Jahre Ullstein 1877–1977*. Frankfurt am Main: Verlag Ullstein GmbH, 1977.

———. *Theodor Wolff; Ein Leben mit der Zeitung*. Stuttgart: Franz Steiner Verlag, 2012.

Spiekermann, Uwe. "Der Mittelstand stirbt! Der Kampf zwischen mittelständischem Einzelhandel und Warenhäusern in Deutschland 1890–1933," in Godela Weiss-Sussex and Ulrike Zitzlsperger (Eds.), *Das Berliner Warenhaus; Geschichte und Diskurse/The Berlin Department Store; History and Discourse,* Frankfurt am Main: Peter Lang GmbH, 2013.

Spoerer, Mark. *C & A; A Family Business in Germany, the Netherlands and the United Kingdom 1911–1961*. Munich: Verlag C.H. Beck, 2016.

Steinberg, Jonathan. *The Deutsche Bank and its Gold Transactions during the Second World War*. München: C.H. Beck, 1999.

Steinweis, Alan and Robert D. Rachlin. *The Law in Nazi Germany; Ideology, Opportunities, and the Perversion of Justice*. New York: Berghahn, 2013.

Stern, Fritz. *Bismarck, Bleichröder and the Building of the German Empire*. New York: Vintage Books, 1979.

Straub, Eberhard. *Albert Ballin. Der Reeder des Kaisers*. Berlin: Siedler Verlag, 2001.

Strutz, Edmund. *175 Jahre Abr. Frowein jun., Abr. & Gebr. Frowein, Frowein & Co. A.G.; Ein Beitrag zur Wuppertaler Wirtschaftsgeschichte*. Düsseldorf: A. Bagel, 1938.

Sudrow, Anne. *Der Schuh im Nationalsozialismus: Eine Produktgeschichte im deutsch-britisch-amerikanischen Vergleich*. Göttingen: Wallstein Verlag, 2010,

Tavernaro, Thomas. *Der Verlag Hitlers und der NSDAP. Die Franz Eher Nachfolger GmbH*. Wien: Verlag für Literatur- und Sprachwissenschaft, 2004.

Tenenbaum, Joseph. "The Einsatzgruppen," *Jewish Social Studies*, Vol. 17 No.1 (January 1955): 43–64.

Tietz, Georg. *Hermann Tietz; Geschichte einer Familie und ihrer Warenhäuser*. Stuttgart: Deutsche Verlags-Anstalt, 1965.

Uhlig, Heinrich. *Die Warenhäuser im Dritten Reich*. Köln: Westdeutscher Verlag, 1956.

Ullstein, Heinz. *Spielplatz meines Lebens; Erinnerungen*. München: Kindler Verlag, 1962.

Ullstein, Hermann. *The Rise and Fall of the House of Ullstein*. New York: Simon and Schuster, 1943.

Unknown author. "Prozesse Abs; Noch'n Ruch," *Der Spiegel*, No. 43 October 19, 1970, pp. 128–131.

Vortmann, Jürgen. "Juristischer Widerstand gegen den Nationalsozialismus," *Zeitschrift für Rechtspolitik*, Vol. 23, No. 5 (May 1990): 193–198.

Wachs, Philipp-Christian. *Der Fall Theodor Oberländer (1905–1998). Ein Lehrstück deutscher Geschichte*. Frankfurt am Main: Campus Verlag GmbH, 2000.

Wagner, Andreas. "Martin Mutschmann; Der braune Gaufürst (1935–45)," in Mike Schmeitzner and Andreas Wagner (Eds.), *Von Macht und Ohnmacht; Sächsische Ministerpräsidenten im Zeitalter der Extreme 1919–1952*. Beucha: Sax-Verlag, 2006.

Wahrig, Gerhard. *Deutsches Worterbuch*. Völlig überarbeitete Neuausgabe. München: Mosaik Verlag, 1984.

Walk, Joseph. *Kurzbiographien zur Geschichte der Juden*. München: K G Saur, 1988.

Warburg, Max. *Aus meinen Aufzeichnungen*. Glückstadt: J.J. Augustin, 1952.

Weber, Fritz. *Vor dem großen Krach; Österreichs Banken in der Zwischenkriegszeit am Beispiel der Credit-Anstalt für Handel und Gerwerbe*. Wien: Böhlau, 2016.

Wehler, Hans-Ulrich. *Deutsche Gesellschaftsgeschichte. Von der "Deutschen Doppelrevolution" bis zum Beginn des Ersten Weltkrieges. 1849–1914*. München: Verlag C.H. Beck, 1995.

Weinreich, Uriel. *Modern English-Yiddish/Yiddish-English Dictionary*. New York: Schocken Books, 1977.

Weizmann, Chaim. *Trial and Error: The Autobiography of Chaim Weizmann*. New York: Harper, 1949.

Wernicke, Johannes."Die gegen die Warenhäuser geforderten Abwehrmittel" in *Kapitalismus und Mittelstandspolitik*. Jena: Verlag von Gustav Fischer, 1907.

———. "Warenhaus, Industrie und Mittelstand," *Rechts- und Staatswissenschaftliche Studien,* Heft XLIV (1911): 17.

Wildt, Michael. *An Uncompromising Generation; The Nazi Leadership of the Reich Security Main Office*. Madison: University of Wisconsin Press, 2009.

Wippermann, Wolfgang. "Eule und Hakenkreuz; Ullstein und Deutscher Verlag im Dritten Reich 1933 bis 1945," in Anne Enderlein and Ulf Geyersbach (Eds.), *Ullstein Chronik 1903–2011*. Berlin: Ullstein Buchverlage GmbH, 2011.

Wistrich, Robert. *Who's Who in Nazi Germany*. New York: Bonanza Books, 1982.

Wixforth, Harald. "Ein Bankier während und nach dem Holocaust. Die wechselvolle Karriere des Hugo Ratzmann," in Jörg Osterloh (Ed.), *Unternehmer und NS-Verbrechen. Wirtschaftseliten im "Dritten Reich" und in der Bundesrepublik Deutschland*. Frankfurt: Campus Verlag.

———. "Die Dresdner Bank im Sudetenland und im Protektorate Böhmen und Mähren," in Klaus-Dietmar Henke (Ed.), *Die Dresdner Bank im Dritten Reich*, Vol. 3. München: R. Oldenbourg Verlag, 2006.

Wohl, Robert. *The Generation of 1914*. Cambridge: Harvard University Press, 1979.

Wojak, Irmtrud. *Fritz Bauer 1903–1968; Eine Biographie*. München: C.H. Beck, 2009.

Ziegler, Dieter. "Die Aufsichtsräte der deutschen Aktiengesellschaften in den zwanziger Jahren. Eine empirische Untersuchung zum Problem der Bankenmacht," *Zeitschrift für Unternehmensgeschichte/Journal of Business History*, Vol. 43, No. 2 (1998): 194–215.

———. "Die Verdrängung der Juden aus der Dresdner Bank," *Vierteljahrshefte für Zeitgeschichte*, Vol 47 (1999): 187–216.

———. "Aryanization and the Role of the German Great Banks, 1933–1938," in Gerald D. Feldman and Wolfgang Seibel (Eds.), *Networks of Nazi Persecution; Bureaucracy, Business and the Organization of the Holocaust*. New York: Berghahn Books, 2005.

———. "Die Nationalsozialisten im Betrieb," in Johannes Bähr (Ed.), *Die Dresdner Bank im Dritten Reich*, Vol. 1. München: R. Oldenbourg Verlag, 2006.

———. "Der Ordnungsrahmen," in Klaus-Dietmar Henke (Ed.), *Die Dresdner Bank im Dritten Reich*, Vol. 1. München: R. Oldenbourg Verlag, 2006.

———. "Entjudung und Nazifizierung 1933–1937," in Johannes Bähr (Ed.), *Die Dresdner Bank in der Wirtschaft des Dritten Reichs*, Vol. 1. München: R. Oldenbourg Verlag, 2006.

———. "Die Arisierung von Kapitalgesellschaften in Fallstudien," *Die Dresdner Bank und die deutschen Juden*. in Klaus-Dietmar Henke (Ed.), *Die Dresdner Bank im Dritten Reich*, Vol. 2. München: R. Oldenbourg Verlag, 2006.

Zinke, Peter. "Er drohte wieder mit der Gauleitung. Gustav Schickedanz und die Arisierung," *nurinst. Beiträge zur deutschen und jüdischen Geschichte*, Vol. 4 (2008): 63–80.

Index

About the Author

William M. Katin earned his PhD from UCLA with a concentration in European history. While serving as a lecturer at California State University in San Bernardino, William became a member of the German Studies Association for which he gave a paper on Johannes Reuchlin for the 43rd Annual Conference in Portland, Oregon.

William is active in scholarship in Germany, having made a presentation contrasting Lion Feuchtwanger with Victor Klemperer. An expanded version is being considered for publication as part of the Feuchtwanger Studies by the Peter Lang Publishing House in a volume tentatively titled *Feuchtwanger und München*.

Katin also participates in conferences conducted by the Technische Universität in Braunschweig. A 2019 lecture concerned the art dealer Galka Scheyer and a forthcoming 2020 lecture concerns the topography of the city of Memel as a nexus between Berlin scholarship in the German language and Kovno music and dance performances.

William is the grandson of Johanna Rülf, who perished in the Kovno Concentration Camp.

www.ingramcontent.com/pod-product-compliance
Ingram Content Group UK Ltd.
Pitfield, Milton Keynes, MK11 3LW, UK
UKHW041841031026
15587UKWH00002B/929

9 781793 606822